The Court of Common Pleas in Fifteenth Century England

Plate I. *Fifteenth Century Picture of the Court.*

This picture, one of four which depict the central courts, appears originally to have been an illustration in a book of abridgments. Miss Putnam (*Early Treatises,* p. 176) has compared the beginning of the table of contents with that in Statham's abridgment and found it almost identical. When the pictures were found by Corner at Whaddon Hall, they had already become separated from the text to which they belonged. Corner presented the originals to the Library of the Inner Temple. Reproductions were published in *Archaeologia,* vol. XXXIX, London, 1863. Langdell Law Library at Harvard has framed copies of a set of these reproductions. The picture of the Court of Common Pleas was described by the late Isobel Thornley in *Y. B. 11 Ric. II,* Ames Foundation, Y. B. series, vol. V, p. xxvii, and by Bolland in *A Manual of Year Book Studies.*

From the fact that there are seven justices of the Common Pleas and that the Chancellor is shown as a cleric, Corner argued that the paintings were originally produced either between 29 and 32 Henry VI or between 34 Henry VI and the end of the reign of Edward IV, for seven justices on the bench of the Common Pleas and a clerical Chancellor do not again coexist after the reign of Edward IV. Two reasons for believing that the painting is not earlier than 34 Henry VI are, first, that the writing which appears below the picture of the Common Pleas is in well-developed bastard and, second, that there are ten clerks sitting around the table of that court. It is difficult to identify these as any but the Custos Brevium or Keeper of the Writs of the court, or his deputy or clerk, and the three prothonotaries and their clerks. The filacers probably were not present in court. In any case there were more than ten of them. According to the ordinance of 35 Henry VI (App. I), the officers expected to attend court were the Keeper of the Writs and the two prothonotaries, each with two underclerks. By 39 Henry VI, however, there were *three* prothonotaries (the addition of a third prothonotary is discussed in Ch. VIII), and each presumably was allowed to have two clerks by him in the court.

A reason for thinking that the picture is not later in the reign of Edward IV than 1462 is that the Chief Baron of the Exchequer court is dressed in scarlet and miniver like a justice of the Common Pleas while the other barons wear plain buff-colored robes and cloaks. Sir Peter Ardern, justice of the Common Pleas, like his predecessors Babington and Juyn, was both Chief Baron of the Exchequer and a judge of the Common Pleas (Foss, *Judges,* vol. IV, pp. 408–409) until 1462, when he appears either to have lost his position in Exchequer court altogether or to have been demoted to the position of second baron. For the remainder of the reign, no one person appears to have held office in both courts at the same time. (See *ibid.,* tables on pp. 395–396.)

The Court of Common Pleas

In Fifteenth Century England

A study of legal administration and procedure

=

By Margaret Hastings

Archon Books
1971

To the memory of N. Neilson whose inspired teaching gave me a zestful introduction to the Middle Ages, and whose friendship sustained me in the long task of preparing this book.

Preface

THIS STUDY of the Court of Common Pleas in fifteenth century England is the outgrowth of work begun in a graduate seminar at Mount Holyoke College under the direction of the late Professor N. Neilson. Miss Neilson had long been interested in the records of the central courts of common law. She had acquired a collection of photostats of plea rolls of Edward IV's reign and had trained students to read and understand them. In her seminar I first conceived the idea that a description of the ways in which a mediaeval court carried on its business would be a useful and possibly interesting addition to our knowledge of mediaeval institutions.

The objectives of this study are two. On the one hand, by collecting in one volume information heretofore widely scattered, about the court in the later middle ages, I have hoped to facilitate the use and interpretation of the records. On the other hand, by studying the workings of the court from these records I have tried to correct erroneous impressions based on secondary materials. Existing descriptions are drawn from Year Book reports or legal manuals or treatises written some centuries later. They do not provide reliable evidence of methods of carrying on business in the court in the mediaeval period. Theory sometimes differed from practice, and legend sometimes submerged historical fact.

I hope also that this study may make it easier for students of social and legal history to use the plea rolls in their research. The rolls are bulky and not easily manageable. The practice of entering continuations of cases without reference to earlier entries and a confusing system of dividing business among the clerks make it difficult to be certain of finding the full record of a case without backbreaking effort. Records published in the Selden Society and other modern editions of Year Books often seem to contribute little to the understanding of the report, and yet they are the only source from which one can hope to discover what was the final disposition of the case.

This study deals with only a very small section of the vast history of the common law, and it stands in an equally modest position in the history of mediaeval public administration. Yet it has a certain value for the middle twentieth century. It is easy today to take for granted the existence of machinery for the administration of justice. In the slight and sometimes irritating contacts of the ordinary law-abiding citizen with the institutions for the administration of justice, he gets little sense of the centuries of slow growth behind the organisms which he sees functioning with varying degrees of efficiency in different parts of the world. Any insight he can acquire into the ways in which procedures for the adjudication of disputes between individuals have developed seems to me to have some value in a time when we are slowly and uncertainly developing procedures for dealing with disputes among nations. We are, as Secretary Bevin has said, "more interested in peace than in procedure," and yet we cannot have the one without first evolving the other.

The acknowledgments I should make for assistance in accomplishing this study are so many that I can mention only some of the more important ones. To Bryn Mawr College I am deeply indebted for encouragement to pursue further the interest in mediaeval legal records awakened at Mount Holyoke and for making it possible for me to spend a year in England working in the Public Record Office. To the late Professor H. L. Gray, of Bryn Mawr College, I owe a debt for which words seem rather inadequate. He was a kind, a wise, and a patient counselor and a good friend to me.

There are many others to whom my thanks are due. Professor Bertha Putnam of Mount Holyoke College has given generously of both her time and her advice based on her many years of experience with legal records. Mr. C. Hilary Jenkinson, Deputy Keeper and Secretary of the Public Record Office, spared time from his many duties and interests to give me valuable help and encouragement. To Professor C. H. Williams and to the members of his seminar in fifteenth century legal history in the year 1933–1934, especially to Miss Marjorie Blatcher and Miss M. K. Dale, I am indebted not only for helpful suggestions and criticisms but also for material on the clerks of the courts in the fifteenth century. Miss Blatcher, who presented for the degree of Doctor of Philosophy at the University of London a thesis on the *Workings of the Court of King's Bench in the Fifteenth Century,* has helped me with warnings and encouragement based on her experience. Miss Dale has answered with expertness and expedition many questions addressed to her from this side of the Atlantic. She has also with great generosity handed on to me certain material which she herself had planned to use in the preparation of a paper on the custody of the records of the court. This material forms the basis for a considerable portion of Chapter IX.

Many people, including the late Richard W. Hale and Professors G. K. Gardner and John M. Maguire of the Harvard Law School, have read the manuscript at various stages. They are responsible for many improvements I have been able to make both in the accuracy and the readability of the completed study. I am grateful also to the staff of Langdell Law Library and especially to the librarian, Mr. Pulling, for their kind help to me in using the rich resources of that library.

To the other friends who have helped me in a difficult piece of work, I can extend my thanks only collectively because of their multitude.

M. H.

Contents

CONTENTS

APPENDICES

Plates

Abbreviations

The following abbreviations of well-known titles have been used throughout the book:

A. H. R.	American Historical Review.
C. C. R.	Calendars of Close Rolls.[1]
C. P. R.	Calendars of Patent Rolls.[1]
D. N. B.	Dictionary of National Biography.
E. H. R.	English Historical Review.
H. E. L.	Holdsworth's History of English Law.
Parlt. Papers	Parliamentary Papers.
P. R. O.	Public Record Office.
R. P.	Rolls of Parliament.
R. S.	Rolls Series.
S. R.	Statutes of the Realm.
S. S.	Selden Society.
Y. B.	Year Book.

The titles of seventeenth century attorneys' manuals [1] to which reference is most frequently made are abbreviated as follows:

C. P. Att. (1648)	The Attourney of the Court of Common Pleas.
Compleat Att. (1652)	The Practick Part of the Law Showing the Office of a Compleat Attorney, etc.
Proposals	Certaine Proposals of Divers Attorneys of the Court of Common Pleas, etc.
Rules, Orders, and Notices	Rules, Orders, and Notices, of the Several Courts.

Postmediaeval lawbooks and law reports are referred to in the form conventional in legal treatises, as follows:

Anderson	Sir Edmund Anderson's reports for the reign of Queen Elizabeth.
Co. Litt.	Sir Edward Coke's Institutes of the Laws of England.[1]
Cro. Car.	Sir George Croke's reports for the reign of Charles I.
Dyer	Sir James Dyer's reports for the reigns of Henry VIII, Edward VI, Mary, and Elizabeth.
F. N. B.	Sir Anthony Fitzherbert's La Novelle Natura Brevium.[1]

[1] Full bibliographical data are given below in "Sources for the Study of the Court of Common Pleas in the Fifteenth Century."

PART I

General Picture of the Court

CHAPTER I

The Fifteenth Century

THE VIOLENT and disorderly tenor of political life during the Wars of the Roses has raised a cloud of condemnation over the fifteenth century which still obscures that troubled period of history from a clear view by modern historians. The prevailing judgment has been that in those "scrambling and unquiet" times, the agencies of government were able to guarantee little security for the enjoyment of life, liberty, and property. According to an extreme statement of the case, the law was worse than no protection for "most men of position, and consequently their hordes of followers, laughed at the law because they knew that they could generally overcome it. . . . To them the law was another pawn in the game, whose pieces were oppression, trickery, and force." [1]

The widespread prevalence of this condemnatory judgment [2] is, in part at least, a tribute to the success of Tudor propaganda. Henry VII, usurper and founder of a new dynasty, had good reason for encouraging the belief that he had saved England from ravaging civil disorder. A dark picture of the years preceding his success at Bosworth Field served to strengthen not only the dynasty but also the monarchy, by providing justification for measures on the French model designed to supply the king with the instruments of power. [3]

Shakespeare undoubtedly did more than any other single in-

---

[1] H. S. Bennett, *The Pastons and Their England* (Cambridge, 1922), p. 165.

[2] See, for example, W. Denton, *England in the Fifteenth Century* (London, 1888), esp. p. 276; A. Abrams, *Social England in the Fifteenth Century* (London, 1909); V. B. Redstone, "The Social Condition of England during the Wars of the Roses," *Trans. Royal Hist. Soc.*, 2nd Ser., vol. XVI (1902), pp. 159–200; C. H. Firth, "Benefit of Clergy in the Time of Edward IV," *E. H. R.*, vol. XXXII (1917), pp. 175 ff.; J. Fortescue, *Governance of England* (ed. Plummer; Oxford, 1885), Intro. pp. 20 ff.

[3] K. Pickthorn, *Early Tudor Government: Henry VII* (Cambridge, 1934), p. 73.

dividual to perpetuate this Tudor version of the period preceding their own and to fix it permanently in the minds of English-speaking peoples. Basing his cycle of historical plays chiefly upon the work of Hall and Holinshed, he gave to the history of the times from 1399 to 1485 the dramatic unity of the Greek trilogies. The Lancastrians, despite the humility of Henry IV and the great qualities of Henry V, failed because of the dishonor on which the dynasty was founded. Henry IV had broken his oath of allegiance to a divinely anointed sovereign and then had acquiesced in his secret murder. The curse of the Lancastrians fulfilled itself in the foreign catastrophe and domestic calamity of Henry VI's reign. The House of York succeeded, only to be engulfed, itself, in retribution for broken pledges and bloody murder. From the welter of turmoil and blood only the uniting of the two roses in the person of Henry VIII could bring forth the greatness of the Elizabethan age.[4]

The parliamentary leaders of the seventeenth century began the work of replacing this "Tudor myth" with another, equally vivid but nonetheless obstructive to a clear view of the times. Their use of Fortescue's concept of limited monarchy in the contest with the Stuarts and their reliance on the mediaeval ideal of the supremacy of law ultimately led to a changed perspective on the fifteenth century. But reverence for the Tudors and pride in England's achievements under their leadership delayed the full development of this new version of fifteenth century history until the time of the Whig historians of the nineteenth century. Its most brilliant expression is to be found in the works of J. R. Green. To him the coming of the Tudors seemed a revolution and a catastrophic one: "The long Parliamentary contest between the Crown and two Houses since the days of Edward the First had firmly established the great securities of national liberty. . . . But with the close of the War of the Succession freedom suddenly disappears. We enter on an epoch of constitutional retrogression in which the slow work of the age that went before it is rapidly undone." [5]

Somewhere beneath the shadows cast by these two dramatic concepts of the fifteenth century lies the complex truth, and his-

---

[4] C. L. Kingsford, *Prejudice and Promise in Fifteenth Century England* (Oxford, 1925), pp. 2-3; E. M. W. Tillyard, *Shakespeare's History Plays* (New York, 1946), *passim.*
[5] J. R. Green, *Short History of the English People* (New York, 1878), p. 302.

torians since the time of Stubbs have been engaged in the work of bringing it into focus. The job is one of digging and dealing imaginatively with the results of digging, transporting ourselves back into a time when words now in everyday use in the countries partaking in the tradition of parliamentary democracy, had not the sharper clarity of meaning they have since acquired. It is a question of trying to look upon the fifteenth century scene with perspective and yet to avoid judgments based on the standards of later ages.

In the constitutional field Dr. Chrimes has accomplished a great deal towards lighting up the obscurities of fifteenth century thought and explaining some of the inconsistencies between fact and theory.[6] In the realm of economics Professor Postan's forthcoming book on *Manorial Profits* will evidently resolve the apparent contradiction between Thorold Rogers' picture of "solid, substantial, unbroken prosperity" and Denton's representation of the period as one of deterioration and insecurity.[7]

Many dark places remain to be investigated. Chief among them are the administrative agencies of government. There is much obvious evidence of administrative breakdown. Contemporary political songs deplore:

> Many lawys and lytylle ryght;
> Many actes of parlament,
> And few kept wyth tru entente.[8]

Hardyng's *Chronicle,* presented to Henry VI in 1457, urges the king to restore the golden days of his father, when England dwelt in peace, for now, he says:

> The lawe is lyke vnto a Walshmannes hose,
> To eche mannes legge that shapen is and mete;
> So mayntenours subuerte it and transpose,
> Thurgh myght it is full low layde vndyr fete,
> And mayntnanse vp in stede of law complete;

---

[6] S. B. Chrimes, *English Constitutional Ideas in the Fifteenth Century* (Cambridge, 1936). Cf. T. F. T. Plucknett, "The Lancastrian Constitution," in *Tudor Studies* (ed. Seton-Watson; London, 1924).

[7] M. M. Postan, "The Fifteenth Century. (A Revision)," *Econ. Hist. Review,* vol. IX (1939), pp. 160–167; Denton, *England;* J. E. T. Rogers, *History of Agriculture and Prices* (Oxford, 1882), vol. IV, pp. 2–23.

[8] *Political Poems and Songs relating to English History* (ed. Wright; R. S., London, 1859–1861), vol. II, p. 252.

5

All, if law wolde, thynge wer by right reuersed,
For mayntenours it may noght bene rehersed.[9]

Political manifestoes such as the Duke of York's petition of 1450,[10] and Jack Cade's proclamation,[11] complain of the failure of justice. Petitions in Parliament, in the Council, and in Chancery describe in vivid terms riots and ambushes committed against neighbors, and extortions and misdemeanors of officials.[12] The Year Books report many cases of maintenance and embracery,[13] and the Pastons lament that justice may be achieved only through money or favor.[14]

These signs led Stubbs to the conclusion that "constitutional progress had outrun administrative order," and that weakness of the central government "made perfect order and thorough administration of the law impossible." [15] There can be little quarrel with Stubbs's main thesis that the government was weak at the top and center. On the other hand, there is still room for questioning how far down and outward the debility extended, and whether conditions complained of by chroniclers, letter-writers, petitioners, and poets were markedly worse in the fifteenth century than they were earlier.

Complaints of abuse were certainly not new in the fifteenth century. Fourteenth century records are full of them. The parliaments of 1372 and 1388 attempted reforms of some abuses.[16] A statute of 20 Edward III, as well as several in the reign of Edward I had attempted to deal with extortions and like misdemeanors of sheriffs and others of the king's officers.[17] Attempts to check

[9] C. L. Kingsford, "Extracts from the First Version of Hardyng's Chronicle," *E. H. R.*, vol. XXVII (1912), pp. 749–750.

[10] *Paston Letters* (ed. Gairdner; London, 1872), No. 114.

[11] *Three Fifteenth Century Chronicles* (ed. Gairdner; Camden Society, London, 1880), p. 96.

[12] See *H. E. L.*, vol. II, pp. 457–459, for an account of these.

[13] P. H. Winfield, *History of Conspiracy and Abuse of Legal Procedure* (Cambridge, 1921), pp. 156–157.

[14] *Paston Letters*, No. 350, postscript of a letter from William to John Paston, May 2, 1460: "Omnia pro pecunia facta sunt."

[15] *The Constitutional History of England* (5th ed.; Oxford, 1893), vol. III, pp. 276–277.

[16] T. F. Tout, *Chapters in the Administrative History of England*, vol. III (Manchester, 1928), pp. 282, 437, 442–443, vol. V (Manchester, 1930), p. 50.

[17] 3 Ed. I (Westm. I), cc. 26–27, 33; 13 Ed. I (Westm. II), cc. 13, 38, 39; 28 Ed. I (*Art. super Cart.*), c. 16; 20 Ed. III, c. 6.

maintenance go back to the third year of Edward I.[18] Moreover, if fifteenth century poets and political leaders decried perversion of justice, so did their fourteenth century predecessors.[19] The actions and manifestoes of the rebels of 1381 indicate that they held the law and its ministers to be among their bitterest enemies.[20] The judicial scandals of Edward I's reign are notorious.[21] They were followed by milder, yet similar, scandals in the middle of the fourteenth century.[22] Perhaps it was with these last facts in mind that the late Professor Holdsworth concluded that there was a rise in the standards of professional honor among the judges from Thomas of Weyland's time to the times of Littleton and Fortescue.[23]

A definitive judgment concerning the extent of the breakdown in government in the years of the century before Henry VII grasped the reins of power requires a more thorough examination of the mass of available legal records than has yet been made. Furthermore, these records should be studied comparatively in relation to similar records of earlier and later periods. It is at least a probability that the breakdown, however serious, began towards the end of the reign of Edward III, and that the later Plantagenets should share in the opprobrium hovering over the Lancastrian and Yorkist rulers.

This study of the Court of Common Pleas in the fifteenth century was begun without intention to enter into the controversy concerning the evils of fifteenth century society and government. Its primary objective was an understanding of the workings of the court. The tremendous bulk and number of the surviving plea rolls, almost the complete set of four hundred for the century, each weighing perhaps fifteen pounds, occupying two to three cubic feet

[18] Statutes concerning maintenance and retainers: 3 Ed. I (Westm. I), cc. 25, 28, 33; 13 Ed. I (Westm. II), cc. 36, 49; 1 Ed. III, stat. 2, c. 14; 4 Ed. III, c. 11; 10 Ed. III, stat. 2; 18 Ed. III, stat. 1; 20 Ed. III, cc. 4, 5, 6; 1 Ric. II, cc. 4, 7, 9; 7 Ric. II, c. 15; 13 Ric. II, stat. 3; 20 Ric. II, c. 1.

[19] *Political Poems and Songs*, vol. I, esp. pp. 272–273, 312, 358, 408–410, and William Langland, *Piers Plowman*.

[20] Charles Oman, *The Great Revolt* (Oxford, 1906), pp. 58–59; George Kriehn, "Studies in the Sources of Social Revolt in 1381," *A. H. R.*, vol. VII, (1902), pp. 254–285, 458–484; Tout, *Chapters*, vol. III, pp. 369–370.

[21] *H. E. L.*, vol. II, pp. 293–299.

[22] Tout, *Chapters*, vol. III, p. 259.

[23] *H. E. L.*, vol. II, pp. 565–566.

of space, and containing an average of about 6,000 entries each, discourages search for anything but specific evidence about readily identifiable persons, places, or subjects, within a limited span of time. A student seeking to corroborate or to confute the thesis in controversy would be faced with a choice between selecting from the mass of monotonous material the more dramatic entries or making a statistical study of a few sample rolls. Either procedure would be misleading in our present state of knowledge and could therefore not contribute greatly to the discussion. It has seemed wiser to attempt first to understand something of how the Court of Common Pleas was expected to function before attempting to judge how well or how ill it did function in practice. False conclusions concerning the health of an institution are easy to draw when its anatomy and physiology are imperfectly understood.

Naturally, however, one cannot avoid attempting to interpret such relevant evidence as comes readily to hand. For example, the plea rolls increased in bulk in the fifteenth century. This may, in part, have been due to the improvement in the methods of enrollment described below in Chapters VIII and X rather than to an increase in the amount of litigation in the court. Certainly the Court of Common Pleas had been very busy in the reign of Edward II.[24] A notable increase in the number of actions of trespass and debt as compared with the number of actions involving rights of ownership and/or possession in land, is probably accounted for by the natural development of the former actions and the successful competition of the central courts with the older local courts.[25]

A search in the rolls for illustrations of the violent tenor of fifteenth century life would prove disappointing. To be sure, the records of pleadings in trespass cases include lists of weapons used in close-breaking, housebreaking, assault, and the like, but the monotonous recurrence of the statement that the offense was committed with staves, knives, arrows, and swords (*baculis, cultellis,*

---

24 F. W. Maitland and G. J. Turner, *Y. B. B. of 3 and 4 Ed. II,* S. S. vol. XXII (London, 1907), pp. xxi, xxiv. See also *C. C. R., 1307–1313,* p. 231.

25 Stat. 12 Ed. I and 6 Ed. I, c. 8, provide that pleas of debt and trespass for sums less than 40s. shall be pleaded in the county court or commote. It is noteworthy that, in the fifteenth century Common Bench rolls which I have examined, the sums asked for in debt and/or damages are never less than 40s. but the sums recovered are often very much less.

sagittis, and *gladiis*), or some combination of two or three of these, even where a woman was defendant or the cause of complaint was the taking away of a few sheep or the plowing up of a strip of land, suggests that the words were a stereotyped expansion of the phrase *vi et armis* rather than a literal description of the method of attack. Furthermore, the major number of entries in the plea rolls give no such interesting detail, misleading or otherwise. With tedious regularity, they tell us that "John Dale" came into court on the fourth day either in his own person or by his attorney, that the defendant did not come, that the sheriff reported that he was not found, or that he had nothing in the county whereby he might be distrained (or, alternatively, that the sheriff did not send the writ), and that Dale therefore sued out further process to the next term. Of a total of over 6,000 entries on the roll for Michaelmas, 22 Edward IV, nearly 5,000 are of this type.[26]

To the proposition that the monotonous repetition of such entries, in itself, proves deterioration or, at least, inefficiency of the legal machinery it can only be answered for the present that the evidence is not conclusive. Judged by modern standards fifteenth century procedure was slow. Nonetheless plaintiffs were willing to pay the necessary fees for it. According to our standards, transportation by oxcart is inefficient. In the fifteenth century, it was the only way to move large objects from one place to another over land, and people paid for it without dreaming that there might be more efficient means of transportation.

While the rolls give no obvious evidence of unusually disturbed social conditions, neither do they offer much testimony to political eruptions and dynastic changes. To be sure, the king's demise, either actual or in construction of the law, interrupted temporarily the ponderous flow of justice.

According to the mediaeval principle, demise meant cessation of all suits begun in the name of the dead or deposed king and the necessity of renewing each case by a writ issued in the name of the new king. This principle had been followed as early as the reign of Edward I, and probably earlier.[27] The rapid changes in the kingship

[26] C. P. 40/882. Cf. N. Neilson's figures, *Y. B. 10 Ed. IV—49 Hy. VI* (S. S. vol. XLVII [London, 1931]), p. xvii.

[27] G. O. Sayles, *Select Cases in the Court of King's Bench under Edward I* (S. S. vol. LV, London, 1936), vol. I, p. 1.

9

between 1460 and 1485 put litigants to the extra trouble of suing out writs of resummons or reattachment, deposition of a king being held by the justices to be the equivalent of death.[28] The many Year Book discussions of procedure on demise make it sufficiently clear, however, that there was never any real question that the suit might be renewed.[29] The rule insisting on a writ of renewal may have had one beneficial effect, that of clearing the docket of cases which had been dawdling term after term for years. The disadvantages were more obvious; at least they were so serious that in the first year of Edward VI's reign a statute was passed which made it unnecessary henceforth to sue out resummons or reattachment, or to begin a case over again merely because the crown sat on a new head. The reason given was that the older principle caused not only greater expense, hindrances, and delay to "playntifs and actors" in suits, but "allso a great lett and hinderaunce of Justice." [30]

One might suppose, too, that a disturbance such as Jack Cade's rebellion would leave some trace in the records of the Common Pleas as well as in those of the local courts and the King's Bench. It is true that all cases from the quindene of the Nativity of St. John the Baptist (July 6) to the end of Trinity term, 1450, were adjourned to the octaves of Michaelmas by a writ close from the king ordering that such adjournment be accomplished with all possible speed "because of certain important and urgent affairs concerning us and the state and defence of our realm of England and the English church." [31] Public proclamation of the adjournment was to be made in court, and the sheriffs were to be ordered to return the writs at a later day. The only direct mention of Jack Cade, however, is a brief note under the heading of the Trinity plea roll, "Tempore Capitanij Kanc' videlicet Jak Cade." One month after the opening of Michaelmas term, 2 Edward IV, there was a similar common adjournment of all pleas to the octaves of Hilary "for certain very urgent and notable causes moving us and our council." [32] The

---

[28] Y. B. 10 Ed. IV—49 Hy. VI, S. S. vol. XVII, pp. 114–120.

[29] See Y. B. 10 Ed IV—49 Hy. VI, S. S. vol. XLVII, p. 115, for a case where reattachment was allowed in a bill of trespass in the King's Bench. The reason given is that "otherwise the plaintiff would lose the advantage of the earlier pleading and his cost, which would be a mischief."

[30] 1 Ed. VI, c. 7.

[31] C. P. 40/758, m. 253d.

[32] C. P. 40/806, m. 350.

"urgent and notable causes" in this instance were Margaret of Anjou's invasion of Northumberland with the help of eight hundred Frenchmen.[33] Other such adjournments might be discovered by a further search of the rolls.

Brief periods of disorder are disclosed by the absence or abbreviation of certain rolls because the court failed to sit during the term. The roll for Easter, 1 Edward IV is missing, and the Trinity roll consists of ninety membranes only,[34] possibly because people were not as yet sufficiently sure that the new regime would endure to sue out process to continue cases or to start new actions. Meanwhile the clerks, attorneys, sergeants at law, and justices of the court seem to have taken the opportunity of a slack season to get their own legal business out of the way. Thomas Littleton, sergeant at law, John Wydeslade, chief prothonotary, John Alderley, attorney of the Bench, and Walter Moyle, justice of the Bench, all figure as plaintiffs in various suits. A further suggestion of troublous times is the entry in this roll of several £2,000 bonds for good behavior given by various knights, esquires, and merchants of Yorkshire.[35] A contraction in the bulk of the rolls similar to that at the beginning of the reign occurred after the death of Edward IV. The Easter roll is slender, and Trinity, 1 Edward V consists of 69 membranes only in comparison to the 617 membranes of Michaelmas, 22 Edward IV and the 449 membranes of Hilary.[36] Since Richard usurped the kingship before the end of Trinity term, there is a roll for Trinity, 1 Richard III, which consists of five membranes.[37]

Nothing of great interest to political and constitutional historians can be got out of this irregularity, which is the only obvious evidence of disorder to be found in the rolls. To balance it, there is an extraordinary continuity of personnel in the offices of the court. Only normal replacements occur among the clerks employed in these offices, even in the most troubled times. Among the justices, king's sergeants, and in the office of king's attorney, personages who would be expected to have closer contacts with the political

[33] C. L. Scofield, *The Life and Reign of Edward IV, King of England and of France and Lord of Ireland* (London, 1923), vol. I, pp. 261–262.
[34] C. P. 40/801.
[35] Mm. 18, 61.
[36] C. P. 40/885A; C. P. 40/882; C. P. 40/883.
[37] C. P. 40/885B.

life of the times, the changes are scarcely more spectacular. All the justices continued in office during the readeption of Henry VI, and all save two, who apparently died at about this time, were either continued in office or transferred to the King's Bench when Edward returned.[38] Evidently some concern was felt lest the even flow of justice be interrupted by political events.

Continuity of personnel and the regularity of the clerks in turning out monotonous and bulky legal records do not, in themselves, prove that the administration of justice in the Court of Common Pleas was little affected by the stresses of the times. They do invite further investigation of the question whether the ponderous machinery of the court rumbled on in relative disregard for the confusion in the upper levels of government.

Other reasons than its controversial character warrant the choice of the fifteenth century as a period for study of the workings of the Court of Common Pleas. There is the advantage of investigating a period nearer to the time of full knowledge than any other within the range of the Year Books. Often it is easier to work back to origins from a middle ground than to begin at the beginning. Of the endless but changing pattern of the administration of the common law, the fifteenth century provides a section which gives some important clues to puzzles of earlier times and some hints as to the reasons for later complexities.

Another characteristic of the period, which appeals to the legal rather than the administrative historian, is what Holdsworth described as the "curious combination of legal development with political retrogression." [39] However deep the "want of governance" may have penetrated into the administrative structure, the age was nonetheless one in which a revolution in legal methods was beginning. Sir Matthew Hale, commenting from the perspective of the seventeenth century, described the times before 1500 as the "golden age of pleading." He lamented the discontinuation of the Year Books during the reign of Henry VIII and ascribed the excellent learning to be found in them to the fact that pleadings were in those days oral. Oral pleadings under the supervision of the justices, he thought, prevented the deceits, subtleties, and complexities which

---

[38] Neilson, *Y. B. 10 Ed. IV—49 Hy. VI*, S. S. vol. XLVII, p. xiv, and below, Ch. VI.
[39] *H. E. L.*, vol. II, pp. 408, 414.

became the rule after paper pleadings were introduced.[40] These demoralizing paper pleadings were first used in the latter part of the fifteenth century. The first mention of one in the Year Book appears in 38 Henry VI. By the middle of the reign of Henry VIII they had probably become the rule.[41]

Concurrent with the introduction of paper pleadings and related to it was another change of greater significance. That was the transformation of the jury from a group of witnesses of fact to a group of judges of evidence.[42] This resulted in a shift of emphasis from pleading to trial. The formal records do their best to conceal from us the history of this transformation. They avoid all mention of the presentation of evidence. This much is clear, however: the change did take place, and it began in the fifteenth century.

A final reason for interest in the fifteenth century arises from its being a time of fundamental changes not only in the forms of pleading and trial but also in the forms of action. Here begins the transition from the time when the law was dominated by the older forms of action to the time when trespass, case, and their derivatives had driven these older actions from the courts. Case for misfeasance had already been admitted at the beginning of the century.[43] Case for nonfeasance, in the latter part of the century, was storming the fortress of the law using all the forces of logic and expediency to batter down conservative resistance. Detinue *sur trover* was the "new-found Halliday" or "cure-all" for persons who wished to recover goods in the possession of third parties although they could not show a delivery of the goods to such parties.[44] Common recovery was rapidly replacing the final concord as a method of evading the restrictions imposed by the statute *De Donis Conditionalibus* on the conveyance of land; in Edward IV's reign was argued Taltarum's, or Talcarn's, case, in which there was discussion of the conditions which made necessary a double voucher.[45] Ejectment

[40] M. Hale, *The History of the Common Law of England* (London, 1713), pp. 172–175.

[41] *H. E. L.*, vol. III, pp. 646–653. Cf. below, Ch. XIII, for paper pleadings.

[42] See below, Ch. XIV, for further discussion of the change in the character of the jury.

[43] *H. E. L.*, vol. III, pp. 429–434.

[44] *Y. B. Trin., 33 Henry VI,* pl. 12.

[45] *Y. B. Mich., 12 Ed. IV,* pl. 25; *H. E. L.*, vol. III, pp. 118–120. This case has sometimes been misinterpreted. A study of the records in connection with the Year Book

was progressing towards the point where, at the end of the century, recovery of the land as well as damages came to be allowed, the first important step towards the ousting of the older and more clumsy real actions. All in all, it is clear that, although developments may not have been so swift and free as they were in the reign of Henry III, and although many of the changes wore the camouflage of legal fictions, the law was neither retrogressing nor going through a winter of hibernation. Lawyers may have been crafty and rapacious, but they read their books and applied their minds with energy to legal problems.

Two fifteenth century lawyers became great figures in the history of the law. It is not possible to speak slightingly of a system of professional training which produced Sir John Fortescue and his younger contemporary, Sir Thomas Littleton. These men are unlikely products of a system altogether decadent. They were pioneers in English constitutional and legal thinking. Fortescue's apologia for the English system of law in the *De Laudibus Legum Anglie* may be colored with prejudice and nostalgic longing for his native land, but his *Governance of England* was a source from which seventeenth century parliamentarians drew arguments for their battle with the Stuarts. Littleton's *Tenures* may have to modern eyes something of the quality of a well-organized museum exhibit, preserving for posterity a picture of an extinct culture, but it was a model of clarity and precision in examining and stating principles of the law, and it became an inspiration to law writers of later centuries.

Some vitality there must have been in the body of precedent and principle which the fifteenth century lawyers handed on to their successors and in the system of professional education to which they had given permanent form. Otherwise neither would have survived the attack in the next century from the supporters of a reception of the Roman law. In the sixteenth century, Roman law was received in Scotland, France, and Germany but not in England. To be sure, new courts were created which were guided by the principles of the Civil Law rather than the common law. Moreover, Henry VIII encouraged the teaching of Roman law in the universities and appointed Civilians to administrative positions. The Year Books

report makes clear that common recovery was already well established and that it was the conditions requiring a double voucher which were under discussion.

14

ceased, and for a time there was probably a falling off in the number of cases brought in the common law courts. To some it seemed a possibility that the spirit of the Corpus Juris Civilis might win supremacy in law as well as in politics and religion. Their forebodings were not realized. The common law survived. Its machinery and principles continued intact. Its devotees turned with renewed energy to the study of their heritage of lawbooks from the past, and the fruits of their studies are exemplified in the constitutional arguments of the seventeenth century.[46]

[46] F. W. Maitland, *English Law and the Renaissance* (Cambridge, 1901); *H. E. L.*, vol. IV, pp. 217–288.

CHAPTER II

The Business of the Court

THE COURT OF COMMON PLEAS had its heyday in the fourteenth and fifteenth centuries. In this time it was much the busier of the two great central courts of common law. The Court of King's Bench had not yet, through the development of the action of trespass on the case and the use of the bill of Middlesex, attracted to itself the major portion of the civil business of the courts, as it did later, in the seventeenth century.[1] For the fifteenth century, the rolls of the Common Pleas are several times as bulky as those of the King's Bench, and there are at least five times as many entries, even if those on the King's side of the King's Bench are included in the count.[2]

The court had three main sorts of jurisdiction. The first and most important was its common law jurisdiction over cases between person and person begun by original writ from the Chancery. This jurisdiction was exclusive in the real actions, that is, those involving rights of ownership and possession in land; in the older personal actions of debt, detinue, account, and covenant; and finally, in the mixed actions, both personal and real, such as ejectment. Jurisdiction was shared with the King's Bench in maintenance, conspiracy, other breaches of statute, trespass, trespass on the case, and their derivatives.[3]

[1] *H. E. L.,* vol. I, pp. 198–200.
[2] See the figures in *H. E. L.,* vol. IV, pp. 255–256, and also N. Neilson's figures in *Y. B. 10 Ed. IV—49 Hy. VI,* S. S. vol. XLVII. I have compared my figures with those of Miss Marjorie Blatcher, collected during her study of the King's Bench in preparation of an unpublished Ph.D. thesis entitled "The Workings of the Court of King's Bench," University of London, 1936.
[3] *H. E. L.,* vol. I, pp. 195–203; A. Fitzherbert, *Diversité de Courtz* (ed. Redman; London, 1523); M. Hale, "Discourse Concerning the Courts of King's Bench and Common

16

Two sorts of jurisdiction by privilege brought a few cases into court each term. On the one hand, the justices as conservators of the peace could try even criminal cases where the cause of action arose within the court or among its records. In exercise of this same jurisdiction they could take surety of the peace from anyone causing a disturbance in the "place" or the Hall within their range of vision.[4] On the other hand, they had jurisdiction by privilege in suits brought by or against officers or ministers of the court.[5]

Fairly frequent entries may be found in the plea roll to illustrate the privilege of officers or ministers of the court to sue there. The form of entry is as follows: "John Doe was attached by his body to reply to Richard Roe, one of the filacers (prothonotaries, attorneys, justices, etc.) of the lord king of the Bench, according to the liberties and privileges of the said court for such filacers, etc., and other ministers of the said Bench used from time beyond memory. . . ." There was, it seems, no need for preliminary summons or distraint in such cases. The plaintiff could proceed immediately by arrest. A curious feature of the privilege, which demands further investigation, is that justices were apparently not excluded from taking part in the discussion of their own cases. The rolls show many entries in which they were sole or joint plaintiffs. In the case of *Rickhill, Brincheley, and Makene v. two parsons of Bromaye,* Rickhill and Brinchley (or Brenchesley), both justices of the Bench, are reported as having expressed an opinion in their own case, although the capacity in which they spoke is not clearly defined. The words of the report are that "afterwards by assent of all the Justices except the plaintiff, viz. Rickhill, and the other plaintiffs, the writ was abated. . . ." [6] On the other hand, in a later case involving privileges of the University of Oxford, Chief Justice Babington and Justice Newton agreed that a man could not be judge in his own case, although Justice Strangeways thought that he could by grant of the king, and Sergeant at law Rolf argued that if a writ was brought

Pleas," in F. Hargrave, *A Collection of Tracts Relative to the Law of England* (Dublin, 1787), vol. I, pp. 357–276.

[4] *Diversité de Courtz;* for instances, see C. P. 40/805, mm. 312, 314, 110d.

[5] For interesting discussions of what constituted an officer or minister of the court, see *Paston v. Jenny, Y. B. Trin., 11 Ed. IV,* pl. 4, and *Wallyng v. Merger, Y. B. 10 Ed. IV—49 Hy. VI,* S. S. vol. XLVII, pp. 38–44.

[6] *Y. B. Mich., 2 Hy. IV,* pl. 48.

against all the justices of the Bench, they would judge their own case.[7] It may be that when justices were suitors in the court, they literally or figuratively stepped down from the Bench for the time being. But, that they were not thereby precluded from the discussion is at least suggested by Rickhill's case.

Although cases in which justices figure as plaintiffs are common in the rolls, I have not happened upon any in which they were defendants. There are, however, many cases in which prothonotaries, filacers, other clerks, attorneys, and sergeants at law were sued in the court. In this case the complaint is by bill and is entered on the roll as "Memorandum that John Doe in his own person (or by A. B. his attorney) on the fifth day of July in this same term showed to the Justices here a certain bill against Richard Roe, one of the filacers (or prothonotaries, clerks, etc., of the court) here present in court, the tenor of which bill follows in these words . . ." or as some variation of this formula. Since the officer of the court was already, if not actually at least in construction of the law, in court, no summons or attachment was necessary. The advantages in this kind of privilege seem to be, at first glance, fairly evenly distributed between plaintiff and defendant. The plaintiff had the advantage of the speedy and less expensive procedure by bill. The defendant, on the other hand, was sued in a court where the procedure was familiar to him, and which was full of his friends, or at least his colleagues. As an illustration of this advantage, one attorney either through favor or his own skill succeeded in having his case postponed during thirty successive terms.[8] On the other hand, there is the more famous case of John Paston against William Jenney, Sergeant at Law, where Jenney argued that he could not be impleaded by such a bill, and that the proper procedure against him was by original writ sued out of Chancery.[9]

---

[7] *Y. B. Hil., 8 Hy. VI*, pl. 6.

[8] C. P. 40/843, Trin., 12 Ed. IV, m. 145.

[9] *Y. B. Trin., 11 Ed. IV*, pl. 4; C. P. 40/840, 145d. referred to by N. Neilson in *Y. B. 10 Ed. IV—49 Hy. VI*, S. S. vol. XLVII, p. xix. Cf. two earlier cases in which William Pole, sergeant at law, was involved. In the first (*Y. B. Hil., 3 Hy. VI*, pl. 26), he sued one T. L. in debt, apparently by original writ. In the second (C. P. 40/659, Mich., 4 Hy. VI, m. 575) J. Warrant brought a bill of conspiracy against him and Pole answered the bill. According to *Cro. Car.*, 84 (1628), a sergeant had privilege of being sued only in the Common Pleas, although it was not certain that he could be sued there by bill.

18

Interesting complications might arise where there was a conflict of privilege among the courts. At least Chief Justice Danby seems to have thought it worth while to take time for speculation on the subject. Among other interesting dicta in an Exchequer Chamber discussion of a case of privilege [10] brought in the King's Bench, involving the servant of a filacer of that court, he delivered an opinion that whenever an officer of the Common Pleas sues an officer of the King's Bench, privilege of the Common Pleas takes priority, "and the reason is that our privilege is as ancient as theirs, each one of them beyond the time of memory, and if we should allow this privilege, we should be affirming that their privilege is older than ours"—and this, he said, is not so.

Parties carrying on suits in the Common Pleas received protection similar to that extended to members of Parliament. This seems, so far as I can discover, to have applied both to plaintiffs and to defendants. For instance in the case of John Stonys, arrested as defendant in a suit in another court while on his way to Westminster as plaintiff in a suit there, the formula was: "because he and any subject of ours, in coming to our court of the Bench to prosecute or to defend any suit there, in remaining there, and in going home, ought to be and customarily is under our protection." [11]

The jurisdiction of the Court of Common Pleas in privilege was its only strictly original jurisdiction. The ordinary common law jurisdiction arose from an original writ from the Chancery directing that the defendant answer the plaintiff before the Justices of the Bench at Westminster. The third sort of jurisdiction, that is, the supervisory jurisdiction over the older local courts and the justices of assize, has left few traces in the rolls. Occasional memoranda of writs of *recordari facias loquelam* and a few entries in land cases brought up from before the justices of assize are the only evidences of this supervisory function of the court. The bulk of the business of the court was based on original writs from the Chancery.

The title "Court of Common Pleas" was not commonly used in

10 *Y. B. 10 Ed. IV—49 Hy. VI*, S. S. vol. XLVII, pp. 38–44, xxxi. The justices of both benches were accustomed to discuss cases of unusual interest in joint meetings in the Exchequer Chamber.

11 C. P. 40/775, m. 617; C. P. 40/805, m. 39; *Calendar of Plea and Memoranda Rolls Preserved among the Archives at the Corporation of the City of London, A.D. 1413–1437* (ed. Thomas; Cambridge, 1943), pp. 199, 241, 292–293, 298.

19

the fifteenth century, although it appears to be based on the famous seventeenth clause of Magna Carta which provided that "common pleas shall not follow our court but shall be held in some certain place." The fifteenth century title or heading of the plea roll was "Placita apud Westmonasterium coram Roberto danby [or another Chief Justice] et sociis suis Iusticiariis domini Regis de Banco de Termino Sancte Trinitatis anno regni Regis Edwardi quarti post conquestum anglie primo [or another term and year]" [12] and the distinguishing feature of the writs and other documents of the court was the incorporation of the phrases *apud Westmonasterium* and *de banco*.[13] King's Bench writs and other records are distinguished by the phrase *coram Rege*, although the king was ordinarily no longer present in the court.[14]

Apud Westmonasterium must not be taken too literally, however, because the court occasionally did move elsewhere. I have found only one reference to its being away from Westminster in the fifteenth century. This was an order for the removal of all pleas to Lincoln during Michaelmas term, 1413.[15] On the other hand, in the sixteenth century it was twice held in other places than Westminster,[16] and it was often at York in the early fourteenth century.[17] One such absence at York lasted five years. Richard II moved it

12 Cf. Plates II and III.
13 See *Y. B. Hil., 5 Ed. IV*, pl. 2, for a bill sued in King's Bench in which the designation of the court was *"coram Justices [sic] de Banco"* without specifying *apud Westm'* or other place. The bill was allowed.
14 See Scofield, *Edward IV*, vol. I, p. 282, for a reference to Edward IV's having sat in the King's Bench. Cf. John Stow, *Annales* (London, 1601), p. 416; C. A. J. Armstrong, *The Usurpation of Richard III* (London, 1936), p. 156, n. 100, quoted by Dr. Chrimes in his edition of Fortescue's *De Laudibus Legum Anglie* (Cambridge, 1942), p. 150.
15 *C. C. R., 1413–1419*, p. 91.
16 *H. E. L.*, vol. I, p. 197; *Black Book of Lincoln's Inn*, vol. I, p. 264.
17 *C. C. R., 1318–1323*, pp. 76, 175, May 1319–Jan. 1320, orders for removal to York and return; p. 417, Feb. 4, 1322, order for transfer to York; *C. C. R., 1323–1327*, p. 42, Nov. 8, 1323, William de Beresford in person or by deputy to see to it that rolls are carried from York to Westminster with proper escort of sheriffs; *C. C. R., 1327–1330*, p. 161, Aug. 18, 1327, order to remove to York; p. 165, Sept. 23, 1327, the King's reply to the mayor, aldermen, and sheriffs of London, who protest against the removal to York, directing them to help with the transfer of the rolls; p. 325, Oct. 20, 1328, transfer back to Westminster; *C. P. R., 1330–1334*, p. 412, Feb. 20, 1333, order for sheriffs, bailiffs, and others to assist William de Herle and the other justices in conveying the rolls, writs, etc., to York; *C. C. R., 1337–1339*, pp. 501–502, Oct. 1, 1338, order for transfer back to Westminster. For discussion of the reasons for these movements, see Tout, *Chapters*, vol. II, p. 178, vol. III, pp. 58–64, and "Beginnings of a Modern Capital," *Collected Papers* (Manchester, 1932–1934), vol. III, pp. 249–275.

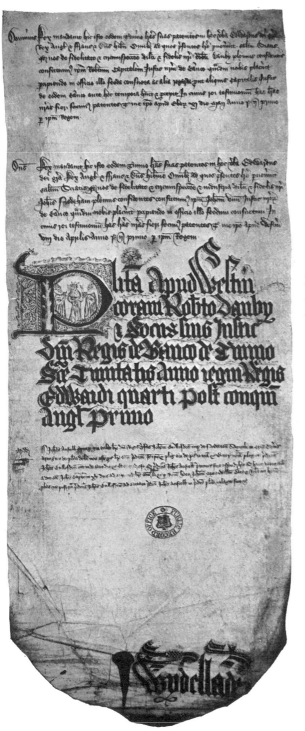

Plate II.
First Membrane of Plea Roll of Trinity Term, 1 Edward IV.

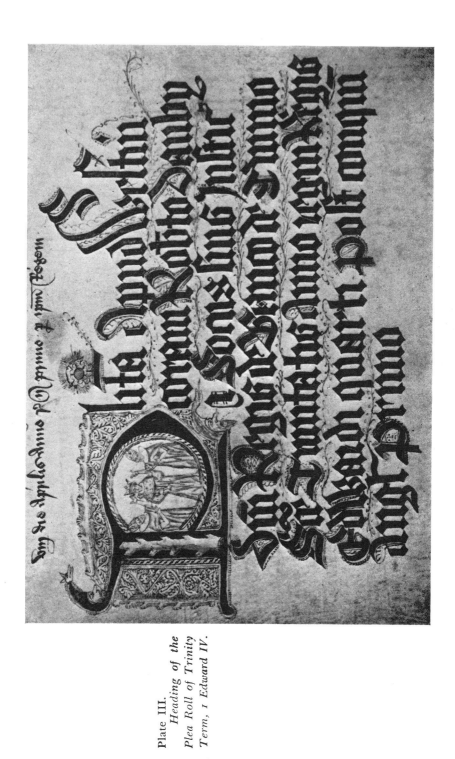

Plate III.
    Heading of the
Plea Roll of Trinity
Term, 1 Edward IV.

again to York for Trinity Term,[18] 1392. I have found no evidence for its sitting elsewhere than at York or Westminster in the fourteenth century save the rather vague assertion in the course of a discussion reported in the Year Book of Michaelmas, 7 Edward III, that "the Common Bench is at one place and another at the will of the King" [19] and the complaint in the statute of Northampton that, by the removal of the Common Bench without sufficient warning, pleas are often without a day, to the great loss of the parties.[20] Neither statement is so phrased that it could not refer merely to the movements to York, which were quite frequent in the period of the statute.[21]

The Court of King's Bench was much more mobile than the Common Bench. Often in the fourteenth century its supervision of the work of the justices of gaol (jail) delivery and of the peace seems to have taken it from Westminster into the various counties of England.[22] This mobility continued into the early fifteenth century. The Commons complained of it, asking that the King's Bench "remain in a certain place at Westminster or at York, there where the Common Bench remains so that no man may be led astray [23] for lack of sage counsel and for non-certainty of place." [24]

To the Commons who presented this petition, removal of the

[18] C. P. R., 1391–1396, p. 63, June 7, 1392, writ of aid, addressed to several, to take horses and carts for carriage from London to York of the king's writs, rolls, fines, writings, records, etc., in the custody of Thomas Haxey; C. C. R., 1389–1392, p. 565, May 30, 1392, order by King and Council that writs, original and judicial, for the octaves, the quindene, and the morrow of Saint John the Baptist shall be made returnable at York. Cf. R. P., vol. III, p. 406; C. C. R., 1392–1396, p. 76, Oct. 25, 1392, order for transfer back to Westminster. See Tout, Chapters, vol. III, pp. 481–482, for discussion of the reasons for this move.

[19] Pl. 47. Cf. L. O. Pike, Y. B. B. 11 and 12 Ed. III (R. S.), p. xxviii; Y. B. B. 12 and 13 Ed. III (R. S.), pp. xxiii–xxv.

[20] 2 Ed. III, c. 11.

[21] See p. 20, n. 17, above.

[22] For a table of the movements of the King's Bench from 1 Edward III to Easter, 9 Henry V, see B. H. Putnam, Proceedings before the Justices of the Peace in the Fourteenth and Fifteenth Centuries. Edward III to Richard III (London, 1938), pp. 29–33. For discussion of the purpose of these movements, see ibid., pp. lvii–lxxvi. The removal of the Common Bench seems sometimes, but not always, to have coincided with the removal of the King's Bench to the northern capital.

[23] The French word is susduit.

[24] R. P., vol. II, p. 286, no. 4; cf. also p. 311, no. 7. These petitions have been cited (H. E. L., vol. I, p. 197) as complaints concerning movements of the Common Bench. It seems, however, to be the King's Bench which is complained of.

Court of Common Pleas to York apparently did not seem an infringement of the provision of Magna Carta that common pleas should be held in a "certain place." Very likely, especially in the troubled periods of the century, they became accustomed to thinking of York as a second capital.[25] With the proper warning of removal provided in the statute of Northampton, there might even have been an advantage to suitors from the midland and northern counties in finding the court nearer home. Moreover, what concerned the Commons was the certainty of the place rather than its fixity. They were near enough to the time of conception of Magna Carta not to be unduly weighed down by tradition and precedent built upon it. By the seventeenth century, however, literal-minded reverence for Magna Carta and its interpretations in the practice of earlier times had grown so great that the court was forced to remain in uncomfortable and inconvenient quarters long after it should, from any sensible point of view, have been moved elsewhere. Roger North says, in his *Lives of the Norths:*

But the air of the great door when the wind is in the north is very cold, and if it might have been done the court had been moved a little into a warmer place. It was once proposed to let it in through the wall . . . into a back room which they call the Treasury. But the Lord Chief Justice Bridgman would not agree to it, as against Magna Charta, which says that the Common Pleas shall be held *in certo loco,* or in a certain place, with which the distance of an inch from that place is inconsistent, and all the pleas would be *coram non judice.*[26]

The sessions of the Court of Common Pleas were held during the four regular law terms. These had long since become fixed at such intervals as to avoid planting, harvest, and other agricultural seasons, as well as the major church festivals from which they were named. The opening and closing days of Michaelmas and Hilary terms were fixed, whereas the dates of Easter and Trinity term varied according to the date of Easter, there being thirty-five possible first days for the opening of each of these terms. Michaelmas was the longest of the terms, beginning on the octave of Saint Michael, or the sixth of October, and ending at the end of the week of the quindene of Saint Martin, that is, the twenty-eighth of

25 Putnam, *Proceedings*, p. lx.
26 Ed. Jessop (London, 1890), vol. I, p. 126.

November.[27] Trinity was the shortest term and also the most likely to be broken off suddenly owing to outbreaks of the plague.[28]

The King's Bench was considered, in the seventeenth century, to have an important advantage in a speedier method of continuation of cases from "day to day" rather than from common return day to common return day as in the Common Pleas.[29] In the fifteenth century, the method of continuation of cases in King's Bench was certainly more efficient and manageable, but it was not inherently more speedy. It is readily understandable that the assignment to a plaintiff in the King's Bench of a particular day in the next term for the return of his writ made it possible for the clerks of that court to draw up a reasonable docket for each day of the term. In the Common Pleas, on the other hand, writs were returnable on the common return days, which were really a whole week of term called by the name of the first day. The parties might appear on any day within the week.[30] This was obviously a clumsy system and, as time went on, must have proved a severe handicap to the court in its rivalry with the King's Bench.

The procedure in the Common Pleas had been much speeded up since the days of Bracton, to be sure, although the statute of uncertain date called *"Dies Communes de Banco"* [31] was still considered to have some theoretical force.[32] According to the rules described by Bracton, which appear to correspond with those prescribed in the statute, Reeves calculated that the whole of the process by distress, from the summons on the original writ to the last *distringas,* would take a minimum of two years and more than eight months. The required time between days in court was from the octaves of Michaelmas to the octaves of Hilary, from thence to the octaves of Trinity, and from thence to the morrow of All Souls.[33] This dilatory proce-

---

[27] H. E. L., vol. III, App. VII; E. A. Fry, *Almanac* (London, 1915), pp. 136–138. For a list of the common return days in the fifteenth century, see below, App. IV.

[28] As, for example, in *Y. B. Trin.,* 4 Ed. IV, pl. 1.

[29] Hale, *Discourse,* ch. ix.

[30] As an illustration of this point, compare the continuations in *Ely and others v. Chertesey* and in *Beyne and others v. Wodecokke and others* in the records quoted in *Y. B. 10 Ed. IV—49 Hy. VI,* S. S. vol. XLVII, pp. 92–95 and pp. 52–55, respectively.

[31] *S. R.,* vol. I, p. 208.

[32] *Y. B. Easter, 8 Ed. IV,* pl. 9. Pigot, one of the sergeants, said that there was no statute affirming the common law with respect to return days, but was contradicted by the justices.

[33] J. Reeves, *A History of English Law* (London, 1783–1784), vol. I, p. 500.

dure had, by the fifteenth century, been abandoned. A later day was often given within the same term, especially in Michaelmas term, which was long, and the usual return was from one term to the next, without, as in Bracton's day, skipping a term in between.[34]

Like Parliament, the court did not begin business on the nominal day of the opening of term. Showing that respect which English administration so often showed for the dignity of the individual or for human weakness, or perhaps in consideration of the hazards and difficulty of travel, the court allowed three days of grace before the business of the term began. During these days parties were allowed to essoin or excuse themselves. Essoins had fallen much into disuse by this time and were certainly not taken in full court before all the justices, who did not take their seats on the Bench in court until the fourth day after the nominal opening.[35]

The rivalry for business between the Courts of King's Bench and Common Pleas has been barely touched upon so far in the mention of concurrent jurisdiction and of the superiority of the King's Bench procedure in continuing cases *de die in diem*. It was, as yet, not very acute. Late in the fourteenth century, the King's Bench seems to have made an effort to cut into the business of the Common Pleas by inducing the Chancery to make trespass writs returnable only in the King's Bench. The Commons, in protest against this change, cynically suggested that the motive behind it was the desire of the King's Bench clerks to get more fees. The royal answer to the petition was merely that writs of trespass should henceforth, as in the past, be awarded in the one Bench or the other at the discretion of the Chancellor.[36] That that discretion eventually led the Chancellor to favor the Common Pleas we may infer, since a greater number of trespass cases was considered by the Common Pleas than by the King's Bench in the fifteenth century.[37]

---

[34] In the plea roll of Mich., 2 Ed. IV (C. P. 40/806), dates for the return of writs range from Michaelmas in one month (i.e., Oct. 27) in the same term to the quindene of Hilary (i.e., Jan. 27) in the next term. The usual "day" given is the octaves of Hilary.

[35] *Y. B. Trin., 4 Ed. IV*, pl. 1.

[36] *R. P.*, vol. II, p. 311.

[37] See N. Neilson's figures, *Y. B. 10 Ed. IV—49 Hy. VI*, S. S., vol. XLVII, pp. xxv–xxviii. Miss Marjorie Blatcher (cf. above, p. 1, n. 2) confirms this statement from her studies.

This abortive fourteenth century attack of the King's Bench on the Common Pleas jurisdiction in trespass was the first bout in a long struggle for power which ultimately, in the seventeenth century, resulted in a monopoly for the King's Bench of the major part of the civil business of the courts. The Common Pleas attempted but failed to regain some of its lost business by using a writ of trespass *quare clausum fregit* as a general writ of summons which could be followed by a new original. This original writ still remained as a prohibitive expense.[38] In Chief Justice Bridgman's time, the Common Pleas resorted to the protection of a statute which forbade the taking of bail beyond the sum of £40 when the specific cause of action was not stated in the writ.[39] This stratagem also failed. The King's Bench showed itself ingenious in getting around the prohibition. It merely added the phrase *ac etiam* and the particular complaint to the wording of the bill, and the Common Pleas was eventually forced to concede victory to its more aggressive rival.[40]

The weapon with which the King's Bench eventually defeated the Common Pleas was already known in the fifteenth century, but was, as yet, little used.[41] It was the bill of Middlesex, a device by which, through the fiction that the defendant was already in custody of the keeper of the Marshalsea Prison (the prison of the King's Bench), the King's Bench could extend its jurisdiction in privilege to forms of action over which the Court of Common Pleas had formerly had exclusive jurisdiction. The bill of Middlesex, to which the marshal would necessarily reply that he did not have the defendant in his custody, but that he was running about in the county of X, was followed by a *latitat* to the sheriff of X, that is, a writ to that sheriff to arrest the defendant in the county of X.

The advantages of this procedure will become more clear when the ponderously slow and costly procedure of the Court of Common Pleas has been described in detail.[42] For the present, let it suf-

---

[38] Hale, *Discourses,* pp. 366 ff.
[39] 13 Car. II, stat. 2, c. 2.
[40] *H. E. L.,* vol. I, p. 221.
[41] Neilson, *Y. B. 10 Ed. IV—49 Hy. VI,* S. S., vol. XLVII, p. xxvi. N. Neilson found thirty in the King's Bench roll for Easter term, 1470. This is few compared to what there would be a century later. There are few discussions of the bill of Middlesex reported in the Year Books.
[42] See Chs. XI–XIV.

fice to say that procedure by bill of Middlesex was like the wave of a magician's rod compared to the Common Pleas procedure at its worst. In his day Chief Justice Hale considered the bill of Middlesex pernicious because, as he said, by giving to them a quick and inexpensive remedy, it encouraged plaintiffs to bring merely vexatious suits.[43]

The evident advantages of the procedure by bill of Middlesex and the fact that a decision of the Court of Common Pleas could be reversed in the King's Bench by writ of error proceedings raise the question why the former court was able to compete effectively as long as it did. Several answers may be suggested to explain why parties were satisfied to trust their interests to a lower court even though a higher jurisdiction and a speedier process were available. The inherent conservatism of a law based on precedent helped at first to curb the ambitions of the King's Bench. The fiction of the custody of the marshal encountered some resistance in establishing itself.[44] Furthermore the Court of Common Pleas had a large prestige built up in the two centuries or more of its existence. Its reputation as a court for the prosecution of civil suits had no doubt grown during the period when the frequent and unpredictable movements of the King's Bench had made the prosecution of a suit there an endurance test to be avoided. Only sergeants at law could plead in the court.[45] For this reason, it was probably still, as in Edward II's reign, the court which the apprentices attended most assiduously for their instruction.[46] It was certainly still the court from which most Year Book reports have come.

Whatever may be the true explanation of its popularity in the fifteenth century, the Court of Common Pleas without question continued throughout the Year Book period to be the busier of the two great central courts of common law. Most of its business had to

[43] Hale, *Discourse,* cap. IX. In Hale's time, a bill of Middlesex cost 2s. 6d. as compared with a minimum charge of 6s. 8d. for an original writ. The *latitat* cost 5s. 1d. The chief savings, however, were in the elimination of the tedious and costly mesne process, described below in Ch. XII.

[44] *Y. B. Trin.,* 7 *Hy. VI,* pl. 15; *Mich.,* 22 *Hy. VI,* pl. 43; *Mich.,* 27 *Hy.* VI, pl. 35; *Mich.,* 31 *Hy. VI,* pl. 5.

[45] *Y. B. Trin.,* 11 *Ed. IV,* pl. 4, *Paston v. Jenney.* Note that Justices Choke and Littleton were both of the opinion that there might be exceptions to the rule.

[46] Maitland and Turner, *Y. B. 3–4 Ed. II,* S. S. vol. XXII, pp. xxi, xli–xlii.

do with recovery of debts.[47] The amounts sought in debt and damages range from 40s. to thousands of pounds. The formal procedure of the court was the same whatever the sum demanded, although the amount of fees expected by the clerks both of the Chancery and the Court of Common Pleas was greater when the amounts demanded were greater.

It is hoped that this general discussion of the business of the court may have prepared the reader for the more particular view of the Court at work which follows in the next chapter.

[47] The figures for four terms of Edward IV's reign are as follows:

Term and roll	Debt	Trespass	Total entries on roll
Easter, 10 Ed. IV C. P. 40/835	2700	650	3800
Mich., 11 Ed. IV C. P. 40/840	5000	1000	6000
Easter, 12 Ed. IV C. P. 40/842	3239	950	4970
Mich., 22 Ed. IV C. P. 40/882	4412	1252	6204

The figures for the first two terms listed are N. Neilson's, *Y. B. 10 Ed. IV—49 Hy. VI,* S. S. vol. XLVII, pp. xix–xxvii. Those for Easter, 12 Ed. IV, are based on a manuscript analysis of this plea roll available at the Mount Holyoke College library. The last set of figures is my own. N. Neilson's figures are estimates. The others are from actual count.

CHAPTER III

A Day in Court

THE COURT OF COMMON PLEAS five centuries ago had little of the somber privacy of the Victorian Gothic law courts of the early twentieth century. Sessions held in the Great Hall at Westminster by the north entrance [1] were patently defenseless against the clatter made by people passing through the door and equally so against the competing sounds made by the Courts of King's Bench and Chancery, in other parts of the Hall. The justices worked under what today would be considered intolerable conditions. In the winter, when the wind was in the north and blew through the cracks round the door or through the opening as people went in and out, matters were much worse. Then both justices and clerks had good reason to be glad of the fur-lined robes which were appurtenances of their office.[2]

Avoiding the discomforts of winter, let us visit a session of the court on Friday of the first week of Trinity term in 1470.[3] This calls for early rising. Fifteenth century Englishmen followed the sun's time more closely than we do in this age of electric lighting. The court opened daily at eight o'clock.[4] As we pass from the morning sunlight through the great door into the dim coolness of the Hall, we see the "place" of the Common Pleas on our right.[5] The clerks are already seated at the green-baize-covered table below the justices'

[1] For the situation of the court, see above, Ch. II.
[2] For the justices' robes, see below, Ch. VI; for the livery of the clerks, see Hanaper Accounts and Jakes's memoranda, below, App. II.
[3] Trinity term began this year on June 25. Friday was the 29th.
[4] John Fortescue, *De Laudibus Legum Anglie* (ed. Chrimes; Cambridge, 1942), cap. 51, p. 129.
[5] The King's Bench and Chancery were at the far end of the Hall under the south window (John Stow, *A Survey of London* [ed. Kingsford; Oxford, 1908], vol. II, p. 118).

28

bench and are arranging their writing implements and parchments in preparation for the morning's session.[6] A wooden barrier separates the table and the area around it from the main part of the Hall. There are nine clerks at the table, all dressed in vivid parti-colored blue and green or buff and green tunics. They make a brilliant patch of color against their somber background, which is lit up only by three shields hanging on the wall above the justices' bench. These nine clerks are the three prothonotaries of the court, each with the two assistants allowed him by the ordinance of Trinity, 35 Henry VI.[7] They are the chief clerks who enter pleadings in the record. Between the table and the bench at the left sits a man dressed in bright blue. He is more difficult to identify but is probably the deputy or clerk of Sir John Fogge, the Custos Brevium or Keeper of the Writs.[8] At either end of the table to left and right stand two tipstaves dressed in blue and green and carrying each a stave in his hand. These are the court criers.[9]

Taking advantage of our privilege as visitors from another century, we discover by asking one of the clerks that the first case on the docket [10] for the morning's session is *Curson v. Curson* in detinue of charters. William Pryce, the plaintiff's attorney, has already arrived. We identify him as the short, bald-headed man standing at the left of the table in earnest conversation with two sergeants at law. His knee-length buff and green tunic and the pen-holder at his belt distinguish him clearly from the sergeants in their long robes of blue and green with great capelike collars and their white

[6] For physical details such as the number and position of people and things, this account relies on the fifteenth century portrait of the court which is preserved in the Library of the Inner Temple (see Plate I, frontispiece). For the account of pleadings, discussion, and decisions of sergeants and justices, it relies on the Year Book reports and the records of the cases for Trinity term, 10 Edward IV (S. S. vol. XLVII, pp. 87–113) or upon general knowledge gained from reading the plea rolls.

[7] The ordinance allowed to "each of the two prothonotaries" two clerks. (See App. I (c).) By 1470, however, there were three prothonotaries. (See Ch. VIII below.)

[8] App. I (c) and (f).

[9] The fifteenth century picture shows these tipstaves standing on the table. It is to be supposed, however, that this is so because the artist knew nothing of perspective rather than because it was the custom of the court that they should stand so. On some occasions at an earlier time, however, the table was apparently used as a kind of stage. Professor Sayles cites a case in which an attorney whose appointment was questioned was asked to stand on the table on which the clerks laid their rolls in order that all might see and remember him (*Select Cases in K. B.,* vol. I, p. xcii).

[10] No docket rolls survive for the fifteenth century. Presumably, however, there was some sort of list of cases for each return day.

coifs. Movement in the crowd behind us attracts our attention, and we turn to see William Curson, the defendant, as he approaches the bar of the court. He is accompanied by a sergeant at law, who, after a final word to his client, takes his place with two others of his order where they stand at the right.[11] As the great bell of the palace clock booms forth the hour,[12] the criers call the court to order for the entrance of the justices. The clerks rise in their places and, for a brief time, the court is a pool of silence within the general hubbub of the Hall. Five justices [13] take their places on the bench, probably in order of seniority, except for Sir Robert Danby, the Chief Justice, who sits in the center. Their scarlet robes lined with white taffeta [14] and their white sergeants' coifs complete a splendid picture particularly impressive to twentieth century eyes unaccustomed to such brilliance of color in everyday dress.

The case of *Curson v. Curson* is called.[15] Pygot, one of the two sergeants standing with William Pryce, the plaintiff's attorney, steps forward, bows to the justices, and delivers the declaration in a rapid monotone which is unintelligible gibberish to us. The language is neither English nor what we recognize as French. It is the special law French reserved for pleadings and discussions among

[11] In the fifteenth century portrait, five sergeants at law are represented. They were probably not all there to plead in the same suit. Parties seem occasionally to have engaged two sergeants as counselors. Commonly, their high fees must have made this impossible. The Year Book reports suggest that sergeants at law often took part in discussions of interesting points of law even in suits in which they were not acting as counsel.

[12] Stow, *Survey*, vol. II, pp. 121–122; *C. P. R., 1429–1436*, p. 184, a grant of the office of keeping the clock to John Lenham, with the fees of 6*d.* a day payable yearly at the exchequer.

[13] The fifteenth century portrait of the court depicts seven justices. In Trinity term, 1470, however, there were only six (Edward Foss, *The Judges of England* [London, 1848–1869], vol. IV, p. 392). They were Chief Justice Sir Robert Danby, Sir Walter Moyle, Sir John Needham, Sir Richard Choke, Thomas Littleton, and Thomas Younge. Younge is nowhere mentioned in the reports of this term. This does not necessarily prove that he was not there. He appears, however, to have become a re-adeptionist after earlier showing strong Yorkist sympathies. It is possible that he was absent in June, 1470, for political reasons. In any case, it was not uncommon for one or more of the justices to be absent during the term. For example, in Easter term, 1464, both Chief Justice Markham of the King's Bench and Danby of the Common Pleas were in the North (*Y. B. Easter, 4 Ed. IV*, pls. 1, 4, 29; *Paston Letters*, No. 281).

[14] The justices' winter robes were lined with white budge or miniver. Their summer robes were lined with taffeta. There seems to have been no fixed rule about color. The contemporary painter dresses them in scarlet.

[15] For the report and record of this case, see *Y. B. 10 Ed. IV—49 Hy. VI*, S. S. vol. XLVII, pp. 104–106.

the lawyers in court.[16] Fluency in it is part of their professional expertness, and the practice of conducting pleadings in this language is one of the means by which they have built up a professional monopoly. As Pygot speaks, Jenney, counsel for William Curson, the defendant, follows closely to see that there is no variation between count or declaration and the writ. This again requires special technical skill since the writ is in Latin. When Pygot has finished, apparently without variation, Jenney steps to the bar and demands judgment of the writ on the ground that his client is son and heir of John Curson, and not, as alleged in the declaration, son and heir of William Curson. This brings a swift rebuke from Justice Littleton, who says that Jenney cannot traverse at one and the same time the statement that he is son and that he is heir of William Curson. Jenney quickly amends his plea to say that the defendant is son and heir of John Curson, not son of William Curson as alleged.[17]

While this exchange is going on, Copley, the first prothonotary, who has the entry of this case, is jotting down memoranda on the parchment before him. From these with the help of the original writ which he will get from the Custos Brevium he will later be able to enter the full record.[18]

Justice Moyle now intervenes in the exchanges between counsel to say that Jenney's plea, even as amended, is not good because the words "son and heir" are not material to the count that the charters came into William Curson's hands at the death of William Curson. The action, says Moyle, is brought against the defendant not as heir but on his possession of the box of charters. Jenney opposes this view, arguing that if the defendant is not allowed this plea, he may, at some future time, be estopped [19] from saying that he is not the son of William Curson as alleged by the plaintiff. Justice Choke

[16] See *H. E. L.*, vol. II, pp. 477–482, and P. H. Winfield, *The Chief Sources of English Legal History* (Cambridge, Mass., 1921), pp. 7–15, for discussions of the language of the law and the reasons why French continued in use after the statute of 1362 enacting that all pleadings should be in English although the record should continue to be entered in Latin.

[17] For the liberality allowed in amending pleadings, see W. S. Holdsworth, "The Development of Written and Oral Pleading" in *Select Essays in Anglo-American Legal History*, vol. II, pp. 614–642.

[18] See below, Chs. VIII and XIII, for further discussion of the method of entering pleadings.

[19] Barred by his own act or admission in not denying or affirming that which he might have denied or affirmed.

31

here assures him that he could not later be estopped from saying what he is not now allowed to plead in traverse or denial. Choke concurs with Moyle in the opinion that the plea is not good. Justices Needham and Littleton, on the other hand, believe that the plea is good and should be allowed. For some time, the point is argued back and forth among the justices. In the course of the discussion, Littleton cites as a parallel situation where the law would be clear, a hypothetical case in which William Curson, son of William Curson, is outlawed and taken by the sheriff on a writ of *capias utlagatum*. In these circumstances, says Littleton, William would have a reversal of the outlawry. Here Chief Justice Danby enters the discussion to say that the situation supposed by Littleton is different from the one under consideration because misnomer in outlawry can result in the arrest of the wrong person, whereas in the case at hand no such mischief threatens. In the end, however, Littleton and Needham prevail. Danby is won to their point of view. The clerk is ordered to enter the plea and the plaintiff to answer it.[20] Thereupon Pygot, in replication to the plea, repeats the allegation that the defendant is the son of William Curson of Brightwell and asks that this matter be submitted to a jury of the country. Jenney similarly asks for trial by twelve men of the country. The parties have now reached an issue of fact, not too closely related perhaps to the essential question whether William Curson is falsely and unjustly detaining something which belongs to John Curson, but nonetheless one which can be determined by the jury. The justices order that the replication be entered, and that a writ of *venire facias* to summon a jury be sent to the county returnable in the first week of Michaelmas term. The prothonotary makes a note of this, and the court is now ready for the next case.

This case, *Halle v. Halle,* involves outlawry in process on an original writ of trespass.[21] While we were absorbed in the first case, Thomas Halle, the defendant, has been brought into the Hall in the custody of a servant of the warden of the Fleet prison, and as

---

[20] This case illustrates the value of the plea roll in supplementing our knowledge of a case reported in the Year Book. So far as the report goes, we are left wondering what was the outcome of the discussion. The record, however, shows that the plea was entered.

[21] *Y. B. of 10 Ed. IV—49 Hy. VI, S. S.* vol. XLVII, pp. 109–110.

William Curson and William Pryce depart he is led forward to the bar of the court. He looks unkempt and ill. His legs are bare, his hair and beard uncut, and his face is pallid and unhealthy. He has apparently been in confinement for some time and has not been able to afford the services of a barber or tailor or to buy from his jailer additional food to supplement his inadequate prison rations. The warden's servant, dressed in a buff-colored tunic and wearing a sword at his belt, offers a jaunty contrast to his charge.

When the case is called, Thomas himself delivers his plea, in English.[22] He says that the outlawry was proclaimed in the county court of Sussex on the preceding twenty-sixth of April and that he was later arrested in Bristol, by virtue of a writ of *capias utlagatum* addressed to the sheriff there, and sent to the Fleet prison, where he has been ever since. He pleads that he ought not to be detained in prison by reason of his outlawry because there was an error in the original writ of trespass. He was not, as alleged in the writ, nor was he ever, living in Westbury on Tryn but was in Thrydland. This is held by the justices to be a good plea, and therefore it is ordered that a writ of *scire facias* be sent out to warn the plaintiff to appear in the second week of Michaelmas term to maintain his writ. Brayne, the prothonotary who has the entry of the case, makes a note of this. Thereupon, Richard Brugge, John Staunton, William Kene, and John White, all of London, gentlemen, offer themselves as mainpernors [23] for Thomas' appearance in the quindene of Michaelmas, and the latter is allowed to go free.

The third case called is *Arweblaster v. Bendysshe* in debt on obligation.[24] The plaintiff is represented by Simon Damme while Thomas Bendysshe is here in his own person. We learn from the declaration (if, by now, we have become sufficiently accustomed to the rapidly spoken law French) that the action is based on a written obligation signed by Thomas Bendysshe on May 16, 1458 (that is, twelve years ago), and that the defendant was bound by the obligation to pay to the plaintiff £200. He has persistently refused to pay despite repeated urgings. Catesby, for the defendant, makes the

---

22 For pleading in person in English, see *Y. B. Mich., 21 Ed. IV*, pl. 4.
23 The mainpernors will be amerced if Halle does not come.
24 *Y. B. 10 Ed. IV—49 Hy. VI, S. S.* vol. XLVII, pp. 96–100.

usual denial of the "tort and force" and asks that the obligation and the condition endorsed upon it be read to the court.[25] Copley, the first prothonotary, takes the *scriptum* from Damme, the plaintiff's attorney, and reads rapidly through its terms. Fortunately, it is in English [26] so that we are able to grasp its contents easily. The condition was that Thomas Bendysshe was to pay the £200 if, within a year from the date of signature, he had not proved that it was the will of John Bendysshe that Arweblaster should make an estate to himself, Thomas Bendysshe, and one J. C. in certain lands and tenements in D. Catesby then pleads, for the defendant, that a bill was drawn up expressing John Bendysshe's will to have the estate conveyed, that John Bendysshe signed this bill, and that Thomas Bendysshe then delivered it to James Arweblaster within the specified time. His plea is, therefore, that the condition of the *scriptum* has been sufficiently fulfilled.

The discussion among the justices turns upon the difficulty of proof of the fulfillment of the condition. Chief Justice Danby thinks that it is sufficiently proved. Pygot argues, however, that the defendant should have shown that the bill was, in fact, John Bendysshe's deed. This raises the question how and where the defendant might have had his proof of the will of John Bendysshe within the time limit specified in the *scriptum*.

The justices appear to agree with Jenney that "no other proof is effective in our law except trial by twelve men." Such proof could not be had except on an action brought in court on a writ of debt, and only the plaintiff could have such an action. Justice Littleton is of the opinion that, if such proof was not made before the end of the twelve-month period, this was the plaintiff's own folly, and that therefore Catesby's plea is good. Because the other justices are not in full agreement, however, the defendant's counsel asks for license to imparl to Michaelmas term in order that he may meanwhile change his plea if he wishes.[27] William Cumberford, the second prothono-

---

[25] This was the usual procedure in debt on a written obligation with condition attached.

[26] Many of the *scripta* quoted in the records are in English.

[27] This is only my own explanation of why, although the Year Book for Trinity term reports a lengthy discussion in the case, only a request for license to imparl is entered in the plea roll.

tary, who has jotted down a memorandum of the plea crosses it out and writes instead "li' lo'." [28]

The pleadings and discussions in these three cases have taken over two hours. It is now after ten o'clock, and there is time for only one more case before the court rises at eleven.[29] Instead of staying to hear this case, let us go through the small door in the west wall of the Hall, through which the justices entered earlier this morning, to see some of the behind-the-scenes activities of the court. Somewhere in the cellar below the Hall or under the Exchequer is the Treasury of the Common Pleas where the plea rolls of earlier terms are kept in case they should be needed for reference in the discussions of pleadings and judgments in the court.[30] It happens that in this morning's session there was no need to refer to entries of earlier terms. On some occasions, however, the clerk or keeper of the Treasury would be ordered to bring in an old roll in order that the justices might "record" what it said.[31]

By inquiring of an usher of the court, we find our way to this Treasury of the Common Pleas, sometimes also called "Hell" in the fifteenth century. There we find the keeper of the Treasury and his secondary. Behind them on shelves are the plea rolls of earlier terms. As we enter the room, an attorney follows close on our heels. He shows to the keeper a writ of *habeas corpora juratorum* which he has procured from the prothonotary's office and asks that a copy of the entry of the pleadings on the roll of Hilary term be made. He gives to the secondary the number of the membrane or "number

[28] The customary abbreviation for *licencia interloquendi* or "licence to imparl."

[29] See Sayles, *Select Cases in K. B.*, vol. II, p. lxxviii, n. 1, for discussion of hours of sitting of the judges. I have found it impossible to estimate satisfactorily how many cases might be considered in a single day's sessions. Judging from the nature of the entries on the plea roll, less than one tenth of them represent happenings in the morning sessions of the court under the direct eye of the justices. This would mean that an average of 10 to 12 cases was considered each day. This is obviously an impossible number if the court, as Fortescue says, sat only three hours each day and all the cases involved as lengthy argument as most of those reported in the Year Books. Presumably, however, many matters, such as routine requests for license to imparl or ordinary judgments to be given on records sent up from the assizes, required little discussion. And if the justices found it hard to give a decision without further consultation of their books, they directed the clerks to make an entry that "the justices wished to advise" and to give to the parties a day in a later term.

[30] For discussion of the location of the Treasury, see below, Ch. IX.

[31] Marginal notes indicating that the justices have examined the roll and "recorded" what it says are not difficult to find in fifteenth century rolls.

rolle," and the latter quickly finds the entry. He makes a fair copy on a suitable piece of parchment. The attorney pays 2s. 5d. (2s. 1d. for the keeper himself, and 4d. for the secondary) [32] and departs on other errands.

This is only one of several sorts of business we might see transacted in the Treasury if we had more time to spend. Here outlawed defendants, who have avoided Thomas Halle's fate of arrest and have secured charters of pardon, may procure their writs of *scire facias* to summon the plaintiff. Here also other defendants who have been exacted in the county court and wish to avoid outlawry appear to offer bail and secure a writ of *supersedeas* to stay the proceedings in outlawry. Here, likewise, are made up the transcripts of the records of cases removed by writ of error into the King's Bench.[33]

Instead of lingering to witness more of the activities of "Hell," we return to the Hall in time to see the court adjourned for the day. The justices leave by the same door through which they entered, presumably to disrobe and go to their dinners. We shall be well advised to follow their example for, although the justices have finished their official day's work and may now retire to their chambers to study or to engage in private discussion, we have not yet finished ours if we propose to have a complete view of the work of the court. If we wait by the great door of the Hall, we may follow the justices and sergeants, clerks and attorneys, as they go down to the landing on the river to the barge which will take them to the Temple landing in London.[34] At the cost of a few pence we may go with them and make our way to a tavern in Fleet Street for dinner.

While we are at dinner, we have an opportunity to reflect on the differences between what we have just witnessed and the proceedings in a session of one of the Common Pleas divisions of the twentieth century High Court of Judicature. Most striking to the eye would be the absence in the court of all save one justice [35] and the presence, in a box especially built to seat them, of a jury of twelve men. These dissimilarities would be only the outward signs

---

[32] App. I (g).
[33] *Ibid.*
[34] Tout, *Collected Papers*, vol. III, p. 269.
[35] The other justices would all be busy presiding in other courtrooms elsewhere in the building.

of fundamental differences in the functions of the court in two periods. In a typical session of the modern court we should be witnessing a trial. The barristers or counselors of the parties would still be wearing the white silk coifs of their predecessors, but they would wear robes of black instead of the gayer colors of earlier centuries. Furthermore they would be engaged not in pleading but in examining or cross-examining witnesses in order to expose the essential facts in the case for the benefit of a jury ignorant of them. In the fifteenth century we should ordinarily have to attend the assizes in the county in order to witness the trial of a civil suit, and the jury we should find there would be theoretically cognizant of the facts.[36] In the twentieth century pleadings are always by exchange of papers. In the fifteenth century only pleadings in the common form could be pleaded by exchanges through the court offices. All special pleadings must be pleaded by sergeants at law in the open court.[37]

Even a modern court must from time to time deal with procedural matters. The judges must rule on amendments of pleas, addition of new defendants, and many other similar details. In the fifteenth century, if we are to rely upon the literal statement of the record, most of the court's time must have been taken up with such business. The question is whether each entry on the plea roll really does represent, as it purports to, a transaction before the judges at Westminster. The tremendous bulk of the plea rolls suggests that the justices did not concern themselves with the details of routine procedure. It would have been physically impossible for them to take individual notice of the several thousands of writs of process sent out during each term in addition to supervising pleadings, giving judgments, and deciding points of procedure where there was no certain rule for the clerks to follow. Moreover, the court was too small and too crowded to contain all the bundles of writs of process and the sixteen or more filacers with their membranes of the plea role and other impedimenta. The fifteenth century portrait of the court does not depict them as present before the justices, nor does the ordinance of 35 Henry VI mention them among the officers

---

[36] Cases from Middlesex were tried at Westminster before the King's Bench (*H. E. L.*, vol. I, pp. 281–285).
[37] See below, Ch. XIII.

expected to attend.[38] Clearly their business must have been transacted elsewhere. The question is where. It is essential that we find the answer in order that we may continue our observation of a day's work in court.

Fortescue says that, after the morning's session, while the justices occupied themselves with reading and contemplation, the parties betook themselves "ad pervisam" to consult with the sergeants at law and their other counselors.[39] Chaucer's reference in the Prologue of the *Canterbury Tales* to the sergeant "that oft had been at the parvys" is well known. The allotting to the sergeants of pillars in the parvis [40] of St. Paul's is first mentioned in the Lincoln's Inn account of the creating of new sergeants in 1547,[41] and the custom seems to have continued until the time of the Great Fire.[42] St. Paul's seems already to have been the haunt of the sergeants and their clients early in the fifteenth century.[43] For the present we are more concerned with the attorneys and clerks. Where were they and the bundles of writs to be found on a day in Trinity term, 1470?

Two cases recorded in the fourteenth century rolls of the Court of Common Pleas offer some help towards the answer to this question. In the first, from 17 Edward III, the plaintiff complained that he had been attacked in the Church of St. Peter the Little, in London, "where the clerks with the rolls and writs of the Common Bench and the attorneys come together after the noon meal." [44] In the second, from 43 Edward III, Edward de Sandeford, a clerk of the court, alleged that the defendant assaulted him in the church of St. Alban of Wodestrete, London, where the clerks, parties, and attorneys were wont to gather every day after dinner to attend to and examine their business as to writs and enroll-

---

38 App. I (c).

39 *De Laudibus,* cap. 51 (ed. Chrimes, p. 128).

40 Webster's dictionary defines *parvis* as "a court or enclosed space before a building, especially a church" and traces the derivation through Old French to the Latin *paradisus.*

41 *Black Books,* vol. I, pp. 276–281.

42 *H. E. L.,* vol. II, p. 490.

43 *Y. B. Easter, 12 Hy. IV,* pl. 10.

44 C. P. 40/333, m. 362, Hil., 17 Ed. III. St. Peter the Little, reputedly the same as St. Peter, Paul's Wharf, was on the north side of Thames Street at the corner of St. Peter's Hill (W. Jenkinson, *London Churches before the Great Fire* [London, 1917], p. 174, and *Victoria Co. Hist. Lond.* [London, 1909], vol. I, map at p. 245).

ments.[45] Sandeford's allusion to the church as the "parish church in the parish in which Robert Thorp, Chief Justice of the Common Bench, has his dwelling" suggests that the choice of the particular church may have been made by the Chief Justice. In 1393 it may have been the chapel at St. Bartholomew's, Smithfield, for Thomas Gaytford, one of the clerks of the bench, was arrested in Smithfield on a private matter while going "towards the chapel of the said court to deliberate on divers business of the king and the common people." [46]

The use of these churches of western London for the transaction of the business between clients, attorneys, and clerks in the Court of Common Pleas is not surprising. Many references may be found in mediaeval documents to the keeping of legal records and the transaction of legal business in churches.[47] Increasingly towards the end of the fifteenth century, however, the officers of the court were settling in the Inns [48] or in that general part of London, and by the nineteenth century, when the times were less turbulent, the offices of the Common Pleas were in Sergeant's Inn and in Chancery Lane.[49] This does not help us much in finding where to go in the fifteenth century, nor does the ordinance of the court made in Trinity, 35 Henry VI. It merely orders noncommittally that officers are henceforth to "attend upon their sayd offices in their places accustomed for the same." [50] The essential requirement from

[45] C. P. 40/436, m. 443, Mich., 43 Ed. III. The trespass took place "ad parochialem ecclesiam infra quam parochiam Robertus de Thorp capitalis Iusticiarius domini Regis de Banco hic tenet hospicium suum videlicet ad ecclesiam sancti Albani de Wodestrete London' que est certus locus ubi clerici partes et attornati predicti pro tempore quo dictus Robertus Capitalis Iusticiarius Regis in Banco his extitit conuenire consueuerunt ad negocia et breuia ac irrotulamenta predicta superuidenda et examinanda post prandium." The plaintiff further explains: "hic uidelicet in ecclesia parochiali eiusdem hospicij ubi in ecclesia clerici de eodem Banco partes et attornati predicti conuenire debent quolibet die post prandium quo Iusticiarij sedent in iudicio hic etc. ad irrotulamenta dictorum negociorum breuia originalia et iudicialia superuidenda et examinanda pro tempore quo Curia Regis hic tenta fuerit." St. Alban's Wood Street was on the east side of the street at the corner of Addle Street (Jenkinson, *op. cit.*, p. 178; *Victoria Co. Hist. Lond., loc. cit.*).

[46] C. P. 40/530, m. 339d. On the other hand this may have been only the place where writs of old terms were kept. (See below, p. 142.)

[47] *H. E. L.*, vol. II, p. 490; *C. P. R., 1381–1385*, p. 394; below, Ch. IX.

[48] Below, Ch. V.

[49] Maugham's testimony in *Parlt. Papers* (1860), vol. XXXI, "Minutes of Evidence," pp. 3–4.

[50] App. I (c).

the point of view of the parties and attorneys was, after all, that whatever place or places were used, they should be known and accessible.

Ultimately, therefore, we are forced to resort to the expedient of all strangers to fifteenth century London and inquire our way to the court offices. Eventually we find ourselves in the forecourt of a church in the midst of a great deal of hustle and bustle. We look first for Copley, the first prothonotary, whom we saw in court this morning. We find him by a column near the entrance, standing behind a trestle table on which are bundles of writs and membranes of the plea roll. Several underclerks sitting on stools are busily scratching away with their pens. In the group before the table we recognize William Pryce, the attorney for the plaintiff in *Curson v. Curson*, the first case we heard this morning. He greets Copley casually, in the manner of men who meet often in their daily work, and asks for the writ of *venire facias* to summon the jury in his client's case. Copley, or one of his clerks, consults the memorandum made in court this morning, and the clerk then writes out the writ. Pryce pays 1s. for the entry of his declaration, 2s. for the entry of the replication pleaded by Pygot, 6d. for the writ, 7d. for the sealing of it and 6d. for a paper copy of the defendant's plea, a total of 4s. 1d., which he will later collect from his client. We also recognize in the group awaiting Copley's attention William Curson, the defendant in the case. We stay to see him ask for the entry of his plea. He pays 2s. for this and 6d. for a paper copy.[51]

Many of the faces around Copley are new to us. Some attorneys and parties are there to have pleadings entered "in the common form." Such pleadings followed the stereotypes established by precedent so completely that, by this time, they need no longer be pleaded before the justices at Westminster. A trained clerk could enter them in the plea roll with only the name of the county, the type of action, the names of the parties, and a few particulars as to places, dates, amounts claimed in debt and damages, goods taken in trespass, etc.

---

[51] For the amounts of the clerks' fees, see App. I (e), (h), and (j); for the fees for sealing writs, see B. Wilkinson, "The Seals of the Two Benches under Edward III," in *E. H. R.*, vol. XLII, pp. 397–401, and *The Chancery under Edward III* (Manchester, 1929), pp. 62 ff.; *R. P.*, vol. II, pp. 170, 229.

Some pleadings in the common form were entered by filacers as well as by prothonotaries. At this time, their functions had not become as completely separated as later.[52] If, therefore, we move on through the crowd to find the "accustomed place" of Chaumbre, filacer for Bedfordshire, Buckinghamshire, Berkshire, and Oxford, we shall see that it looks not so very different from Copley's. Chaumbre's files of writs are larger and his membranes of the plea roll fewer, but his "office" is equally busy. The chief business here, however, is not the enrollment of pleas nor the making of memoranda from which the record may later be drawn up at leisure, but the entry of appearances of plaintiffs and the writing of judicial writs of process to make the defendant come.

We watch and listen closely as one of the attorneys approaches Chaumbre and asks for the return of his writ of *capias* in *Burton v. Gough* in trespass for assault and battery at Abingdon.[53] Chaumbre searches through the bundle of writs for the county specified, finds there the writ with a return endorsed by the sheriff that the defendant was not found. The attorney, therefore, asks for a writ of *sicut prius capias,* pays 3d. for this, and for the entry on the plea roll, and 7d. for the sealing of the writ. If he is a careful man, he waits to see the entry made and asks to have the number of the membrane of the plea roll entered on the face of the writ. Often, according to the evidence of the fifteenth century plea rolls, the filacer cannot find the writ because it has not been returned by the sheriff. In this event, in order to avoid a discontinuation of the case, the attorney asks that a note of his appearance and the sheriff's failure to return the writ be made in the plea roll. He pays 3d. for the entry and goes about his other business.

We might include other officers such as the chirographer or the clerk of the fines in our day's visit to the court, but perhaps we have already seen enough to be aware of some of the more obvious similarities and differences between the fifteenth century Court of Common Pleas and its twentieth century successors, whether in England or America. Except for the fact that they are no longer housed in churches, and that typewriters, fountain pens, and paper have replaced goose quills and parchment, the offices have perhaps changed

---

[52] Cf. below, Ch. VIII.
[53] C. P. 40/835, m. 242.

less than any other part of the court. Docket books and filing cases have eliminated much unnecessary labor in finding records of old terms. The attorneys rather than the clerks now write out the pleadings and deliver copies to the attorney for the other party. Law French and Latin have been abandoned, except for the most technical terms, and with them the bulky plea rolls of former centuries. Yet it is probable that, if William Copley were transported through time and space from his "accustomed place" in fifteenth century London to the office of the clerk of the Superior Court of the Commonwealth of Massachusetts, he would find himself in no altogether alien environment. He would certainly be able to find a common ground of conversation with the clerk and his assistants, and he would undoubtedly recognize many of the forms, terms, and abbreviations which they use every day in their records.

CHAPTER IV

The Records

O NE NEED NOT complain of scarcity of records from which to study the workings of the Court of Common Pleas. In the six hundred years or more of its independent existence, the court produced tons of rolls, barrels of writs, bushels of essoin rolls and of feet of fines, concords of fines, notes of fines, as well as stacks of paper books. Although the earlier records are more obscure, their bulk and variety are not quite so great as in later centuries. Beginning about 1500, a number of new kinds of records were added to the output of the court. The introduction of the action of ejectment, the growing use of common recovery, the development of *assumpsit,* and many other like changes led to the adoption of new types of record. Some new records, such as the docket and remembrance rolls, were intended to improve administrative efficiency. Some were perhaps introduced in consequence of the growing use of paper and of paper books, which were more manageable and less expensive than parchment rolls.

Various records of the Common Pleas have accumulated in other departments. For instance, among records of the Exchequer are the fines and amercements, or estreats of the Bench. Of these there are three groups: the fines for licenses to agree, the amercements, and the returns on writs of distraint. All three for the fifteenth century are in poor condition. Among the records of the Chancery are the so-called "County Placita" or "Brevia Regis et Recorda," [1] which include transcripts of Common Pleas records sent to the Chancery

[1] M. S. Giuseppi, *Guide to the Manuscripts Preserved in the Public Record Office* (London, 1923–1924), vol. I, p. 61; C 47/47–88.

43

in reply to writs of *certiorari* addressed to the Chief Justice and the Custos Brevium of the court.

In the hanaper accounts may be found the lump sums received for the sealing of writs, judicial and original, special notes of payment for pardons of outlawry, as well as notes of payments of "fees and regards" [2] to the justices from the issues of the Bench. Among the Exchequer Miscellanea are oddments of a rather miscellaneous but useful nature, such as attorney's bills of costs and bills of payments to justices. It is chiefly, however, in the court's own records, that is the files of writs and rolls, that one must look for an understanding of the way the court worked in the fifteenth century.

A necessary first step in discussion of the records of the court is a definition of terms. For example: in discussing plea rolls it should be observed that the word *roll* or *rotulus* in the Latin, *rolle* or some variation of it in the Anglo-Norman French, was used in the fifteenth century to mean a single parchment membrane which was rolled up when not in use. Such are the rolls which we see on the green table in the contemporary picture of the court,[3] single membranes on which the clerks are making entries. References on writs are in the form "Ro' CIX" and references from the Rex rolls to the plea rolls are similar. The whole plea roll of a term is referred to in the plural of *rotulus*, or by the word *filacium, ligula,* or *bundell.*[4] The number of a single membrane is sometimes called in English "the number rolle."[5] It is because Pike ignored this mediaeval use of the word "rolle"[6] that he was led into misinterpretation of a case reported in 39 Henry VI.[7]

There are usually from three hundred to more than six hundred of these membranes in a fifteenth century plea roll, piled one on top of the other, sewed together at the top, and bound tightly with stout cord. Each membrane is about eleven inches wide and two and one-

2 For explanation of these terms, see below, Ch. VI.

3 See Plate I, frontispiece.

4 For this usage, see indentures quoted in Palgrave, *Ancient Kalendars,* vol. III, pp. 148–154, 196, 255–257, 300–301, 370, 427.

5 See Table of Fees, App. I (g).

6 L. O. Pike, *Y. B. 20 Ed. III* (R. S.), Pt. 2, p. xxi.

7 *Y. B. Mich., 39 Hy. VI,* pl. 43. The case had been entered in "two rolls" and there was disagreement between the two entries. Pike thought that this meant that there were still Rex rolls of the Court of Common Pleas in the fifteenth century, that is, duplicate rolls. What is more probably meant is that the case was entered on two different membranes of the plea roll for the same term.

half feet long. The foot of each membrane is rounded off. The parchment is often of poor quality and sometimes so badly cured that there is a good deal of oil left in it. Many rolls have been chewed by rats, some have disintegrated from damp-rot, and many show signs of having soaked in water, probably at the time when they were kept in the basement of Westminster Hall.[8]

The writing covers both sides of the membrane beginning on both at the top or sewed end, so that the whole roll must be turned in order to read what is on the dorse. In the early sixteenth century some imaginative clerk apparently saw that it would be easier to read a roll if the writing on the dorse were to begin at the bottom. Even so the discovery was applied only to two new types of rolls, the docket and the remembrance rolls, not to the formal and time-honored plea roll.

The reason for this clumsiness of the plea rolls obviously is that the rolls were not made up until after term. The filacers and pro-thonotaries kept their single membranes with them during term time, being expected, according to an ordinance of the court of 23 Henry VII, to deliver them within seven or eight days after term to the clerk of the estreats. This clerk kept them for two days to take out the list of persons owing fines and amercements to the king and then delivered them to the clerk of the essoins, who bound them up and gave them to the clerk of the Common Pleas treasury, or the clerk of "Hell" as he was sometimes called.[9] It was not inconvenient either to read or to write on the dorse of membranes so long as they remained unbound. In the early days, when the roll for a term was comparatively slim, it was not inconvenient even after they were bound up. As the rolls increased in bulk administrative habit was apparently too strong to allow a change for convenience's sake.

Each membrane is numbered at the foot. In the fourteenth century the numbering was by Roman numerals written with a pen; in the fifteenth, strange figures clearly derived from Roman numerals but more conspicuous and probably painted on with a brush were substituted. Two of these have been reproduced in Plate IV (p. 46).

[8] *Deputy Keeper's Reports,* Second Report, App. I; *Parlt. Papers* (1837), Report from the Commissioners on the Public Records, App. F, 1 (a) and (b).

[9] Ord. 23 Hy. VII, Recoveries 7 Hy. VIII to 22 Hy. VIII, f. 9. See below, App. II (d).

In addition to the number at the foot of the membrane is the name of a clerk of the court. Whether these are signatures in the modern sense or not, there is an invariable association of certain handwritings on the membranes with the same names at the foot and occasionally there are characteristic decorations of the names. The first twenty-two membranes of the roll are a kind of index to it. The "signatures" on them form a list of the prothonotaries and filacers of the court and give some indication of the groups of counties which are associated with the names of particular filacers.

Plate IV. *Method Used in Numbering Plea Roll Membranes, Numbers 613 and 146.*

In the plea rolls of Edward IV's reign and later it is obvious that there were three chief clerks. On the membranes of these three are found the entries of pleadings and process in cases which have come to the issue to be settled by the trial. These three chief clerks regularly "sign" definite groups of membranes in each roll, and their entries are from all counties. For instance, in the rolls of Easter, 12 Edward IV, Trinity, 12 Edward IV, Easter, 22 Edward IV, and Michaelmas, 22 Edward IV, are to be found the following groupings:

C. P. 40/842 Easter, 12 Edward IV

Copley	m. 1(?), mm. 102–120, 301–320, 451, 452	All counties
Cumberford	m. 2, mm. 121–138, 321–338	All counties
Brayne	m. 12, mm. 141–160, 193–202, 210–229, 399–404, 441–446, 453	All counties

46

C. P. 40/843 Trinity, 12 Edward IV

Copley	mm. 1, 101–120, 301–320, 451–458, 491–496	All counties
Cumberford	mm. 2, 121–136	
	No further "signatures" of Cumberford. On m. 494 (Copley, Midd.) is a memorandum that Cumberford died June 15 and that Roger Brent replaced him in the office of "one of the prothonotaries of the Bench."	
Brent	mm. 137–140, 212–214, 321–339, 421–433	All counties
Brayne	m. 12, mm. 141–160, 341–370, 402–409, 410 shared with Praers, 513–515	All counties

C. P. 40/880 Easter, 22 Edward IV

Copley	mm. 1, 101–120, 301–320, 401–408	All counties
Brent	mm. 2, 121–140, 321–340	All counties
Conyngesby	mm. 12, 141–160, 341–360, 441–460, 474–479	All counties

C. P. 40/882 Michaelmas, 22 Edward IV

Copley	mm. 1, 101–120, 301–320, 401–420	All counties
Brent	mm. 2, 121–140, 321–340, 421–435	All counties
Conyngesby	mm. 12, 141–160, 341–360, 436–460, 541–560, 609–611, 613–615	All counties

All the membranes listed are filled, as has been said above, for the most part with entries of stages in the proceedings after issue has been joined, though an occasional entry of some earlier stage in process intrudes itself. An additional sign that these three clerks are of special importance is the fact that they are the only ones to whom, after the first twenty-two membranes, definite groups of membranes of the plea roll are allotted. There seems little question that these "chief clerks" are the "prothonotaries" referred to in Year Books and in other records.

As to the remaining names on the first twenty-two membranes, seventeen seem to be rather irregularly associated with the entries, chiefly of process, from particular counties and seem to take, again more or less regularly, definite position among the first twenty-two between 3 and 20. The list is as follows:

47

mm.	Clerk	Counties	mm.	Clerk	Counties
	C. P. 40/842			C. P. 40/882	
	Easter, 12 Edward IV			Michaelmas, 22 Edward IV	
3	Chaumbre	Beds, Berks, Bucks, Glouc, Oxon, Suff	3	Lyster	Beds, Berks, Bucks Oxon, York, Yorks
4	Danby	Cornwall, Oxon, Suff Worc, York	4	Knyght	Beds, Bucks, Cornwall, Glouc, Oxon, Suff Worc
5	Cheke	Suffolk	5	Cheke	Suffolk
6	Praers	Cornwall, Heref, Glouc, Staffs, Worc	6	Praers	Cornwall, Glouc, Heref, Worc
7	Forster	Coventry, Derby, Leics, Notts, Warw	7	Staynford	Coventry, Derby, Leics, Nottingham, Notts, Warw
8	Harvy	Leics, Norfolk, Notts	8	Harvy	Essex, Herts, Leics, Lincoln, Norfolk, Norwich
9	Ferrers	Essex, Herts	9	Ferrers	Essex, Herts
10	Beell	Essex, Kent, Norfolk, Yorks	10	Beell	Coventry, Kent
11	Orston	Lincoln, Lincs	11	Orston	Lincoln, Lincs
13	Conyers	Kent, Surrey, Sussex	13	Acton	Cambs, Kent, Surrey
14	Pulter	Cambs, Devon, Hunts, Kent, Lond, Midd, Somers	14	Pulter	Bristol, Cambs, Devon, Dorset, Hunts, Kent, Lond, Midd, Somers, Surrey, Sussex
15	Glyn	Bristol, Devon, Dorset, Somers	15	Wydeslade	Devon, Dorset, Somers
16	Vaus	Lond, Midd	16	Elryngton	Berks, Cambs, Dorset, Essex, Hunts, Lond, Midd, Oxon, *pro Eliz. regina* in several counties
17	Elryngton	Norfolk, Norwich	17	Vaus	Norfolk, Norwich
18	Elryngton	Southampton, Wilts, Hants	18	Adam	Hants, Southampton
19	Burton	Northants, Rutland Salop, Staffs	19	Burton	Northants, Rutland, Salop, Staffs
20	Acton	Yorks	20	Danby	Yorks, York, Hull
21	Waldyene	*Licencia concordandi* from all counties	21	Bedford	*Licencia concordandi* from all counties. Short entries from Cumberland, Hants, Northants, Northumberland
22	Snayth	Juries in respite from all counties	22	Underhull	Juries in respite, all counties

48

With the exception of the clerks whose names are signed on mem-branes 21 and 22, these are without doubt the filacers. The division of business among them, however, is not so clear and tidy as the printed lawbooks and later documents would lead us to expect.[10] Some of the overlapping may have been due to rivalry for business between offices. Some offices, such as that of Cambridge, Hunting-donshire, London, and Middlesex, or that of Devon, Dorset, Somer-set, and Bristol, must have had a good deal more business than others, and the clerks of these offices must have received cor-respondingly more in fees. It would be natural for those who had little business to try to get some from those who had much. Such rivalry would help to explain why, although there were apparently recognized and definite offices as early as 43 Edward III,[11] there is such obvious trespassing from one county group to another. There is also evidence of occasional borrowing of space here and there in changes of handwriting midway on a membrane and of oc-casional coupling of names at the foot of membranes; but these are infrequent and do not explain the vague lines of demarcation be-tween large and important groups indicated in the table above.

Certain offices are, to be sure, better defined than others. The Suffolk cases and those from Essex and Hertfordshire and from Lincoln and Lincoln City seem to be found pretty regularly on the membranes of whatever clerks occupy m. 5, m. 9, and m. 11 re-spectively; but that does not prevent Suffolk entries from being en-rolled frequently on the membranes of the clerk who occupies m. 4, or Essex and Hertfordshire entries from being enrolled on the membranes of the clerk who occupies m. 8. Further, m. 10 is often without a "signature," or has one which does not appear again in the roll or at best only once or twice. Altogether the impression given is that this system of enrollment had grown up without direc-tion, was still somewhat in process of becoming, and was badly ob-

---

[10] *H. E. L.*, vol. I, App. XXX. Professor Sayles suggests that there was already a clear division of counties between the various filacers' offices (*Select Cases in the Court of King's Bench,* vol. I, p. lxxix and note 1). The rolls of the Court of Common Pleas do not entirely support his supposition. The King's Bench was evidently more efficient in this respect than the Common Pleas. Miss Marjorie Blatcher found in her study of the fifteenth century King's Bench rolls a more regular grouping.

[11] See C. P. 40/436, m. 443, for a case of assault against the king's clerk of Devon, Dorset, and Somerset; cf. C. P. 40/790, Trin., 36 Hy. VI, m. 561d., a case of debt by an underclerk of the filacer of Warwick, Leicester, and Derby against his master.

served in any case, probably because of rivalry between clerks for business.

The two clerks whose names are usually associated with mm. 21 and 22 do not fit into the above classification of filacers. Their entries tend to come from all counties rather than from any special group. Furthermore, the clerk occupying m. 21 seems to make most of the entries of notes of fines, and the clerk occupying m. 22 most of those of juries in respite; both also make entries of stages of process of the type which is most frequently found on filacers' membranes. Presumably, they are not filacers but, respectively, the Clerk of the King's Silver and the Clerk of the Juries. On the other hand, their functions had not yet become so specialized that they could not do a little filacer's business on the side. The clerk who has m. 21 in particular seems to make entries of process from out-of-the-way counties like Rutland, Westmoreland, and Cumberland.

Finally, a group of membranes at the end of the roll, not numbered but all "signed" by the same clerk, bears the charters and other deeds enrolled and the warrants of attorney. The "signature" is that of the clerk of the warrants and estreats, for William Skypwyth's name appears on the rolls of charters and warrants for the later years of Henry VI and early Edward IV, and he was Clerk of the Warrants and Estreats at the time.[12]

Next in importance to the plea rolls as records of the court are the writs. These were, until they were delivered into the Treasury of Receipt, in the custody of the Custos Brevium. Jacob, referring to the files of writs at a much later date, says, "A file is a record of the court; and the *filing* of process of a court makes it a record of it." [13] The principle was the same in the earlier period, and the sanctity of the files was protected. From 1311 comes an instance of a pardon granted to one of the clerks of the Bench, "convicted before the justices of the Bench and committed by them to the Fleet prison for cutting off a writ from the files of the Bench at Westminster, with the intention of carrying it away in his bosom." [14]

---

12 C. P. 40/799–848; *C. P. R., 1452–1461*, p. 366, June 28, 1457.
13 Jacob, *Law Dictionary*, under title "File."
14 *C. P. R., 1307–1313*, p. 362, April 13, 1311.

These files of writs are as yet only in process of being sorted and classified.[15] Those which I have examined are done up in bundles of several hundred covered by a heavy parchment envelope. The writs inside are both judicial and original,[16] and to some are attached panels, transcripts of records, and *"posteas."* All are creased from having been folded and show traces of red wax where they have been sealed. Most seem to have a second filing hole, probably the one made at the time of filing in the deputy sheriff's office.[17] In the lower right-hand corner of each writ is a "signature" which in the case of judicial writs is that of a filacer or prothonotary from whose office the writ issued, and in the case of original writs that of a cursitor of the Chancery. After the *teste* of judicial writs there is usually a reference to the entry on the plea roll of the current or a preceding term which provided the warrant for issue of the writ. Sometimes the clerk helpfully gives a reference to the term as well as the "number rolle"; occasionally there is no reference at all. The dates of the writs, with the exception of originals which were available at all times, are within the four legal terms.

Sheriffs' returns and other endorsements appear on writs both original and judicial. Additional pieces of parchments containing panels of jurors and *posteas* are often attached to writs of *venire facias juratores* and *habeas corpora juratorum. Posteas* are transcripts from the plea roll of the record in the case. These were sent into the county before trial where the Clerk of the Assizes entered an account of the proceedings before the justices of assize. On the dorse of original writs there is usually, at the top in the position of an endorsement on a check, the name of the underclerk of the cursitor. Sometimes there is an endorsement that the writ was delivered to the deputy sheriff *de recordo* with a reference to the membrane of the plea roll on which the enrollment of the writ was to be found.[18]

On the covering membrane of two of the bundles examined is a

[15] For the opportunity to see several bundles of writs, I am indebted to Mr. Hilary Jenkinson, Deputy Keeper of the Public Records, and to Mr. Wardle, his assistant.

[16] A judicial writ is one issued by the justices of the court and represents a stage in process. An original writ was issued from the Chancery in the king's name. The first step in bringing an action was to secure an original writ from the Chancery. See below, Ch. XI.

[17] See below, Ch. XI.

[18] Ch. XI, below.

phrase beginning with the word "Oxon." Though this might arouse the hope that the contents of the bundles would show some special county grouping, related perhaps to the groupings of counties in the filacers' offices, the contents turn out to be a rather miscellaneous assortment of writs. The places from which they come and the "signatures" of the clerks are, in the three bundles examined, as follows: [19]

Oxon de Octabis sancte Trinitatis anno regni
Regis Edwardi quarti post conquestum Secundo

Yorks and York	Audeley and Waldyene
Lincs and Lincoln	Hervy
Derby and Leics	Forster
Coventry and Warwick	Forster, Hervy, Vaus, Conyers
Salop	Burton and Waldyene
Staffs and Rutland	Burton
Northants	Burton, Pittes, Pulter, Waldyene
Beds, Berks, Bucks, Oxon	Hethe and Broun
Wilts	Waldyene
Devon and Midd	Pulter
London	Pulter, Holme, Conyers
Glouc and Heref	Broun
Hants	Waldyene
Cambs, Sussex, and Surrey	Pulter
Suffolk	Broun
Norfolk, Essex, and Herts	Hervy
Cornwall	Broun
Hull and York	Waldyene

Prothonotaries' writs from all the counties listed.[20]

---

[19] These lists are made up by examining the file from top to bottom and hence are in an order the reverse of that in which the writs from various counties were filed, since the writs at the bottom were obviously filed first. In the Michaelmas quindene group, for instance, the writs from Oxford, Berks, Bucks, and Beds, were filed first. There tend to be more solid blocks of writs from particular groups of counties at the bottom of the file, whereas the top of the file comprises a mixture of writs which may have straggled in, some of them possibly late, even after the file had been made and bound up.

[20] There are a great many writs of *exigi facias* and no *posteas* in this bundle.

Oxon de Quindena Sancti Michelis anno regni
Regis Edwardi quarti post conquestum secundo

Westmor, Cumb, Northumb	Waldyene
Hull, Yorks, York	Audeley, Copley
Lincs, Lincoln	Gegge
Derby	Forster
Leics	Forster and Conyers
Staffs and Rutland	Burton
Rutland	Pittes
Northants	Burton, Vaus, Pittes
Beds	Hethe, Cheker
Bucks, Berks, and Oxon	Hethe
Bucks	Cheker

Prothonotaries' writs from all the counties listed.

Breuia de Crastino Animarum anno regni Regis
Edwardi quarti post conquestum secundo
adiornata vsque in Octabis sancti hillarij
per breue de communi adiornamento

Northumb and Yorks	Waldyene
Lincs	Gegge
Notts	Hervy
Derby, Leics, Coventry, and Warw	Forster
Staffs and Salop	Burton
Northants	Waldyene
Beds	Hethe
Bucks	Forster
Berks	Broun
Oxon	Hethe and Forster
Glouc	Praers, Broun
Worc	Praers
Devon	Glyn
Bristol	Forster
Somers	Glyn
Hants	Elryngton
Sussex, Surrey and Kent	Fililode
London	Conyers, Vaus and Pulter
Midd	Pulter, Vaus

53

Herts and Essex	Hervy, Ferrers
Suffolk	Aleyn
Norwich	Hervy
Norfolk	Conyers and Elryngton

Prothonotaries' writs from all counties listed.

The relation between names of clerks and county groups is obviously the same as that found in the plea rolls, since for every writ there is or should be an entry on the plea roll to warrant it, and that entry is on the membrane of the clerk in whose name the writ is issued. One or two names, such as Pittes, Holme, Conyers, and Cheker, do not appear on the membranes of the plea roll. The writs issued in their names, however, appear to be either writs of *exigi facias* or writs of process in stages after joinder of issue. They are quite probably either exigenters or prothonotaries' clerks, according as the writs they signed are of *exigi facias* or of process following upon joinder of issue.

The system used in the Custos Brevium's office for filing and doing up the bundles of writs does not emerge clearly from this examination of three bundles only. The two bundles labeled Oxon obviously include writs from many other counties following no easily discernible principle. Without examining the bundles of writs for a whole year at least it seems impossible to say more than that there must have been, in busy terms, several files for each return day.

Another group of records of the court which is interesting from the historical point of view is the series of Rex rolls. Although few have survived for the fifteenth century, their importance in helping us to an understanding of the offices in the court is such that they are included here. A glance through the lists of early Curia Regis and Common Pleas rolls [21] is sufficient to show that at intervals there are rolls marked "Rex." These apparently begin in 51 Henry III and grow numerous in Edward I's reign. There is an almost complete set for Edward II's reign, after which they apparently disappear altogether. Pike, however, discovered that the continuation of the series was in his time concealed under the erroneous classification "Extract Rolls of the Queen's Bench." This error was

21 *P. R. O. Lists and Indexes*, Plea Rolls, p. 4.

promptly rectified and the Rex rolls for Edward III's reign may now be found listed among Common Pleas documents.[22] The series is continued with some gaps to 10 Henry IV.[23] That for Easter, 10 Henry IV appears to be the last of them. The mere fact that no more have come down to us would not necessarily prove there are none after the early fifteenth century; but from various other indications, to be discussed later, we may judge that the series probably disappeared at about that time.

Pike described very fully the nature of these early "Rex" rolls. They are near duplicates of the ordinary plea rolls except for variations in the order of enrollment, the adding of cross-references to the Chief Justice's roll in the margin, and, far more important, the lack of continuations. This last difference, as Pike has shown, is due to the fact that the matter of *posteas* was entered on the roll of the current term in a new record and not, as on the Chief Justice's roll, in a continuation of the original entry. For instance, an entry on the Rex roll of Trinity term, 16 Edward III [24] begins as follows: "Termino Hill' ultimo rotulo CCXLV. Inter Robertum de Ufford Comitem Suff' et Henricum de Wolcote . . ." and goes on to record the matter which is found on the Chief Justice's roll of Hilary term as a *postea*. This method of continuation and their unimportance even at the time when they were written makes the Rex rolls of little value to us except for what they reveal concerning the history of offices and methods of enrollment.

Although other records of the courts such as the fines and the rolls of estreats of the Bench might be discussed here, the foregoing are the most important ones and are those from which the materials for this study have been mainly drawn. Fines have received more attention from scholars than have other records of the court and in any case had their greatest importance in earlier centuries before the invention of common recoveries. The estreat rolls of the later fifteenth century are in such poor condition as to discourage examination.

These are the "remains" of the court in the fifteenth century, the sources in which this search for an understanding of the workings

---

22 Pike, *Y. B. 16 Ed. III* (R. S.), pt. II, p. xxv; C. P. 23/1–162; *C. P. Class Lists,* p. 61.
23 There is one undated roll for an earlier year of Henry IV.
24 C. P. 23/33, m. 66d; cf. C. P. 40/329, m. 245. See below Ch. VII.

of the court began. For many purposes they explain their own secrets, and there is no need to consult other records or secondary accounts in order to understand them. Their importance lies in their authoritative character. In the course of discussions at the bar the lawyers sometimes stated, for the sake of the argument, that a certain practice was followed. Only the records will tell us authoritatively whether this was so. Often the Year Book reporters fail to tell us the outcome of a discussion. Only the record of the case will tell us what actually happened. On the other hand, the records are not infallible either. Sometimes there is no answer to our question. Sometimes the answer is there but not where we expect to find it. For this reason a more thorough acquaintance with the officers of the court and their methods of work seems both useful and important.

PART II

Personnel of the Court

CHAPTER V

Bench and Bar:

APPRENTICES AND SERGEANTS AT LAW

THE COURT OF COMMON PLEAS in the fifteenth century required the services of a hundred or more people to carry on its work. These ranged in rank and importance from the Chief Justice sitting in scarlet splendor on the bench to the lowly under-clerk of a filacer employed in writing writs and enrollments in some dingy chamber in the lawyers' colony of western London. Included in the number were justices, sergeants at law, attorneys, clerks, ushers, custodians of records, and all under-clerks, assistants, and deputies of these many servants of the court and the King.

The number of justices varied during the century from four to eight. Until 1471 it was most commonly six. After that there were never more than five, and four was the usual number. As for the sergeants at law, there seems to have been a general policy of keeping the number up to eight or nine but it is impossible to tell without more vital statistics how many there were at any given time.

Of all these people only the attorneys and clerks were technically officers of the court. The justices were officers not of the court but of the King, and their functions were more judicial than administrative (although the distinction is modern and altogether foreign to fifteenth century modes of thought). Sergeants at law, owing to their monopoly of the power to plead in the court,[1] could be termed by Chief Justice Bryan "ministers without whom the court could not be properly served," but they were not its officers in any tech-

---

[1] Y. B. Trin., 11 Ed. IV, pl. 4, Paston v. Jenney. In this case Littleton, J., suggests that the rule would not always be adhered to. In Y. B. Hil., 17 Ed. IV, pl. 4, a plea in bar was pleaded by "un petit serjeant" (presumably an apprentice) but was later disallowed in favor of a plea in abatement pleaded by a sergeant.

nical sense.[2] Their fees and their relations with their clients were regulated only by the rather inadequate contemporary law of contract,[3] not by court ordinance, and, as Justice Choke maintained in Jenney's case, their oath, in contrast to the attorney's oath, bound them, not to attend and serve the court but to serve well and truly their clients' interests.[4]

On the other hand, although the individual sergeant was not an officer either of the court or of the King, the sergeants' order as a whole had a public and official character. King's sergeants and justices were chosen only from among the sergeants at law. Election to the order was thus a prerequisite for appointment to the highest legal and judicial offices. Moreover, the normal expectation on becoming a sergeant was that one would eventually fill a vacancy on the Bench. Fifty-eight of the eighty-six apprentices who became sergeants between 1400 and 1500 later rose to the Bench.[5] The figure would probably be more impressive yet if we knew how many of the twenty-eight failed only because they died before there was a vacancy to which they might have been appointed. If additional evidence is needed to establish the public character of the order, it may be found in the fact that the degree of sergeant was conferred by the King's justices in public ceremony, and that the call to take the degree was by royal writ close based on an order in council.[6]

---

2 In *Cro. Car.* 84 (1628) several precedents were cited, among them Sergeant Martyn's case, where a writ of privilege was said to have been issued reciting that sergeants at law were to be attendant to the said court *"ex officio plus quam alibi,* and that their service was necessary at this Bar." After protracted search I have been unable to find this case in the Year Books of Henry V. Martyn was a sergeant only from 18 to 20 Henry V. See James Manning, *Serviens ad Legem* (London, 1840), 230–237 for cases involving sergeants' privilege.

3 In *Paston v. Jenney* the plaintiff sued in debt for 25 marks owed by *scriptum.* For the record, see C. P. 40/840, m. 145d. In *Y. B. Hil., 3 Hy. VI,* pl. 26 William Pole, sgt., sued his client, T. L., for £20 due him for acting as counsel. The defendant was allowed to wage his law and Pole got nothing. In *Y. B. 14 Hy. VI,* pl. 58, Justice Paston said in the course of a discussion of trespass on the case: "And if you as a sergeant at law undertake to plead my plea and do not do it or do it other than as I direct you, by which I lose, I shall have an action on my case."

4 *Y. B. Trin., 11 Ed. IV,* pl. 4, *Paston v. Jenney.*

5 These figures are based on Foss's tables (*Judges,* vols. IV and V). For the rule that justices must be chosen from among the sergeants at law, see *H. E. L.,* vol. II, pp. 485–486.

6 For examples of the writ, see *C. C. R., 1409–1413,* p. 258; *C. C. R., 1414–1419,* pp. 176, 216; *C. C. R., 1422–1429,* p. 163.

Justices and sergeants, then, were homogeneous in background and education. Justices were sergeants who rose to the top, adding public office to professional rank. What then were the personal and educational qualifications necessary to be admitted to the order of sergeant at law in the fifteenth century? The subject of mediaeval legal education has received a good deal of attention both from social and from legal historians, and it is not within the scope of this present work to add any new information or new solutions to old problems. On the other hand, for the sake of rounding out a full picture of the court, it has seemed a good idea to summarize briefly the knowledge already available in printed sources concerning the professional training of fifteenth century judges.

In the thirteenth and early fourteenth centuries justices had often been clerics or lay officials with a varied educational background.[7] By the fifteenth century not only were they appointed exclusively from the ranks of the sergeants at law, but also the educational requirements for entrance into that order had become stereotyped. Fortescue's account of the course of professional training offered by the Inns of Court, although incomplete and in some respects unduly eulogistic, is nonetheless authoritative and, for scarcity of other evidence, must be heavily relied upon in any account of fifteenth century legal education.[8]

In the first place, what sort of people undertook the difficult training for a lawyer's career? Fortescue says that none but the "sons of nobles" could afford to study at the Inns of Court because of the large annual expense involved.[9] This is an exaggeration. It is true that there were no stipends, and that the student or his family must therefore bear the whole cost. But this was no deterrent to ambitious gentlemen or their sons or to an occasional son of a merchant. Of the twenty-eight men who were justices of the Common Bench in the reigns of Henry VI, Edward IV, Edward V, and Richard III,

---

[7] W. C. Bolland, "The Training of a Mediaeval Justice," in *Cambridge Legal Essays* (Cambridge, Mass., 1926), pp. 57–70. According to Tout (*Place of Edward II in English History* [Second ed. rev., Manchester, 1936], p. 327) there were no clerical judges after 1316.

[8] See Chrimes, *De Laudibus*, pp. ciii, 197, and R. G. Fletcher, *Pension Book of Gray's Inn* (London, 1901–1910), vol. I, p. xxii, n. 1, for estimates of Fortescue's reliability.

[9] *De Laudibus*, cap. 49.

one was a merchant's son [10] and most were members of the upper gentry or the lesser nobility. Many, like Thomas Littleton and William Paston, were founders rather than descendants of titled families.[11] Law as a career offered excellent opportunities for the accumulation of landed wealth.

The road to eminence on the Bench was long and hard although not without rewarding pleasures of companionship and intellectual stimulation. Maitland has put it that English law was "tough law," and that the system of education had perforce to be tough in order to train students adequately in the knowledge of it.[12] Fortescue encouraged his royal pupil to gain as much knowledge of the law as was possible for a scholar or a learner in the course of a year. He warned him, however, that to understand the hidden mysteries of the law required much longer and more profound training, and that he would do better to administer justice through his sergeants at law than to attempt to give judgments himself.[13] Coke's admonition to James I was a belligerent echo of this mild *caveat*. He warned James that even his "excellent science and great endowments of nature" were inadequate tools for the understanding of the "artificial reason and judgment" of the English common law.[14]

Legend has it that both Littleton and Fortescue were sent to university before they went up to London to study the law. Modern research into the lives of these two great lawyers has cast doubts upon the claims in both cases.[15] Nonetheless many students did spend several years at Oxford or Cambridge before they went up to the Inns of Court for specialized training. For example, Justice Paston's sons, John, Clement, and William, Jr., all studied at Cam-

---

[10] This was Thomas Yonge, one of the liveliest and most interesting of the mid-fifteenth century justices of the Common Pleas. His father was a merchant of Bristol and once mayor of the town. His brother became Lord Mayor of London. All three were elected to the House of Commons and seem to have been active in the factional politics of the day (Foss, *Judges*, vol. IV; *D. N. B.*; J. Wedgewood and A. Holt, "Biographies of Members of the House of Commons, 1453–1509," *History of Parliament* [London, 1936]).

[11] The founding of titled families by ambitious lawyers might prove to be an interesting topic for research in social history.

[12] *English Law and the Renaissance,* p. 18.

[13] *De Laudibus,* cap. 8.

[14] E. Coke, 12 *Co. Rep.,* 65.

[15] E. Wambaugh, *Littleton's Tenures in English* (Washington, D.C., 1903), p. xx; Chrimes, *De Laudibus,* pp. lxx, 195.

bridge before studying the law.[16] His grandson, Walter, took a degree at Oxford in preparation but died before he could go up to London for legal studies.[17] University training must have been invaluable to the mediaeval student of the law, for he needed to know three languages. Some deeds and bonds as well as everyday conversation and letters were in English. Writs and records and some ancient statutes were in Latin, while pleadings and new statutes were in French. Latin grammar, an important study at the universities, was a useful if not essential discipline for mediaeval lawyers. French also could be studied at Oxford. A university statute of 1432 provided that "the art of writing and composing and speaking the Gallic idiom" and also the art "of composing charters and other scripts and of holding lay courts, or the English mode of pleading," should be taught.[18] H. G. Richardson has described the work of Simon O. who taught forms of conveyancing, accounting, and elementary legal procedure, as well as rhetoric, at Oxford in the fifteenth century.[19]

Whether or not one had attended Oxford or Cambridge, the first step in the professional study of the law was to attend an Inn of Chancery. There, according to Fortescue, one learned "the originals [20] and something of the elements of law." [21] How long a time was required for this he does not say, but it was probably no more than a year or two.[22] In Stow's time, the Inns of Chancery were "chiefly furnished with Officers, Atturneyes, Solicitors, and Clarkes." [23] For the young students beginning the study of the law

16 *Paston Letters*, Nos. 29, 66, 311.

17 *Ibid.*, No. 829.

18 H. Rashdall, *Universities of Europe* (new ed. by F. M. Powicke and A. B. Emden; Oxford, 1936), vol. III, p. 162 and notes; S. Gibson, *Statuta Antiqua Universitatis Oxoniensis* (Oxford, 1931), pp. 240–241, lxxxvii.

19 "An Oxford Teacher of the Fifteenth Century" in *Bulletin of the John Rylands Library*, vol. XXXIII, No. 2, Oct., 1939, pp. 436 ff.

20 Original writs.

21 *De Laudibus*, cap. 49.

22 Thomas Roberts of Willesden, later coroner of London, remained at Clement's Inn for four years (from Nov., 10, to Aug., 14 Henry VII) before he was admitted to the Inner Temple (B. H. Putnam, *Early Treatises on the Practice of the Justices of the Peace in the Fifteenth and Sixteenth Centuries* [Oxford, 1924], pp. 129–130, n. 8).

23 *Survey* (Kingsford ed.), vol. I, p. 78. In 1555, the four greater Inns began to restrict admission of attorneys (*Black Books*, vol. I, pp. 315, 318, 425; *Calendar of Inner Temple Records*, vol. I, pp. xlvii, 190, 191, 469; *Pension Book of Gray's Inn*, pp. 213, 296, 324; *Middle Temple Records*, vol. I, p. 104).

this immediate contact with practicing lawyers, even though of the lesser ranks, must have been invaluable experience. Whether it was available to fifteenth century students is impossible to say without more contemporary evidence. It seems very likely.[24] And it is more than likely that some of the more impecunious or less ambitious students were diverted into apprenticeship to clerks or attorneys of the court instead of going on to the more arduous study for the degree of sergeant at law. An anonymous treatise of Henry VIII's time speaks of those who, because there were no stipends for study at the Inns of Court, had to give over study and become "tipplers in the law" instead of serious students.[25]

When a student had learned enough about writs and rudiments, he was admitted to one of the greater Inns. Here, provided he did not weary of his studies or abandon them for active practice, he could expect to remain for twenty years or so in order to become sufficiently expert to be ordained a sergeant.[26] Lest the reader conceive of this as a wasteful and unprofitable prolongation of immaturity, it should be explained at once that students in the Inns usually married and frequently held public office and engaged in private practice long before they finished their studies. Thomas Littleton, for example, was married in 1444,[27] nine years before his call to the degree of sergeant in 1453. He seems to have given "good and notable" counsel to clients at least as early as 1450.[28] He was appointed to commissions of the peace in Worcestershire in 1443, 1444, 1446, and 1451,[29] to commissions of gaol delivery in the same county in 1447 and 1451,[30] and to various other special commissions in 1448 and 1450.[31] In 1449 he was appointed to succeed Donyngton as Recorder of Coventry,[32] an office of great honor and im-

---

[24] There were ten Inns of Chancery in Fortescue's time and only four Inns of Court. This proves nothing in itself about numbers and kinds of people living in them but, with the help of Inn regulations of the next century and other scattered evidence, it does suggest occupancy by clerks and attorneys in the fifteenth century.

[25] W. Herbert, *Antiquities of the Inns of Court* (London, 1804), p. 211.

[26] In *De Laudibus*, cap. 50, Fortescue sets the minimum at sixteen years; in cap. 8 and in *De Natura* (vol. I, cap. 44) he says twenty (cf. Chrimes, *De Laudibus*, note on p. 150).

[27] Foss, *Judges*, vol. IV, p. 440.

[28] Wambaugh, *Littleton's Tenures*, p. xxiv.

[29] *C. P. R., 1441–1446*, p. 481; *C. P. R., 1446–1452*, p. 597.

[30] *Ibid.*, pp. 136, 534.

[31] *Ibid.*, pp. 139, 436.

[32] Putnam, *Early Treatises*, p. 78, nn. 2 and 4, p. 178, n. 4.

portance and one requiring considerable knowledge and wisdom in legal matters. In any case, the requirement of sixteen to twenty years' preparation applied only to practice in the Court of Common Pleas, since other courts were open to mere apprentices in the law. William Ayscogh, appointed Justice of the Common Pleas in April, 1440, seems to have begun to practice in the central courts eight years before his call to be a sergeant.[33] Finally, the modern reader should be reminded that the young men who entered the Inns of Court were very young compared to first-year men in American law schools or beginning students at the present-day Inns. Thomas Marowe was between fifteen and eighteen when he was admitted to the Inner Temple, while his friend, Thomas Frowyk, later Chief Justice of the Court of Common Pleas, was not much more than fifteen.[34]

Education at the Inns was a matter of learning by doing. There being few treatises and no one great text to provide an easy knowledge of the essential principles of the law,[35] the student learned by example and by practice. He listened both to arguments in court by experienced practitioners and to "mootings" in the Inns by the older students. He also attended "readings" or lectures given during the "learning" vacations by the most advanced students. When he had acquired sufficient knowledge by listening and discussion with his contemporaries, he began to take part—first in mootings, where no one's life or fortune depended on his expertness. When he had become sufficiently skilled at these, he was called to the bar and allowed to practice in the courts. Eventually he was called upon to "read" and by reading became a Bencher of the Inn, a rank which required him to act on occasion as judge at the mootings of younger fellows. [36]

To say that this system of professional education was practical,

---

[33] Foss, *Judges*, vol. IV, pp. 282–283.

[34] Putnam, *Early Treatises*, p. 129, n. 8.

[35] For the sources available to a fifteenth century student of the law, see Putnam, *Early Treatises*, pp. 173 ff. Miss Putnam gives a complete list of the sources available to Marowe at the time of his reading in 1503, with dates of publication for those in print.

[36] Except where other references are given the account of the course of study in the Inns is taken from a report on the subject presented to King Henry VIII about 1540 by Nicholas Bacon, Robert Cary, and Thomas Denton. This was printed by Waterhouse in his *Fortescutus Illustratus* in 1663.

and that the alternation of discussion of hypothetical cases with actual practice and the constant association of students with lawyers actively engaged in the profession gave it vitality is not to contribute a new and original interpretation.[37] On the other hand the point is sufficiently important to bear a good deal of repetition.

The law student's learning year was adjusted to the legal year, and the fact that he did a good part of his learning during "vacations" followed from this. There were three parts to his year, as follows: the law-terms when the courts were sitting, learning vacations, and mesne or dead vacations. During the law-terms, Inn activities were confined to afternoons and evenings, the mornings presumably being devoted to attendance at Westminster or other courts. The afternoons were spent in argument and discussion and the evenings in the more formally conducted arguments of mootings. During the "learning vacations" readings replaced the court sessions in the morning, and the rest of the day was continued as in term time. During mesne or dead vacations no program was prescribed for the morning; otherwise study continued as during the law terms and the learning vacations, although attendance was not required. Christmas vacation, lasting from Christmas eve until the day after Epiphany (January 7), was occupied with elaborate revels and general merriment, and only the younger students were required to attend.[38] Including the two weeks of the Christmas vacation the whole time of required attendance was only about twenty-eight weeks out of the fifty-two. The serious and ambitious student may often have resided many more weeks at his Inn during the comparative quiet of the mesne vacations, but even he must have frequently needed to spend this time in attending to his estates or to other family business. In the summer the Inns were probably very sparsely populated because of the danger from plague, and sometimes Easter and Michaelmas vacations had to be shortened because of it.[39]

The Inns had no "curriculum" in the modern sense of the word. They did, however, offer varied techniques for learning the law and

---

[37] *H. E. L.*, vol. II, p. 508.
[38] There were revels in Lincoln's Inn four times in the year, but the Christmas revels appear to have been the most elaborate (*Black Books*, vol. I, pp. xxx–xxxiii, 12).
[39] *Black Books*, vol. I, pp. 31, 46, 86, 93, 97, 121.

ranks from which one graduated to higher ranks. Mootings provided some opportunity for learning to all ranks. Two utter barristers appointed for each evening were responsible for presenting an argument of a doubtful case before two Benchers of the Inn who acted as judges. After this exercise two inner barristers delivered in law French a declaration, "even as the Sergeants doe at the bar in the King's Court to the Judges." The utter barristers and Benchers then took up the discussion, and the Benchers gave a decision.

"Readings" were lectures on a statute "old" or "new" with discussion of difficult points of interpretation. The Reader chose one statute on which to base the whole series of fifteen or sixteen discourses which he gave throughout the learning vacation. First he expounded the meaning of the words of the text. Next he showed "such inconveniences or mischiefs as were unprovided for." Then he discussed doubtful points of interpretation. After each lecture in the series general discussion followed, the youngest utter barrister having the privilege of speaking first. This was the procedure described in the mid-sixteenth century report on the Inns, and there seems little doubt that the general scheme followed in the preceding century was the same, although detailed requirements concerning length and numbers of lectures may have been different.[40]

The student began his career as an inner barrister. In this rank he attended mootings and probably also visited the courts at Westminster. He took very little direct part in argument himself, although on occasion he had to deliver a declaration at a mooting. After six to eight years [41] he became an utter barrister. In this rank wider opportunities and responsibilities were open to him. He might be called upon to be a Reader or Bencher in one of the Inns of Chancery. Also, when the Benchers of his Inn decided he was ripe for it, he might be called to the bar and so begin to practice in any court save only the Common Pleas. The highest distinction conferred upon him by the Inn was the call to read. This call automatically elevated him to the Bench of the Inn and thus made him a voting member of the society and a potential officeholder. For this

40 For the whole subject of readings see Miss Putnam's *Early Treatises.*
41 Putnam, *Early Treatises,* p. 129, n. 8.

honor he must usually wait ten or twelve years after his rise to the rank of utter barrister.[42] The rank of Bencher involved new responsibilities as well as honor. In Lincoln's Inn by an ordinance of 1466, new Benchers were required to attend readings during six whole vacations immediately following their elevations to the Bench. Benchers must also carry the responsibility of office in the Inns and must act as judges of the mootings.

Before a Bencher could be raised to the rank of sergeant at law, he must read a second time.[43] The second call to read was usually for the Lent vacation [44] and, if the call to take the degree of sergeant came as it sometimes did, before the second call to read, the Inn had to alter its election, allowing the sergeant-elect to take precedence over a reader already chosen.[45]

Life in the Inns was not always purposeful, sober, and sedate. Living quarters may have been for the most part cramped and austere,[46] and emphasis, as Fortescue says, may have been placed on "cultivation of virtues and the banishment of all vice," but his idyllic picture of peace unbroken by "turbulence, quarrels, or disturbance" was the nostalgic exaggeration of an old man in exile. On the other hand, in comparison to the violence of life illustrated in the *Paston Letters,* the life in the Inns was peaceful. At least the evidences of lawlessness and violence in the Lincoln's Inn records for the fifteenth century are few and slight, no more than would be expected where a group of high-spirited young men, many of them not serious students but only, like the young Pastons, scions of landholding families anxious to learn enough law to defend their

---

[42] W. Dugdale, *Origines Juridiciales* (London, 1666), cap. 56. There are certain difficulties about Dugdale's chronology. If the call to the bar came five years or so after the call to the rank of utter barrister, and the call to read five years or so after that, making ten years in all, and the second call to read nine to ten years later, it is difficult to see how Frowyk finished the whole course of study in nineteen years or, for that matter, how Marowe finished in twenty-four (Putnam, *Early Treatises,* p. 135, n. 1).

[43] Bacon, Cary, and Denton, p. 545; Putnam, *Early Treatises,* pp. 167–168; *Black Books,* vol. I, p. 312.

[44] Putnam, *Early Treatises,* pp. 167–168. Frowyk's second reading was in the autumn term of 10–11 Henry VII (*ibid.,* pp. 179–180).

[45] *Black Books,* vol. I, p. 353.

[46] Two fellows were expected to share one room. A special fine must be paid for the privilege of having a room to one's self or even for picking one's roommate. A fireplace or a garden also involved extra expense (*Black Books,* vol. I, pp. 30, 32, 34, 40, 53).

estates, were crowded together in a household surrounded by the excitements of the City of London.

There were, to be sure, chronic difficulties about card-playing and dice-throwing in the hall out of hours.[47] Some, presumably of the younger fellows, were caught chasing rabbits in the coney garth belonging to the Inn.[48] Students were not always respectful in speaking to officers of the society.[49] Arguments sometimes became unduly heated, and the daggers customarily carried by young gentlemen of the time made such altercations dangerous.[50] Some fellows were light-fingered. One stole a cup belonging to another fellow.[51] Another stole a rosary from the wife of a capper of London, or so the husband said.[52] One fellow was caught in a house of ill fame; several were found to have smuggled women into their chambers at night. [53]

The penalty for all these offenses was, as Fortescue says, expulsion from the society or, in the case of lesser offenses, expulsion from commons. Readmittance could be bought, however, and rather easily. The fines range from 20d. for unseemly language or chasing coneys to 40s. for attacking a member of the society with a dagger or seizing a woman in Chancery Lane and bringing her into the Inn.

Sometimes brawls occurred between "the men of Court," that is the lawyers, and the townspeople or members of the king's household. The forays between members of the Inns and the townspeople [54] were probably similar in cause to the town and gown controversies in the university towns. They were perhaps given an added edge because of the age-old ever-recurring hatred of the layman towards the lawyer, whose specialized competence he distrusts and fears but cannot on some occasions do without. What caused

---

[47] Ibid., pp. 4, 44, 45, 57, 76.

[48] Ibid., pp. 45, 79.

[49] Ibid., pp. 63, 66, 71, 77, and elsewhere.

[50] Ibid., p. 43, a case in which the victim nearly died of the wounds inflicted; p. 40, a less serious case of attack with a dagger; p. 63, a case of slapping; p. 91.

[51] Ibid., p. 58.

[52] Ibid., p. 68.

[53] Ibid., pp. 40, 66, 68, 71, 74, 77, 79.

[54] Chronicles of London (ed. Kingsford; Oxford, 1905), p. 154 (1441); p. 169 (1458); "A Short English Chronicle," Three Fifteenth Century Chronicles (ed. Gairdner; Camden Society, Westminster, 1880), p. 71; R. Holinshed, Chronicles of England, Scotland, and Ireland (ed. Johnson; London, 1807–1808), vol. III, p. 246.

the "discord and trouble between those of the King's house and Lincoln's Inn" in the later years of Edward IV the records do not explain, but a member expelled for slapping another was readmitted without fine when the governors were reminded of his diligence in procuring arms to enable the Fellows to defend themselves against the king's men.[55] Items like this are a useful reminder of the prevailing violence of the age.

Serious candidates for the degree of sergeant at law were a minority of the whole number of persons living in the Inns or taking some part in Inn activities. These were not yet narrowly professional communities. Members of the king's household were admitted and pardoned attendance during learning vacations.[56] King's officers, as for example, John Best, the coroner of England,[57] were admitted on similar terms. Others seem to have been admitted in a spirit of good fellowship, for the gift of a doe or a buck once or twice a year.[58] One, Gloucestre, was admitted in Michaelmas, 1464, to repasts in Lincoln's Inn until his daughter should marry, die, or take the veil.[59] One wonders whether Gloucestre's daughter was a shrew or merely a poor cook.

Many clerks and attorneys seem either to have let chambers or to have been admitted to commons, or both. Vaus, filacer of Middlesex and London in the Court of Common Pleas, was admitted to Lincoln's Inn in Easter term, 1465, with permission to have a clerk in commons and to be absent during the learning vacations.[60] Thomas Orston and Peter Staynford, also filacers of the Common Pleas, were admitted on similar terms ten years later.[61] John Nethersole and Simon Damme, attorneys in the Common Pleas, seem both to have been prominent members of Lincoln's Inn. Nethersole, indeed, remembered the Inn in his will, leaving forty marks towards

55 *Black Books,* vol. I, p. 63 (1476–1477).
56 *Ibid.,* pp. 60, 64.
57 *Ibid.,* pp. 22, 40.
58 For example, see *ibid.,* p. 22.
59 *Ibid.,* p. 38.
60 *Ibid.,* p. 39.
61 *Ibid.,* p. 58. Although Vaus, Orston, and Staynford are not referred to as filacers, the special terms of their admission and the fact that in the sixteenth century filacers and prothonotaries were admitted to chambers on the same terms suggest that these are the men whose names appear in the plea rolls as those of filacers.

the building of a library.[62] There are many entries of admissions of both filacers and prothonotaries in the sixteenth century Inn records.[63] Also admitted as "clerks," but evidently men of far less experience and eminence in their vocation than Vaus and Orston, were those whom the fellows were allowed to keep in clerks' Commons on payment of the appropriate fees. Some of these seem to have been neither serious students of the law nor even persons able to wield a pen. At any rate, it was necessary in May of 1506 to ordain that "in future noone may be in clerks' commons unless he exercises himself about the study of the law of the land" and dresses himself decorously.[64] And in June, 1535, it was further provided that clerks must be able to read and understand Latin and also to write "or entend to learne to wryght." [65]

The busy life and varied companionship of the Inns surrounded by the teeming vitality of one of the largest cities in Europe can scarcely have seemed dully academic to the green younger sons of the country gentry or even to the riper graduates of the universities.

Elevation to the rank of sergeant at law meant leaving behind the youthful fellowship of the Inns of Court and moving into the more soberly homogeneous atmosphere of the sergeants' inns. There were two of these, one in Fleet Street, another in Chancery Lane.[66] Sergeants at law did not, however, altogether abandon their old allegiance for the new. The Black Books of Lincoln's Inn offer many evidences of their continued contact. Chief Justice Fortescue, for example, sometimes dined at his old Inn,[67] and Chief Justice Robert Rede of the Common Pleas was, "for the love that he bore the Inn," given the nomination of the butler whenever the office should fall vacant.[68] Sergeants at law sometimes interceded on behalf of trans-

[62] *Ibid.,* pp. 74, 135, 136, 138.
[63] *Ibid.,* pp. 149, 151, 163, 165, 167, 168, 172, 198, 216, 234, 325, 388, 441; *Middle Temple Records* (ed. Hopwood; London, 1904), vol. I, pp. 6, 12, 38, references to Thomas Jubbes, John Jenour, and William Mordaunt, clerks of the Common Bench in the early years of Henry VIII.
[64] *Black Books,* vol. I, p. 140.
[65] *Ibid.,* vol. I, p. 241. For other references to fellows' clerks, see *ibid.,* pp. 9, 276.
[66] Kingsford, *Prejudice and Promise,* a map of fifteenth century London; Foss, *Judges,* vol. IV, pp. 401–402.
[67] *Black Books,* vol. I, p. 15.
[68] *Ibid.,* p. 152.

gressors against the rules of the society.[69] But the sergeant ceased to be a member and could no longer take part with the same easy informality.

The call to take the order of sergeant came by royal writ close. After the second decade of the century, it seems to have been customary to summon eight or nine apprentices at a time, distributed fairly evenly among the four Inns.[70] Who decided which apprentices were worthy of the call is not altogether clear. Fortescue says that the sergeants were chosen by the Chief Justice of the Common Bench on advice of the other justices.[71] This seems an eminently reasonable method of choice since the practice of the sergeants was chiefly in the Common Pleas. On the other hand, the evidence from memoranda of the council and from the Close Rolls is that the council drew up the list of names.[72] Possibly the explanation is that the Chief Justice, on advice of the other justices, presented a list to the council which then issued the order for the writ of summons.

Like other mediaeval celebrations of beginnings and endings, the initiation of sergeants at law combined splendor, solemnity, and revelry. Fifteenth century accounts of the ceremonies are meager. Fortescue concerns himself mainly with the expense involved, leaving the steps in the ceremony to the imagination of his pupil. The chroniclers give fairly full accounts of two fifteenth century feasts, those of 1464 [73] and 1495,[74] but fail to describe the proceedings leading up to these feasts. The earliest complete account of the conferring of the degree is for 1503, the year in which Sir Thomas More's father and Sir Thomas Marowe were made ser-

---

69 *Ibid.*, p. 229.

70 See Foss, *Judges*, vols. IV and V.

71 *De Laudibus*, cap. 50 (ed. Chrimes, p. 121).

72 N. H. Nicolas, *Proceedings and Ordinances of the Privy Council of England* (London, 1834–1837), vol. V, p. 80; Manning, *Serviens ad Legem*, p. 200; *C. C. R., 1409–1413*, p. 258; *C. C. R., 1413–1419*, p. 176; *C. C. R., 1422–1429*, p. 163.

73 "Gregory's Chronicle of London," *The Historical Collection of a Citizen of London in the Fifteenth Century* (ed. Gairdner; Camden Society, Westminster, 1876), p. 222; Holinshed, *Chronicles,* vol. III, p. 283; Stow, *Survey,* vol. II, pp. 35–37; *Y. B. Mich., 3 Ed. IV,* pl. 7.

74 F. Bacon, *History of the Reign of King Henry VII* (ed. Lumby; Cambridge, 1902), p. 131; *Chronicles of London,* pp. 207–208; R. Fabyan, *The New Chronicles of England and France* (Reprinted from Pynson's edition of 1533; London, 1811), p. 685. Miss Putnam has corrected an error in the dating of this feast in Dugdale and in the Year Books (*Early Treatises,* pp. 131–132).

geants. The events of that year are fully described in the Middle Temple records.[75] The ceremonies of 1521 [76] and 1547 [77] are likewise fully reported in contemporary sources.

From these sixteenth century accounts, it appears that the essentials of the proceedings were, first, the sergeants' farewell to the Inn. In the great hall of each of the four Inns the fellows and the sergeants-elect in their new parti-colored robes gathered to meet the king's messengers. With an appropriate speech of congratulation and farewell, the treasurer presented to each man a purse collected from among the members.[78] The sergeants-elect then thanked the company for the purse and for past benefits received. All drank together, and the Inn fellowship escorted the sergeants-elect to the great house where the ceremony was to be performed.[79] There, before the justices of England assembled in the chapel or the hall, the sergeants knelt and delivered declarations based on writs presented to them by the prothonotaries. The Chief Justice then tied on their coifs and placed their hoods upon their shoulders.[80] Then justices and sergeants feasted together, the justices at the high table with such great men of the realm as were present, the sergeants below. Next came the formal introduction of the sergeants to the Court of Common Pleas. For this they rode in splendid procession to West-

[75] *Middle Temple Records,* pp. 7–9. See Putnam, *Early Treatises,* p. 135, n. 2, for a correction in the dating of these proceedings. Dugdale's account (*Orig. Jurid.,* cap. 43) is based on the Middle Temple account.

[76] *A Calendar of the Inner Temple Records* (ed. Inderwick; London, 1896), vol. I, p. 62.

[77] *Black Books,* vol. I, pp. 276–281.

[78] In 1486 Lincoln's Inn gave £6 9s. 4d. to each of the sergeants-elect (*Black Books,* vol. I, p. 85). This seems to have been about the usual amount (cf. *ibid.,* pp. 199, 234; Dugdale, *Orig. Jurid.,* cap. 50).

[79] In 1464 it was Ely House, and again in 1495 and 1521. In 1503 it was Lambeth, and in 1547, Lincoln's Inn Hall.

[80] Nothing is said in the Middle Temple account of the administering of the oath. That an oath must have been part of the fifteenth century ceremony is evident from Choke's remarks in Jenney's case. (Cf. above, p. 60.) The appropriate time for its administration would seem to have been during this ceremony of conferring the coifs and hoods. The copy of the oath given by Dugdale is the same as that reprinted in the *First Report of the Committee on the Public Records* (p. 219) from the Red Book of the Exchequer, and is as follows: "Well and truly ye shall serve the King's people as one of the sergeants at the law, and ye shall truly councill them that ye shall be retained with after your cunning, and ye shall not defer, tract, nor delay, their causes willingly for covetousness of money, or other thing that may turn you to profit, and ye shall give due attention accordingly: As God you help and by the contents of the Book." (Cf. Chrimes, *De Laudibus,* notes on cap. 50, p. 202; *The Book of Oaths* [London, 1649], p. 247.)

minster, accompanied by their friends wearing their livery and by all the justices of England, and escorted by the Warden of the Fleet and a sergeant at arms carrying a great mace. In Westminster Hall, before the Chancellor and Treasurer of England, the sergeants again demonstrated their skill in pleading and, this time, were answered by experienced pleaders. Last came the sergeants' feast to which came the great of the realm, sometimes, as in 1495, even the King and Queen.[81]

In 1503, the various parts of this ceremony were spread over four days, from Friday until the following Monday. Such elaborate and extended celebration was expensive, and the sergeants themselves paid the cost of it. Fortescue says that in his day no one could satisfy the requirements at less than £226 13s. 4d.,[82] and by 1503 the cost was very likely greater. One important item of expense was the gold rings which must be given to every lord, prelate, or knight who attended the solemnities, to the Chancellor and Treasurer of England, to the Keeper of the Privy Seal, to all the justices of both benches, to the barons of the Exchequer, to the Keeper of the rolls in Chancery, to the Chamberlains and "officers and notable men serving in the king's Courts," and finally to every clerk of the king's courts, especially the Court of Common Pleas, down to the least of them—to each a ring varying in value according to his estate and rank, Fortescue, himself, spent £50 for rings alone.[83] Besides rings the sergeant must give liveries, not only to his servants, but also to all his friends who attended the ceremony.[84]

If this expense is translated into modern terms, it is easy to see why certain apprentices, in 1412, tried to avoid taking the degree, and why, after that year, a money penalty was imposed for refusal. In that year, John de Preston, James Strangeways, and six others were threatened with disbarment if they did not accept the degree.[85] Preston and Strangeways complied, but John Martyn, John Barton, the younger, and William Wynarde apparently refused. These three, with John Juyn and Thomas Rolfe, were called again in

---

[81] *Chronicles of London,* pp. 207–208; Bacon, *Henry VII,* p. 131.
[82] *De Laudibus,* cap. 50.
[83] *Ibid.*
[84] *Ibid.* The sergeants were exempted from the statutes of livery and maintenance "for the time when they take the degree upon them" (8 Hy. VI, c. 4).
[85] *C. C. R., 1409–1413,* p. 258.

1415, this time on pain of paying 500 marks.[86] Still they resisted, and a third writ was issued adding William Babyngton to the list and increasing the penalty to £1,000.[87] Despite the severity of this penalty, the apprentices continued recalcitrant, and in 1417 a petition was presented to Parliament complaining that the suits of the people of the realm were delayed because there were not enough sergeants. This time the contumacious apprentices were commanded by the Duke of Bedford, as King's Lieutenant, and by the Lords assembled in Parliament to take the degree without delay. Still protesting, they appeared before the Lords on the fifth of November and asked to be excused until the following Trinity. On their solemn promise to make no excuses at this later date, the ceremony was respited, and we hear no more of their obstinacy.[88] The penalty of £1,000, however, remained in the writ of summons as a permanent reminder of this episode and, it would be supposed, an effective inducement to comply with the call.[89]

If the costs of becoming a sergeant were high, the financial rewards of the rank were also high. Fortescue says, "Nor is there any advocate in the whole world who enriches himself by reason of his office as much as the sergeant." [90] Now, while Fortescue's knowledge of the world was limited, his knowledge of the opportunities of a sergeant were immediate and personal. And William Ayscogh seems to have agreed with him concerning the happy position of the sergeant. Ayscogh petitioned the Council in 1441 that he should have certain tenements of the annual value of £25 12s. and 10d. as recompense for having been made a justice only two years after his elevation to the degree of sergeant. Thus he had been deprived of "all his winnings that he should have had" as a sergeant.[91]

Although I have not found it possible to calculate in any satisfactory way the annual income of any of the leading sergeants at law, there are various references to the rate of pay which may be useful to others in the same search. In 1500 John Yaxley signed an

<hr>

[86] *C. C. R., 1413–1419*, p. 176, Feb. 15, 1415.
[87] *Ibid.*, p. 216, July 11, 1415.
[88] *R. P.*, vol. IV, p. 107.
[89] See the writ issued in 1424, *C. C. R., 1422–1429*, p. 163; *C. C. R., 1441–1447*, p. 87.
[90] *De Laudibus*, cap. 50.
[91] *Archaeologia*, vol. XVI, No. II. Although he complained in the petition of failing eyesight, Ayscogh seems to have remained on the Bench until 1454 (Foss, *Judges*, vol. IV, pp. 282–283).

indenture with Sir Robert Plumpton to act as his counsel at the assizes at York, Nottingham, and Derby. Yaxley was to receive £5 in hand and the remainder of 40 marks plus expenses at a later date.[92] Earlier (Hilary, 3 Henry VI), William Pole, sergeant at law, brought suit against a client for failure to pay him a sum of £20 which he was to receive annually during two years of service as his counsel.[93] Later in the same reign (31 Henry VI), in a case of maintenance, Moyle, apprentice, announced that if no certain sum of money were promised to a sergeant for his services, he should have "by common right" 40d. as compared with 20d. for an attorney.[94]

The work of a sergeant at law was not confined to private practice. He was also called upon for public service. For example, William Boef and Thomas Littleton, both made sergeants in 1453, were appointed to many commissions in the early years of their careers as sergeants at law.[95] They were among those appointed to assign archers for Devon and for Warwickshire, respectively, in December, 1457.[96] In July, 1458, Boef was appointed with Sir John Fortescue, Chief Justice of the King's Bench, and John Giffard to a commission to deliver Exeter jail.[97] In April, 1459, he was appointed to a commission to inquire into felonies, trespasses, etc., against the priory of SS. Peter and Paul at Montacute, in Somerset.[98] In June, 1460, his name appeared in a long list of commissioners of oyer and terminer for Somerset, Devon, and Cornwall.[99] The list included all the justices of both benches, several lords, gentlemen, and two other sergeants at law. Finally he was appointed to commissions of the peace for Devon five times from June 29, 1458, to August 19, 1460.[100]

Littleton's list of appointments for the same period is longer and more impressive than Boef's, perhaps because he was abler than Boef, who never became a king's sergeant or a justice, and who died

---

92 *Plumpton Correspondence* (ed. T. Stapleton; Camden Society, London, 1839), p. 152, note to letter CXIX, Ser. II; Foss, *Judges*, Vol. IV, p. 403.

93 *Y. B. Hil., 3 Hy. VI*, pl. 26.

94 *Y. B. Mich., 31 Hy. VI*, pl. 1.

95 Littleton had been appointed to several commissions as an apprentice.

96 *C. P. R., 1452–1461*, pp. 406–410; *R. P.*, vol. V, pp. 230–233.

97 *C. P. R., 1452–1461*, p. 443.

98 *Ibid.*, p. 496.

99 *Ibid.*, p. 613.

100 *Ibid.*, p. 664.

about 1461.[101] In the same year that he became a sergeant Littleton was made one of the commissioners to raise a loan for the relief of the Earl of Shrewsbury at Bordeaux,[102] and in 1455, for the relief of Calais.[103] Seven times between June, 1454, and August, 1468, he was appointed to commissions of the peace for Worcestershire and Yorkshire [104] and five times between September, 1456, and April, 1460, to commissions of gaol delivery in the counties of Warwick and Worcester.[105] In 1460 he was appointed to various commissions of oyer and terminer to inquire into the lands of Richard of York (killed at the battle of Wakefield in December of the preceding year) [106] and of Sir William Oldhall, attainted by parliament on the twelfth of October, 1459.[107]

Although such references to Littleton and Boef in the *Calendars of Patent Rolls* are formal, factual, and brief, they are by no means dull and colorless. They suggest long rides on horseback in fair weather and foul, stops at inns by the wayside and inns in the towns, the close companionship of travel with justices, with other sergeants at law, and gentlemen serving on the same commissions, the drama of clashes of local rivalries at the sessions. Always when justice was administered crowds looked on, sometimes disinterested enough but sometimes ready to threaten the lives of those who made justice go against them or their "good lords." [108] In some ways the law terms at Westminster must have seemed dull and peaceful compared to the strenuous and possibly dangerous jauntings in the country. On the other hand London and Westminster offered the civilized

<hr>

[101] Wedgewood and Holt, *Biographies*, p. 89.
[102] *C. P. R., 1452–1461*, p. 53.
[103] Nicolas, *Privy Council*, vol. VI, pp. 235, 240.
[104] *C. P. R., 1452–1461*, pp. 680–685.
[105] *Ibid.*, pp. 343, 345, 347, 517, 566.
[106] *C. P. R., 1452–1461*, p. 564, Feb. 4; p. 562, March 13, 1460.
[107] *Ibid.*, p. 561, Feb. 13; p. 604, March 12.
[108] Firth gives an account taken from Ancient Indictments of how the justices were prevented from holding an oyer and terminer in Cambridge in 1464 by Thomas Parson and others, who threatened to stop them by force, if necessary (*E. H. R.*, vol. XXXII [1917], p. 177). In Edward Hall's *Chronicle* (London, 1809), pp. 234–235, is an account of how justices of oyer and terminer appointed for London in 1456 were frightened into leaving the Guildhall by "diverse light-witted and less-brained persons in the City" who got together a band of citizens to free certain defendants who were being taken from Newgate to their trial. Thomas Howes, in a letter to Sir John Fastolf (*Paston Letters*, No. 158, May 9, 1451) describes how Heydon and Tuddenham, two of John Paston's bitterest enemies came to sessions of oyer and terminer with four hundred mounted retainers.

pleasures of discussion with fellow members of the bar, a lively social life, and for Littleton, the opportunity he needed for the study which led to his book on *Tenures.*

A sergeant who was on his way up the ladder to the Bench was likely to receive two permanent appointments in addition to the many temporary commissions. One was that of king's sergeant. Although experience in this office seems not to have been an essential prerequisite to appointment to the Bench, more than half the justices during the reigns of Henry VI, Edward IV, Edward V, and Richard III had been appointed to it. And most seem to have had experience as justices of assize.[109] Each of these offices brought an additional £20 a year to add to the sergeant's income from fees, and the king's sergeant received a further increment of 26s. 11d. for a robe at Christmas time.

King's sergeants were, like the justices, called to Parliament.[110] There they were expected to assist the lords and judges in the trials of petitions.[111] They were also associated with the justices as advisers to the council in its deliberation on judicial matters.[112] As legal advisers to the Crown they outranked the king's attorney.[113] In the last Parliament of Henry VI this responsibilty brought them temporarily into the main stream of political events but only for the briefest of moments. On Wednesday, October 20, 1460, they were called upon to give an opinion on the Duke of York's claim to

---

[109] Nowhere is the need for revisions of Foss clearer than in such matters as patents of appointment to offices like that of king's sergeant at law and to commissions of assize. Richard Choke, for example, is nowhere listed in Foss as a king's sergeant, yet his patent appears in the patent rolls for July 4, 1453 (*C. P. R., 1452–1461*, p. 85). The commissions of assize are not listed in the Index of the *Calendars of Patent Rolls* but they may be found by searching under the names of individual justices, sergeants, and apprentices of the law.

[110] Dugdale, *Orig. Jurid.,* p. 110; *R. P.,* vol. III, p. 455a, vol. V, p. 42a, 240a, 376.

[111] Manning, *Serviens ad Legem,* pp. 206–208; *R. P.,* vols. III–V, *passim,* among lists of names of triers of petitions.

[112] For petitions that justices and king's sergeants advise the council, see *R. P.,* vol. III, p. 15; vol. IV, p. 201. For late fourteenth and fifteenth century evidence of their presence in the council as advisers, see J. F. Baldwin, *The King's Council in England during the Middle Ages* (Oxford, 1913), pp. 490, 492, 510–511; I. S. Leadam and J. F. Baldwin, *Select Cases before the King's Council,* S. S. vol. XXXV (Cambridge, 1918), pp. ci, cxvi–cxvii, 72 ff.; *C. C. R., 1435–1441,* pp. 22, 81–82; *C. C. R., 1441–1447,* pp. 183–185, 332–334. For discussion of the position of the justices and king's sergeants in the council, see Baldwin, *op. cit.,* pp. 70–71, 122, 205–206; Leadam and Baldwin, *op. cit.,* pp. xvi–xvii.

[113] Fortescue, *Governance of England* (ed. Plummer), p. 45, n. 3.

the throne. Their reply was discreet if it was not courageous, and it makes clear to us the limits which they themselves saw to their responsibilities. They answered "that the said matter was put unto the king's justices and how, the Monday then last passed, the same justices said and declared to the said lords that the said matter was so high and of so great weight that it passed their learning and also they durst not enter any communication in that matter to give any advice or counsel therein; and since that the said matter was so high that it passed the learning of the justices, it must needs exceed their learning, and also they durst not enter any communication in that matter, and prayed and besought all the Lords to have them excused of giving any advice or counsel therein." When pressed further by the Lords on the ground that they received their fees and wages for giving the king counsel, they said "that they were the King's counsellors in the law in such things as were under his authority or by his commission, but this matter was above his authority wherein they might not meddle." In the end the Lords were forced to make their own defense of the King's title.[114]

This seems to have been the one occasion on which the king's sergeants were directly involved in the turbulent political events of the times. Ordinarily they were occupied with more obscure duties of representing the king's interests in the law courts and of pleading poor men's causes before the council. By an ordinance of 1423 the council required the clerk each day to select for consideration the poorest suitor's bill. Then the king's sergeant was to be sworn to give him counsel "without any good taking of him on pain of discharge" of his office.[115]

Appointments to a commission of assize meant a considerable increase in public activity for the sergeant since the justices went on circuit twice during the year.[116] Meanwhile, in the case of men like Littleton, there was no abatement in the number of other commissions, special and general, to which he might be appointed.[117]

[114] *R. P.*, vol. V, pp. 375–376.
[115] *R. P.*, vol. IV, p. 201 b, 2 Hy. IV, no. 17.
[116] The *nisi prius* dates in the plea rolls fall between Hilary and Easter and Trinity and Michaelmas terms.
[117] If Littleton, for example, actually worked on all the commissions to which he was appointed between 1460 and the time of his elevation to the Bench, it is hard to see how he found enough time for private practice.

To Littleton elevation to the Bench came in middle age, thirteen years after his election to the order of sergeant at law and eleven after his appointment as king's sergeant. In this respect he seems to have been fairly representative of his contemporaries, although some rose to the Bench after fewer years of pleading in the courts and some had never been king's sergeants.

Clearly fifteenth century judges of the central courts were no novices in the law. Their varied experiences as students, as practicing lawyers, as administrators, and as judges prepared them, if any training could, for the variety of problems which came before them as judges.

CHAPTER VI

Bench and Bar:

THE JUSTICES

T O BECOME A JUSTICE and sit upon the Bench was a thing more glorious to the onlooker than impressive to the sergeant himself. Elevation to the Bench brought no revolution in his way of life. He exchanged his parti-colored robes furred with white lamb and his round cape with tappets for a plain-colored robe furred with miniver and a cape that fastened on one shoulder.[1] His white coif, however, he kept upon his head as a sign of his degree and, like the sergeant at law, never doffed it even in the presence of the king himself.[2] From a standing position on the floor below he ascended to the bench upon the raised dais, and his functions, too, were changed. He was to decide rather than to plead. Yet in the discussions reported in the Year Books his part was not strikingly different. Without previous knowledge it is often hard to tell whether a justice or a sergeant at law is speaking. His daily life also was little altered. He continued, if he wished, to reside when in London in one of the sergeants' inns. And the many appointments to commissions of special inquiry, of assize, of oyer and terminer, of gaol delivery, etc., were showered upon him as before, the only change being that there were more of them, and that his responsibilities were greater.

There was a ceremony to create a new justice and an oath to be taken, but the inauguration was simple compared with that of a

---

[1] Fortescue, *De Laudibus*, cap. 51. Cf. *R. P.*, vol. II, p. 593 (1406).
[2] *Ibid.*, cap. 50.

sergeant at law. The king appointed new justices by letters patent issued on advice of the council.[3] The Chancellor himself went to the court where the vacancy was to inform the sergeant of his new office. The letters patent were read openly in the court, and then the justice was sworn. The essentials of the oath seem to have been that he would do "justice without favour, to all men pleading before him, friends and foes alike," and that he would not "delay to do so even though the king should command him by his letters or by word of mouth to the contrary," that he would "not receive from anyone except the king any fee or other pension or livery nor take any gift from any pleaders before him, except food and drink of no great price." [4]

There was obviously a change in the sources and amount of his income, and, if Ayscogh is to be believed, the change was at least temporarily for the worse.[5] Three parts of his income came from the king. The first was the salary. The amount of this had not increased since the time of Edward I. For the Chief Justice it was £40 annually; for a puisne justice, 40 marks.[6] In addition, there was a grant by letters patent: for the Chief Justice, £93 6s. 8d., and for a puisne justice, 110 marks yearly.[7] Finally, there was an allowance for robes of 106s. 11¼d. and the sixth part of a halfpenny at Christmas, and 66s. 6d. at Whitsun. This was the same for the Chief Justice as for puisne justices.

The grant by letters patent was an innovation introduced by the Ordinance of 20 Edward III with definite intent to reduce the incentives for bribery by providing for the justices "in such manner as ought reasonably to suffice them." [8] The amount had been twice increased since the ordinance.[9] The payment for robes was a commutation of an earlier grant of the robes themselves, a change introduced in response to a petition of 18 Henry VI.[10]

---

3 *Ibid.*, cap. 51. Littleton's patent was "by the King by word of mouth" (*C. P. R.*, *1461–1467*), but see Nicolas, *Privy Council*, vol. IV, pp. 4, 265.

4 For the form of the oath see stat. 20 Ed. III, c. 1 (1346); *R. P.*, vol. III, pp. 158, 623; *First Report on the Public Records*, p. 236; Baldwin, *The King's Council*, pp. 345 ff.; Fortescue, *De Laudibus*, cap. 51.

5 Above, p. 75.

6 Foss, *Judges*, vol. IV, p. 227; *H. E. L.*, vol. I, pp. 252–255.

7 *C. P. R.*, *1461–1467*, pp. 128, 190.

8 20 Ed. III, c. 1.

9 Foss, *Judges*, vol. III, pp. 357–358; vol. IV, 227.

10 *R. P.*, vol. V, p. 14; Nicolas, *Privy Council*, vol. IV, p. 265; *C. P. R.*, *1429–1436*,

Also in response to this petition (a complaint of the justices that, as often before, their payments were in arrears) [11] a further innovation was introduced. It was provided that henceforth they should collect the grant by letters patent, not, as formerly, from the Treasurer direct, but from the keeper of the hanaper or from the customs collectors of the ports of London, Bristol, or Hull.[12] Action on this ordinance seems not to have been immediately effective for sizable sums were still in arrears in 1443, three years later.[13]

Fifteenth century judges supplemented this income for their services at Westminster by serving on commissions of assize, of the peace, of gaol (jail) delivery, of oyer and terminer, and other similar commissions. The sums they got for these services were probably not very large. Justices of the peace, for example, could earn a maximum of only 48s. a year and anyone of the rank of banneret or above was forbidden to take even this pittance.[14] Justices of assize got only £20 a year.[15] I do not know what amounts, if any, were paid to justices of gaol delivery and other commissioners. They were probably never enough to induce judges to compete for the appointments.

The most important source of a justice's income was neither his salary and other rewards from the king for his services at Westminster nor his salary for service on special and general commissions. It was the fees which he received from the parties to suits in court.[16] The chief part of these came from payments for the sealing of judicial writs. Lump sums received from this source are recorded in the accounts of the Clerk of the Hanaper. For the year 12 Edward IV they totaled £269 14s. 12d.[17] Presumably the total annual receipts were divided among the justices according to

p. 347; *C. P. R., 1436–1441,* p. 238, evidence that the robes themselves were granted until 1440.

[11] For earlier and later references to arrears due to the justices, see *R. P.,* vol. IV, p. 437; *Y. B. 8 Ed. II* S. S. vol. XXXVII), p. xiv; *Y. B. Mich., 1 Hy. VII,* pl. 4. For accounts with J. Stonor, see Exchequer Accounts Various: E 101/508/1; for accounts of payments to J. Cokayn, temp. Henry IV, see E 101/513/22.

[12] *R. P.,* vol. V, p. 14 (1439); 10 Hy. VI, stat. 2.

[13] *C. C. R., 1441–1447,* pp. 191–193.

[14] 12 Ric. II, c. 10; 14 Ric. II, c. 11. Cf. Putnam, *Proceedings,* pp. lxxxix–xc; *Early Treatises,* pp. 65–66.

[15] *C. C. R., 1441–1447,* pp. 191–193.

[16] *H. E. L.,* vol. I, p. 254.

[17] E 101/216/15.

some established principle of rank and seniority. Without knowing this principle and without more totals of receipts from which to draw an average, it is impossible to estimate a total average income for a fifteenth century justice. In 1522, however, the subsidy assessments accredit Chief Justice Brudenell with an income of 650 marks, the two senior puisne justices, Pollard and Brooke, with 500 marks, and Fitzherbert, newly appointed to the court, with £240.[18]

An additional source of income for the Chief Justice, and possibly also for the puisne justices at this date, was what today would be considered a kind of "graft." The Chief Justice had at his disposal a number of valuable offices in the courts, for example, the offices of first and third prothonotaries and the office of filacer. By the end of the seventeenth century the proceeds from the sale of offices were highly prized perquisites of judicial office, but the Chief Justice had got them largely into his own hands as against the king and the puisne justices. In the fifteenth century the price for one of these appointments was probably not so great as it later became, and "brocage" was perhaps still frowned upon, but there is little reason to doubt that sums were paid and that justices received them.[19]

In their private capacity justices, like other men with legal training, had further opportunities for income. They were often called upon as trustees of estates and presumably received some reward for such service. For example, Littleton and several others received a grant of land in 1468 "to the use of Dame Isabel Shottesbrook, late wife of John Barton, the younger, late lord of Thornton of Thornton" (co. Bucks), that they might found a chantry in the parish church of Thornton.[20] Again, in 1476 Littleton with Humphrey and Thomas Stafford, esquires, and John Catesby, one of the king's sergeants at law, received a similar grant to the use of Eleanor Stafford, widow of Sir Humphrey, to found a chantry in the parish church of Bromsgrove (co. Worc),[21] John Paston, son of William,

---

18 Foss, *Judges*, vol. V, p. 99. Cf. Assessments of 2 Ric. II (*R. P.*, vol. III, p. 58). Justices were assessed 100s. as compared with 10 marks for barons and 40s. for bannerets.
19 See below, Ch. VII.
20 *C. P. R., 1467–1477*, p. 112.
21 *C. P. R., 1476–1485*, pp. 11, 57.

the judge, had known how to make a good thing for himself of his trusteeship of Caister Castle, although he came into possession of the castle only after protracted altercation, litigation, and arbitration. One of the ways of safeguarding one's family against forfeiture of estates by attainder seems to have been to create a trusteeship in the hands of lawyers as a precautionary measure. Littleton and several others are referred to as having received such an estate-in-trust created by the Earl of Wiltshire some years before his attainder by the first parliament of Edward IV.[22] This subject of trusteeships and also the more general subject of accumulation of landed estates by men of the law deserve further investigation.[23] Many fifteenth century judges appear to have been founders of landed and titled families of later centuries.

The daily life of a justice cannot have been quite so idyllic as Fortescue's description of it. The sessions of the court, he says, began each morning in term time at eight and were over by eleven. The rest of the day the judges passed "in studying the laws, reading Holy Scripture, and otherwise in contemplation at their pleasure."[24] This may be an accurate description of certain intervals in the life of a fifteenth century justice. The question is whether he was ever allowed long periods of enjoyment of so peaceful and pleasant a manner of living.

No answer can be given to this question within the limits of this present work. Many detailed biographies of fifteenth century judges using the record sources available since the time of Foss would provide the best answer to it. On the other hand, some of the problems can be suggested in a summary of the facts available concerning the life of Justice Thomas Littleton during one year of his active life on the bench.

The year 1468, beginning twenty months after Littleton's appointment as a justice, seems a good one to consider. It is early in his career on the Bench of the Common Pleas, but not too early for him to have become accustomed to his duties. It is also a year in which, although there were rumblings of the upheaval to come in

---

[22] *C. P. R., 1461–1467,* pp. 549–550, appointment of a commission to inquire into the claim of petitioners to parcels of the manor of Ashby la Zouche. Cf. *R. P.,* vol. V, pp. 476–483, and Scofield, *Edward IV,* vol. I, p. 220.

[23] Miss M. K. Dale, M. A., has collected materials for such a study.

[24] *De Laudibus,* cap. 51.

1470, there was at least no open civil war. Edward had spent Christmas at Coventry in the abbey there with his beautiful but selfish wife and his false brother, the Duke of Clarence. It had not been a holiday without cares, however. A bodyguard of two hundred or more men had escorted him to Coventry because of alarms of Lancastrian plots in which Warwick was suspected of complicity. Warwick was in Yorkshire where he had been since August, sulking at his failure to influence Edward against the Burgundian alliance and at a jibe from Edward over the preference to a cardinalate of the Archbishop of Canterbury rather than Warwick's brother, the Archbishop of York. Edward's distrust of Warwick had been aroused by the discovery that the latter had been negotiating at the papal court for a dispensation to allow marriage between his daughter Anne and the Duke of Clarence and by revelations of a messenger of Margaret of Anjou, captured by Lord Herbert in Wales. This messenger accused many persons of treason and reported that, across the Channel, people believed that Warwick was sympathetic with Margaret and had gone to Yorkshire to raise troops to assist her. There was widespread unrest in the kingdom, much of it due to popular reaction against Edward's favor to his wife's family and to Warwick's popularity.[25]

These developments touched Littleton's life early in the year. On the third and thirteenth of January successively he was appointed to two commissions of oyer and terminer to deal with "great riots and oppressions done unto our subjects" in Nottingham, Derby, Stafford, Salop, Hereford, Warwick, and Worcester. On both commissions with him were Markham, the Chief Justice of the King's Bench, Billing, puisne justice of the same bench, and Catesby and Neell, sergeants at law, as well as a long list of magnates and household favorites beginning with Clarence, Warwick, the Earl of Rivers, and Lord Scales, the very men whose rivalries were causing the unrest.[26] It seems probable that most of the work of the hearings fell upon the men of law. Clarence, a rather addlepated lad of eighteen, was engaged in the secret negotiations for Warwick's return to favor.[27] Warwick himself was in Yorkshire until late in

25 Scofield, *Edward IV*, vol. I, pp. 433–435.

26 *C. P. R., 1467–1477*, p. 55; Scofield, *Edward IV*, vol. I, p. 435.

27 W. Worcester, "Annales Rerum Anglicarum," Great Britain, Exchequer, *Liber Niger Scaccarii* (Oxford, 1728), vol. II, pp. 512–513.

January when he went to Coventry to make his peace with the King. After that, he returned with the King to London for a meeting of the council in February.[28] The Earl of Rivers and Lord Scales were being kept out of Warwick's way. Both Benches were in session at Westminster during Hilary term, and Markham and Catesby are reported as having taken part in discussions there.[29] This suggests but by no means proves that the brunt of the work of the hearings and determinings ordered by the king was borne by Billing, Littleton, and Neell. Apparently they had not finished their task by the end of Hilary term for on February 13 a new commission was appointed for the same counties, this time including all the justices of both Benches.[30]

Whether Littleton served actively on this particular commission or not, he seems to have been busy in the interim between Hilary and Easter terms. He was appointed on February 16 with Byngham, one of the justices of the King's Bench, and Cumberford, second prothonotary of the Court of Common Pleas, to a commission of inquiry into the complaint of John Sutton, Lord Dudley, that he was wrongly deprived of the manor of Warsshop in Nottinghamshire. After the attainder of Lord Roos, the king had granted this manor to Lady Roos and her brother, the Earl of Worcester.[31] Littleton must also have gone on circuit as justice of assize for the northern counties with Richard Illyngworth, Chief Baron of the Exchequer.[32] And on January third and March twentieth he was appointed to commissions of the peace for Warwickshire.[33]

During the Easter term he was back at Westminster, if we are to believe the Year Book reporter. His name appears frequently in the reports both of that term and of Trinity. Between Easter and Trinity terms he must have been called with the other justices to advise the Lords in the final session of the Parliament of 7–8 Ed-

28 Scofield, *Edward IV*, vol. I, pp. 443–445.
29 *Y. B. Hil.*, 7 *Ed. IV*. The Year Books are unfortunately rather unreliable evidence of the presence or absence of a justice or sergeant. See printer's note on p. 25 of *Y. B. 7 Ed. IV*.
30 *C. P. R., 1467–1477*, p. 69.
31 *Ibid.*, p. 70.
32 He had been appointed to this circuit in February, 1466 (*C. P. R., 1461–1467*, p. 477.)
33 *C. P. R., 1467–1477*, p. 634.

ward IV, which met late in May at Reading only to adjourn to London where it sat until June 7.[34]

In the second week of June, however, political events once more interrupted the quiet order of his judicial existence.[35] A man named Cornelius, servant to Sir Robert Whityngham, Lancastrian exile at Margaret of Anjou's court, was arrested at Queensborough. He had packets of letters from Lancastrians to their friends in England, among them Thomas Danvers. One Hugh Mille was already in the Fleet prison on suspicion of treason. Danvers was arrested and committed to the Tower. And Cornelius, while hot irons were applied to his feet, implicated many other persons including Hayford, sheriff of London, Plummer, an alderman, Nicholas Huse, former victualler of Calais and lieutenant of Guisnes, Sir Gervase Clifton, Peter Alfray, a London draper, and John Hawkyns, servant to Lord Wenlock. Hawkyns, when questioned, accused both his master and Sir Thomas Cooke, wealthy draper and former mayor of London.

Two commissions of oyer and terminer were appointed to deal with these developments, one for London,[36] the other for Middlesex, Surrey, and Essex.[37] Littleton's name was on both in an impressive list, including magnates, household favorites, gentlemen, the lord mayor of London, and all the justices of both Benches. According to Dr. Scofield, the mayor, Chief Justice Markham and Thomas Littleton did most of the work.[38] Both Markham and Littleton, however, are represented in the Year Book as having taken part in the discussions at Westminster during Trinity term (June 22 to July 13). Perhaps they divided their time between Westminster Hall and the Guildhall. Clarence, Warwick, and Gloucester, who topped the list, had gone with the king to Margate to see Princess Margaret safely on her way to Burgundy for her wedding, but they were back in London in time for the hearings.

The results of the trials at the Guildhall are significant. The king, strengthened in his suspicions by the landing of the Earl of

34 Scofield, *Edward IV*, vol. I, pp. 450–453; *R. P.*, vol. V, pp. 571 ff.

35 For an extended account of the events summarized here, see Scofield, *Edward IV*, vol. I, pp. 453–462.

36 *C. P. R.*, *1467–1477*, p. 103, June 20, 1468.

37 *Ibid.*, p. 102, July 3, 1468.

38 Scofield, *Edward IV*, vol. I, p. 457. Miss Scofield quotes Warrants for Issue and Issue Rolls as authority for the statement.

Pembroke in Wales, had had Cooke's wife committed to the custody of the mayor and had ordered Sir John Fogge to search both his town and country house for evidence. This Fogge did and took the opportunity also to carry off many valuable household goods, including a gilded saltcellar, spoons, plate, and hangings. Nonetheless, despite Edward's evident desire for a conviction, the jury found Cooke guilty of misprision of treason only. Plummer, Hayford, Pakenham, and Portaleyne were acquitted outright but did not escape fine by the king. Hugh Mille, probably the least innocent of all since he was among the rebels in Wales a few months later, successfully pleaded a pardon granted to him by the king in the previous year. Huse was outlawed and only Hawkyns, Alfray, and Norris were condemned to be hanged. Alfray was saved at the foot of the gallows by a pardon procured through the intercession of the archbishop of York and in the end only Hawkyns and Norris paid the penalty at Tyburn. A general pardon was offered to all others who would ask for it before St. John's Day (August 29). Many did so, and from the fines and the sums paid for pardons the king may have got enough money to console him for the jury's failure to convict more victims.

This was the lively beginning of a busy summer for Littleton, if we are to believe the evidence of appointments. There were the summer assizes to be held in the northern counties. Moreover, Littleton had been appointed with Sir John Needham, another justice of the Common Pleas, and several others to a commission to inquire who was the next heir of John and Thomas Haryngton, deceased, and what land they held in Yorkshire.[39] This commission was perhaps to be accomplished while Littleton was in Yorkshire for the assizes. Meanwhile, the unrest stirred up in June by the accusations of Cornelius and the landing of the Earl of Pembroke continued. Godfrey Grene wrote to Sir William Plumpton that "the yeomen of the Crowne bene riden into divers countries to arrest men that be apeched."[40] Littleton, early in August, was appointed with all the other justices of both Benches and the mayor of Exeter to a commission of oyer and terminer for Devon and Gloucester.[41]

[39] *C. P. R.*, *1467–1477*, p. 103, June 30, 1468.
[40] *Pl. Cor.*, No. XIII, pp. 19–20.
[41] *C. P. R.*, *1467–1477*, p. 126, Aug. 3, 1468

Michaelmas term began on 10 October and lasted until 28 November. According to the Year Book, Littleton was at Westminster for this term. On 12 December, however, he was appointed to another commission of oyer and terminer, this time for the counties of Hampshire, Wiltshire, Devonshire, Southampton, and Salisbury.[42] On the commission also were the King's brothers, the earls of Warwick, Arundel, and Rivers, all the justices of both Benches, and the mayors of Southampton and Salisbury. The matters to be heard and determined were probably consequent upon the discovery of another plot. This time Sir Thomas Hungerford and Henry Courtenay had been arrested and imprisoned at Salisbury.[43]

Altogether, if we are to believe the evidence of his appointments and the Year Books, Littleton, in 1468, lived a life much more active than contemplative. The question is whether he actually served on all the commissions to which he was appointed. A casual study of the appointments of justices to commissions in relation to the background of their regular judicial work suggests that there may have been some system of division of labor by arrangement among them. Even so the life of a fifteenth century justice cannot have been one of ease or, as Fortescue says, "free from all worldly cares." The long rides on horseback, the hazards of road and weather, the discomforts of strange beds and bedfellows, and the constant demand for his services to deal with the chronic unrest among the upper ranks of society suggest to us a strenuous rather than a contemplative life. Perhaps our standards are different, or perhaps Fortescue's picture was the product of nostalgia for old companionships and regret that he had abandoned the relatively peaceful life of a judge for the more violent vicissitudes of politics and ultimate exile.[44]

Fortescue's choice of the active political life raises the general question of the extent to which justices were drawn into partisan

---

[42] *Ibid.,* p. 128, Dec. 12, 1468.

[43] Scofield, *Edward IV*, vol. I, p. 480.

[44] A casual glance at the chronology of Fortescue's life compiled by Dr. Chrimes is sufficient to show that he was just as busy as Littleton throughout the time he was Chief Justice of the King's Bench. Moreover, on at least one occasion, he accomplished his duties with pain and difficulty. In January, 1444, he had to ask the council to excuse him from holding the assizes at East Grinstead because William Paston, his associate, was ill and he himself had sciatica and could not sit a horse. Even so, he planned to cover the part of the circuit which could be reached by water (*Paston Letters,* vol. I, no. 37, Jan. 29, 1444).

controversy either by reason of their office or because of personal preference. The two notable occasions when the judges as a group were drawn out of their seclusion in the purlieus of the common law were in 1460, when the lords called upon them for an opinion concerning the Duke of York's claim to the throne,[45] and in 1485, when Henry VII asked them for advice concerning the pacification of the kingdom and for their opinion concerning the legal effect of his attainder.[46]

On the earlier occasion they burked the responsibility thrust upon them, giving two reasons for their refusal to venture an opinion. The first was that as judges they could not act as counsel between party and party. The second was that the matter they were asked to consider "touched the King's high estate and regality, which is above the law and passed their learning." This sounds more like James I than like Sir Edward Coke and is as good an illustration as can be found of the difference in spirit between fifteenth century common lawyers and their seventeenth century successors. The questions referred to them in 1485 were not so delicate and were well within the province of their competence. For the improvement of the state of the realm, they said, the enforcement of statutes already enacted was the great necessity. Concerning the king's attainder their view was that kings were above such disabilities imposed by Parliament.

As private individuals very few of Littleton's contemporaries on the Bench of the Common Pleas appear, so far as my present knowledge is concerned, to have taken an active part in the partisan controversy of their times. Of the twenty-eight judges of the Common Pleas during the reigns of Henry VI, Edward IV, Edward V, and Richard III, six had served as members of the House of Commons before they were raised to the Bench, but only three had acquired a distinct party label. Sir John Needham is mentioned as a Lancastrian sympathizer in the parliament of 1450.[47] Sir Robert Danby, appointed Chief Justice in 1461, was known as a Yorkist.[48] Sir Thomas Yonge, member of a Bristol family of merchants, served in

---

[45] *R. P.*, vol. V, p. 376; Chrimes, *English Const. Ideas*, pp. 22–23; Pickthorn, *Early Tudor Govt. Henry VII*, p. 3.
[46] *Y. B. Mich., 1 Hy. VII*, pls. 3 and 5.
[47] Foss, *Judges*, vol. IV, pp. 446–447; Wedgewood and Holt, *Biographies*.
[48] Foss, *Judges*, vol. IV, pp. 426–428; Wedgewood and Holt, *Biographies*.

every Parliament from 1435 to 1471, until 1465 as a member of the House of Commons, after that, in his capacity as justice of the Common Pleas, with the Lords. Yet his record is inconsistent. In the Parliament of 1451 he presented a petition that the Duke of York should be recognized as heir to the throne. For this he was committed to the Tower but was later released and pardoned; and he successfully petitioned the Parliament in 1455 for compensation for unjust imprisonment. In 1470, however, he supported the readeption, and this fickleness may have been the reason why he was not reappointed to the Bench in 1471. On the other hand, his annual tun of wine from the port of Bristol was exempted in the Act of Resumption of 1473 and he was described in the act as "our well-beloved Thomas Yonge, late one of the justices of the Common Bench." [49]

The conclusion to be drawn from the record of Littleton's contemporaries and particularly from a comparison of the career of Littleton himself with that of Fortescue is that if one wished to avoid involvement in politics one could, but that if one became involved one paid a price. That price was not prohibitive, however. Even Fortescue, good Lancastrian that he was, returned to England after the Restoration and was received back into the king's good graces, although he was not reappointed to his former office.[50]

The most important question raised by the careers of Fortescue, Danby, Needham, and Yonge is that of tenure and independence of fifteenth century judges. To what extent could they count on permanency on the Bench, once they had achieved that dignified position? Technically, of course, they had no security at all. Their appointments were "at the king's pleasure." On the other hand, as a matter of practice, there was extraordinary continuity even during the most troubled years of the fifteenth century. All the Common Pleas justices of Edward IV were reappointed by Henry VI in 1470, and Littleton and Choke were again reappointed by Edward IV on his return.[51] Moyle is supposed to have died in 1471.[52] Needham

---

[49] Foss, *Judges,* vol. IV, pp. 464–467; Wedgewood and Holt, *Biographies. R. P.,* vol. VI, p. 82.
[50] Chrimes, *De Laudibus,* p. lxxv.
[51] Foss, *Judges,* vol. IV, pp. 238, 395.
[52] *Ibid.,* p. 445; Wedgewood and Holt, *Biographies.*

was raised at that time to the King's Bench.[53] What became of Chief Justice Danby is not altogether clear. Foss and others have thought that he, not Hankford, was the justice who committed suicide by ordering his gamekeeper to shoot anyone entering the park at night.[54] Richard III reappointed all the justices of Edward IV [55] and Henry VII all those who had held office before Bosworth Field.[56]

Several explanations are possible of this continuity of judges in office despite their technically weak position. Foss suggested that since "it cannot be supposed that the judges were indifferent spectators of the stirring events of the time, nor that all preserved their opinions in silence, the non-removal of any of them on the success of the royal aspirant speaks strongly of the respect which was paid by the people to the law and the reverential estimation with which they were generally regarded." [57] Foss seems here to be drawing rather comprehensive conclusions from flimsy evidence. It is a long jump from continuity in office to general "reverential estimation," especially by the people, and one is not certain after reading the *Paston Letters, Stonor Letters,* and *Plumpton Correspondence* that the justices were not indifferent spectators. The class of society to which most of them belonged appears to have been more concerned with local controversies and matters of immediate personal interest than with rivalries in court circles. To be sure, it was often important to the Pastons in their controversy with the Duke of Norfolk over Caister Castle to know which faction was in the ascendant at court, but such considerations engaged their self-interest rather than their devotion to a cause.

A more plausible explanation of the continuity of tenure is the very practical one that there were only a few men with the necessary qualifications to become justices. Once the rule became established that candidates for the Bench must come from among the sergeants at law, the king's power of appointment and dismissal became

[53] *C. P. R., 1467–1477*, p. 258.
[54] Foss, *Judges*, vol. IV, p. 426; *D. N. B.*; J. Gairdner, review of Calendars of the Patent Rolls of Edward IV, Henry VI: 1467–1477, *E. H. R.*, vol. XVI (1901), pp. 142–143.
[55] Foss, *Judges*, vol. IV, p. 483.
[56] *Ibid.*, vol. V, p. 13.
[57] *Ibid.*, p. 1.

limited by factors not entirely within his control. To be sure, the king had the final authority in creating sergeants at law, but he could not do so at will. The ceremony of conferring the degree itself required long preparation, and there would without question have been vehement protests from the Inns of Court had the King attempted arbitrarily to elevate to the degree men who had not been through the stiff course of professional training of which the Inns had a monopoly.

The question of independence of the judges in their decisions is more complex. The chief interest and significance of the story related above of Sir Thomas Cooke and the sessions of oyer and terminer at the Guildhall in 1468 is its bearing on this subject. Edward was so certain of Cooke's guilt, or at least so determined to seize Cooke's wealth, that the outcome, had he judged the case himself, would have been a foregone conclusion. Yet Markham dared to charge the jury to acquit Cooke of all but misprision of treason. Through the machinations of Earl Rivers and his wife Markham was removed from the Chief Justiceship,[58] but Littleton did not suffer. And Markham's dismissal is the one clear instance of royal arbitrariness in this respect during a whole century of confusion and uncertainty. Fortescue, on one occasion at least, set the law above the king's will and suffered no loss of his office. Early in his career as Chief Justice he defied the King's order to release Thomas Kerver, who had been convicted of treason and committed to Wallingford Castle prison. He said that he had no power under the law to free him.[59] In the trial of Stacy, Burdett, and Blake, Edward IV perverted the law to his own uses, but the case was one of high treason and was tried before the Lords.[60] The fate of these three unhappy men has little to do with the general question of independence of common law judges.

What little direct evidence we have concerning the king's relations with the courts of common law seems to show that, in attempting to influence them where his own interest or favor was engaged, he resorted to much the same tactics as his subjects. The terms of their oath and fourteenth century statutes required the judges to

---

[58] Scofield, *Edward IV*, vol. I, pp. 461–462.
[59] Chrimes, *De Laudibus*, p. 204. Cf. *C. P. R., 1441–1446*, pp. 278, 295.
[60] Scofield, *Edward IV*, vol. II, pp. 188–189, 208.

ignore royal commands by privy seal or letters patent intended to influence the course of justice.[61] Perhaps it was this restriction which forced the king, like any other suitor, to resort to "laboring juries" and putting pressure on sheriffs. Dr. Scofield found in the Tellers Accounts a note of the payment of 26s. 8d. to John Tailour for part of his reward "for labouring the jury" which "passed with the King in Devonshire against Philip Atwell and others." [62] Shocking as this may be as an illustration of Edward's willingness to abuse the machinery of justice, it is nonetheless surprising that a jury should have had to be labored on behalf of the king. In a century in which might is supposed to have made right the king would have been expected to use his position rather than his purse to get a favorable verdict. And Henry VI, in writing to the sheriff of Norfolk directing him to find a panel of jurors to acquit Lord Moleyns from the charges leveled against him by the Pastons in 1450,[63] was stooping to employ a method used by his subjects rather than depending upon special royal prerogative. Other great men also used their influence with sheriffs and, abusive as the practice was, it did not controvert the common law principle of trial by twelve men of the country.

On the general question of integrity of fifteenth century justices, I can make no original contribution from the plea rolls or other record sources. Justice Paston was charged with taking corrupt rewards and Chief Justice Prisot with unjudicial partiality, but accusations do not prove guilt, especially when made by enemies.[64] Furthermore, the standards of the day were different and, although in the later fourteenth century serious efforts had been made to prevent the giving and taking of gifts to justices, the custom died hard and lingeringly.[65] No such judicial scandals as the exposure of Edward I's judges and of Chief Justice Thorpe in Edward III's day disturbed the dignified atmosphere of Westminster Hall in the

---

[61] See below, Ch. XV; R. P., vol. III, p. 44.

[62] Scofield, Edward IV, vol. II, p. 373. There seems no reason to assume without further proof that the 6s. 8d. "paid to John Widslade for his labour in making of a return of a verdite which passed with the king," etc., was anything more than Wydeslade's fee as clerk of assizes for making the record of the verdict which was sent to Westminster.

[63] Paston Letters, No. 155, Debenham et al. to John Paston, May 2, 1457.

[64] Paston Letters, Nos. 19, 158.

[65] 14 Ed. III, stat. 1, c. 5; 15 Ed. III, c. 3; 20 Ed. III. c, 1; 8 Ric. II, c. 3.

fifteenth century.[66] The late Professor Holdsworth believed that professional standards were higher in that century than earlier.[67] Fortescue and Littleton certainly lived out their official lives well above the level of corruption. Moreover, the Year Book reports of the century convey an atmosphere of earnest and honest although laborious and intricate reasoning about the law.

The predominant impression one gains from reading fifteenth century materials on the legal profession is that the time was one in which the standards of a relatively new professional group were being consciously built up, and that, while "the cultivation of virtues and the banishment of all vice," was not as complete as Fortescue would persuade us to believe,[68] there was nonetheless an effort to reserve the highest positions for the men of the greatest learning, wisdom, and virtue.

[66] H. E. L., vol. II, pp. 295–299, 565.
[67] Ibid., p. 566.
[68] De Laudibus, cap. 49.

CHAPTER VII

Officers of the Court

OFFICEHOLDING as service to the public is a modern conception and even now is all too often more an abstract ideal than a matter of conviction and practice with officeholders. Comparatively modern, also, is the idea that service to the government should be compensated by a salary paid out of the public treasury. In mediaeval times, and even as late as the early nineteenth century, offices in English courts of law were looked upon as freehold or property which, like freehold in land, gave to the holder certain rights and placed upon him certain responsibilities.[1] The chief of the rights was to receive fees and other perquisites of the office. The responsibility was to see that the duties attached to the office were properly performed.

These duties need not, however, be performed in person. In the fifteenth century the office of Custos Brevium of the Common Bench, for example, was held by household favorites who could not have performed all of their many duties in person. The office of Chirographer, also, was let to farm and continued to be so despite Commons protests and royal promises.[2] The justices made an effort midway in the century to restrict the appointment of deputies in other offices of the court to suitable and duly authorized persons.[3] These efforts were not permanently successful, however. The practice was continued and extended, so that by the nineteenth century, when a parliamentary commission investigated the conditions of

---

[1] *H. E. L.*, vol. I, pp. 246–247, 259–261.
[2] See below, Ch. IX.
[3] App. I (c) and cf. stat. 2 Hy. VI, c. 13.

tenure of offices in the law courts, they found more than half of those in the Court of Common Pleas to be exercised by deputy.[4] The emphasis on right rather than service involved some other consequences which are at variance with present-day ideas. For example, one could bring an assize for the recovery of an office, or for the profits of it.[5] One could ask for and receive a money compensation for its loss.[6] One could come into possession of it by inheritance or through a final concord or common recovery.[7] One could even, as in the case of the office of Custos Brevium of the Common Pleas after 29 Charles II, hold it in trust from generation to generation, to the use of another person and his heirs in tail.[8] One could also continue, as did the prothonotaries of the Court of Common Pleas, to receive fees for duties which had long since come to be performed by other officers.[9]

All offices in and about the courts were not necessarily alike in the conditions of their tenure, however. Certain ones, such as that of usher and crier of the Bench, came very early to be held under feudal conditions of inheritance and subinfeudation. This office was in the grant of the usher of the Exchequer who held by sergeanty tenure of the king himself.[10] Another such office was that of Warden of the Fleet and Keeper of Westminster Palace. This also was a sergeanty, held in chief of the king.[11] By Edward IV's time, it had come by grant in fee tail into the hands of Elizabeth Venour, widow of William.[12] A case of trespass for the rescue of certain

4 *Parlt. Papers* (1810), Misc.; (1819), vol. II, Report on Fees in the Common Pleas.

5 For examples, see *Y. B. 5 Ed. II.*, S. S. vol. XXXIII, p. 229, third part of profits of bailiwick of the marshalcy of justices in Eyre; *Y. BB. Mich., 7 Ed. III*, pl. 47; *Hil., 8 Ed. III*, pl. 47, a case involving the office of usher and crier in the Common Bench; *Hil., 5 Ed. IV*, pl. 1, the office of King of Heralds; *Mich., 6 Ed. IV*, pl. 20; *Easter, 9 Ed. IV*, pls. 2, 20; *Trin., 9 Ed. IV*, pl. 3, Bagot's case for a clerkship in the Chancery; *Mich., 8 Ed. IV*, pls. 21, 37, office of Clerk of Essoins in the Common Bench; 2 Dyer, 114b., Easter, 2 and 3 Phil. and Mary, office of filacer in the Common Bench.

6 *C. P. R., 1413–1416*, p. 333; Nicolas, *Privy Council*, vol. II, Petition to the King, June 15, 1415.

7 *Y. B. Easter, 4 Ed. IV*, pl. 7.

8 *Parlt. Papers* (1819), vol. II, Report on Fees in the Common Pleas, pp. 9–23.

9 *Ibid.*, pp. 24–48.

10 *C. C. R., 1327–1330*, p. 507; *C. C. R., 1333–1337*, p. 151; *Y.BB. Mich., 7 Ed. III*, pl. 47, *Hil., 8 Ed. III*, pl. 47.

11 *C. C. R., 1313–1318*, pp. 186–187. The office is discussed in Tout's account of the burglary of the king's treasure in 1303 ("A Mediaeval Burglary," in *Collected Papers*, vol. III, pp. 98–99 and note 2).

12 *C. P. R., 1461–1467*, p. 512, March 12, 1466.

prisoners was brought against her servants in Easter, 4 Edward IV by William Babington, who was remainder-man under the terms of the grant. In the course of the discussion of the case by the Bench Justices Ashton and Danvers agreed that the office of Warden of the Fleet lay in inheritance "by matter in the deed," and that it could therefore be alienated by fine, lie in grant, be recovered by record, or "come to a man by descent and inheritance in the manner of lands and tenements." [13]

Such inheritable tenures had developed by the fifteenth century only in these two offices of the Court of Common Pleas. Neither of them required any technical training or other special qualification for its exercise. It may be that a deliberate policy kept the other more technical offices connected with the court from coming under such grants. Certainly the discussions of fifteenth century cases involving office show gropings for a concept of office tenure different from the concept of tenure of land. On the other hand, the distinctions are not clearly made and the language used is the language of the law of real property.

For example, when the Duke of Norfolk attempted in 1460 to dismiss John Brandon from the office of Marshal of the King's Bench prison on the ground that he had allowed certain prisoners to escape, and to appoint in his place Thomas Bourchier, the justices assembled in Exchequer Chamber agreed that if an officer who holds for life or for a term of years performs his duties badly or does not perform them at all, he may forfeit the office. On the other hand, the parallel which Chief Baron Arderne cited in asserting this proposition was that of a tenant of land for life or for a term of years, who alienates the land contrary to right. Moreover, the final decision that the Duke's second patent to Thomas Bourchier was good was given on the ground that John Brandon, instead of exer-

---

[13] *Y. BB. Easter, 4 Ed. IV*, pls. 7, 12, and *Hil.*, note at the end of the year. William Babington later brought an assize to recover the office and tenements in Michaelmas, 5 Edward IV, and the case is reported at some length in the *Long Quinto* (fols. 58 ff. and 109–110). Babington claimed that Elizabeth had forfeited her right in the office by consenting to her ravishment by John Worth after the death of William, her first husband. Littleton, then a sergeant at law, led the case for Elizabeth, and both the legal arguments and the facts of the story are of considerable interest. The jury gave a verdict for the plaintiff, but, in view of the later patent to Elizabeth referred to in note 12 above, it seems likely that the matter was referred to the arbitration of a group of justices and sergeants and that Elizabeth, apparently a ward of the king, eventually recovered her right.

cising the office himself, had appointed a deputy, which he had no right to do under the terms of the Duke's patent.[14]

In another case discussed in Exchequer Chamber in Trinity, 11 Edward IV, clearer glimmerings of a distinction between office and other freehold were made, only to be obscured finally by discussion of the law relating to discontinuance by a tenant in tail. In this case Pygot and Fairfax, two of the sergeants at law, had been asked to arbitrate the rights of two men in the office of one of the Chamberlains of the Exchequer. A certain J. L. claimed under a life grant from Humphrey Bourchier, Lord Cromwell, who held the office under royal letters patent [15] to himself and the heirs male of his body. William de Hastings, on the other hand, claimed by letters patent made to him on the alleged death of Humphrey Bourchier without heirs male of his body.[16] In the early stages of the discussion in Exchequer Chamber, when the question was raised whether Lord Cromwell had the power to assign the office, it was "clearly held that in such offices which are granted by the King to a man in trust and confidence . . . the grantees cannot make assigns unless it is clearly stated in the patent 'to him and his assigns,' etc. because he could then grant the office to one in whom the King has no confidence and whom he does not wish to have occupy the office, or one who is negligent, etc. and, Sir, this office is a great office, because he guards the King's treasure, that is his records, which is good reason that none have this office except one in whom the King has confidence, etc. and such offices are not like land because the profits of land belong all to the grantee and not to the King, but in this office, the exercise of it is to the profit of the king. . . ." [17] This was a promising opening for the development of a concept of office which might have escaped the bonds of the feudal land law, but the discussion was not followed up.

In relation to a second group of offices, that is, those which were granted by the king not in fee tail or other inheritable tenure but

---

[14] Y. B. Mich., 39 Hy. VI, pl. 45. Cf. citation of this case in Easter, 5 Ed. IV (Long Quinto, fol. 28) in which it was asserted that Brandon lost his office because he allowed prisoners to escape.

[15] Q. v. in C. P. R., 1461–1467, p. 460, July 17, 1465.

[16] C. P. R., 1467–1477, pp. 310–311. Humphrey was apparently killed at the battle of Barnet (D. N. B. under title "Henry Bourchier, 1st earl of Essex").

[17] Y. B. Trin., 11 Ed. IV, pl. 1.

only for life, the idea that competence for the office was essential to the validity of the letters patent was twice advanced by the justices in Edward IV's reign. They rejected two royal patents on the ground of unfitness. In 18 Edward IV, the justices of the Common Pleas refused to enroll a joint grant for life of the office of Custos Brevium of the Common Pleas to Sir John Fogge and his son on the ground that two men could not competently fulfill the duties of the office.[18] In the more famous case of Thomas Vynter (or Wynter) the point was more clearly made. The justices of the King's Bench rejected a joint grant for life to Thomas Croxton and Thomas Vynter to the office of Coroner and Attorney of the King in that court on the ground that Vynter was untrained for the office. According to Chief Justice Billing twenty to thirty years of training was little enough to fit a man for it.[19]

In the sixteenth century the idea that competence was essential to the maintenance of right in an office was discussed again in relation to appointments by the Chief Justice but not in relation to royal grants.[20] There the issue was between royal and judicial patronage. The Crown on several occasions between 1550 and 1650 attempted to invade with royal grants the third and largest group of offices in the court, that is, those in the grant of the Chief Justice. Into this classification in the fifteenth century fell most of the offices of the court, and their sale had probably already become an important source of income to the Chief Justice.[21]

According to mediaeval concepts the right to sell followed logically from the right to appoint. Shocking as this may seem by modern standards, the practice was so re-enforced by usage and vested interest that reform did not come until the nineteenth century. I have found no direct mention of the sale of Common Pleas offices in the fifteenth century. On the other hand, statutes both before and after the fifteenth century attempted to check the practice. In 1388 the Merciless Parliament enacted a rather general and probably ineffectual provision that the king's officers, including the

[18] *Y. B. Trin., 18 Ed. IV*, pl. 6. See below, Ch. VIII, for further discussion of this grant.
[19] *Y. B. Easter, 9 Ed. IV*, pl. 20. Cf. 2 Dyer, 150b., Mich., 4 and 5 Phil. and Mary. For the patent which was rejected, see *C. P. R., 1461–1467*, p. 457.
[20] *Vaux v. Jefferen*, 2 Dyer, 114b., Easter, 2 and 3 Phil. and Mary; Memorandum, 2 Dyer, 150b., Mich., 4 and 5 Phil. and Mary.
[21] *H. E. L.*, vol. I, p. 255.

two Chief Justices, who had the grant of other offices should not appoint to them "for any Gift or Brocage, Favour, or Affection . . . but that they should make all such Officers and Ministers of the best and most lawful Men and sufficient to their Estimation and Knowledge." [22] This was followed in 1423 by an even weaker provision that they should be held answerable for the sufficiency of their appointees.[23] In 1552, over a century later, a more specific statute was passed "for avoiding corruption in offices in those Courtes, Places, or Romes wherein there is requisite to be had the true admynistracion of Justice or service of Truste," but all the offices in the grant of the Chief Justices of both Benches and of the justices of assize were exempted from the effects of the act.[24] This suggests that their "brocage" was well-entrenched in usage. A curious list of the "Names of the officers in the Common Pleas and the number of the rolls each officer occupies and the value of these" [25] compiled by Thomas Jakes, Clerk of the Treasury and of the Warrants and Estreats in the time of Chief Justice Frowyk, is most plausibly identifiable as a list of the patronage values of these offices.[26]

The bout already alluded to between the Crown and the Chief Justices for this patronage in Common Pleas offices began in Michaelmas of the first year of Queen Elizabeth. Chief Justice Browne was forced to defend against the Queen his right to appoint one of the exigenters of the court.[27] Later in the reign, in the more famous case of Richard Cavendish, the justices resisted the creation by letters patent of a new office of Clerk of the *Supersedeas* on the ground that such a grant would disseise of their "free tenement during their life-time" the prothonotaries and exigenters of the court. But there was more at stake than the fees of the prothonotaries and exigenters. Acceptance of the grant would have been a dangerous precedent for further invasion by the Crown of the Chief Justice's patronage of office. Elizabeth tactfully dropped the matter when she discovered the strength of the justices' opposition.[28] James

22 12 Ric. II, c. 2.
23 2 Hy. VI, c. 13.
24 5 and 6 Ed. VI, c. 16.
25 App. II (a).
26 The values listed appear to be far less than the annual values of the fees from these offices. See below, Chs. VIII, IX, and X.
27 *Skrogges v. Coleshill,* Dyer, 175a., Mich., 1 and 2 Eliz.
28 1 Anderson, 152.

I renewed the attack in the interests of John Murray, Groom of the Bedchamber and court favorite. Despite the able arguments based on a prerogative writ *de non procedendo* presented by Sir Francis Bacon, the king was forced to a compromise. He did succeed in getting recognized the appointment of John Michell, Murray's client, but only on a promise not to admit thereafter any petition for office which would tend to grant away, abate, or diminish "any of the profits, or preeminences of the Judges." [29] Charles I was not bound by his father's promise, however, and the filacers of the court resorted to a petition in the House of Lords against his efforts to raise money through selling patents granting office in the patronage of the Chief Justice.[30]

This attack of the Crown on judicial patronage seems not to have been planned or premeditated. Mary Tudor's appointment of Coleshill as exigenter of the court was made during the vacancy of the Chief Justiceship. Elizabeth's patent to Cavendish was granted at his own suggestion and without full knowledge of the facts. James's appointment of Michell was in response to the suit of Murray and was probably granted without knowledge of Cavendish's case and without preconsidered intent to assert the prerogative. Charles's actions were doubtless dictated by financial necessity. On the other hand, as Holdsworth pointed out, neither were the justices resisting on principle.[31] The war was one between vested interests and, from the vantage point of the twentieth century, it seems that it might have been better if the Crown had won. So might the disgraceful condition of office tenure in the law courts have come sooner to the attention of Parliament.

If the form of appointments to offices in the Court of Common Pleas was neither simple nor uniform, neither was the method of payment. Fees paid by the parties to suits constituted the chief source of income for all, high and low. Almost every transaction in the court or its offices involved the payment of a fee to one or more officers, and the number and size of the payments seem gradually to have increased in the course of centuries in spite of all attempts

[29] Bacon's *Works* (ed. Spedding; London, 1859), vol. VII, pp. 683–686.
[30] Petyt MS, No. 538, vol. 17, fol. 261. This reference was given me by Miss Marjorie Blatcher.
[31] *H. E. L.*, vol. I, pp. 260–262.

to check the tendency.[32] In addition to their fees, some officers received a salary or "regard" from the king. This kind of grant was not confined to the Custos Brevium and the Chirographer, who held their offices by letters patent, but applied also to the Clerk of the Warrants and Estreats, who was appointed by the Chief Justice. Some officers increased their income by acting as deputy sheriffs and thereby getting for themselves fees for the return of writs.[33] In the fourteenth century, many had received regular pensions, gifts, and liveries from corporate religious houses and towns or cities.[34] This practice did not have the odor of corruption which it would have today. Despite statutes against livery and maintenance, public morality in these matters was not very highly developed.[35]

Damages clere (or *cleer*), or *damna clericorum*, were, for some clerks, another source of income. According to seventeenth century authorities, these were a tenth part of all damages recovered by the plaintiff in excess of five marks.[36] In their proposals for the reform of faults of the law in 1650, the attorneys asked for their abolition and explained that they were "originally, as is conceived, exacted by the Clergy as a personal Tythe, the Clergymen being the Clerkes that Writ to all or the most of the Courts at Westminster."[37] This explanation fits the facts except that the amounts taken by the clerks in the fifteenth century seem to have sometimes exceeded and sometimes been less than one tenth.[38] They were taken only by the

---

32 For inquiries into fees into the offices of the law courts before the nineteenth century, see *H. E. L.*, vol. I, pp. 262–264, and *Parlt. Papers* (1819), vol. II, Report on Fees in the Common Pleas, pp. 2–3.

33 Stat. 23 Hy. VI, c. 9; *Rules, Orders, and Notices*, Mich., 15 Eliz.

34 P. de Thame, *The Knights Hospitallers in England* (ed. Larking; Camden Society, London, 1857), pp. xlii–xliii, 58, 100–101, 193, 203; *R. P.* vol. III, p. 588; below, App. II (b).

35 See T. F. Tout, "The English Civil Service in the Fourteenth Century" in *Collected Papers*, vol. III, pp. 191–221.

36 G. T. of Staple Inne and T. P. of Barnard's Inne, *The Attourney of the Court of Common Pleas* (London, 1648); G. Jacob, *A New Law Dictionary* (London, 1772), under title, "Damage-cleer."

37 *Proposals*, 1650.

38 Assize Roll, 158, Derbyshire, 34 Ed. I, case of trespass, breaking into chapel and taking ornaments. An entry below is as follows: "Dampna 1 m' unde C. di M'." In another trespass case entered on the plea roll of Easter, 31 Hy. VI (C. P. 40/769, mm. 372 ff.) appears the following subscription: "Dampna Mille libras vnde Henrico Fylongley et Iohannem Wydeslade clericis xx marca." Fylongley and Wydeslade were respectively Custos Brevium and Chief Prothonotary at this time. Cf. W. C. Bolland ed., *Eyre of Kent*, vol. III, 6 and 7 Ed. II, S. S. vol. xxix (London, 1913), pp. xliii–xlix.

Custos Brevium, the prothonotaries, and the clerks of the assizes, who filled in the sittings in the county the same relative positions as the Custos Brevium and the prothonotaries in the central court. The petition of 1650 was answered belatedly in the reign of Charles II by a statute which forbade them henceforth to be taken.[39]

The mediaeval concept of office as freehold giving to the holder title to certain fees and other perquisites is responsible for a good deal of complexity in the history of offices of the court from their earliest origins to the nineteenth century. New offices were created or evolved out of old ones without plan or express intention of any responsible authority. Neither legislative supervision nor budgetary limit restrained the proliferation of offices. The only effective check was what the traffic would bear, and this proved an unreliable one. The ultimate outcome was the veritable jungle of salable sinecures inhabited by a "banderlog" of clerks or deputies of clerks all clamoring for their fees, which the parliamentary commissioners discovered when they began their work in the early nineteenth century.[40]

Some new offices were created by act of the king, motivated by good sense, cupidity, or the desire to reward service. The office of Chirographer seems to have originated in the early fourteenth century from the need for one responsible clerk to make out the chirograph in final concords and to keep a record of it.[41] The office of Clerk of the Hanaper of the Common Bench seems to have come into being as the result of various financial expedients of Edward III.[42] The attempts of Elizabeth and James to create the new office of Clerk of the Supersedeas on behalf of favorites seem to have resulted ultimately in the creation of such an office within the patronage of the Chief Justice.[43]

New offices more commonly came into being by a slower evolu-

---

[39] 17 Car. II, c. 6.
[40] *Parlt. Papers* (1810), Misc.; (1819), vol. II.
[41] See below, Ch. VIII.
[42] For a description of these and of the origin of the office of Keeper of the Seal of the Common Bench, see Tout, *Chapters*, vol. III, pp. 154–155; H. W. C. Maxwell-Lyte, *Historical Notes on the Use of the Great Seal of England* (London, 1926), pp. 329 ff.; Wilkinson, "Seals of the Two Benches," pp. 397–401, and *Chancery*, pp. 60–63.
[43] In the list of clerks of the court which appears in the *Attorney of the Common Pleas*, published in 1648, is a Clerk of the Supersedeas. According to the parliamentary commission reports, he was appointed by the Chief Justice.

tionary process. As the work of a particular clerk increased or because he found it inconvenient or impossible to perform some or all of the duties himself, he appointed a farmer, deputy, or assistant to whom he paid a salary, or wage, or an allowance from the fees. But, because the accepted custom was that all those who worked in the courts should be compensated by fees and also, no doubt, through tipping by attorneys or parties in order to expedite their suits, the deputy or assistant soon established a right to take a fee for himself as well as for his master.[44] In time he came to be recognized as a separate officer. As the result of such a process, no less than twelve new offices had by 1770 grown out of the three offices of the prothonotaries of the Court of Common Pleas which existed at the end of the fifteenth century.[45] The office of Clerk of the Treasury similarly generated two new offices whose functions were so interconnected that one deputy acted for all three with respect to part of their duties, while one of the principals acted as deputy for one of the other principals with respect to another part of the duties.[46]

On the other hand, the story is not entirely one of burgeoning of new offices. In the Court of Common Pleas a reverse tendency operated also. In the fifteenth century there were sixteen or seventeen filacers. By the nineteenth there were no more than eight. Furthermore, the "clerks of the prothonotaries and filacers," referred to in the Black Book list of fees,[47] of earlier times, have disappeared or acquired specialized functions. The reduction in the number of filacers was probably due to the decline in the amount of work available for them consequent upon the increased popularity of the bill of Middlesex and other pressures which transferred business to the King's Bench.[48] As business declined, filacers, in competition with one another, built up amalgamations of older offices. And as often in such free competition, the greatest rewards went to the strong. In 1819, the eight offices of filacer of the Common Bench varied in average annual value from £30 in the office of Derby, Leics, Notts, and Warwick to £1,299 5s. 0d.

[44] In the case of the Chirographer's deputy, this development was resisted, perhaps because the sum involved, i.e., 4s., was a considerable sum. See below, Ch. IX, p. 139.
[45] Parlt. Papers (1819), vol. II, pp. 60–61.
[46] Ibid., pp. 87–94.
[47] App. I (j).
[48] See above, Ch. II.

in the office of London, Middlesex, Beds, Berks, Bucks, Oxon, Cornwall, Gloucester, Hereford, and Worcester.[49]

There were in all over thirty clerks who had work in and about the Court of Common Pleas in the fifteenth century. No complete contemporary list has been found in the course of this study. The list made by Thomas Jakes,[50] Clerk of the Treasury and also of the Warrants and Estreats under Chief Justice Frowyk in the early years of the sixteenth century, omits the Clerk of the Essoins, the Clerk of the Outlawries, the exigenters, and the Clerk of the King's Silver, all of whom have left some traces of their existence in records or memoranda of the court or other branches of the government. Smith's list, in the *Republic* (written at Toulouse in 1565),[51] is likewise incomplete, for it omits the Clerk of the Treasury and the Clerk of the Outlawries. A list compiled from the evidence of fifteenth century records is given in the following table.

Officers of the Court of Common Pleas
in the Reign of Edward IV

Officer	*Source of appointment*	*Source of income*	*Conditions of tenure*
Custos Brevium	King by letters patent	Salary from Exchequer, 10 marks; fees	For life during good behavior; exercised by deputy
First and Third Prothonotaries	Chief Justice	Fees	For life during good behavior; exercised in person
Second Prothonotary	Chief Justice on nomination of the Custos Brevium	Fees	Exercised in person
Keeper or Clerk of the Treasury	Chief Justice	Fees. (Salary from Chief Justice?)	At pleasure of Chief Justice; exercised in person and com-

49 *H. E. L.*, vol. I, App. XXX, p. 688.
50 App. II (a).
51 T. Smith, *De Republica Anglorum* (ed. Alston; Cambridge, 1906), App. A, c. 15, p. 159. Maitland, *English Law and the Renaissance*, is my authority for the date and place of writing.

Officers of the Court of Common Pleas (*continued*)

Officer	Source of appointment	Source of income	Conditions of tenure
			bined with the office of Clerk of the Warrants and Estreats
Filacers	Chief Justice	Fees	For life during good behavior; exercised in person
Exigenters	Chief Justice	Fees	Same as filacers'
Clerk of the Essoins	Chief Justice	Fees. (Salary from Chief Justice?)	Same as filacers'
Clerk of the Juries	Chief Justice	Fees	Same as filacers'
Chirographer	King by letters patent	Fees	For life during good behavior; exercised by "servant" but theoretically not by deputy
Clerk of the King's Silver	Chief Justice	Fees	Same as filacers'
Clerk of the Outlawries	King's attorney	Fees	Same as filacers'
Clerk of the Warrants and Estreats	Chief Justice	Fees and salary of £10 a year from the king	Same as filacers'
Keeper of the Hanaper of the Common Pleas	King by letters patent	Salary of £4 annually	(?)

Added to this list should be an indeterminate number of attorneys, for not only clerks but also attorneys were officers of the court in the fifteenth century. Many discussions of the court's jurisdiction emphasize this fact.[52] Before this time, when attorneyship had only been on its way toward becoming professionalized, this had not been true. In the early fourteenth century, attorneys sued and were sued by original writ rather than by bill of privilege.[53] Furthermore, it seems that even in the fifteenth century, when they became officers of the Court of Common Pleas, they did not become at the same time officers of the upper bench.[54] The privileges and responsibilities of officers of the Common Pleas seem to have been thrust upon them by perseverant effort of the Commons in the early years of the century. In the Parliament of 1402, the Commons petitioned that, because "falsifications, deceits, and disinheritances" occurred as a result of the great number of attorneys, some of them "little or entirely unlearned in the law and some of tender age," the justices should assign no more than four, five, or six attorneys to each county. They were to examine attorneys for fitness and to require an oath of those to be enrolled on the lists of the court.[55] If the statute enacted in this Parliament did not exactly fulfill the Commons' demands in all particulars, it did at least insure the official status of attorneys. They were to be examined and sworn in numbers at the discretion of the justices and were to be banned from the court if they acted in suits in "foreign" counties, or if they committed any of the offenses complained of in the petition.[56]

The Commons returned to the attack in the Parliament of 1410. They again petitioned for a specific limitation of the number, but this time not so stringently. Six to twelve were to be allowed for each county. On the other hand, the penalties they asked for were much more severe. Not only were attorneys to be banned from the court, but also they were to be imprisoned for a year, and they were to make fine and ransom to the king.[57] The clerks and attor-

---

[52] See especially *Y. BB. Mich., 22 Hy. VI,* pl. 43; *Mich., 3 Ed. IV,* pl. 21, and *Trin., 11 Ed. IV,* pl. 4.

[53] See *Y. BB. Trin., 12 Ed. III* (R. S.), pp. 586–587 and *Mich., 17 Ed. III* (R. S.), pp. 138–141, for cases in which attorneys sued or were sued by writ rather than bill of privilege.

[54] *Y. B. Hil., 1 Hy. VII,* pl. 17.

[55] *R. P.,* vol. III, p. 504, 1402, 4 Hy. IV. A much earlier petition (*R. P.,* vol. I, p. 84, 1292) asked that the number of attorneys and apprentices for each county be limited but did not ask that they be sworn as officers of the court.

[56] 4 Hy. IV, c. 18.

[57] *R. P.,* vol. III, pp. 642–643, 1410, 11 Hy. IV. See stat. 33 Hy. VI, c. 7, for a later effort to limit the number of attorneys for Norfolk, Suffolk, and Norwich.

neys themselves countered this petition with one of their own in the parliament of 1413, and the whole matter was finally referred to the discretion of the justices.[58] This outcome clearly placed the attorneys among the officers of the court whose doings were subject to rules and orders issued by the justices.

As a consequence of their new professional status, there must have followed a changed relationship to clients. So long as attorneys were, or might be, untrained representatives appointed by statutory or other permission, warrants of attorneyship were important. So soon as they became officers of the court, warrants were far less important. By 1650 the attorneys themselves entered their own warrants and were in a position to complain that this was a useless inconvenience to themselves and an unnecessary expense to the parties.[59] Already in Edward IV's reign they entered their own warrants except in special cases,[60] and the strictness of the rules regulating the time when such warrants must be entered was also beginning to break down.[61]

Despite the increasing complexities of the law and the professionalization of attorneyship, parties nonetheless continued to appear in person. At least the rolls show frequent entries that the plaintiff or defendant came "in propria persona," and there is no good reason to doubt the literal truth of the words.[62] In many instances, appearance in person was required, as, for example, by the defendant when he had been arrested.[63] Moreover, a party might, at will, appear in person on one day and by attorney on the next.[64]

The association between clerks and attorneys was close and stronger than the relationship of either group with apprentices and sergeants at law. In subsidy assessments of Richard II attorneys were classed with "apprentices of least estate" and expected to pay only 6s. 8d., as against the 40s. required of sergeants at law and "great apprentices." Neither clerks nor attorneys were admitted to the bar

58 *R. P.*, vol. III, p. 666, 1413, 13 Hy. IV.
59 *Proposals*, 1650.
60 *Y. BB. Easter, 4 Ed. IV*, pl. 21; *Easter, 7 Ed. IV*, pl. 20.
61 *Y. B. Easter, 4 Ed. IV*, pl. 21.
62 See C. P. 40/880, m. 371, Easter, 22 Ed. IV, for a case in which John Alderley, attorney, appeared in his own person while his wife appeared by him as her attorney.
63 *F. N. B.*, 26D; stat. 7 Hy. IV, c. 13; *Y. B. Easter, 7 Ed. IV*, pl. 20, in which a plaintiff was required to enter a warrant in person on a writ of right.
64 *Rither v. Sayer*, C. P. 40/751, m. 501; C. P. 40/753, m. 355.

in later mediaeval times although they were admitted to both Inns of Court and of Chancery.[65] Both clerks and attorneys were admitted to their office by the court itself, while sergeants, justices, and "great apprentices" received their rank by royal grant or by decision of the Benchers of the Inns. Both groups appear to have got their training primarily by apprenticeship rather than by attending moots and readings in the Inns of Court.[66]

The most cogent proof of the intimacy of their association, however, is the fact that clerks frequently acted as attorneys and attorneys as clerks. The Commons protested against this practice as early as 16 Richard II and the protest was repeated in each of the petitions relating to numbers and qualifications of attorneys which have been discussed above. The king, no doubt on the advice of his justices, remained unmoved. In the reign of Edward IV, many of the names recognized as those of prothonotaries and filacers of the court appear also in the roll of warrants of attorneys. Furthermore, the clerks frequently entered cases in which, as attorneys, they were taking out writs of process. Special attorneys, such as the queen's attorney and the king's attorney for the duchy of Lancaster, seem customarily to have been appointed from among the leading clerks of the court.[67]

The Commons complained in 1402 not only that clerks acted as attorneys, but also that attorneys made out writs of *capias* and *supersedeas*. A court ordinance of Trinity, 35 Henry VI forbade

[65] See *Black Books*, vol. I, pp. 149, 151, 163, 165, 167, 198, 216, 234, 441, for admission of Edward Stubbe, Robert Kypping, William Tassell, Master Roper, and Master See, filacers, and Edward Stubbys, Nicholas Rookwood, "Mr. Leonard," and Zachary Scott, prothonotaries; *Middle Temple Records*, vol. I, pp. 6, 12, 38, 54, for evidence of membership of William Mordaunt, prothonotary, and Thomas Jubbes and John Jenour, filacers. The best evidence that attorneys earlier were members of the four great Inns is the effort to exclude them in the latter part of the sixteenth century. They were still to be allowed admission to the Inns of Chancery. See *Black Books*, vol. I, pp. 315, 320, 391; *Middle Temple Records*, vol. I, pp. 13, 66, 87, 88, 121. By the seventeenth century this effort seems to have been given up. They were then required to be members of either Inns of Court or of Chancery. See *Rules and Orders for the Common Pleas*, 1654.

[66] The study of the forms of writs in the Inns of Chancery would obviously be useful to them and it is quite likely that they took a fairly full part in the study at these inns before their admission as attorneys of the court.

[67] Elryngton, the queen's attorney in 22 Ed. IV, was filacer of Middlesex and London (C. P. 40/882, mm. 54–57). William Cumberford, second prothonotary in 32 Hy. VI, was, with William Armeston, attorney of the king for the duchy of Lancaster (C. P. 40/771, m. 566).

this practice,[68] but both the Commons and the court were attempting to check the inevitable. The court was busy. Attorneys encountered delays in getting their writs and enrollments made. They knew the proper forms of writs and enrollments, having studied them at the Inns of Chancery and often, no doubt, been apprenticed as clerks to officers of the court. What could be more natural than that they should increasingly undertake to write their own writs and entries? By the seventeenth century, they customarily made out all their own writs and engrossed their entries on the plea rolls as well.[69]

A final word is necessary concerning the estate of persons who held office in the Court of Common Pleas in the fifteenth century. Further research into the lives and family histories of the clerks should make possible many interesting generalizations. Some few facts emerge even from this general study of the administration of the court. For one thing, the days of the clerical officer in the court were over. Among the names of the clerks of the Court of Common Pleas in the fourteenth century may be found many which are recognizable in the patent rolls as those of holders of benefices. This was particularly true of the clerks who compiled the Rex roll as long as it lasted.[70] Both the *Custos Brevium* and the Chirographer appear often to have been clerics and sometimes persons with really substantial training in the canon law.[71] By the fifteenth century, as will become clear in succeeding chapters, all this had changed. The royal patentees were then drawn from the secular members of the king's court and the appointees of the Chief Justice from the swarming ranks of students in the Inns.

[68] App. I (c).
[69] *C. P. Att.* (1648), p. 33; G. T. of Staple Inne and T. P. of Barnard's Inne, *The Practick Part of the Law Shewing the Office of a Compleat Attorney* (London, 1652), p. 26.
[70] See below, Ch. VIII.
[71] See for example Master John de Shordich, who was sent on several diplomatic missions abroad (*C. P. R., 1321–1324*, p. 426; *C.P.R., 1327–1330*, p. 440; *C. P. R., 1330–1334*, p. 91). Shordich is referred to as "Advocate of the Court of Arches" (see *R. P.*, vol. II, p. 41a) and "professor of both laws" (*C. P. R., 1321–1324*, p. 426).

CHAPTER VIII

The Prothonotaries

AT THE TOP of the hierarchy of officers who carried on the adminis-trative work of the court in the later fifteenth century were three prothonotaries. They were the chief clerks in charge of enter-ing the records of cases in the plea roll and of making out judicial writs of process. Seventeenth century books make a clear distinction between their work and that of the filacers.[1] According to later editions of Cowell's *Law Dictionary* this distinction was recent, no earlier than 14 James I, when, by agreement between the pro-thonotaries and filacers, the former only were to enter pleadings and all stages after the defendant had appeared in court to answer, while the latter were to enter all mesne process, that is, process to induce the defendant to appear.[2] In the fifteenth century there existed no such clear division of labor (or fees). Prothonotaries, although primarily responsible for pleadings and later develop-ments of a case, sometimes entered earlier stages. And filacers, although commonly confined to entries of mesne process, were allowed to enter not only pleadings in the common form but also verdicts, judgments, and final process.[3]

[1] *C. P. Att.* (1648), pp. 7, 47–49; *Compleat Att.* (1652), p. 1; G. Gilbert, *History and Practice of the Court of Common Pleas* (London, 1761), p. 46; G. Jacob, *The Com-pleat Attorney's Practice in English in the Court of King's Bench and Common Pleas at Westminster* (London, 1674), vol. II, p. 307.

[2] J. Cowell, *A Law Dictionary* (London, 1727). Cf. Jacob, *Law Dictionary*, and R. Boote, *Historical Treatise of an Action or Suit at Law and of Proceedings Used in the King's Bench and Common Pleas* (London, 1823), p. 129. For the order of 14 Jac. I, see *Rules, Orders, and Notices of the Several Courts of King's Bench, Common Pleas, Chancery, and Exchequer* (London, 1724).

[3] For examples, see C. P. 40/882, m. 250, *Richardson v. Durem*, verdict and writ of error into King's Bench entered by Elryngton filacer; 287d., *Dekyn v. Roche*, verdict entered by Danby, filacer for Yorks; 511d., *Kirkeby v. Alton*, verdict, judgment, exe-cution, and writ of error into King's Bench entered by Ferrers, filacer for Herts.

113

A principle of division obtained, however, and in the King's Bench was so well defined that counsel could argue that entry of a special judgment on a filacer's roll was ground for reversal.[4] The basis of division in the Common Pleas was probably not the stage which the action had reached so much as the more practical one of where the transaction represented by the entry took place. Special pleadings were at this time still pleaded orally before the justices at Westminster. They would, therefore, be entered on the rolls of the prothonotaries, the only clerks besides the Custos Brevium and the Clerk of the Estreats who were permitted to come into the "place" at Westminster.[5] Pleas in the common form, on the other hand, need not be pleaded in court. They could be entered directly on the rolls in the court offices as well by filacers as by prothonotaries or their clerks. Need for definition of the boundaries between the duties of the prothonotaries came with the introduction of pleading—even of special pleas—by exchange of papers through the court offices. It is obvious that this system offered an opportunity for an ambitious and sufficiently learned filacer to compete with the prothonotaries for business. So, in Michaelmas, 15 and 16 Elizabeth, we find the court ordaining that henceforth filacers shall enter only pleadings in the common form.[6] Perhaps this order did not satisfy the prothonotaries. Whatever the cause, they seem to have won a further concession in 14 James when the filacers were excluded altogether from the entry of stages after the first appearance of the defendant.

Prothonotaries were persons of considerable dignity and importance in the court. They were frequently called upon by the justices for expert knowledge or opinion concerning technical matters. They were acknowledged authorities on the forms of writs and entries.[7] And, through their special familiarity with records and their knowledge of the forms to be followed in compiling them, they had acquired a higher kind of authority. They were sometimes consulted concerning the technicalities of pleading, the special field of expertness of the sergeant at law. For example, in a case of an-

[4] *Y. B. Easter, 9 Ed. IV*, pl. 12.
[5] Cf. above, Ch. III, p. 37.
[6] *Rules, Orders, and Notices.*
[7] *Y. BB. Mich., 2 Hy. IV*, pl. 44; *Mich., 33 Hy. VI*, pl. 43; *Mich., 39 Hy. VI*, pl. 22; *Long Quinto*, fol. 23.

114

nuity brought by the Prior of Shene against the Prior of St. John of Jerusalem, when Collow, counsel for the defense, called in question the declaration because it did not show matter of record for the title, "Copley, le chief Prothonotary" said that all entries in such cases (where property had been seized in war) were like the one under discussion, and that no matter of record need be mentioned. The court, therefore, held the count good, and Collow went on to plead other matter.[8]

Prothonotaries were often consulted concerning details of procedure. For instance, in a discussion of the proper steps in reviving a case after demise of the king, Brayne, "one of the prothonotaries," showed a precedent for the use of a writ of *certiorari*.[9] Many more illustrations from the Year Books could be adduced. To those familiar with these old reports or with early nineteenth century court procedure such emphasis is not necessary. By the time of the parliamentary investigations of 1810 and 1819 the giving of technical advice and the taxing of costs (a task divided in the fifteenth century between the jury and the judge) had come to be the chief remaining active functions of the prothonotaries.[10]

All the work of entering records and making out writs had by this time long since come to be performed by the attorneys. The prothonotaries, to be sure, continued to take the ancient fees. Moreover, the fees had both multiplied and increased since the fifteenth century. In 1802, a rebellious attorney objected to paying the prothonotary for an entry which he himself had made. The court cowed him with a decision that the fee claimed "was an ancient as well as a just fee."[11] The justification for this patently inequitable decision was doubtless that the prothonotaries performed essential functions as advisers to the court, and since there was no other source of income for them save the fees for duties anciently performed, these must be continued despite their irrationality. The parliamentary commissions which investigated the offices soon after this incident recognized the incongruity of the situation and pro-

8 *Y. B. Hil., 22 Ed. IV*, pl. 6. The annuity was an appurtenance of a French priory taken in the French wars of Edward III.
9 *Y. B. Mich., 49 Hy. VI*, pl. 1 (S. S. vol. XLVII, p. 114).
10 *Parlt. Papers* (1810), Report on Saleable Offices in the Common Pleas; (1819), Report on Fees in the Common Pleas, p. 25.
11 *Parlt. Papers* (1819), Report on Fees.

posed that the prothonotaries should henceforth be paid for their advice and for taxing bills of cost rather than for entries of pleas and other disused tasks.[12]

In the fifteenth century the problem was still far off. Wydeslade, Brown, Cumberford, Copley, Brent, Conyngesby and the others who held office then were busy clerks as well as expert lawyers. Although they must have spent much time in the study of forms and precedents, they had also to attend court daily and to supervise the work of a flock of underclerks. Whatever income they took in fees was probably still well earned.[13]

In their official capacity the prothonotaries are a little more than shadows, but they do not emerge either from the records or from the Year Books as full-blooded human beings. William Copley's exclamation, "Thynk and thank God," [14] reiterated in the Edward V plea rolls, suggests several disparate portraits of the man. Was he, for example, an old sobersides, was he an imaginative but timid soul, or was he just a good and charming man? Records of litigation concerning property suggest that several of the prothonotaries were men of wealth and dignity.[15] Local records may perhaps yield some facts concerning their private lives. Further details may also be gleaned from the plea rolls. Such human detail, however interesting, is not essential to the understanding of the workings of the court and has therefore been ignored in making this study.

On the other hand, the title "prothonotary" does require some further discussion. Both this designation and that of "Chief Clerk" seem to have been shared with the Custos Brevium or Keeper of the King's Writs and Rolls. Neither is exact or specific. Moreover, "prothonotary" is a hybrid Greek and Latin word and seemingly out of place in an English common law setting. Cowell, writing in the early seventeenth century, was sufficiently troubled by the exotic character of the word to explain that the office derived from

[12] *Ibid.*
[13] With the help of the fifteenth century table of fees, it would be possible by tabulation of the numbers and types of entries made in the four terms of an average year to estimate their annual income. The task would be lengthy and full of statistical and other pitfalls. I have not had the courage to attempt it.
[14] App. III.
[15] Miss Marion Dale has collected a number of cases in which their property interests are involved.

the later Romans.[16] He did not attempt to trace the derivation. "Notarius" was, of course, a familiar word in mediaeval Latin, but it applied normally only to persons appointed by papal letters.[17] "Protho" (derived from the Greek prōtos), on the other hand, is certainly out of place in thirteenth century England where it first appears. There were "prothonotaries" at the papal court, however, and it seems probable that the term came into the English law courts from this source at a time when the writing in the courts was done by clerics.[18]

The word means nothing more obscure than principal or chief clerk, but the latter designation was more often reserved for the Custos Brevium whose full title was "Chief Clerk and Keeper of the King's Writs and Rolls of the Bench." An entry in the Year Book of Trinity, 18 Edward IV illustrates the casualness with which the two titles were applied. It recites that the justices rejected letters patent granting to Sir John Fogge and his son, for the term of their two lives, the office of "Chief Prothonotary" of the Common Bench.[19] This note presents insurmountable difficulties unless an interchangeability of the titles "Chief Clerk" and "Prothonotary" is assumed. For one thing, the grant does not appear either on the patent rolls or among the canceled letters patent. In the second place, prothonotaries were appointed by the Chief Justice, not by the king. In the third place, the grounds on which the patent was rejected relate to the duties, not of the prothonotaries, but of the Custos Brevium. The plausible explanation seems to be, therefore, that the patent referred to is the one which was issued in 12 Edward IV to Sir John and his son, granting to them in survivorship the office of "Keeper of our Writs and Rolls in the Common Bench." [20] Sir John secure in the receipt of the fees of the office under an older grant of the office to him alone dating from the first

---

[16] J. Cowell, *The Interpreter or Booke Containing the Signification of Words* (Cambridge, 1607).

[17] Mr. Hilary Jenkinson brought this fact to my attention.

[18] Mr. Jenkinson has also suggested that the term may have been introduced by the Norman kings, since there was a prothonotary at the Norman court in Sicily.

[19] *Y. B. Trin., 18 Ed. IV*, pl. 6.

[20] C 66/529, 12 Ed. IV, pt. I, m. 10, July 11. Cf. C 202, H 63/35, the canceled letters patent of 1 Ed. IV granting the office to Sir John alone. According to a marginal note on the patent roll, the grant to the two Fogges was not canceled until 1 Ric. III.

year of Edward IV, may have neglected to present the later patent until four years after it was given to him. Alternatively, the report may have strayed from its proper chronological place in the Year Books. In any case, the reporter has used the somewhat redundant phrase "Chief Prothonotary" to refer not to the clerks who later acquired exclusive rights to that title but to the chief keeper of the records.[21]

A more puzzling connection between the two highest offices in the court lies in the method of appointment of the second prothonotary. The first and third prothonotaries were appointed directly by the Chief Justice without restriction on his choice of candidate. The second prothonotary, on the other hand, was appointed only on nomination of the Custos Brevium. This method of appointment is substantiated by fifteenth century records as well as by the later books. In the plea roll for Trinity, 1472, appears a memorandum that on the eleventh of June William Cumberford, the second prothonotary, died. Then Sir John Fogge, "to whom by reason of his office belonged the presentation to the office of one of the prothonotaries of this court," came into the court in person and presented Roger Brent. Chief Justice Bryan, having regard to Brent's diligence and regularity of attendance in the court (presumably as an underclerk or deputy of some sort, for his name does not appear in the plea rolls before this date), admitted him to the office. Cumberford, the record goes on to say, had succeeded Thomas Brown, who, in his turn, was successor to William Wakefield.[22] Another fifteenth century demonstration of this special tie with the second prothonotary is the license issued in 1449 to Thomas Brown authorizing him to hold his office by deputy for the remainder of his life "provided that this grant be not to the prejudice of the keeper of the writs of the Bench in conferring the office when void." [23]

Pursuit of an explanation of this close relationship between the

<hr />

21 See Ch. IX.
22 C. P. 40/843, m. 494. Cf. Neilson, *Y. B. 10 Ed. IV—49 Hy. VI*, S. S. vol. XLVII, p. xviii. Ordinarily one prothonotary succeeded another with no comment either in the records or elsewhere, the change in "signature" being the only evidence of change in incumbent. From an historical point of view Cumberford's death in term time is fortunate.
23 *C. P. R., 1446–1452*, p. 263, March 22, 1449.

offices of Custos Brevium and of prothonotary takes us back into the early history of the court to a time when the term "record" did not ordinarily mean a written document, and when the methods of making and caring for written records were more casual and haphazard than they later became. Before the reign of Edward I the customary usage of the word "record" in the law courts was to refer to the collective or individual memory of the justices. This, as Professor Woodbine has pointed out, is the sense in which Bracton used the word. For what we would call the "record," that is the written parchment on which was entered the account of the proceedings before the justices, he used the term "rotulus." When he says that the "first" roll was the authoritive one from which all others derived their origin and authority, but that this authority would not stand against the "record," he means simply that the memory of the justices was the final and highest authority.[24]

This authority to correct misprisions of the clerks the justices kept throughout the mediaeval period.[25] Moreover, in the marginals of the plea rolls, the older usage of the word "record" survived even as late as the fifteenth century. Often the clerks had occasion to enter in the margins such notes as the following: "Recorded by the Court that [this case] was not continued beyond the Octaves of Michaelmas in the seventh year of Edward fourth," [26] or "This declaration is recorded by the Chief Justice." [27] Confusingly enough, the word was also used in fifteenth century marginals to mean a viewing of the written record and making a statement concerning its condition. Illustrations of this usage are such notes as "the justices record that in this plea there is no interlineation beyond the word 'penitus' in the thirty-third line . . ." [28] or that the entry is "recorded to be without erasures and interlineations to the end . . . by Asshton and Danvers and afterwards by the Chief

24 F. 352b. Cf. G. E. Woodbine, review of Sayles, *Select Cases in the Court of King's Bench* (vol. I), *Yale Law Journal*, vol. XLVI (1937), pp. 1264 ff.; and S. E. Thorne, "Courts of Record and Sir Edward Coke," in *Toronto Law Journal*, vol. II (1937), pp. 24–49.
25 See statutes of 14 Ed. III, stat. 1, c. 6; 9 Hy. V, c. 4; 4 Hy. VI, c. 3; 8 Hy. VI, cc. 12, 15. Cf. *Y. BB. Easter, 4 Ed. IV*, pl. 23, *Mich., 7 Ed. IV*, pl. 7.
26 C. P. 40/797, m. 273d.
27 C. P. 40/797, m. 370.
28 *C. P.* 40/882, m. 552.

Justice." [29] Here it is not the memory but the present intelligence of the justices which is called upon for a "record." But Justice Cottesmore made the theory clear when, in a case argued in Easter, 7 Henry VI he said: "But the record is at all times in the heart of the justices and the roll is nothing but a remembrance for better certainty." [30]

It is easy to see why the written document rapidly took the place of the older kind of "record" for most of the practical purposes of the court. Surviving rolls of the *Curia Regis* dating back to the reign of Richard I indicate that the justices had already begun to follow the practice of older administrative bodies and to employ clerks to set down on a roll an account of the proceedings before them which would aid their memories if they were called upon for a "record." With the division from the *Curia Regis* of the King's Bench and Court of Common Pleas, a development which, despite interruptions, was completed during the reign of Henry III,[31] the making and keeping of the written records seems to have been temporarily erratic and haphazard. Entries in Bracton's *Notebook* refer to a roll *in thesauro* or *apud scaccarium*, or to a roll in the keeping of a particular clerk, in such terms as to imply the existence of a principal roll and several others. For example in Hilary, 1222, the authority of the roll kept by William of York was maintained against that of "all the other rolls." [32] In a case from 1224 several rolls in the treasury are referred to.[33] And in 1219 the roll of the treasury was compared with the roll of Richard de Heriet, one of the justices, and found to be the same.[34] Confirming the impression that there were several parallel rolls are the lists of those which still survive for the period in the Public Record Office. They are a mixed batch, bearing the names of various justices.[35]

The difficulties and inefficiencies of a system depending on the memory of mortal men and providing no reliable assistance to

[29] C. P. 40/787, m. 302d.
[30] *Y. B. Easter, 7 Hy. VI,* pl. 22.
[31] Sayles, *Select Cases in K. B.,* vol. I, pp. xi–xl.
[32] *Bracton's Notebook* (ed. F. W. Maitland; London, 1887), vol. II, p. 124; cf. p. 393.
[33] *Ibid.,* vol. III, p. 238.
[34] *Ibid.,* vol. II, pp. 62–63.
[35] *P. R. O. Lists and Indexes,* Plea Rolls. Thorne (*Toronto Law Journal,* vol. II [1937], pp. 24–49) has commented on the difficulty of distinguishing public from private records in this early period.

that memory are probably more obvious to a twentieth century observer than to a thirteenth century justice. Memories were more reliable in the days before pencil and paper came into common use, and more could be and was expected of them. Also, in the pioneer days of the courts there was not so much business to remember. On the other hand, as time passed and justices died and cases accumulated, the need to rely on written documents must have been progressively obvious.

Just when the Court of Common Pleas began to introduce greater method into the making and keeping of its records is not immediately clear from the available sources. Some sort of change in the direction of greater system is suggested by an order of June 21, 1253, commanding Roger de Whitcestre to deliver to Roger de Thurkelby "the first roll" of pleas of the Bench and to keep the "second roll with the writs of the King in the Bench." [36] Roger de Whitcestre was a King's clerk and in 1246 had been appointed keeper of the Writs and Rolls in the Bench, receiving £10 annually at the Exchequer for as long as he continued in the office.[37] Bracton, in the passage already referred to, identifies the "first roll" with the roll of the prothonotary.[38] Thurkelby, in 1253, was not a prothonotary but a justice.[39] On the other hand, the order refers not to drawing up but to the custody of the two rolls and, even at a later date, the roll compiled by the three prothonotaries and the filacers was considered to be in the custody of the Chief Justice.[40] It seems possible, therefore, to conjecture that this order to Roger de Whitcestre either established or confirmed a new practice concerning the plea rolls. There were to be two principal rolls. The first and most authoritative was to be the one compiled by the prothonotary (with the help, no doubt, of underclerks) and remaining in the custody of the justices. The second was to be compiled under supervision of the Keeper of the King's Writs and Rolls and to remain in his custody.

This hypothesis would fit with the known facts for the period from 51 Henry III on. From that date until early in the fifteenth

[36] *C. C. R., 1251–1253,* p. 374.
[37] *C. P. R., 1232–1247,* p. 480.
[38] F. 352d.
[39] *C. C. R., 1251–1253,* pp. 196, 266.
[40] See below, Ch. IX.

century,[41] as Pike demonstrated, there is a fairly complete set of duplicate rolls marked "Rex." It would also help to explain the meaning of the ordinance of 1309. In that year Sir John Bacon (who had been Keeper of the King's Writs and Rolls of the Bench since 1292),[42] was charged to keep a "counter-roll" of all the pleas which are pleaded in the Bench and also of the essoins.[43] Apparently the intention was to re-enforce something old rather than to en-act something new. Perhaps Sir John, who was a busy man, had been neglecting his duties. In 1306 he had gone on a personal mis-sion to Rome and had been allowed to leave his court duties in the hands of a deputy.[44] Perhaps, on the other hand, the Rex rolls had been somewhat neglected because their usefulness was no longer so evident after a Chief Justice's roll came to be regularly kept. There is no clear evidence of there being a Chief Justice until 1 Edward I. After that, however, there is not only a clearly designated Chief Justice but also a fairly complete set of plea rolls bearing his name.

The ordinance of 1309, whatever its relation to earlier practice, seems to have been only temporarily effective. A fairly complete set of Rex rolls survives for the middle years of Edward II, and these rolls, although not exact duplicates of the justices' roll, are nonetheless fairly full.[45] Soon after 20 Edward III,[46] however, they begin to decline, and by 39 Edward III neglect had gone so far that there were only three membranes of the Easter roll. William de Sandeford, the Custos Brevium, explained on the covering mem-brane that "there were no more rolls of this term because the King's clerks would not write anything more." For Trinity, he said, they would not write anything at all.[47]

Sandeford did not explain the reasons for the clerk's delin-quency, but it is easy to guess at some of them. For one thing, it had been clearly demonstrated in the Abbess of Berking's case in 16 Ed-ward III and the Rex roll no longer had any value as a check on the principal roll. In that case counsel for the defense, after a prelimi-

41 See above, Ch. IV.
42 C. P. R., 1281–1292, p. 485, April 17, 1292.
43 C. C. R., 1307–1313, p. 231, 3 Ed. II.
44 C. C. R., 1302–1307, p. 391, June 6, 1306.
45 See P. R. O., Lists and Indexes, Plea Rolls.
46 C. P. 23/50—67.
47 C. P. 23/67.

nary imparlance in an earlier term, answered in the later term by challenging the count as self-contradictory. Examination of the Chief Justice's roll, however, showed that the questionable passage in the declaration had been amended. Defendant's counsel then asked to have the Rex roll searched. Here the declaration was unamended. In spite of that, the court held the amended count good and required the defendant's counsel to go on to plead other matter.[48]

To the clerks responsible for writing the king's rolls a more important consideration than this uselessness of their task was, no doubt, the fact that they were not paid for it. The clerks who compiled the justices' roll took fees from the parties. The king's clerks who made the Rex roll had no opportunity to do so. From the form of their roll it would appear to have been compiled from the bundles of writs and other records which were returned from the sheriff's office into the office of the Custos Brevium and remained there after the term was over.[49] The king's clerks probably did their work after the end of term and without contact with the parties. No source of income was therefore open to them except a salary or wages paid by the king or the Custos Brevium. The Custos Brevium alone seems to have had a salary from the King and he received only £10 a year. If he paid his underclerks a wage, it is unlikely to have been a large one. Many of them seem, to be sure, to have held livings of which the disposition was in the Chancellor's hands, but these, however adequate, would not provide the needed incentive for the performance of a useless task in the court.[50]

In this same period, while the Rex roll was progressively falling into disuse, the Chief Justice's roll was progressively becoming a more orderly and systematic record of the proceedings in the court. And in this history of greater systematization of the roll lies the explanation of the existence in the late fifteenth century of three prothonotaries where, a century earlier, there had been only one. The rolls of Edward I and II show only a rough sort of chrono-

[48] Y. B. Trin., 16 Ed. III, pl. 32 (R. S. p. 119). Cf. pp. 594 and xxvi–xxix.
[49] This statement is a conjecture only, since, owing to the unsorted state of the bundles of writs, it was impossible for me to compare a Rex roll with the appropriate collection of writs.
[50] For the whole matter of clerical livings and king's clerks see Wilkinson, *Chancery*, p. 31.

logical arrangement by return days. Entries of appearances in mesne process, records of trial in the county, records of pleadings, and memoranda of writs of final process follow one another with no apparent classification. By 10 Richard II, however, some effort to separate pleadings and later stages from routine entries of appearances is evident. Two clerks, Wakefield and Brown, are beginning to "occupy" the membranes later associated with the first and second prothonotaries and are making these entries of pleadings and other later stages. This change may represent a corresponding one in the court's methods of doing business. It may show, for example, that from this time on the sessions at Westminster were less and less concerned with the routine sending out of writs of mesne process and that transactions involving matters of this sort were already taking place in some one of the churches of western London. It would be impossible to come to such a conclusion without further proof.

For our immediate purpose Wakefield's emergence as one of two prothonotaries at the same time that the Rex roll is falling into neglect has more importance. It suggests a hypothesis concerning the special relationship of the Custos Brevium and the second prothonotary which, while not capable of proof, seems worthy of discussion. It will be remembered that Brent, who was presented to the office of second prothonotary in 1472 by Sir John Fogge, the Custos Brevium, traced his official ancestry to Wakefield. It seems a possibility that Wakefield was originally appointed as a kind of king's prothonotary, whose special function was to see that the files of writs and *posteas* in use by the justices' clerks during term time were properly turned over to the Custos Brevium at the end. Legal tradition in Roger North's time supports this explanation. He says that the second prothonotary was added to the first to take care of crown business.[51]

North's account of the origin of the third prothonotary is equally simple and equally without substantiation or indication of date. He says that a prothonotary was needed to take care of poor men's

---

[51] Roger North, *Lives of the Norths* (London, 1890), vol. I, p. 127. A difficulty about this explanation is that Wakefield "occupied" the position of first prothonotary in the rolls of Richard II. On the other hand, Brown, referred to as his successor in the memorandum of Brent's appointment, was second prothonotary.

causes. The two chief prothonotaries were too busy, and poor men's causes brought no fees. Therefore, says North, a third prothonotary was added, but the distinction between his duties and those of the others was soon forgotten.

The true explanation of the addition of a third prothonotary appears to be not quite so simple as this, and it is easier to discover when a third prothonotary was appointed than to discover why. There were two only in Richard II's reign and still only two as late as Trinity, 35 Henry VI. A court ordinance of that year provided that "everych of the ii prenotaries" was to be allowed to bring only two clerks to sit with him in the court.[52] On the other hand, a Year Book report of Michaelmas, 39 Henry VI mentions three prothonotaries by name. In a discussion of the method of entering assizes, Wydeslade, Cumberford, and Copley each testified concerning his own practice.[53] Seemingly a third prothonotary had been appointed sometime between Trinity, 35, and Michaelmas, 39 Henry VI.

The rolls show such an appointment but, as often is the case in mediaeval records, they do not make a direct statement of it. Wydeslade and Cumberford were clearly the first and the second prothonotaries, respectively, in Trinity, 35 Henry VI.[54] In addition a third clerk, Copley, had already begun to do some prothonotary's work, that is, he was entering mainly records of pleadings and later stages rather than records of mesne process. He "occupied" membrane 12 and was beginning to gather to himself other blocks of membranes. By Michaelmas, 39 Henry VI he had thoroughly settled into the position occupied by the third prothonotary in the rolls of Edward IV. A search in the rolls immediately preceding that of Trinity, 35 Henry VI shows, however, that at least two years before that term Copley had already begun to emerge as a third prothonotary.[55] When and why the decision was made to give him the title as well as the work of prothonotary the rolls do not tell us.

No mention has been found of North's prothonotary of the poor until 15 Edward IV when a puzzling note in the Year Book relates

[52] App. I (c).
[53] Y. B. Mich., 39 Hy. VI, pl. 22.
[54] C. P. 40/787, Trin., 35 Hy. VI.
[55] C. P. 40/778, Trin., 33 Hy. VI.

that "J. Bron'" was appointed to this position and was sworn to keep his office in person or by one clerk, the two being forbidden to come to the court together presumably because of overcrowded conditions. He was to enter cases for men who could swear that they were not able to pay, and he was to take no fees.[56]

This note raises a good many difficulties. No J. Bron' has been found among the clerks who "signed" the plea roll either in 15 Edward IV or in subsequent years. William Brayne was third prothonotary in that year, and a clerk named Brown was temporarily appointed to succeed Brayne sometime between Michaelmas, 17, and Michaelmas, 18 Edward IV, but was soon, in Michaelmas, 20, replaced by Conyngesby.[57] Neither William Brayne nor Brown will answer the description of a new officer appointed in Trinity, 15 Edward IV to take care of poor men's causes, nor is there any evidence in the rolls of the existence of a fourth prothonotary.

Perhaps this is one of the puzzles which a modern edition of the Year Books will help to solve. A possible, although not very satisfactory, explanation is that J. Bron' is a Year Book mistake for W. Brayne (worse distortions of names do occur), and that what happened in 15 Edward IV was that Brayne, the third prothonotary, was given the additional job of taking care of poor men's causes. This does not explain the provision that he should come to court in person or by his clerk but never with his clerk. Another possibility is that Brown, who succeeded Brayne in 17–18 Edward IV, may have been temporarily appointed earlier as a fourth prothonotary to take care of poor men's causes, but, because he could not get enough fees, later asked for and got an appointment to the vacancy left by Brayne. In this case a more thorough search of the plea rolls for Trinity, 15 Edward IV and the terms immediately following should reveal Brown's name somewhere. Some support of the conjecture that the prothonotary of the poor was the third prothonotary rather than a new appointee in the term mentioned is to be found in an increase in the amount of the latter's business in these years. He began to "occupy," temporarily at least, more rolls than either of the other two prothonotaries.

[56] Y. B. Trin., 15 Ed. IV, pl. 2. Cf. Neilson, Y. B. 10 Ed. IV—49 Hy. VI, S. S. vol. XLVII, p. xix, n. 1.

[57] C. P. 40/874. Cf. App. III, below.

The history of the office of the prothonotary illustrates as well as any the lack of any conscious administrative concept behind the growth of offices in the court. This office originated, developed, and proliferated in response to immediate needs and pressures. Successive divisions of the duties and multiplications of the fees required of suitors began in obscurity and achieved the confirmation of usage before official notice has been taken of their existence. Rules and orders of the court dealt only with minor matters of method and procedure and successive investigations of fees took as their only standard of measurement the "ancient and accustomed" payments. Not until the nineteenth century was there any attempt to assess the value of the office in terms of its efficiency in serving the public. By that time, there were nine "officers" and an indeterminate number of underclerks performing the duties carried out in the early thirteenth century by one or two clerks, and these men all had a vested interest in obstructing the overhauling of the organization which guaranteed them a livelihood. It took fifty years of effort to abolish the old office of prothonotary and to set up in its place a new set of offices designed primarily for service.

CHAPTER IX

The Keepers of the Records

MEDIAEVAL CUSTODY of records appears strangely lax and inefficient by modern standards. Indeed, England's wealth of surviving records is a miracle of the accumulative instinct rather than a monument to archival science.

Two fundamental differences in concept account for important differences in the mediaeval treatment of records. For one thing, a "record" in the days of Henry III, when system first was introduced into the care of the rolls of the Court of Common Pleas, did not ordinarily mean a written document. Its thirteenth century meaning has been discussed above in connection with the early history of the prothonotary's office.

Secondly, even after "records" in the modern sense came to be regularly made and preserved, custody of them was personal rather than geographical. When Bracton collected the materials now called his *Notebook*, he used the word "thesaurus" to indicate the royal treasury where rolls in the king's custody were kept, but the term lacked geographical concreteness. Later mediaeval documents relating to the transfer of records make only incidental mention of places. Their primary concern is with who gives and who receives.[1] References to places of custody are confusing in their variety and disparity. Professor Sayles found, for example, that in the late thirteenth and the fourteenth centuries records of the central courts and eyres were being kept in such various places as a tenement in Chedgrave, a chest in the New Temple, London, St. Bartholomew's,

[1] F. Palgrave, *The Antient Kalendars and Inventories of the Treasury of His Majesty's Exchequer* (London, 1836), vol. III, pp. 99–122, 148–163, 196, 255, 370, 427.

Smithfield, the castles of Pontefract, Tutbury, and Tonbridge, and the House of the Friars Preachers in London.[2] Such a state of affairs would have been impossibly confusing had it not been for the principle of personal responsibility. Wherever the records were some officer was responsible for producing them if called upon to do so.

Even the personal responsibility for Common Pleas records had not always been clear. In the preceding chapter an attempt has been made to sketch the early history of the making and keeping of those records. Professor Sayles has described the efforts made during the reign of Edward I to get all instead of a few of the plea rolls into the treasury and has published an interesting set of documents illustrating these efforts.[3] These seem to me to reveal a new concept, that is, that not only the rolls written especially for the king, but also all the records of the courts belonged ultimately to the king and should eventually find their way into his treasury.[4] A long series of indentures between officers of the Court and the Treasurer and Chamberlains of the Receipt dating from 7 Edward I to 22 Charles II testify to the persistence of this idea; [5] and the Public Record Office, staffed with skilled archivists working according to scientific principles, is its modern culmination.

The idea that custody was personal rather than geographical also persisted throughout the mediaeval period. To be sure, an attempt was made in the reign of Edward II to establish the Chapel of the Pyx and the Tower as the two final repositories of those records which had been turned over to the officers of the treasury. This did not lead, however, to a permanent concentration of all records in those places. Since "formal delivery to the Treasurer and Chamberlains was held to constitute deposit in the Treasury," and since the effort to check up on what these officers did with records after they had received them was not continued after Edward II's

---

[2] Sayles, *Select Cases in K. B.*, vol. I, pp. cxvi–cxxvii and App. IX.

[3] *Loc. cit.*

[4] Professor Sayles explains the delivery of legal records into the Treasury of the Receipt by the close connection between the Exchequer and the law courts, which persisted even after the Exchequer Court began to confine itself chiefly to financial matters. I confess that I do not see the need to explain the turning over of these records by any more complex principle than that records of the king's courts were the king's records and therefore belonged in the treasury with his other records.

[5] Palgrave, *Antient Kalendars*, vol. III, *passim*.

reign, there was some carelessness about removing them to the Chapel of the Pyx and the Tower. Various places in their own department, for example, the Chapel of St. Stephen, a "coffer of the Treasurer and Chamberlains in the window behind their backs," and a chest "of the Tellers' chamber beyond and above the Receipt," were used by the Treasurer and Chamberlains for storage.[6]

Moreover, despite this effort to establish certainty as to the final resting place of the king's records, the principle of personal responsibility held its ground, and there were at least three places where Common Pleas records might be found in the fourteenth and fifteenth centuries. Some records were in the chapel of St. Bartholomew's, Smithfield;[7] some were in a vaulted chapel next the Temple church;[8] some in a cellar called "Hell" at Westminster,[9] for which a lock and six keys were bought in 1352; and others were in no certain place but were in the personal keeping of the Chief Justice.[10]

The key to an understanding of this apparent chaos is knowledge about the officers who had custody of the records of the Court of Common Pleas, and what their responsibilities were with regard to them. Responsibility was distributed among the Custos Brevium, the Chief Justice,[11] and the Chirographer, although the last officer was held answerable only for writs of covenant and notes of fines.[12] As a matter of convenience the Chief Justice appointed a servant to take care of his records for him, but the official accountability remained with the master, and if he died without turning over his records to his successor, his heirs and executors became responsible.[13] In the contemporary list of fees the Chief Justice's servant

6 V. H. Galbraith, "The Tower as an Exchequer Record Office in the Reign of Edward II," in *Essays in Mediaeval History Presented to T. F. Tout* (ed. Little and Powicke; Manchester, 1925), p. 232, n. 2.

7 *Loc. cit.*

8 Where fourteen hundred bundles were found in 1809 (Palgrave, *Antient Kalendars*, vol. I, p. xl; J. Hunter, ed., *Fines sive Pedes Finium.*, A.D. 1195–A.D. 1214 (Record Commission; London, 1835), vol. I, p. xviii.

9 E 101/471/6. I owe this reference to Miss M. K. Dale.

10 This seems to me the only possible explanation of their coming into the hands of administrators and executors of Chief Justices. See below, note 13.

11 The indentures printed by Palgrave are between these two "officers and the Treasurer and Chamberlains.

12 5 Hy. IV, c. 14.

13 *C. C. R., 1435–1441*, pp. 294–295, an order to the administrators of John Cottesmore to deliver over the records to Richard Newton, the new Chief Justice; C. P.

is referred to as the "Clerk of the Treasurehouse." [14] His name and his function will be more fully discussed later in this chapter. Before we turn to him we should first consider his more prominent colleagues, the Custos Brevium or Keeper of the King's Writs and Rolls of the Bench, and the Chirographer. Both these officers were servants of the king, appointed by letters patent.

The position of Custos Brevium was one of some consequence. Many distinguished or notorious persons held it. For example, Ellis de Beckingham, Custos Brevium from 1278 to 1285, later became a justice of the court.[15] So did John Lovel and John Bacon.[16] Master John de Shordich, who held the office from 1323 to 1327, was a "professor of civil law," an advocate of the Court of Arches, and several times an ambassador to the court of Charles IV of France.[17] Thomas Haxey, Custos Brevium from 1387 to 1397, achieved notoriety for his attack on the expenses of the royal household in the last parliament of Richard II.[18] John Fogge, Custos Brevium during the reign of Edward IV, was a favorite of Edward IV as well as a person of some prestige in his own county.[19] Moreover, the office, along with that of the Chancellor, the two Chief Justices, the Treasurer, the Chamberlains, the Chief Baron of the Exchequer, and a number of others, was among those which the barons in 1311 asked to have granted only by consent of Parliament.[20]

The type of incumbent and the conditions of tenure changed notably during the period from the earliest mention of the office in the middle of the thirteenth century to the appointment of

---

40/801, m. 59, order to Margaret Prisot, widow and executrix of John Prisot, to deliver the rolls, writs, and other memoranda to Chief Justice Danby; cf. Thomas Jakes' memoranda Recoveries 7 Hy. VIII—22 Hy. VIII, re the death or withdrawal of each chief justice from 1449 to 1506 with comments on the delivery of the records. These memoranda were discovered by Miss M. K. Dale.

[14] App. I (g).

[15] Sayles, *Select Cases in K. B.*, vol. I, p. cxxxvii.

[16] *Ibid.*, pp. xlvi, lx; *C. P. R., 1307–1313*, p. 552.

[17] *C. P. R., 1321–1324*, pp. 340, 426; *C. C. R., 1327–1330*, pp. 500, 510, 586; *C. P. R., 1327–1330*, pp. 440, 491; *R. P.*, vol. II, p. 41a.

[18] *R. P.*, vol. III, pp. 339, 341, 430; vol. IV, p. 63. He was condemned for treason but later pardoned by Richard for having introduced a bill for the reduction of the King's household expenses. The judgment was annulled and his lands, goods, and other possessions were restored by Henry IV.

[19] *C. P. R., 1461–1467* and *1467–1477, passim* for grants to him.

[20] *R. P.*, vol. I, p. 282, 5 Ed. II.

Richard Decons in 1501. Fourteenth century grantees are usually referred to as "king's clerks." [21] What precise status or function is indicated by the term "king's clerk" is difficult to say. In the early fourteenth century there seems to have been a large group of clerks who not only worked in and about the law courts, but, like John of Shordich, were sent on missions at home and abroad, and held livings of the king's grant.[22] Fifteenth century appointees, on the other hand, were nonclerical and usually had some connection with the household. John Hotoft, "king's esquire," who succeeded Robert Darcy in 1413, was later Treasurer of the Household, Keeper of the Wardrobe, Chamberlain of the Receipt of the Exchequer, and War Treasurer of Henry VI.[23] John Ulveston and Thomas del Rowe, who received a grant in survivorship in 1444,[24] were called in their patent "king's servants." John was receiver of Eton College, while Thomas was referred to as "one of the clerks of the Common Bench." John Fogge, esquire and later knight, appointed in 1461 and already mentioned above as one of the more notorious incumbents, was Treasurer of the royal Household.[25]

Tendencies towards tenure for life or even by inheritance appear

[21] The only ones not so designated are William de Herlaston, William de Culham, and Sir Thomas Haxey, *q.v.* below, App. V (A).

[22] See *Calendars of Close and Patent Rolls,* indices, for references to king's clerks in administrative positions, as envoys abroad, and as incumbents of livings in the king's grant. See *R.P.,* vol. II, p. 41, for provision that the Chancellor shall grant these livings to clerks of long service in the Chancery, the Exchequer, and the two Benches, and not to other persons.

[23] *C. P. R., 1413–1416,* p. 1; *C.P.R., 1422–1429,* p. 101; Issue Roll, 1 Hy. VI, Easter, r. 8; 20 Hy. VI, Mich., r. 8, Dec. 11; 25 Hy. VI, Mich., Feb. 18. The references to the Issue Rolls were given me by members of Professor William's seminar in fifteenth century legal history in the University of London.

[24] For his grant, see *C. P. R., 1441–1446,* p. 316. For his failure to get it recognized in the court, see C. P. 40/738, Trin., 24 Hy. VI, m. 528d; C. P. 40/739, Mich., 24 Hy. VI, mm. 337–339d, a suit brought by Robert Darcy and Henry Fylongley, Keepers of the Writs and Rolls of the Bench, against Thomas del Rowe because, whereas by letters patent Oct. 16, 19 Hy. VI, the plaintiffs were granted the office, Thomas on Oct. 3, 23 Hy. VI, took away thirteen bundles of writs returned to the Bench in the octave of Michaelmas, "in the great hall at Westminster" in the custody of the plaintiffs. They claim £600 damage for the taking of the writs and other disturbances to their exercise of the office. Thomas pleaded the grant to him and John Ulveston referred to above. The plaintiffs replied by producing a petition in which their claim to the office was granted by the king in the parliament of 23 Henry VI. Although judgment is not recorded in this roll, it is apparent from the later records that the plaintiffs were successful. On m. 371 of the plea roll for Mich., 36 Hy. VI (C. P. 40/787) a debt case notes the delivery of a *scriptum* to Henry Fylongley.

[25] *C. P. R., 1461–1467,* pp. 187, 191, 215.

in the course of the fifteenth century. Until 1381 the office had been granted "during pleasure." In that year Richard II altered Richard de Treton's grant to one "during good behaviour,"[26] and in 1386 William de Culham received a life grant.[27] Though John Hotoft's grant in 1413 was again "during pleasure" only,[28] Robert Darcy, who, at the death of Henry V, recovered the office under a life grant from Henry IV, held it from 1440 to 1461 in survivorship with Henry Fylongley.[29] Sir John Fogge was sole incumbent for a time and then received a grant in survivorship with his son.[30] John Kendale held it alone from 1483 to 1485,[31] and then it was granted to John Heyron and John Fogge, esquire (son of Sir John), again in survivorship. This patent was vacated in 17 Henry VII because John Fogge's name had apparently been inserted without the King's knowledge.[32] Meanwhile Richard Decons had got a grant which was to take effect at the death of John Heyron.[33] The tendency for the office to become an incorporeal hereditament probably continued through the Tudor and early Stuart reigns, for we know that in 29 Charles II the office was granted by letters patent "to certain persons named in the letters patent and their heirs and assigns in trust for the earl and countess of Litchfield and the issue of the countess in tail" and continued to be so held until the reforms of the nineteenth century.[34]

The office must have been usually exercised by deputy in the fifteenth century. Sir John Fogge, for example, was too heavily burdened with other duties to have been able to go to court daily, taking with him the writs and other memoranda. There are occasional references in fact to attorneys of the court acting as deputies for him. Thomas Torold, attorney, delivered the fines for 21 to 29 Henry VI into the Treasury as deputy of Sir John in 4 Edward IV,[35]

---

[26] *C. P. R., 1374–1377*, p. 590.

[27] *C. P. R., 1385–1389*, p. 211.

[28] *C. P. R., 1413–1416*, p. 1.

[29] *C. P. R., 1406–1413*, p. 219; *C. P. R., 1413–1416*, p. 333; *C. P. R., 1422–1429*, p. 101; *C. P. R., 1436–1441*, p. 471.

[30] *C. P. R., 1461–1467*, p. 11; *C. P. R., 1467–1477*, p. 339.

[31] *C. P. R., 1476–1485*, p. 463.

[32] *C. P. R., 1485–1494*, p. 123.

[33] *C. P. R., 1494–1509*, p. 265.

[34] *H. E. L.*, vol. I, p. 258; *Parlt. Papers* (1819), Report on Fees in the Common Pleas, p. 9.

[35] Palgrave, *Antient Kalendars*, vol. III, p. 388; E 101/336/12.

133

and in the plea roll for Easter, 1482, we find a note that John Elryngton, deputy of Sir John (and also queen's attorney, common attorney, and filacer for Cambridge, Huntingdonshire, London, and Middlesex), delivered a *scriptum* to Richard Cok, Clerk of the Assizes.[36]

The appointment of a deputy received official sanction by the middle of the century. Beginning with John Fogge's grant in 1461, the letters patent include the phrase "per se vel per sufficientem deputatum suum." [37] Earlier than this a deputy seems to have been admitted by the Chief Justice. The ordinance of the court issued in Trinity, 35 Henry VI provides that no one shall exercise an office in the Common Pleas by deputy except those who have special license of the Chief Justice and specifies the number of clerks which each of the officers of the court may have with him in the court; it concludes with the provision that the "keeper of the writtes or his deputie" may have one clerk.[38] In virtue of special royal license the office had sometimes been exercised by deputy at a much earlier date. Master John Luvel, when beyond the seas or employed on the king's business, appointed deputies.[39] John Bacon was allowed to exercise the office by deputy when he went to Rome to expedite certain of his affairs there.[40]

The Custos Brevium's salary from the king was not sufficient to enable him to pay a deputy. In the fifteenth century it was apparently never more than 10 marks,[41] although in the thirteenth and early fourteenth centuries it had on several occasions, for reasons not specified, been £10.[42] But even £10 would not have enabled the Chief Clerk to pay a deputy.[43] The greater part of his

---

[36] C. P. 40/880, m. 117d.; cf. a similar note in C. P. 40/878, m. 306.

[37] Patent Roll, 1 Ed. IV, pt. I, m. 15.

[38] App. I (c). The italics are mine.

[39] C. P. R., *1281–1292*, pp. 339, 419.

[40] C. C. R., *1392–1397*, p. 391.

[41] Issue Roll 725, Mich., 1436, r. 7, Nov. 27; 1 Hy. VI, Nov. 30; 1 Hy. V, Nov. 15. And see C 47/87/5/83, return of the Treasurer and Chamberlains to a writ of *certiorari* from the Chancery in which they report that the accustomed salary of the office in the time of "William Wandeford" and Richard de Treton was ten marks. William Sandeford was Custos Brevium from 1354 to 1375 and Richard de Treton from 1375 to 1387. Cf. E 404/84, 19 Hy. VII.

[42] Sayles, *Select Cases in K. B.*, vol. I, Intro., App. VI (f); C. P. R., *1232–1247*, p. 480, May 23, 1246; E 403/152, 2 Ed. III, Dec. 9.

[43] The deputy may, of course, have received his income entirely in fees.

income, as in the case of the justices and other officers of the court, must have come from fees. They were what made the office a prize to be bestowed on royal favorites. In the parliament roll of 1330 is a petition of Master John de Shordich, Advocate of the Court of Arches, that he should have compensation for the loss of the office of *"Cheif Clerk en le Commune Bank qe le poait valer par an cent marcs."* [44] One hundred marks was at the time a sizable income, especially when supplemented by other grants from the king. This sum was still the approximate official estimate of the value of the office in the early fifteenth century, for Robert Darcy received an annunity of £60 from the issues of the hanaper in recompense for its loss when Henry V, either in ignorance or in disregard of Darcy's patent, gave the office to John Hotoft in the first year of his reign.[45] Again in 1430 John Hotoft received a grant of 100 marks a year from the fee farm of the City of Lincoln in compensation when Robert Darcy recovered the office on the death of Henry V.[46]

This need not mean that it was never worth more than 100 marks at any time in the fifteenth century. Fluctuations in the amount of business in the court must have resulted in corresponding fluctuations in the profits. No satisfactory estimate of the average return for a year can be made because, while the list of fees from the Black Book [47] tells how much the Custos Brevium got for each exercise of his office, it does not and cannot tell how many times he was called upon in any given term to produce writs of an old term for inspection nor how many writs came in after the return day, these being the main occasions on which he received fees. Furthermore, the fees listed are not necessarily the only ones received.[48] Our only course, therefore, is to accept the valuation of the office with which Robert Darcy and John Hotoft were content in the early fifteenth century, remembering that there were probably seasonal fluctuations.

The functions of the fifteenth century Custos Brevium are less

---

[44] *R. P.*, vol. II, p. 41a, 1330.

[45] *C. P. R., 1413–1416*, p. 333; Nicolas, *Privy Council,* vol. II, p. 169, Petition to the King, June 15, 2 Hy. V, 1414, asking for compensation for loss of office.

[46] *C. P. R., 1429–1436*, p. 101, Nov. 1, 1430.

[47] See App. I (f).

[48] See *R. P.*, vol. III, p. 543, 5 Hy. IV, for mention of an accustomed fee of 1s. 10d., owed to the chief clerk of the Bench "pur lentree d'accorde de chescun Fyn."

difficult to determine than the amount of the fees which he received for fulfilling them. He was, as his name implies, the custodian of the writs original and judicial, but he had the custody of other records as well. In 1392 a writ directing Roger Westwood, clerk, John Barnetby, Thomas Belwood, and William Northope to supply horses and carts for the carriage from London to York of the records in the custody of Thomas Haxey, Keeper of the Writs and Rolls of the Common Bench, lists king's writs, rolls, fines, writings, records, certificates of bishops, and "other memoranda and evidences" as being in Thomas' keeping.[49] Indentures of delivery of fines, writs, and rolls of the Bench to the Treasurer of the Receipt testify to his custody of those records.[50]

In addition to bringing writs and other documents into court for other officers to examine, "without payeing anything therefore."[51] the Keeper of the Writs was expected to make copies of documents in his custody when directed to do so by a writ of *certiorari* from the Chancellor.[52]

---

[49] *C. P. R., 1391–1396*, p. 63, June 7, 1392. Just a century earlier (Sayles, *Select Cases in K. B.*, vol. I, pp. cxxi, clix), Robert de Littlebury, then chief clerk and Custos Brevium, delivered to the Treasurer and Chamberlains of the Exchequer Rolls of the years 50–56 Henry III and 1–17 Edward I, essoin rolls for the same years, all the writs original and judicial to Michaelmas, 17 Edward I except those sent out with the justices in eyre, a hamper containing statutes of the king and episcopal letters, three sacks in which were contained notes of fines levied and records without a day (*recorda sine die*), and twenty-nine boxes in which were contained charters denied by parties (*carte dedicte*). In the octave of Hilary in the following year, he handed over to his successor, John Luvel, the roll for Michaelmas, 17–18, writs of that term in eight bundles, certain *scripta dedicta*, two bundles of records *sine die,* and sixteen notes of fines. Essoin rolls are not mentioned in the late fourteenth century list, probably because the Custos Brevium no longer kept duplicates of those in the Chief Justice's custody. John Bacon had been charged in 1309 to keep a counterroll of essoins as well as of the pleas (*C. C. R., 1307–1313*, p. 231). Whether he or his successors did so or whether any such rolls have survived is impossible to tell. The Record Office lists include only one set of these rolls, and the ones available are torn, dirty, and chewed by rats, so that they are almost unrecognizable as rolls of any kind.

[50] Palgrave, *Antient Kalendars,* vol. III, *passim.*

[51] App. I (f).

[52] In Chancery Miscellanea, County Placita, C 47/47–88, are many examples. Although Cowell (*Interpreter*), calls these returns of the Custos Brevium "exemplifications," Mr. Jenkinson tells me that that term is properly used only to refer to copies of Chancery documents made in the Chancery and sealed with the great seal. The endorsement on C 47/59/6/242, a copy of the writs and records relating to the trespass action *Forthay v. Catesby*, 4–5 Ed. IV, explains that it is the tenor or the process and enrollments in the case which the king ordered to be sent into the Chancery so that an exemplification might there be made of them on request of the defendant. Many, on the other hand, are copies of the record of outlawry of a defendant which may have been called for in the Chancery before the issue of a pardon of outlawry or a *supersedeas.*

136

In the plea rolls are frequent notes of the delivery to him or his deputy of *scripta dedicta* and other documents in evidence.[53] He in turn delivered them to the Clerk of the Assizes before the trial of the case in the county.[54] The certificates of bishops listed in the writ of 1392 were probably also documents in evidence such as certificates of marriage, baptism, or other facts in the cognizance of the bishop.

Although the Custos Brevium's function as Keeper of the King's Rolls of the Bench had been given up early in the fifteenth century, the memory of this function survived in the formal title "Custos Brevium et Rotulorum nostrorum de Banco."

The Chirographer, unlike the Custos Brevium, was not primarily a record keeper. The reasons for discussing him in this context are the similarities in conditions of tenure and type of incumbent between the two offices, and the help we may gain in trying to understand why there were so many places of deposit of Common Pleas records in the period under consideration.

The Chirographer was appointed by royal letters patent to note fines and to engross them. As a matter of practice, he kept the original writs of covenant and *dedimus potestatem* and, as the result of petitions of the Commons early in the century, these and the notes of fines which he made were given the status of records in case the chirographs themselves should be lost. A chirograph was, of course, an indenture conveying land from one party to another, written three times on a single piece of parchment which was then cut into three pieces. Each party received a copy, and the third part or "foot of the fine" was delivered into the custody of the Custos Brevium. As an additional safeguard against loss, the Commons asked in 5 Henry IV that a roll of fines be made in the Bench before the writs of covenant and *dedimus potestatem* were taken out of the files of the Bench by the Chirographer. This roll was also to be given into the custody of the Custos Brevium.[55]

Conditions of tenure of the office appear to have been somewhat

---

[53] In *Kelyng v. Pratte,* m. 276d., C. P. 40/842; *Dayrell v. Dayson,* m. 108d., C. P. 40/843, for example.

[54] In *Wyche v. Wederby,* m. 111d., C. P. 40/842; *Bury v. Ulff,* m. 193d.; *Cokfeld v. Pomeys,* m. 125, etc.

[55] *R. P.,* vol. III, pp. 495–496, 543; stat. 5 Hy. IV, c. 14. I have not been able to find the rolls on which, in compliance with the statute, are supposed to have been entered the writs of covenant and concords of fines. The Enrollments of Writs for Fines and Recoveries do not, according to Giuseppi (*Guide,* vol. I, p. 252), begin until

similar to those of the office of Custos Brevium, although the change from grants during pleasure to grants for life had taken place much earlier and was less complete. As early as 1313 Robert de Foxton had been given the office "for life during good behaviour" [56] and as late as 1483 Richard III granted it to Robert Worthington "during pleasure." [57] Grants in survivorship became common after 1438 when William Pope and Ralph Legh received such a patent.[58] Unlike the office of Custos Brevium, however, that of Chirographer never became inheritable. In 1819 it was still held under life grants in survivorship.[59]

Concerning the question whether the office was exercised in person or by deputy the evidence is obscure. In answer to a Commons petition of 1401 complaining of the taking of extortionate fees, the King had promised that after the death of the current incumbent, "Monsieur Piers de Bukton," the office would be exercised only in person.[60] Nevertheless, the letters patent continue throughout the century to include the phrase "per se vel per sufficientem deputatem suum." It is true, however, that William Pope had difficulty in enforcing a patent of 1421 which included this phrase and was forced in 1424 to get a new grant which included a *non obstante* clause to obviate the effect of the provision of 1401. In 1445, when Chief Justice Fortescue brought action against Pope for taking twice the authorized 4s. in a fine between himself and Nicholas Aysston (or Ashton), Justice of the Common Pleas, and others, John Gerveys, "servant and minister" of William Pope, answered for him in court.[61] But in 1497 Sir William Vampage asked that Thomas Wodyington receive a joint grant with him since, as Knight of the Body to the King, he found it impossible to attend court daily himself.[62] Sir William's petition seems unnecessary unless personal attendance was required.

The persons appointed to the office in the fifteenth century were,

---

23–24 Elizabeth. In the fifteenth century, notes of fines were made on the plea roll, on membrane 22, and elsewhere. See above, Ch. IV, and below, Ch. X.

56 *C. P. R., 1313–1317*, p. 31.
57 *C. P. R., 1476–1485*, p. 463.
58 *C. P. R., 1436–1441*, p. 170.
59 *Parlt. Papers* (1819), Report on Fees in the Court of Common Pleas, p. 150.
60 *R. P.*, vol. III, pp. 495–496.
61 C. P. 40/737, Easter, 23 Hy. VI.
62 C 82/170, Nov. 28, 13 Hy. VII.

like the keepers of the writs, persons of some rank and consequence, most of whom had some connection with the royal household.[63] Moreover, in the fourteenth century the incumbent, like the writ keepers, had been a king's clerk, on two occasions the king's confessor.[64] The income of the office seems to have been entirely from fees, although John Gardyner, Chirographer from 1500 to 1508, was given in 1504 a reward of £6 to be taken out of the fines in any of the courts.[65] By the fifteenth century the fees must have greatly diminished because of the decreasing importance of fines and their replacement by common recoveries. Recurring complaints of extortion are probably explained by this diminishing income.[66] As in other offices, moreover, deputies or subordinates apparently attempted to eke out the pittance paid them by their masters by taking fees for themselves.[67] The sum allowed by statutes going back to that of Westminster II [68] was 4s. for each chirograph. The extent to which the revenue had fallen off since 1330, when Master John de Shordich was appointed to the office in lieu of £50 paid at the Exchequer,[69] is indicated by a petition of William Pope in 1444. He had surrendered grants of £23 6s. 4d. a year for life by the hands of the Chamberlain of Chester and the Receiver of Lancaster in exchange for the office of Chirographer of the Bench, and he evidently regretted his bargain. He was compensated with an additional £10 yearly from the subsidy and ulnage of cloth in London.[70]

The chief record keeper of the Court of Common Pleas was the Chief Justice himself. It was he who had the official responsibility for the plea rolls, which we think of as the most important records of the court. In his custody, also, were acknowledgments of fines,

---

63 John Rodenhale was a knight, a justice of the peace in Yorkshire East Riding, served on various other commissions, and was Deputy-Treasurer in the absence of the Earl of Arundel in 1413 (*C. P. R., 1399–1401* and *1401–1405, passim; C. P. R., 1413–1416,* p. 14; *C. C. R., 1413–1416,* p. 111). Sir William Vampage and John Payn were household officers (*C. P. R., 1485–1495,* pp. 41, 429; Chancery Warrants, C 82/107, June 24, 8 Hy. VII; C 82/170, Nov. 28, 13 Hy. VII).

64 *C. P. R., 1371–1374,* p. 199; *C. P. R., 1377–1381,* p. 559.

65 E 404/85, 20 Hy. VII.

66 *R. P.,* vol. II, pp. 312–313; vol. III, pp. 471, 495–496.

67 Above, Ch. VII.

68 C. 44.

69 *C. P. R., 1330–1334,* p. 36.

70 *C. P. R., 1444–1446,* pp. 297, 350.

139

writs, the seal, and various memoranda,[71] as well as recognizances and summonses.[72] As a matter of practical convenience these records fell into two groups. There were the rolls, writs, and other memoranda of old terms, and there were the ones in current use. The old records were kept in the Common Pleas Treasury under the care of the Clerk of the Treasury; the current ones, as, for example, the membranes of the current plea roll which had not yet been bound up into a roll, must have been scattered around London and Westminster in the hands of whatever clerk or officer was using them in his work. By the nineteenth century, the Chief Justice had appointed an officer called the Treasury-keeper to take care of these records.[73]

The earliest reference I have found to a clerk who kept the records in the Treasury is the mandate addressed in October, 1374, to Hugh de Wombewell, appointed "Keeper of the Rolls of the Common Bench" by William Fyncheden, late Chief Justice, directing that Hugh deliver to Robert Bealknap, Fyncheden's successor, "all rolls, records, and processes touching the office, in his keeping." [74] Wombewell and Thomas Jakes are the only two Clerks of the Treasury in the fourteenth and fifteenth centuries whose names I have been able to find. Jakes, whose memoranda concerning the court offices have several times been referred to, was also Clerk of the Warrants and Estreats under Chief Justice Frowyk, and a man of parts and possessions. He married Frowyk's widow and left behind him a number of books including a manuscript volume of Year Books and a volume of statutes.[75]

The duties of the Clerk of the Treasury, other than the keeping of the records, were to search for and make transcripts of records of old terms to be sent into the county for trial at *nisi prius,* to make similar transcripts of cases called into the King's Bench by writs of error, to make out writs of *scire facias* on charters of pardon and

71 *C. C. R., 1435–1441,* pp. 294–295.

72 C. P. 40/801, m. 59.

73 *Parlt. Papers* (1819), Report on Fees in the Common Pleas, pp. 100–106.

74 *C. P. R., 1374–1377,* p. 3; cf. *C. C. R., 1339–1341,* p. 604, an order to Nicholas de Greseleye to deliver "rolls, writs, and memoranda of the Common Bench which are in his custody" to Roger Hillary, newly appointed Chief Justice (*C. P. R., 1340–1343,* p. 75).

75 *D. N. B.* under title "Thomas Frowyk"; G. J. Turner, *Y. B. 4 Ed. II,* S. S. vol. XXVI, pp. li–lii; App. II.

writs of *supersedeas* and bills of bail when a defendant outlawed in process appeared in person to stop further process. For doing this work the clerk and his secondary were paid fees by the suitors of the court. They were not paid for searching for and copying records to be sent to the Chancery on writs of *certiorari*, nor were they allowed at this time, as they were later, to take fees for search by others of records in the Treasury. The clerk was enjoined in the list of fees from 35 Henry VI to allow officers and attorneys to see essoin and plea rolls of old terms "for the assurances of their matters and processes without anythinge payinge therefore." [76] A parliamentary petition of 1384 suggests that this injunction was necessary because there had been difficulty, as in the case of other officers, in preventing the Clerk of the Treasury from taking fees for every transaction within his office. The complaint was that officers were charging fees for bringing old rolls into court for officers to examine, and the proposed remedy was that those found guilty should make fine and ransom with the king. The King answered merely that anyone who had a grievance should apply to the Chancellor for redress.[77]

According to Cowell, the Clerk of the Treasury was the only officer of the court who was removable at the pleasure of the Chief Justice. His unique tenure was no doubt due to the character of his original appointment as a servant to the Chief Justice rather than an officer of the court. At Frowyk's death there seems to have been one of the periodic attempts of the King to take away some of the Chief Justice's patronage by conferring the office on John Kyrton by letters patent. Thomas Jakes jotted down in a paper book an account of the death or withdrawal of each Chief Justice from 1449 to 1506, with comments on the turning over of the records by writs addressed to the Chief Justice and the Clerk of the Treasury, and concluding with a remonstrance against his own removal by the patent to Kyrton. These memoranda may be the substance of a petition presented to the King, but Jakes did not record the outcome.[78]

Jakes refers to himself as the "Clerk of Hell," and in a pardon issued to him early in the reign of Henry VIII he is styled "late

[76] App. I (g).
[77] *R. P.*, vol. III, p. 202.
[78] Recoveries 7 Hy. VIII to 22 Hy. VIII.

clerk of Hell, otherwise called Thomas Jakes, late keeper of the records of King Henry VIIth and of other his lieges, of the common bench, existing and being within the place called hell." [79] The title "Clerk of Hell" is likewise used in a Year Book discussion of the offices in the appointment of the Chief Justice.[80]

The mention of Hell leads us to a general consideration of the places where the various officers responsible for the records of the Common Bench kept them in the fifteenth century. In the early fourteenth century the Custos Brevium had kept his records in the chapel of St. Bartholomew's, Smithfield.[81] He continued to keep them there until 1384, for in that year Richard de Treton, then Keeper of the Writs, came into Chancery and produced ten files of writs of 45 Edward III, all damaged, and said that the prior was bound to appoint a place in his church "sufficient for safe keeping of all writs and memoranda returned in the said Bench the keeping whereof pertains to the said Richard's office, and at his own cost to repair and maintain such place—and that the now king was seised of such place in time of the now prior, and the king's forefathers in the times of the prior's predecessors, in right of the crown as founders." Despite the King's right and his own obligations, however, the prior had carelessly allowed the rain to soak down through the roof and into the chest containing the King's writs to their damage. The prior at first disclaimed knowledge of the King's right to a place of custody for his records in the priory but finally pleaded a sudden tempest which had come up and blocked the gutter with a dislodged stone. The damage, he said, had been repaired as quickly as possible. He was let off with a fine of 6s. 1d., and Richard was exonerated from responsibility.[82] The writs may still have been at Smithfield in 1393, for Thomas Gaytford, one of the clerks of the Bench, was arrested in Smithfield on a private matter while going "towards the chapel of the said court to deliberate on divers business of the King and the common people." [83] Whether they were still at Smithfield in the fifteenth century I have not been

79 *Cal. Latin Papers*, Hy. VIII, vol. I, pt. I, p. 206.
80 *Y. B. Trin.*, 22 Ed. IV, pl. 43.
81 Galbraith, *Essays in Mediaeval History*, p. 232, n. 2; Exchequer, Accounts Various, 332/12.
82 *C. C. R.*, *1381–1385*, p. 428; C. P. 40/492, m. 15.
83 *C. P.* 40/530, m. 339d. Cf. above, p. 39.

able to discover. It seems a place unnecessarily distant from Westminster in which to keep records frequently needed there.

The places where the other responsible officers in the Court of Common Pleas kept their records are more difficult to discover. According to Hunter, the Chirographer's records were those found in the vault under the Temple Church in 1809, while the fines in general were stored in presses in the gallery of the Chapter House at Westminster.[84] One would have to make a careful check of all the indentures concerning delivery of fines by the Custos Brevium with the lists of the records found in the Chapter House in order to know whether these last were the ones which had been turned over to the Treasurer and Chamberlains or the ones still in the custody of the keeper of the writs.

According to a Commons petition of 1440, the proper place for records in the custody of the Chief Justice of the King's Bench was "within the abbey of Westminstre," while the Common Pleas treasury was "in a place therto ordeyned and accustomyd." [85] Thomas Jakes's title gives us the hint that this place was called "Hell." Now, there are many references to "Hell," beginning with one in 1310 to an affray which took place "here in the hall in the place which is called Helle, under the Bench." [86] Maitland found that Hell was originally a tenement in Westminster under the great hall, but that in later days there were two taverns adjoining the hall, one called "Heaven," the other "Hell." [87] In *London Lanes* Alan Stapleton says that "Heaven" was a tavern formerly on the site of the committee rooms of the House of Commons, and that "Hell" and "Purgatory" were two subterranean passages under the old Exchequer Chambers, once used, according to Fuller, as a prison for king's debtors.[88] One of the subterranean passages under the Exchequer may have been the cellar for which a lock and six keys were bought in 1352, along with two locks and a key for "a certain chest of the king in the house called 'helle' under the

[84] Hunter, *Fines,* vol. I, p. xvii.
[85] *R. P.,* vol. V, p. 29, 18 Hy. VI. In 1398 four "bookbinders" were paid for mending the records of the Common Pleas "whose writing and binding were much disfigured by rain and other mischances through the defects of the roof of certain houses within Westminster Palace where they were kept (E 403/561, m. 14).
[86] C. P. 40/180, m. 69.
[87] Maitland, *Y. BB. of 2 and 3 Ed. II,* S. S. vol. XIX, p. xvi.
[88] *London Lanes* (London, 1930), pp. 210–211.

Exchequer." [89] The act of resumption of 1485 refers to "the Keping of the Houses called Paradyse and Hell, within the Hall of Westmynster . . . with the Hous under the Exchequer called Le Puttans Hous . . ." which had been granted to Piers Carvanell, one of the gentlemen ushers of the chamber.[90] Whatever the exact location of Hell, it seems to have been in Westminster Hall, and it is quite certainly the place where the Chief Justice kept the records of old terms.

The whole question of custody of legal records is one requiring further study. Places naturally came to be more important as more records accumulated so that they could not be readily moved. On the other hand personal responsibility continued to be an important factor and should be kept in mind in further study of this subject in order to avoid increasing confusion.

[89] E 101/471/6.
[90] *R. P.*, vol. VI, p. 372, 1 Hy. VII.

CHAPTER X

Filacers and Other Clerks

THERE REMAINS to be considered a miscellaneous assortment of lesser clerks and servants of the court who worked either in Westminster Hall or in the offices in London. Few of them emerge as more than names. Yet the names themselves encourage some interest. A Danby was filacer for Yorkshire, the city of York and Hull throughout the latter part of the reign of Edward IV.[1] Was he perhaps a younger relative of Robert Danby, Chief Justice from 1461 to 1471, who belonged to a Yorkshire family? Again, a Wydeslade was filacer for Devon, Dorset, Somerset, and Bristol from 12 Edward IV to 2 Richard III. What relation was he to John Wydeslade, first prothonotary in the later years of Henry VI? Then there are the two John Elryngtons. They were filacers for Norwich and Norfolk and for Wiltshire, Hampshire, and Southampton in the early years of Edward IV. One survived to become, at the end of the reign, queen's attorney and filacer for Cambridge, Middlesex, and London, a richer prize than his earlier office. Are these John Elryngtons the same as the king's servants of that name who are mentioned in the patent rolls? One was Treasurer of the Household, and between them they held many offices, including that of Clerk of the Hanaper, King's Cofferer, Parker of Hundesdon forest, as well as several wardships of castles and manors in the king's grant.[2]

The most numerous group among these lesser clerks were the filacers. Their work, as their name implies, was mainly with the files

---

[1] App. III.

[2] *C. P. R., 1467–1477*, pp. 349, 396, 441, 477, 489, 537, 568, 596; cf. C. P., 40/882, m. 488.

of writs. They made out writs of common process and also made the entries in the plea roll which were to warrant these writs.[3] In the fifteenth century, as has been said above, they were still also allowed to enter pleadings in the common form.[4]

The nineteenth century commissioners who investigated the salable offices in the court of Common Pleas recommended that the "offices of filacers for the several counties may be well executed by one person." At that time there were eight such officers.[5] In the seventeenth century there had been from fourteen to seventeen, and they were taking fees for work which was already then being done by the attorneys.[6] In the fifteenth century there seem to have been sixteen, and they probably performed the work for which they were paid. The plea rolls of Edward IV's reign have been described in some detail above,[7] and it has been shown that the first twenty-two membranes of each roll constitute a sort of rough index and provide a list of the names of the enrolling clerks. The three prothonotaries occupy membranes 1, 2, and 12, respectively. The Clerk of the Fines and of the Juries occupy 21 and 22. Membrane 10 is signed by a clerk whose name does not usually appear elsewhere in the roll. I have been at a loss to identify him. The other sixteen are evidently the filacers.

In the nineteenth century there was a wide range in value of the offices, from £30 in the office of the shires of Derby, Leicester, Nottingham, and Warwick, to £1299 5s. in the office of London, Middlesex, Bedford, Berkshire, Buckingham, Cornwall, Gloucester, Hereford, and Worcester.[8] In the fifteenth century the range in value seems not to have been so great. The filacers received either 3d. or 6d. for each writ of process, depending on its type. For entries of declarations and pleas they were presumably paid at the same rate as the prothonotaries according to the type and length of the entries. The least lucrative office seems to have been that of Essex, Norfolk, Norwich, Hertford, Leicester, and Lincoln, and the most

---

3 App. I (h) and (j).
4 The division of work between them and the prothonotaries is discussed above in ch. VIII.
5 *Parlt. Papers* (1810), Report on Saleable Offices in the Common Pleas.
6 Cowell, *Dictionary;* Jacob, *Law Dictionary* and *Attorney's Practice*, Vol. II, p. 309.
7 Above, Ch. IV.
8 *H. E. L.*, vol. I, App. XXX. The sums given are net average receipts for three years, with taxes and allowances to deputies deducted.

lucrative that which included London and Middlesex. In the roll for Michaelmas, 22 Edward IV, Hervy, filacer for the former counties, was responsible for 230 entries, while Elryngton, filacer for the latter group and also the queen's attorney, was responsible for 746.[9] In Thomas Jakes's list of patronage values of the offices [10] (if that is what it is) the office associated with membranes 8, and 189 to 200 (Essex, Herts, etc.) is listed at £5 while that associated with membranes 14, and 86 to 100 (London and Midd) is listed at £20.[11]

Filacers were appointed by the Chief Justice, probably for life during good behavior as they were later, although I have found no specific statement to this effect. They were forbidden by the ordinance of 35 Henry VI to exercise their office by deputy, but the list of fees and the plea rolls testify to their having had underclerks to assist them in their work. The "Clerkes of the Prothonotaries and Philizers" received fees for making the paper copies of pleadings and other matters entered in the rolls.[12] They also received wages from their masters, but if Robert Buk, underclerk to Robert Beaufitz in the office of Warwick, Leicester, Nottingham, and Derby, is typical, the wages were not very large. Robert, who had been retained by his master to "write the writs and enroll them in the king's rolls," brought action in debt for arrears of a salary of 20s. at Christmas and at Easter.[13] Perhaps it was his master's lack of generosity which made some underclerk write "Olde Shrewe" above the name of Wauclyn, filacer of the Bench a century earlier.[14]

In addition to the three prothonotaries, the two record keepers, the Chirographer, and the filacers, seventeenth century books list eight other clerks or groups of clerks. Of these, the Clerk of the Warrants and Estreats, the Clerk of the Essoins, the Clerk of the Outlawries, the Clerk of the Juries, and the exigenters are directly mentioned by name in fifteenth century records or reports. I have

---

[9] The difficulty in drawing a clear line between the various offices has been discussed above in Ch. IV. Not only Elryngton but also Pulter entered cases from London, Middlesex, Cambridge, and Huntingdon, as well as several other counties.

[10] App. II.

[11] If the allocation of membranes was the same at Jakes's time as earlier, Smyth, whose office is valued at £5 was the successor to Hervy, while Agmondesham is successor to Pulter, who shared the entries from London, Midd, Cambridge, and Hunts with Elryngton.

[12] App. I (j).

[13] C. P. 40/790, m. 561d., Trin., 36 Hy. VI.

[14] C. P. 40/284, m. 327, Hil., 5 Ed. III.

found no direct mention of the Clerk of the King's Silver, but he can be identified by his work in the plea roll. The Office of the Clerk of the *Supersedeas* did not exist before the seventeenth century, when it was devised by James I in order to reward his Groom of the Bedchamber.[15] The office of Clerk of the Errors had apparently not yet branched off from that of Clerk of the Treasury.

Of the six offices which did exist before 1500 that of Clerk of the Warrants and Estreats was probably the most important. This clerk was a kind of hybrid among the officers of the court. As Clerk of the Warrants, he was appointed by the Chief Justice to enroll warrants of attorney in a special roll which was added as a kind of appendix to the plea roll. As Clerk of the Estreats, he was a servant of the king and was paid a salary or "regard" of £10 a year for making a roll of "estreats" of fines and amercements owed by parties to suits in the Bench.[16]

The method of making estreats is quite fully described by Fitzherbert in the *New Natura Brevium* in 1534.[17] From this description, the court ordinance of 23 Henry VII,[18] the two statutes relating to estreats,[19] and the remains of his work in the plea roll, we can reconstruct his duties quite completely. The prothonotaries and filacers were required to deliver to him the membranes of the plea roll within seven or eight days of the end of term. He was to make the estreats within two days and deliver the membranes to the Clerk of Essoins for binding. The filacers and prothonotaries helped him in his task by entering in the margin beside the record a *mia'* where an amercement was authorized and a sum of money where distress was to be collected. The Clerk of the Estreats had only to run down the margin until he came to one of these notes, take out the names of the parties and the cause of action. He must then have made up a set of lists by counties, which he delivered to the Clerk of the Assizes. The latter delivered them to the coroners, who assessed the amercements and delivered the lists back to the Clerk of the War-

15 The case of Murray, Groom of the Bedchamber, was discussed above in Ch. VII.
16 Issue Roll, Mich., 3 Hy. IV, r. 9, Nov. 21; *C. P. R., 1436–1441*, p. 302; *C. P. R., 1441–1446*, p. 56; *C. P. R., 1446–1452*, p. 552; *C. P. R., 1452–1461*, p. 302.
17 *F. N. B.*, vol. I, fols. 75–76.
18 App. II (d).
19 27 Ed. I, Stat. de Finibus; 7 Hy. IV, c. 3.

rants and Estreats. He then made up the estreat roll, which he delivered into the Exchequer.

In addition to his reward from the king, the Clerk of the Warrants and Estreats received fees for entering charters, indentures, and *scripta* of various sorts which had been acknowledged in court, and for entering warrants of attorney. These fees are not listed among the others taken from the Black Book, but Thomas Jakes set down in his memoranda, under the date 21 Henry VII, the fees as they were in his time. For entering the warrants of the Mayor of London he received a coat, and an additional 20*d*. from the Mayor himself and 13*s*. 4 *d*. paid by the secondary of the county in Trinity term.[20] His income from all sources seems to have been sufficient to pay two assistants. In Michaelmas, 1471, William Skypwyth brought suit by bill against Thomas Gouselle in trespass for committing assault on his servants William Pryce and Robert Palmer "so that they were unable to go about the business of the said William Skypwyth, that is, to keep and exercise" his office of Clerk of the Warrants and Estreats.[21]

A suggestion that the office of Clerk of the Estreats may have branched off from that of first prothonotary is to be found in the ordinance of 1309 already quoted in the discussion of the latter office. It provided that "le clerk la justice" should have of the gift and grace of the king twenty-five marks yearly "because he has more to do than heretofore and because he is charged with making all the estreats of the bench to be delivered to the Exchequer." [22]

The office of Clerk of the Juries seems also to have been an offshoot of the office of prothonotary. Through Michaelmas, 8 Edward IV the entries of juries in respite on m. 22 are above the signature of Cumberford, the second prothonotary. After that date the names of Snayth and various others appear successively.[23] In the nineteenth century list of offices, this one is joined with that of second prothonotary as being in the grant of the Chief Justice on nomination of the Custos Brevium.[24] In the files of writs examined,

[20] App. II.
[21] *Y. B. 10 Ed. IV—49 Hy. VI*, S. S. vol. XLVII, p. 115.
[22] *C. C. R., 1307–1313*, p. 231.
[23] App. III.
[24] *H. E. L.*, vol. I, p. 687.

those of *habeas corpora juratorum,* which were later made out by the Clerk of the Juries, are signed with the name of a prothonotary, or that of a clerk whose name does not appear in the rolls. On the other hand, a Clerk of the Juries is mentioned in a Year Book report as early as 34 Henry VI. The plaintiff brought action by bill in trespass on the case against John Ceveront, Clerk of the Juries. The complaint was that, whereas the plaintiff had paid a certain sum of money for the enrollment of "le Jur' et le Nisi prius," the defendant had made no such enrollment and, despite the verdict of the jury in his favor, the plaintiff got no judgment.[25] Apparently there was at this time a clerk called the Clerk of the Juries, but his office had not yet become completely distinct from the prothonotaries' offices.

The Clerk of the Essoins had originally had as his chief duty the entering of essoins in a special essoin roll. By the fifteenth century, essoins were falling into disuse.[26] Perhaps for this reason the Clerk of the Essoins had been given the task of cutting, marking, and binding up the membranes of the plea roll.[27] The Chief Justice provided the parchment, but was probably, as later, reimbursed from the fees for the sealing of writs under the green wax and for judicial writs in the Bench.[28] The Clerk of the Essoins was entitled to 4d. for every essoin he entered, 2d. for an adjournment, 6d. for a bill of exceptions, 2s. 4d. for a *supersedeas,* and 4d. for every nonsuit. In addition, he got a reward of 13s. 4d. from the Chief Justice for putting the plea roll together and delivering it to the Clerk of the Treasury.[29]

Fees are listed for the Clerk of the Outlawries in the Black Book table, but I have found no trace in the fifteenth century plea rolls or files of writs of work done by him. Jacob says he was a servant of the Attorney-General for making out writs of *capias utlagatum* which were issued in the latter's name.[30] Smith does not mention him as a special officer, but ascribes his duties to the king's at-

[25] *Y. B. Mich., 34 Hy. VI,* pl. 12.
[26] See below, Ch. XV. There are only thirty-three essoin rolls altogether from 11 Henry III to 38 George II and these are in such poor condition that they are almost impossible to examine. The fifteenth century ones are very meager.
[27] Ordinance of 23 Hy. VII (App. II).
[28] Jacob, *Attorney's Practice,* vol. II, p. 160; *Compleat Att.* (1652), p. 2.
[29] App. I (k).
[30] Jacob, *Attorney's Practice,* vol. II, p. 311; *Compleat Att.* (1652), p. 2.

torney.[31] The table of fees, however, lists payments due him for a number of transactions. He was entitled to 6*d.* for every writ of *capias utlagatum,* 4*d.* for making a traverse, error, or pardon of outlawry in his remembrance, 6*d.* for a *certiorari* upon an outlawry, and 6*d.* for a fine on a writ of rescue to be returned by the sheriff.[32]

In the fifteenth century plea roll, entries relating to reversal of outlawry after the writ of *capias utlagatum* had been issued are on the membranes of the prothonotaries and filacers, and writs of *capias utlagatum* in the files of writs which I have examined are issued in the name of prothonotaries or filacers. Writs of *certiorari* from the Chancery, asking for a transcript of the record of an outlawry, are returned in the name of the Chief Justice.[33] A possible explanation is that, although there was a Clerk of the Outlawries, he was considered merely a servant of the King's Attorney, representing him in the court, and not an officer in his own right.

Of the exigenters the only traces I have found are a grant of the office for Lincoln and other counties to William Jaques in 1439,[34] and in certain bundles of writs the "signature" of writs of *exigi facias* by three clerks whose names are not those of filacers or other clerks of the court.[35] The duties ascribed to the exigenters in the later attorney's books are the making out of exigents, writs of proclamation, and writs of *supersedeas,* until that duty was taken away by letters patent of James I.[36] I have not come upon their names on any but writs of *exigi facias*. Writs of proclamation were not required until 4 Henry VIII.[37]

The duties of the Clerk of the King's Silver in the seventeenth century were to enter the effect of a writ of covenant in a paper book and also in the rolls of the court, putting the shire in the margin and in the text the following: "A. S. dat Domino Regi dimidiam marcam [or more according to the value] pro licencia concordandi cum C. D. pro talibus terris in tali villa [etc.] habet chirographum per pacem admissum [etc.]." [38] The king's silver books, according to

---

31 Smith, *De Republica,* App. A.
32 App. I (i).
33 Chancery Miscellanea, County Placita.
34 *C. P. R., 1436–1441,* p. 319, Sept. 15, 1439.
35 The bundle for Trinity quindene, 2 Edward IV is particularly full of them.
36 Jacob, *Attorney's Practice,* vol. II, p. 311; Smith, *De Republica,* p. 159.
37 4 Hy. VIII., c. 4; 6 Hy. VIII., c. 4; 31 Eliz., c. 3.
38 Cowell, *Interpreter.* Cf. *Compleat Att.* (1652), p. 2; *C. P. Att.* (1648), p. 7.

Giuseppi,[39] do not begin until 3 Elizabeth, but entries in the form given above are fairly numerous in the plea rolls of the later fifteenth century, especially on the membranes of the clerk whose name is signed at the foot of membrane 21.

The only other officer whose fees are listed in the fifteenth century table of fees are the criers of the court. The duties of these officers are indicated in their title. Their fees from the parties, however, were in the nature of tips which had received official sanction. They were paid 4d. for nonsuits, 8d. for fines, and 1s. for final judgments. In addition they were allowed to take something "of Courtesye at the pleasure of the partye" for taking custody of juries and assizes while they were considering their verdict.[40] Earlier, their fees had been regulated by statutes applying to all such officers in the royal courts.[41] The office was then and apparently remained a third part of the ushership of the Exchequer which was held in chief of the king.[42] By Edward IV's time the criers had added to their official functions a service to parties in common recovery for which they were probably liberally tipped. They acted as common vouchees in these actions, and a full list of the names of those who held the office in the later part of the fifteenth century could probably be drawn up from the records of recoveries.

The Keeper of the Seal of the Common Bench is a shadowy figure who received annually £4 from the king, paid from the receipts of the hanaper. Robert de Ragenhille, who held the office from 1399 to about 1417,[43] is the only incumbent in the office who is more than a name. He was a king's clerk and seems to have been a person of some importance. He held a commission of oyer and terminer in 1401 [44] and a prebend in the cathedral church of St. Mary, Salisbury, before that time.[45] The duties of the clerk were obviously to seal all the judicial writs of the court and all other

---

39 Giuseppi, *Guide,* vol. I, p. 252.

40 App. I (l).

41 3 Ed. I (Westm. I), c. 30; 13 Ed. I (Westm. II), c. 44.

42 *C. C. R., 1333–1337*, p. 151; *C. P. R., 1354–1358*, p. 3; *C. P. R., 1367–1370*, p. 326; *C. P. R., 1370–1374*, p. 155.

43 *C. C. R., 1396–1398*, p. 358; *C. C. R., 1399–1402*, p. 24; *C. C. R., 1405–1409*, p. 8; *C. C. R., 1413–1419*, pp. 25, 172; *C. P. R., 1446–1452*, pp. 473–475.

44 *C. P. R., 1399–1401*, p. 545.

45 *C. P. R., 1405–1408*, p. 317.

documents which required the court seal.[46] He is always referred to as keeper of part of the seal of the Bench. The other half of the seal seems to have been in the keeping of the Chief Justice of the court.[47]

The clerks and attorneys of the Bench, especially the prothonotaries and filacers, acted also as Clerks of Assize. For this purpose they received commissions or patents of association with the justices.[48] John Wydeslade and William Copley, prothonotaries of the court, both had experience as Clerks of Assizes, especially Copley.[49] John Wydeslade, the younger, filacer for Devon and Dorset and other southern counties, was also Clerk of Assize in the southern circuit.[50] Richard Cok [51] and Thomas Elyot [52] both attorneys, also acted as Clerks of Assize. The office involved duties similar to those of the filacers and prothonotaries of the central court and was therefore one for which they were peculiarly well suited. For those who liked an active life service at the assizes would provide a welcome diversion from the sedentary life of Westminster and London.

By the nineteenth century the offices described here had multiplied and divided so that there were half again as many officers as existed in the fifteenth century. More than half were exercised by deputy, and in many the duties had fallen into obsolescence. Small wonder that parties complained of the multitude of fees, some paid for work no longer performed and most to officers they never saw.

---

46 Cowell, *Interpreter;* Jacob, *Law Dictionary.*
47 *C. C. R., 1435–1441,* p. 294.
48 *Y. B. Mich., 32 Hy. VI,* pl. 17.
49 *Y. B. Mich., 39 Hy. VI,* pl. 22; C. P. 40/842, m. 276d; 843, 47d, 108d.; 880, m. 310.
50 C. P. 40/842, m. 193d.
51 C. P. 40/880, m. 117d.
52 E 101/123/2.

PART III

Method of Bringing a Personal Action

CHAPTER XI

The Original Writ

THE GREAT BULK of the mediaeval plea rolls is a monumental testimonial to the litigiousness of the English people. The prosecution of a suit at law in the fifteenth century was a long and tedious business, seemingly not one which a man would undertake for frivolous reasons. And yet despite the difficulties and delays the Court of Common Pleas did not lack business.

Historians have "burked the task" of tracing through its many stages the intricate procedure in civil litigation, and they have done so with reason.[1] On the other hand, the key to many mysteries of mediaeval common law is an understanding of the steps by which an action was carried through from its beginning to its conclusion. Many Year Book discussions are hopelessly obscure without this knowledge, and the plea rolls themselves often conceal rather than reveal what happened in an action. The history of attorneyship is closely tied to the history of procedure since knowledge of its technicalities was that which gave the professional attorney ultimate advantage over the amateur who had acted on behalf of parties in the early days. Moreover, understanding of the causes of the abuses which Dickens and others decried in the early nineteenth century is impossible without some cognizance of mediaeval forms and the elaborate fictions which came to be based upon them.

This is my justification for attempting the difficult task of tracing the steps taken in bringing a personal action in the fifteenth century Court of Common Pleas. The endeavor may be rash, but it is undertaken in a spirit of humility and awareness of the probable inac-

[1] Sayles, *Select Cases in K. B.*, vol. II, p. xcvii.

curacy of some of the results. Attention is given only to procedure in personal actions because in the period under consideration the real actions were long past their prime in importance. Moreover, they were full of archaic ritual which cannot properly be understood except in its original setting. It would be both useless and confusing to attempt to discuss here the elaborate anachronisms of the ordeal of battle and the many essoins earlier allowed in the land assizes. They were not important to most fifteenth century suitors to the court and therefore need not concern us in this study.

The first step in bringing a personal action to the fifteenth century Court of Common Pleas, save in the few cases begun by bill of privilege, was to get an original writ from the Chancery. This was essential in order to give the court jurisdiction of the case. The plaintiff or his attorney went to the cursitor [2] of the proper shire and gave to that officer the necessary information for writing the writ, that is, the names, styles, and residences of the parties, the cause of the action, and the place where it arose. Great precision was required in the setting down of all these items, especially if the plaintiff proposed to resort to outlawry to get the defendant into court.[3] The cursitor then drew up a writ on a small strip of parchment eleven to twelve inches long and varying in width according to the substance of the writ, folded it, sealed it with the great seal,[4] and delivered it to the plaintiff or his attorney on payment of the proper fee. The writ was "tested" (i.e., witnessed) at Westminster, in theory by the king himself, although in fact writs returnable in the central courts were writs *de cursu*, that is, writs issued without the king's special knowledge or consent.

There were two general forms of original writ in the fifteenth century. One was the writ called *Praecipe* referred to in Magna Carta. This was the form used in real actions and in the older per-

[2] Officer in the Chancery who made out writs *de cursu*, q.v. below.

[3] For the necessity of particularity in the writ in naming of plaintiff and defendant, see *Y. B. B. Ed. IV, passim*, especially *Mich., 2 Ed. IV*, pl. 4; *Mich., 3 Ed. IV*, pls. 10, 21; *Easter, 5 Ed. IV*, pl. 13; *Easter, 4 Ed. IV*, pl. 13. In debt on obligation, it was especially important to make the writ agree with the bond, and in any action where process of outlawry was used the slightest error in the original writ or the count on the original might be sufficient cause for the reversal of the outlawry (1 Hy. V, c. 5, 1413).

[4] According to Mr. C. Hilary Jenkinson, the great seal was probably no more than barely touched to the red wax sealing the writ.

sonal actions such as debt, detinue, and account.[5] It ordered the sheriff to command the defendant to do right to the plaintiff, and, if the defendant refused and the plaintiff produced sufficient suit, to summon the former to answer before the king's justices at Westminster on a day given in the writ. The other and newer form of writ was one which allowed the defendant no alternative to coming to Westminster. It ordered the sheriff, on the plaintiff's producing sufficient suit, to attach the defendant by gage and pledge to appear in court on the day mentioned in the writ.[6] Of this type were the various writs of trespass and its derivatives: case, trover, and ejectment—all of them actions in which no sum certain or performance of a specified act could satisfy the plaintiff's claims.[7]

Both forms of originals and suits by bill of privilege as well required that the plaintiff give to the sheriff pledges of his good faith in beginning the suit. These pledges may have come to be fictitious by the fifteenth century. The names found on the dorse of writs are pairs like "R. Dere" and "W. Est," or "Ino Man" and "Johannes Robert." It is impossible without more examples to decide whether such names belonged to living beings. Names of pledges to prosecute bills seem more real but are not surely so. For example, J. Warant in suing William de la Pole in conspiracy offered as pledges John Breton and John Campyon,[8] and John Paston in his suit against Jenny gave the names of Thomas Mason and John Chaundeler.[9]

The plaintiff had to determine the venue of the action, that is, the county in which he wished to lay it, before he went to the Chancery to get his writ, for only so would he know to which cursitor's office to go. He had not much choice in the matter, since all actions were still required, in the fifteenth century, to be brought in the county where the cause of action arose, even though the defendant might be known to be dwelling in the opposite corner of England.[10]

---

[5] *H. E. L.*, vol. III, App. I, A: 1–17; B: 1–4 for examples of this type of writ.
[6] For examples, see *ibid.*, App. I, B: 5–9.
[7] Blackstone (*Commentaries*, bk. III, p. 274) calls these two forms the writ "optional" and the writ "peremptory," respectively. The second writ was more advantageous to the plaintiff because it provided for immediate attachment, while the first writ made necessary a preliminary summons.
[8] C. P. 40/659, m. 575.
[9] C. P. 40/840, m. 145d.
[10] In plea roll entries, the place mentioned in the declaration always corresponded to the marginal designation of the county.

The reason for what seems like a stupid limitation was the principle that the jurors must come from the vicinity of the place where the cause of action arose, since they were still thought of primarily as witnesses of fact rather than judges of evidence.

Debt was the first action to break away from this restriction. A statute of 6 Richard II,[11] providing that writs of debt and account "and all other such actions" not laid in their proper counties shall "utterly abate," suggests that plaintiffs were already, at that early date, trying to lay their actions in the county where they knew the defendant to be. In debt the law allowed them to do so by 15 Elizabeth [12] and probably earlier, but other actions seem to have remained local for some time to come.

Another matter of interest in trying to see clearly the progress of an action through the mediaeval Court of Common Pleas is the time allowed the plaintiff for getting his writ returned. Apparently since the Chancery was open during vacations as well as during the law terms, one might get an original at any time before the term in which one wanted it returned, always provided that sufficient time was allowed between *teste* and return day for the writ to be served. Although more time was frequently allowed, from two to three weeks seems at this time to have been the required minimum.[13] Conceivably, therefore, a very energetic attorney or party might get two successive writs returned in the same term, or possibly even three in Michaelmas term.

The final transaction in the Chancery was the payment of the

---

[11] 6 Ric. II, c. 2.

[12] *Rules, Orders, and Notices,* Mich., 15 Eliz., forbids attorneys to sue out original writs in personal actions *other than debt* anywhere but "in the proper shire where the cause of the Suit shall grow and arise."

[13] In the bundle of writs for the quindene of Michaelmas, 2 Edward V, for instance, the thirty-eight originals range in date of issue from early May to September 24. The latter date would allow just over three weeks between the issue of the writ and the end of the return day period, which would be October 20. An examination of the rolls supports the conclusion that three weeks was the usual minimum at this time. Thomas Powell's *Attourney's Academy* (London, 1623), p. 97, and other seventeenth century books mention fifteen days as the necessary minimum time. The statutes *Dies Communes in Banco* and *Dies Communes de Dote,* however, allow for the passage of as many as eight return days between the return of one writ and the return of the next, except in dower, where the time is shorter. The statutes of 43 Hy. III, c. 12, and 52 Hy. III, c. 12, on the other hand, give fifteen days as the required time between *teste* and return, in assizes of *darrein presentment* and in actions of *quare impedit,* or three weeks "according as the Place may be far or near."

fees. For the seal the charge was 6*d*.[14] For the fine paid to the Chancery clerks for their work in making out the writ the charge was 6*s*. 8*d*. where the thing demanded was of the value of £40. Above that amount the rate was roughly one two-hundredth of the value of the thing demanded: 1 mark for amounts between £40 and 100 marks; £1 for amounts between 100 and 200 marks, etc. For instance, at the foot of the face of a writ of debt for 500 marks sued out by the Deacon and Chapter of the Blessed Mary of Lincoln against John, bishop of Coventry and Litchfield and others, appears a note as follows: "pro triginta et tribus solidis et quatuor denariis solutis in hanapario." An endorsement on the back says: "per R. Kirkeham pro fine infrascripto et quia affirmauit quod clarum debitum non excedit D marcas." [15] In the hanaper accounts the same ratio prevails wherever the amount paid for the original is mentioned. In general, lump sums paid for as many as thirty originals returnable both in King's Bench and Common Pleas are the only note of fines for originals in these accounts. As in the files of writs, however, there is special mention of the cost in case of writs demanding things of high value. For instance, in the case of the writ mentioned above there is a note in the hanaper accounts as follows: "De fine facto xij die Septembris de Decano et Capitulo Lincoln' pro breui de debito habendo . . . xxxiijs.iiijd." [16]

Later law books, including Fitzherbert's *Novelle Natura Brevium*, corroborate the conclusion based on the records that where the value of the thing demanded was £40 or above, the rate was 1 to 200, but they do not tell us what the charge was where the amount demanded was less.[17] In such cases it may have been based on the nature of the writ, as in the Common Pleas offices.[18] The charge for a writ of waste in 9 Henry VI was 1*s*.; and the charge for a writ of trespass against the statute of 5 Richard II brought in 9 Henry VIII was 18*d*.[19]

The cost of the original writ was a serious handicap to the Court

[14] Wilkinson, *Chancery*, p. 60; Maxwell-Lyte, *The Great Seal*, p. 331.
[15] File of quindene of Mich., 2 Ed. IV, "Oxon."
[16] E 101/215/2, third from the last membrane.
[17] *F. N. B.*, 96; *C. P. Att.* (1648), p. 18; *Proposals* (1650), p. 1; Hale, *Discourse*, p. 360.
[18] App. I (h).
[19] E 101/514/17, 4 Hy. VI, law expenses of Hugh Dalby; E 101/518/4, 9 Hy. VIII, law expenses of Thomas Roche and others against William Fawke and others.

of Common Pleas in its struggle for business against the King's Bench, the charge for the bill of Middlesex being very much less.[20] Because of this prohibitive cost, the practice developed in the eighteenth century of getting in the first instance a writ of *capias* and waiting to sue out the original until after the verdict. As Boote says, the result of this was that suits were generally determined before they were begun.[21] The reforming spirit of the Commonwealth period in the seventeenth century had produced a proposal that the original be abolished altogether, but, perhaps owing to the opposition of King's Bench and Chancery officers, whose fees would have been threatened, nothing came of it.[22] An attorney who had attempted in 20 Henry VI the eighteenth century practice of starting an action with a *capias* was disbarred from practice in any of the king's courts.[23]

The next stage in the progress of a case through the Bench is one of some interest and of corresponding obscurity. The plaintiff, having procured his writ from the Chancery, must get it to the sheriff to have it acted upon. Mr. G. H. Fowler discovered that in the early fourteenth century Exchequer messengers were frequently employed to deliver and return to Westminster writs for both benches.[24] He does not show, however, that all writs were so delivered. The statute of Westminster II implies by its terms that the responsibility lay with the parties or their attorneys,[25] and the lawyers acting for the Pastons and Plumptons seem commonly to have sent their writs by private messengers.[26]

The problem was to find a safe method of delivery, one which insured the plaintiff against loss or embezzlement of his writ. Writs were essential records in his case, and if even one was lost he might

---

[20] Hale, *Discourse*, cap. 9.

[21] Boote, *Historical Treatise*, p. 109. Blackstone (*Commentaries*, bk. III, p. 282) explains that the plaintiff might wish to sue out the *capias* in the first instance, especially where the defendant might abscond if he had warning of the arrest. If he did abscond, the plaintiff could file his original and proceed by outlawry.

[22] *Proposals* (1650), p. 1. Poor men could get their writs free of charge (*R. P.*, vol. II, p. 170; 11 Hy. VII, c. 12).

[23] *Y. B. Trin.*, 20 Hy. *VI*, pl. 6.

[24] G. H. Fowler, *Rolls from the Office of the Sheriff of Beds and Bucks*, 1332–1334 (Beds. Hist. Soc., vol. III, 1929), pp. 3–12.

[25] 13 Ed. I, cc. 10, 39.

[26] *Paston Letters*, Nos. 102, 467; *Plumpton Cor.*, Ser. I, No. XXVIII; Ser. II, No. LXIV.

find himself seriously handicapped in carrying on his suit. The sheriff's office was apparently the chief danger spot, for his office was the place from which writs most commonly disappeared. Several statutes were enacted in attempts to remedy this evil. In the statute of Westminster II provision was made that parties should deliver their writs, original and judicial, "in the open County, or in the County where the Collection of the King's Money is," and that, to insure responsibility, they should take from the sheriff or his deputy a bill containing the particulars of the writ, sealed by the sheriff or his deputy. The abuse continued,[27] however, and in the statute of 23 Henry VI a new expedient was proposed. Every sheriff was to make annually "a Deputy in the King's Courts of his Chancery, the King's Bench, the Common Place, and in the Exchequer of Record, before that they shall return any Writs, to receive all manner of Writs and Warrants to be delivered to them. . . ."[28] The statute was carried out so far as the appointment of deputies is concerned. In the later fifteenth century appointments of deputies appear in the rolls of warrants of attorneys at the end of each plea roll. The men appointed are invariably clerks or attorneys of the court, sometimes both. The formula used in these entries suggests that the deputy not only received the writs but also broke the seal and sent into the county, not the writ itself, but some note of it.[29] Seventeenth century practice books, describing the usual method of getting a defendant arrested on a *capias*, instruct the attorney to deliver the writ to the deputy sheriff and "procure a warrant thereupon and get him arrested by the Sheriff's bailiffs."[30] In other words, the writ itself remained with the deputy sheriff in London, while a warrant or order based on it was sent to the county. It is possible that this method was already in use in the fifteenth century. John Paston on one occasion wrote that he had sent a warrant for the sheriff "to warn the persons in Flegge and Yarmouth impanelled between the king and me."[31]

[27] Stat. 4 Hy. VI, c. 1.
[28] Stat. 23 Hy. VI, c. 9.
[29] For example, in the roll of attorneys for Michaelmas, 2 Edward IV (C. P. 40/806, Atts. m. 1) is the following: "Johannes Albertson, vicecomes Bristoll', ponit in loco suo Ricardum Brugge ad recipiendum et frangendum omnia et singula breuia ac warantia ei ut viccomiti comitatus predicti directa."
[30] C. P. Att. (1648), p. 16; *Compleat Attorney* (1652), pp. 7-8.
[31] *Paston Letters*, No. 871.

A further insurance against embezzlement was provided in the method of delivery of writs "de recordo." Certain writs in the files are marked as having been so delivered, and *posteas* to entries of process on the plea roll frequently note that a writ in the case has been delivered "de recordo." Moreover, on the rolls themselves are numerous memoranda of writs delivered to deputy sheriffs in open court, each memorandum including the full tenor of the writ delivered.[32] John Bocking, attorney for John Paston, wrote to his master on June 7, 1456, that he had had "attachments granted in open court with the help of Litelton and Hewe at Fen." [33] Delivery of writs in open court in the presence of the justices (and that appears to be the meaning of "de recordo") would supply the most inescapable kind of evidence with which to hold the sheriff responsible. Not only the plea roll but also the memory of the justices would be available as a record in case the writ disappeared.

Original writs seem to have been less tempting to embezzlers than others, no doubt because they were neither very threatening not very effective. Writs of *habeas corpora juratorum, distringas juratores,* or of *exigi facias* or *supersedeas* in outlawry were the types most commonly embezzled.[34] Perhaps this accounts for the fact that originals were almost invariably returned on their proper return day, the note that the sheriff did not send the writ seldom appearing in the record. The proper return was that the defendant had been summoned "by good summoners," and on at least one occasion, where the sheriff had made a mistake in his return, the court amended it.[35] Sometimes, however, the sheriff made some sort of excuse, such as that he had delivered the writ to the bailiff of a liberty to be executed, and that the latter had not done his duty.

In the seventeenth century original writs were returned *de cursu* by the attorney in the case, except where the defendant was a free-

---

[32] Three hundred and fifty-two such memoranda appear in the roll for Mich., 22 Ed. IV, on which there are altogether 6,205 entries (C. P. 40/882). A court ordinance of 15 Eliz. requiring that sheriffs and sheriffs' deputies return all writs of common process "that shall be delivered to their hands, or of record" within the required return days indicates that the usage continued into the sixteenth century (*Rules, Orders, and Notices*).

[33] *Paston Letters,* No. 285.

[34] These were the types most commonly enrolled *de recordo* and also those most commonly mentioned in the statutes concerning embezzlement.

[35] *Y. B. Mich., 33 Hy. VI,* pl. 6.

holder of the shire. In the latter event the books instruct the attorney to deliver the writ to the undersheriff to be properly executed, for otherwise the defendant, "if he have sufficient in the same County, and a Nihil be Returned, may bring an action on the case, for disabling of him and his estate, against the Attorney for the Plaintiffs, or against the Sheriffe of the same County, that shall so disable him by returning a nihil." [36] No direct evidence of such returns *de cursu* has been found in fifteenth century rolls or files of writs. On the other hand, Sir John Paston wrote to his brother in 1476 that the undersheriff of Norfolk in Hastings' time as sheriff was ready, in order to avoid prosecution, to give a noble or a royal in amends for having returned a *nihil* against the latter. This undersheriff's behavior had obviously been irregular, but one wonders, in view of the regularity of the returns to originals as compared with other types of writs, whether the deputy sheriffs in London did not keep some sort of list of freeholders of the county in order to avoid the trouble and expense of sending the writ into the shire merely to be endorsed that the defendant had nothing in the county by which he might be summoned. It is to be remembered in this connection that, since actions were required to be brought in the county where the cause of action arose rather than where the defendant dwelt, in many cases everyone concerned knew very well that the defendant was not a freeholder nor even a resident of the county to which the original writ must be sent.

Where an original writ of the second type (called by Blackstone the writ "peremptory"),[37] directing the sheriff to take gage and pledge from the defendant for his appearance, was sent down to the county to be executed against a freeholder, the gage or *vadium* taken seems to have been real. A Year Book report proves the point. In this case the defendant, on the day of the return of the writ, was allowed an essoin and got a writ of deliverance of his goods which had been attached.[38] The sheriff refused to deliver them but sent the writ back to Westminster with a return that he had made delivery. Littleton for the defendant asked for a second writ of deliverance. This was refused on the ground that the court could not

---

[36] *C. P. Att.* (1648), pp. 14–18; cf. Powell, *Academy*, p. 94. *Compleat Att.* (1652), pp. 8–9, seems to imply that process *de cursu* was used even against men of worth.
[37] *Commentaries*, bk. III, p. 274.
[38] *Y. B. Mich., 3 Ed. IV*, pl. 14.

mistrust the word of a king's officer. Although this case shows that the gage taken by the sheriff was real, the pledges, on the other hand, bore such sets of names as the following: [39]

London

J. Inn R. Wynn Rob. Sloo Richard Roo	*or*	J. Rose Ric. Wyse Th. Sloo Wm. Roo	*or*	J. Gun R. Wyse R. Ryse J. Wyse

Yorks

G. Clyff J. Firsh Adam Sand R. Landmote	*or*	J. Hunter J. Brown Wm. Freman R. Clay

Sussex

J. Hunt J. Dyn	*or*	J. Hert R. Dyn

The sheriff of Yorkshire apparently had a more fertile imagination than the sheriffs of Sussex or London, but that these pledges were living human beings is difficult to believe. It appears from the statutes of Westminster that the safe pledges had once been as real as the gage, and that the sheriff in executing the process had taken issues from "Rents, Corn in the Grange, and all moveables, except Horse Harness, and Household Stuff" and delivered them to the sureties or pledges, from whom the defendant might redeem them provided he put in an appearance before the writ of *distringas* was issued against him.[40] In the fifteenth century the pledges being no longer real people, the goods probably remained in the sheriff's hands until they were redeemed.

Whether the writ itself or only a copy or warrant based on it was sent into the county, it must ultimately get back to the office of the Custos Brevium. The sheriff and his subordinates were responsible for seeing that it got there, and the Custos Brevium was allowed

---

[39] These names are from the plea roll of Mich., 2 Ed. IV.
[40] 3 Ed. I, c. 45; 13 Ed. I, c. 39.

to take a fee for returns which came in late.[41] The ordinance of 35 Henry VI required that he "give attendance in his Owne person or by his sufficient deputy at all convenyent times that Officers may take out writtes for proces and other necessary causes without any mony payinge therefore." [42] For purposes of practical convenience the files of writs for each return day must have remained in the hands of the filacers during the working hours of the court. The plaintiff or his attorney would therefore go to the office of the proper filacer, ask him to consult the files for the returned writ and to enter his appearance on the plea roll, and on the warrant of this entry to make out a writ of further process against the defendant.[43]

On the return of the original writ the Court of Common Pleas had official cognizance of the case. The next writ was therefore a judicial writ issued in the name of the justices of the court and sealed with their seal rather than a royal writ sealed with the great seal. If the original writ was the peremptory sort giving the defendant no alternative to appearing, as in trespass and its derivatives, the next writ was one of *capias* or *distringas*. If, on the other hand, the original was the optional type ordering the defendant either to give satisfaction or to appear, the next step was an attachment. This was like the original writ in trespass. The advantage,

[41] App. I (f).

[42] *Ibid.*

[43] The principle that the entry on the plea roll was the warrant for the issue of the writ is made clear in the *postea* in Beauchamp v. Fadyr (C. P. 40/806, m. 162d). The record says that the sheriff returned a writ of *exigi facias* with the endorsement that the defendant had been exacted and did not come and had therefore been outlawed. This writ was filed. The defendant, in attempting to reverse the outlawry, asked that "the roll which should warrant this writ be seen and examined by the court." It was examined and the justices found that the process in the case had been discontinued from Easter to Michaelmas, 3 Edward IV. The outlawry was therefore quashed. In the file of writs examined almost every writ bears in the lower right-hand corner a reference to the plea roll entry which was warrant for its issue. The infrequent errors in the numbers probably occurred because the numbering of the membranes was sometimes changed at the time when they were bound together after the end of term. They were numbered once when they were distributed to the clerks and again when they were returned to the clerk of the essoins at the end of term. The suggestion has been made that the filacer made his entries from the files of writs at the end of term. If this were true, there would be a correspondence between the order of the writs in the files and the order to the entries on the plea roll. There is no such correspondence. An ordinance of Mich., 15 Eliz. (*Rules, Orders, and Notices*) implies that attorneys had tried to get clerks to continue their cases automatically. This was forbidden. Powell warns attorneys to see to their continuations themselves if they do not wish the proceedings to be quashed (*Academy*, pp. 99–100).

therefore, of process in trespass was that it omitted one step which had to be taken in the older forms of action. If the defendant did not appear in response either to the original or to the first writ of *capias* or *distringas* (and he seldom did), getting him into court was usually a long and difficult business. The measures which the plaintiff had to take under such circumstances are better left therefore for discussion in another chapter.

CHAPTER XII

Mesne Process

MESNE PROCESS, the name given to all writs and returns between the original and the defendant's appearance, was the longest and most exhausting part of an action in a fifteenth century court of law. The laying of actions in the county where the cause of action arose, rather than where the defendant resided or had lands and chattels, was only one of the many obstacles to the plaintiff's success in making the defendant come to court to answer his complaint. The wonder is, considering the obstructions, the many delays, the tedious procedure, even where no extraordinary hurdles had to be surmounted, and the considerable expense of writs, attorneys' fees, and so forth, that anyone ever had the courage to go to law in a mediaeval court except for large debts, extensive lands, or chattels of great value. Either attorneys were persuasive salesmen of the law, or men were willing to pay much to gratify litigious proclivities.

There were two main types of mesne process. They were process by distraint and process by arrest and, if necessary, outlawry. Process by distraint was the older of the two and was associated by later writers with the personal actions of debt, covenant, and account, while process by arrest and outlawry is associated with the newer action of trespass and is supposed to have been allowed in the older actions only by statute.[1] There is little doubt that *capias*

---

[1] *Co. Litt.*, 128b; Blackstone, *Commentaries*, bk. III, p. 281; Hale, *Discourse*, p. 359; *H. E. L.*, vol. III, p. 626. Coke says that a statute was necessary to make it possible to use the *capias* process in "Account, Debt, Detinue, Annuity, Covenant, *Action sur le statute de 5 Richard II, Action sur la case,* and in divers other common or civil actions." Blackstone assumes that only *capias* would issue in trespass except against those

process came in with the action of trespass. What is not certain is that it was not extended to other actions before such extension was officially authorized by act of parliament. The statutes on this subject which were effective during the period of this study are those of Marlborough and Westminster II [2] authorizing the use of *capias* and outlawry in account; of 25 Edward III, stat. 5,[3] making it available in debt, detinue, and replevin; and of 34 Edward III,[4] extending it to breaches of the Statute of Laborers. A statute of 19 Henry VII, c. 9, authorized it in case, in which its use had been forbidden by 18 Edward III, statute 2, c. 5.

Oddly enough the fifteenth century plea rolls are full of instances of the use of *capias* in actions on the case and in other actions not mentioned in these statutes. The Michaelmas, 2 Edward IV plea roll, for instance, shows *capias* and outlawry writs being issued not only in trespass *vi et armis,* account, debt-detinue, replevin, and breaches of the ordinance of laborers, but also in waste, case, covenant, all breaches of statutes, and refusal to do services attached to land. Perhaps, as often in the middle ages, administrative practice was a leap or two ahead of statute law.

Of course, certain persons were privileged to be free from arrest. Members of the nobility and members of parliament were exempt.[5] Process against them must be by distress infinite. Officers of the court were sued by bill,[6] in which case no process was issued against them because they were assumed to be present in the court. Persons attending court as parties to suits were likewise privileged from arrest,[7] as were members of convocation and clergymen performing divine service, in distinction to those lurking fraudulently in churches to avoid arrest.[8] Certain places also carried privilege from arrest: churches, the king's presence, the verge of his royal palace, and the place where the king's justices were sitting.[9]

privileged from arrest. Hale says that process by *capias* lay originally only in trespass *vi et armis,* for the king's debts, in pleas of the crown, and for deceits or contempts in the king's courts.

[2] 52 Hy. III, c. 23; 13 Ed. I, c. 11.

[3] 25 Ed. III, stat. 5, c. 17.

[4] 34 Ed. III, c. 10.

[5] Powell, *Academy,* p. 104; Blackstone, *Commentaries,* bk. III, p. 288.

[6] This type of privilege is discussed in Ch. II.

[7] *Y. B. Easter, 4 Ed. IV,* pl. 27, fol. 15; C. P. 40/805, Trin., 2 Ed. IV, m. 39, quoted above, Ch. II.

[8] 50 Ed. III, c. 5; 1 Ric. II, c. 15; *Y. B. 6 Hy. IV,* pl. 11, fol. 2; stat. 8 Hy. VI, c. 1.

[9] Blackstone, *Commentaries,* bk. III, p. 289.

From the writs and rolls it is clear that process by arrest and out-lawry was commonly used both in the older personal actions and in trespass and its derivatives, and that distraint was used quite as often in trespass *vi et armis* as in debt-detinue.[10] The status of the defendant rather than the nature of the action seems to have been the factor which determined the process. Powell says that in his day it was the defendant's possession of freehold within the shire which determined whether distress or *capias* issued. In the plea rolls the phrase used in recording the sheriff's report that the defendant's goods have been exhausted by distraint is "nulla plura bona habet," and the next process is either *capias* or a writ of distraint into another county,[11] no mention being made of land. On the other hand, in a Year Book discussion of a return on a writ of distraint issued in an action of trespass against a prior, reporting that the defendant had nothing further by which he might be distrained, Hankford, sergeant, said, "Prior is a name of dignity, and although he *may not have land there, he may have some elsewhere.*"[12] The conclusive proof that the status of the defendant, whether based on land tenure or on some other qualification, rather than the nature of the case determined the process to be used lies in the fact that frequently in cases where action was brought against several de-fendants, *capias* process was used against some, while process by distress was used against the others.

Capias process was not inherently more effective than distraint, for it might only lead to the long-drawn-out ritual of outlawry. It was probably never thought of as a better method of getting the de-

---

[10] In the rolls of Mich., 2 Ed. IV, 2,726 of 3,204 entries of some stage of process to secure appearance are of *capias,* while only 458 are of distraint. Twenty more were begun by distraint but changed to *capias* in this term or the succeeding one because the defendant had nothing more by which he might be distrained. Even among the 458, ninety-seven were cases in which, although distraint was the process used against one or more defendants, the others were to be arrested. (On this point, see also *Y. B.* 2 *Hy. IV,* pl. 13, fol. 4.) Of the whole number of cases in which process by distraint was employed, 305 were actions of debt and 105 actions of trespass, whereas the number of debt to trespass actions among the 3,204 entries of process was 2,430 to 655.

[11] See for example C. P. 40/882, m. 46, where a writ of distraint went to the sheriff of London. He returned that the defendant had nothing in London. "Et super hoc testatus est in Curia Regis hic quod satis habet in Comitatu Warr'." Therefore a writ went to the sheriff of the latter county. In twenty entries on the Mich., 2 Ed. IV plea roll, the return "nulla plura bona habet" was made to a writ of distraint. In fifteen of them process continued by way of *capias;* in the other five "it was testified that the defendant has enough in" another county whereby he may be distrained, wherefore a writ was sent to the sheriff of that county.

[12] *Y. B. Mich., 7 Hy. IV,* pl. 7.

fendant into court. To a freeholder, the prospect of long-continued loss of small amounts in distraint would probably be quite as unpleasant as would be the prospect of arrest to a man unencumbered by worldly goods. Even where outlawry followed after process by *capias*,[13] the consequences were not so serious as might be imagined. There were a good many ways of reversing outlawry for a man who found himself inconvenienced thereby.[14] The clear advantage that process by *capias* and outlawry had over process by distraint was that it was the only way to proceed against the man who had nothing by which he could be distrained. This was the reason for its introduction with the new action of trespass in the thirteenth century and for its rapid spread with or without statutory permission to other forms of action.

All the steps in process by distraint are not completely clear.[15] When the writ reached the sheriff, he seems merely to have made an assessment of an amount sufficient in his opinion to make the defendant answer. At the time of returning the writ he took nothing either in money or goods. The amount of the distress was entered in the plea roll by the filacer, when the attorney came to see whether the defendant had entered an appearance. If the latter had not appeared, the attorney proceeded to get his next writ. At the end of the term the Clerk of the Estreats went through the roll and took out the amounts of the distresses with the names of the parties and the cause of action. These amounts he delivered to the Exchequer in a roll in which were also included the fines and amercements. In the Exchequer writs of "green wax" were made out ordering the sheriff to collect the sums previously assessed.[16]

The rolls and writs do not make clear how the warning was

---

[13] See *Y. B. Hil., 8 Hy. VI*, pl. 24, for an inconclusive discussion as to whether an exigent would be allowed in detinue of charters.

[14] See below, p. 180, for reversal of outlawry. Distraint was sometimes of more effect than *capias*. For example, in *Y. B. Mich., 2 Hy. IV*, pl. 13, distraint had issued against one defendant, *capias* against others. The defendant who was distrained appeared in this term but the others had not yet come, although the first writ of *exigi facias* had gone out.

[15] Miss Marjorie Blatcher studied with some care the estreat rolls of the King's Bench. Some of the results of her study are presented in an article entitled, "Distress Infinite and the Contumacious Sheriff," which appeared in the *Bulletin of the Institute of Historical Research*, vol. XIII, (1935–1936), pp. 146–150.

[16] Stats. 3 Ed. I (Westm. I), c. 45; 13 Ed. I (Westm. II), c. 39; 42 Ed. III, c. 9; 7 Hy. IV, c. 3; *F. N. B.*, fol. 96. Cf. above, Ch. X.

given to the defendant or how the amount of the issues was assessed. The amounts of issues show a regular gradation, seemingly according to the wealth of the defendant with some possible exceptions. They range from 6d. (to be taken from the widow of Justice Passelewe) [17] to 8 marks. It is possible that the sheriff or undersheriff merely consulted a list of the freeholders of the shire with the valuations of their lands and returned an amount in some customary ratio. Whether, when the distresses were ultimately collected, they were taken, as earlier, in the form of "Rents, Corn in the Grange, and all moveables, except Horse Harness, and Houshold Stuff," [18] or in money cannot be ascertained from the materials available for this study. There is mention in the rolls of mainpernors for the payment of the issues to the king, but the names are obviously fictitious.

The entry in the record at the return of the first *distringas* was that the plaintiff appeared on the return day, the defendant did not, the sheriff reported that the defendant was distrained by a certain amount, and, finally, that the defendant was to be distrained again and the pledges were to be amerced. The marginal bringing to the attention of the Clerk of the Estreats the amount of the distress has already been mentioned. The *mia'* (for *misericordia*) which always accompanied it was by this time merely a vestigial ornament since the names of the mainpernors were fictitious.

Process by distress continued until the goods of the defendant were exhausted. Then, if the plaintiff's patience were not also exhausted, he might resort to process by arrest. According to a note in the *Year Book* for Michaelmas, 8 Edward IV, the theory was that the latter process was necessarily from term to term, while in process by distress a term might intervene, that is to say, a writ of distress might be sued out in Michaelmas term returnable in Easter. The reason given for the difference was that, if a term were allowed to intervene in process by arrest, the defendant might have to stay too long in prison while this objection would not hold in distress.[19] The ordinary practice, as often, seems to have been different from the theory. In the Michaelmas, 2 Edward IV plea roll process by

[17] C. P. 40/806, m. 187d. There were two defendants in this case. The other was to lose two marks in issues.
[18] Stat. 13 Ed. I (Westm. II), c. 39.
[19] *Y. B. Mich.,* 8 Ed. IV, pl. 10.

distraint, like process by *capias*, is continued from term to term. In fact, many writs of distraint issued in that term were returnable in the same term, on the morrow of All Souls, or the morrow, octave, or quindene of Saint Martin.

Mr. G. H. Fowler describes a scheme of three summonses, three attachments, three distraints, and three writs of arrest as being followed, although with a good deal of irregularity, in the early fourteenth century.[20] The evidence of the fifteenth century plea rolls is that writs of summons and attachment were issued only once, after which followed either a distraint or a *capias*, *capias* being much the commoner of the two. Sometimes, it appears from the rolls, the defendant belatedly responded to the summons or attachment and appeared in court in answer to the original writ after the first writ of mesne process had gone out but before it had been served. In this case, he put in bail for his appearance on the later day.[21]

The writ of *capias* directed the sheriff to arrest the defendant and have him ready to bring into court on the day appointed. The proper return was that the sheriff had taken the defendant and was ready as required in the writ.[22] If the sheriff made this return but failed to produce him, the plaintiff got a writ of *habeas corpus* to the sheriff appointing another day. To this the proper return was fulfillment of the order. Sometimes, however, the sheriff returned that he could not bring the defendant into court because he was languishing in prison and was too ill to be moved. There are four entries of the latter type on the roll of Michaelmas, 2 Edward IV. One would be inclined to weep for the defendant and to reflect on mediaeval inhumanity were it not that the *Returna Brevium* directs the sheriff to make this return either if the defendant is ill, or if the sheriff does not wish to "go to the trouble and expense of taking him to Westminster before the justices according to the pur-

---

[20] *Sheriff's Roll of Beds and Bucks,* pp. 16–17.

[21] In five cases on the roll of Mich., 2 Ed. IV, the defendant appeared in response to the original writ after the first writ of *capias* had gone out. The main part of these entries is in the usual form, recording the appearance of the plaintiff, the failure of the defendant to appear on the day. A *postea* records the late appearance.

[22] Powell, *Academy,* p. 98. The *Returna Brevium* (ed. Redman, 1538) gives the following model for the return: "Virtute istius breuis cepi J. W. infrascriptum cuius corpus coram iusticiariis infrascriptis sic ad diem et locum interius contentos habeo paratum prout breue istud exigit et requiret," etc., or more briefly, "Infrascriptus J. W. captus est per corpus suum cuius corpus ad diem, etc. habeo paratum prout interius recepi. . . ."

174

pose of the writ." [23] Among the writs themselves there is evidence that this return was sometimes "frivolously" made.[24]

The defendant was not ordinarily kept in prison. Except for certain persons listed as exceptions in the statute of 23 Henry VI, c. 9, he was allowed to go free on giving bail. The exceptions were persons taken after outlawry in execution of final process, those taken on a surety of the peace, persons committed to ward by command of the justices, or vagabonds refusing to work, and excommunicated persons. In Elizabeth's reign, special bail, that is bail examined by the justices, in distinction from common bail which could be received by the sheriff and entered with the filacer, was required in cases where debt and damages amounted to £20 or more.[25] Whether this was true a century earlier is not apparent from the plea rolls. If the defendant did not appear after giving bail, his mainpernors were amerced. If he did appear and the plaintiff did not, he must take care to have his appearance recorded so that his mainpernors should not suffer.[26]

The usual return to a *capias* was that the defendant was not found in the sheriff's bailiwick. When this return was made, the clerk entered it in the plea roll, and a *sicut alias* or *sicut prius*

---

[23] Redman ed.: ". . . si le vic' ne voiet faire ascuns exposic' ou cottages pur luy amen' all westmestr' deuant les iustic' solonque le purpose de breue. . . ."

[24] See C. P. 40/804, Easter, 2 Ed. IV, m. 202, *Alice, Countess of Salsbury v. Danell.* The sheriff returned that he took the body of the defendant, but that the latter was languishing in prison so that he dared not move him for fear of his death. He was ordered to bring him later in the same term. This second writ was, as a precaution, delivered to the deputy sheriff *de recordo.* In the file of writs for the quindene of Michaelmas is a writ beginning, "cum nuper tibi precipimus," and reciting the previous writ. It goes on to say: ". . . since you returned to our Justices there on the day that you had taken the body of William and, although the said William was well and healthy and able to work as we have heard from trustworthy evidence, you nevertheless, permitting the same William to wander at large, further returned to our same Justices that the same William was languishing in prison, for which reason he could not be moved for fear of his death, and that therefore you could not have the body of the said William there at Westminster on the day, then delaying by your frivolous return the reply of the said William to the said writ unjustly." The sheriff is ordered to produce the defendant in Michaelmas quindene on pain of paying £20. The sheriff's reply was that his predecessor was the guilty one. This must often have been the case, since sheriffs changed office in the middle of Michaelmas term. Powell's advice to the attorney in such a case was to get a *distringas nuper vic (Academy,* p. 99).

[25] *Rules, Orders, and Notices,* Trin., 24 Eliz., sect. 1.

[26] C. P. 40/842, Easter, 12 Ed. IV, m. 1, *Upon v. Josson'* in trespass. The defendant appeared and asked "for the safety of himself and his friends" that his appearance be recorded. The court directed that this should be done.

capias was sent to the sheriff. Then followed a *sicut pluries capias.* Usually only three writs of *capias* were sent out, but there are 171 entries in the Michaelmas, 2 Edward IV plea roll (among 2,727 entries of appearances in process by *capias* and outlawry) in which, on the return of a *sicut pluries capias* with a *non inventus,* a further writ of *capias* went out.[27] These may be cases in which the attorney, for want of instructions from his master, merely continued the case to avoid the necessity of having to begin over again. Or perhaps they are cases in which the plaintiff had not yet made up his mind to begin the long process of outlawry and thought perhaps that another *capias* might by chance be the one which would bring the defendant in. Outlawry, which was the next expedient, was long and expensive and frequently ineffective.

Most plaintiffs seem nonetheless to have chosen to proceed to outlawry. For them, the next step on return of the *sicut pluries capias* was the suing out of a writ of *exigi facias.* In order to get this writ, the attorney must first have the filacer look up the returned writ of *capias* and enter the appearance on the roll. Then he must take some sort of note of the return of the writ and the entry on the plea roll to one of the exigenters,[28] whose duty it was to make out the writ of *exigi facias.* For this writ the charge was 6*d.* in all actions except trespass on the case and breaches of statute, for which twice that sum was charged.[29]

The attorney or the party must enter the warrant of attorney in the term in which the first writ of exigent issued. Two statutes of Henry VI's reign provided a penalty of 40*s.* to be taken from attorneys who failed to enter their warrants before proceeding to process of outlawry,[30] and later books are particularly insistent on this rule, although the attorneys in 1650 complained that it was a

---

[27] There are thirty-three more in which another writ of *capias* was sent out because the sheriff had not returned the previous writ. In these cases the plaintiff apparently took the trouble to have the entry made in order to avoid question that his process was continued from term to term.

[28] *Q.v.* above, Ch. X.

[29] App. I (h).

[30] 10 Hy. VI, c. 4; 18 Hy. VI, c. 9. The complaint which the statutes were intended to answer was that persons were outlawed where there was no real plaintiff, the fraudulent entry being made in the plea roll that the plaintiff "optulit se in propria persona." The statutes provide that clerks shall not receive such entries unless the plaintiff or some one of his counsel shall swear to his existence and the prosecution of the suit in his name. The clerks as well as the attorneys are to be fined 40*s.*

useless bit of red tape.[31] A comparison of the attorneys' roll for
Michaelmas, 2 Edward IV with the entries on the plea roll of the
same term which recorded the sending out of writs of *exigi facias*
shows that, for the most part, the statutes must have been obeyed,
although in a few cases the warrant must have been entered earlier
or later.[32]

Between the issue and return of the *exigi facias* there must be
time for five county courts, not to mention a little extra time at
both ends for the delivery and return of the writ. Since the county
court met only once a month, a whole term was always allowed to
intervene between the issue and return of the writ of *exigi facias*
and sometimes more than one term. If the return was that the defendant had been exacted in five county courts and had failed to
appear, the plaintiff got from the clerk of the outlawries on payment of 6d.[33] a writ of *capias utlagatum* to have the defendant arrested if he should appear publicly after the outlawry. This was not
specially entered on the roll, unless it was delivered "of record," [34]
or unless the defendant appeared and put in a plea to have the outlawry reversed. If, as seems often to have been the case, the sheriff
did not return the writ or returned that the defendant had been
exacted in one, two, three, or four county courts, but that there had
not been time for more, the plaintiff had to get another writ of
exigi facias, in the former case, a simple *de novo exigi facias,* in the
latter case, an *allocatis.* The *allocatis* was a writ which mentioned
the number of county courts at which the defendant had already
been exacted and commanded the sheriff to exact him in the number of county courts further required to make up the five. Which-
ever process was followed, a *postea* was added to the original entry
on the plea roll to record the plaintiff's appearance and the issue of
the new writ. The return day of an *allocatis* was usually in the term
following. Outlawry was theoretically more speedy in London
than in other counties because the hustings sat oftener than the
county courts.

31 Powell, *Academy,* p. 98; *C. P. Att.* (1648); Gilbert, *History and Practice of C. P.,*
p. 18; *Proposals,* pp. 6, 7.
32 See below, Ch. XIV, for reversal by error in the King's Bench for failure to enter
a warrant of attorney in process by outlawry.
33 Table of Fees, App. I.
34 See above, Ch. XI.

The defendant sometimes appeared in court and entered bail before the return of the exigent. There are nine such appearances recorded on the Michaelmas, 2 Edward IV roll. The Clerk of the Treasury was the officer to whom the defendant went to apply for his bill of bail and the writ of *supersedeas* which would warn the sheriff to discontinue proceedings on the writ of *exigi facias*. The bill of bail cost only 4*d.*, the writ of *supersedeas* 2*s.*, a very heavy charge for a single writ. The *supersedeas* was never issued, however, unless the defendant appeared in person.[35] For some reason the Clerk of the Essoins seems also to have received a fee of 2*s.* 4*d.* for every *supersedeas* upon bail.[36] According to Danby, Chief Justice of the Common Pleas, bail might be put in and the writ of *supersedeas* procured in vacation time as well as during term,[37] and even if the outlawry had been proclaimed in the county, it was annulled if the writ of *supersedeas* went out before the writ of *exigi facias* endorsed with the proclamation of outlawry had been received by the court.[38] Another way in which the defendant might forestall his outlawry was by surrendering himself to a local jail before the return of the *exigi facias*.[39]

[35] Table of Fees, App. I (g). By Trinity, 24 Elizabeth it appears that the attorney might put in bail and get the *supersedeas*. The job of making out writs of *supersedeas* and of making out bills of bail was probably given to the Clerk of the Treasury because it had to be done on the authority of the records which were in his keeping and because he was peculiarly the Chief Justice's clerk (see above, Ch. IX). Bail was a special concern of the Chief Justice.

[36] Table of Fees, App. I (k).

[37] *Y. B. Mich., 7 Hy. IV*, pl. 2. But see *ibid.*, pl. 32, in which a *supersedeas* issued from the Chancery was ineffective because, as Rickhill said, the Chancery has no knowledge of the record in the case. See also *Y. B. Easter, 7 Ed. IV*, pl. 19, which confirms the preceding case. But see *Y. BB. Mich., 4 Ed. IV*, pl. 14, and *Hil., 4 Ed. IV*, pl. 3, case in King's Bench of *Jenney v. Paston*, in which Paston on an outlawry after judgment got a writ of *supersedeas* to the justices under the Privy Seal. Markham, Chief Justice of the King's Bench, issued in obedience to the king's command a *supersedeas* to the county. Discussion followed in the Exchequer Chamber as to whether the *supersedeas* was good. It was finally agreed that it was, after the prothonotaries of the Common Pleas had affirmed "that it was the common course for such a writ of *supersedeas* to issue for the vexation and trouble of the party."

[38] *Y. B. Hil., 4 Ed. IV*, pl. 3, fol. 41 ff., *Jenney v. Paston* quoted above.

[39] In the roll of Mich., 2 Ed. IV, there are five such cases in addition to the nine in which appearance was made at Westminster. In four of the five cases, the defendant was too infirm to go to court, at least so the sheriff said. In the other case, the sheriffs confessed that they did not have the defendant ready and were amerced 26*s.* 8*d.* The entries in these cases are not in the usual form noting the plaintiff's appearance, but in the form of memoranda of orders to the sheriff beginning, "Preceptum fuit vicecomiti," and concluding with a record of the issue of a writ of *habeas corpus* to the

If the defendant did not appear, enter bail, and get his writ of *supersedeas,* the plaintiff sued out against him a *capias utlagatum* from the Clerk of the Outlawries, for which he paid 6*d.*[40] Presumably this clerk consulted the files for the returned writ of *exigi facias* and entered the plaintiff's appearance on the rolls. Frequently, also, such writs were entered *de recordo* on the plea roll as an insurance against embezzlement. The *capias utlagatum* ordered the arrest of the defendant if he appeared publicly after the sheriff had received the writ. By later statutes,[41] whenever outlawry was effected in a county other than the one in which the defendant resided, proclamation was also to be made in the defendant's county.[42] This was a remedy devised for the circumstances, which earlier must have been fairly common, that a defendant did not even know that he had been outlawed,[43] a consequence, of course, of the requirement that the plaintiff's original writ must be directed not to the county where he knew the defendant to be, but to the county where the cause of action arose.

The consequences of outlawry were forfeiture of goods to the king and loss of the protection of the law. That goods were actually taken when there were any in the county where the action lay is proved by statutes of the later fourteenth and early fifteenth centuries providing for persons whose goods have been taken erroneously.[44] That it must have been an inconvenience to some people is evident from a statute allowing sick persons to get reversal of outlawry by attorney,[45] and from another making similar provision for persons out of the country on the king's service.[46] There are only three cases in the Michaelmas, 2 Edward IV roll in which, so far as the record goes, the defendant did not appear after the outlawry and secure a reversal. Even in these cases he may have come a number of years later and have got a pardon which he did not take the trouble to

sheriff. No entries which I have seen appear to accord with Danby's description of appearances during the vacation.

40 Table of Fees, App. I.
41 4 Hy. VIII, c. 4; 6 Hy. VIII, c. 4; 31 Eliz., c. 3.
42 The proclamation was to be returned on the same day as the *exigi facias.*
43 See *Y. B. Mich.,* 7 *Hy. IV,* pl. 6, for such a case.
44 37 Ed. III, c. 2; 9 Hy. VI, c. 4. See also *Y. B. Mich.,* 7 *Hy. VI,* pl. 27, in which counsel requests a writ for return of goods.
45 7 Hy. IV, c. 13.
46 2 Hy. VI, c. 11.

have recorded as a *postea* to the original entry in the plea roll. There were a good many ways of reversing an outlawry in the fifteenth century and even more by the seventeenth.[47] The commonest method at the later date was by a writ of error in the Common Pleas itself on the ground of some mistake in the return of the exigent, in the proclamation, or of failure to file the proclamation with the Custos Brevium, of failure to return a writ of *capias,* or of a mistake in such a writ. The attorney for the defendant was instructed to search with the Custos Brevium for such errors. There were at least four methods of reversal in use in the fifteenth century, the most common being reversal by pardon.[48]

To secure pardon the defendant must surrender himself to the Warden of the Fleet, and get a certification from him to the Chancellor [49] and a certificate of the record of the outlawry from the Keeper of the Treasury. On the basis of these he got a pardon, which cost 16*s.* 4*d.*, paid the Clerk of the Hanaper.[50] For the certificate of the record of the outlawry he paid 2*s.* 1*d.* to the Clerk of the Treasury; to the Warden of the Fleet he paid 2*s.* 4*d.* and "for his favour xxd.," and to the Clerk of the Treasury 6*d.* for a *scire facias* to warn the plaintiff to appear, and 4*d.* for a bill of bail.[51] The pardon he proffered in the court.

Another method of reversal was to appear in court in person and challenge the outlawry on the ground of misnomer in the writ.[52] There are thirteen entries of such challenges in the roll of Michaelmas, 2 Edward IV as against twenty-two reversals by pardon. The defendant had to enter bail, as in other appearances on *capias* and outlawry procedure, and to get a *scire facias* to warn the plaintiff.

---

[47] See Powell, *Academy,* pp. 110–111, and *C. P. Att.* (1648), pp. 25–32 for discussions of seventeenth century methods.

[48] Twenty-two examples in Mich., 2 Ed. IV.

[49] Stat. 5 Ed. III, c. 12.

[50] *Accts. Various* E/101/217/8, Particulars of Accounts of J. Elryngton, Clerk of the Hanaper. He distinguished two types of pardon, those of special grace and those of common grace. The same sum was paid for both. Common Pleas pardons of outlawry were probably of common grace.

[51] Table of Fees, App. I (g).

[52] Stat. 1 Hy. V, c. 5, 1413, requires that additions shall be made of the "estate or Degree, or Mystery, and of the Towns or Hamelets, of Places and Counties, of which they were or be, or in which the Defendants be or were conversant," in original writs, appeals, or indictments in which the exigent is awarded. If such additions are not made, the writ or indictment or appeal abates on exception of the party.

Sometimes the plaintiff appeared and defended the writ, sometimes he did not come. In the latter case, the king's attorney defended the writ, the king's interest in the outlaw's goods being at stake. Issue was joined on the misnomer, and the case went to trial in the county in which the fact at issue was likely to be known, before a jury of the neighborhood.[53] Of the thirteen entries of challenge on the Michaelmas, 2 Edward IV roll, six have *posteas* recording a successful reversal. In the seven others the entry does not get beyond the *scire facias* to the plaintiff. It would be impossible to tell without laboriously going through the plea rolls in many subsequent terms whether anything further happened in each of these cases.

A third method of reversal was by error into the King's Bench. By this method some error in the procedure, such as a failure to put in a warrant of attorney, was alleged. A *certiorari* was issued to the Chief Justice of the Common Pleas to return the record into the King's Bench.[54] The Clerk of the Treasury found the record in the rolls in his keeping and made a copy thereof, for which he was paid 12s. 1d.[55]

A final method of reversal of which one example may be found in the Michaelmas, 2 Edward IV roll seems to have been the ancestor of that commonly used in the seventeenth century, that is, reversal by error in the Common Pleas itself.[56] In this instance, the defendant appeared on October 30 in 3 Edward IV and entered bail for his appearance on the return day, that is, the morrow of St. Martin's Day. On that day he appeared and challenged the outlawry on the ground that process in the case had been discontinued from

[53] See case in *Y. B. Easter, 5 Ed. IV*, pl. 9, in which defendant pleads in abatement of a writ of debt that he was a draper of London, not a yeoman of Middlesex. The question whether to try the case in London or Middlesex was settled by trying it in London. Cases of reversal by challenge to the writ in the plea rolls frequently show that the *venire facias* went to the sheriff of another county than the one in which the principal action was brought, because the question of the defendant's degree or "mystery" is a matter ascertainable in his place of residence or origin rather than in the place where he contracted a debt or committed a trespass.

[54] See K. B. 27/604, m. 23, *Master of Hospital of St. Leonard of York v. Topclyff*, for a good example of this kind of reversal. The error alleged is that the plaintiff did not enter a warrant of attorney. On the record sent by *certiorari* into the King's Bench judgment was given that outlawry be annulled "et quod predictus Robertus Topclyff ad communem legem regni Anglie et ad omnia que ipse occasione predicta amisit restituatur etc. Et quod ipse eat inde sine die," etc.

[55] Table of Fees, App. I (g).

[56] C. P. 40/806, Mich., 2 Ed. IV, m. 162d., *Beauchamp v. Fadyr*.

181

Easter month to the morrow of St. Martin's Day. This was found to be true on examination of the rolls, and he was therefore quit of the outlawry.

Selection of the best method of reversal would depend on the facts of each separate case. The last one was probably the least expensive and for that reason became the most common as time went on. It was possible, however, only where the plaintiff or his attorney had made some error. Perhaps fifteenth century attorneys were more careful to guard against error than later clerks. Perhaps we have merely not yet arrived at the point when outlawry was looked upon only as a method, somewhat clumsy but sometimes necessary, of getting the defendant into court and nothing more. In the fifteenth century there seems to have been some idea of making the defendant suffer for his contumacy in not appearing. Pardon and error into the King's Bench must have been the most expensive method of reversal. Pleading in abatement of the writ was possible only where there was some misnomer within the provisions of the statute. It is called "a troublesome and chargeable way" by the author of *The Common Pleas Attorney;* [57] and the clerk is instructed to look into the book of entries to find precedents for his plea and warned that he must get the hand of the king's attorney to the pleas in the case. In the fifteenth century the clerks were no doubt familiar enough with the form of the pleading so that this method would not have been so difficult as it was later.

When the defendant put in an appearance to reverse his outlawry, he was given a day on which to answer the plaintiff in the principal action. At the least, this process by arrest and outlawry would have taken a year and a half,[58] even where the defendant had resorted to no special tricks to delay the process. Process by distraint varied in length according to how long it took to exhaust the defendant's goods or to wear down his resistance. At best the plaintiff might hope for success after the first distress, a matter of a few weeks; at worst he might have to resort to *capias* and outlawry after the goods had been exhausted—a matter of years.

The advice of seventeenth century experts to attorneys in their

[57] Page 29.
[58] The sequence of writs and returns described by Reeves, *H. E. L.,* vol. I, pp. 499–500, must have been given up before the fifteenth century.

time was to take the first writ of *capias* to the deputy sheriff of the county, get a warrant issued on it, and get the defendant arrested immediately. If the defendant resided in a foreign county, they were advised to get a *testatum capias* into the second county.[59] This was, of course, in the time when the original writ was returned by the attorney himself *de cursu* so that the defendant could have no warning before the arrest and would therefore have no opportunity to abscond.[60] To a fifteenth century attorney such advice would seem unduly lighthearted. He could not return his original *de cursu* and so could not avoid giving the defendant warning of arrest. Even a *testatum capias* into another county might prove a useless expense. In seven out of sixteen cases where a *testatum capias* had been issued returnable in Michaelmas, 2 Edward IV, the plaintiff had to ask for another *capias* addressed to the original county. In the nine other cases we are not told in this term's record whether the *testatum capias* was successful.

Entries of mesne process take up the greater part of space in the plea rolls. For example in the roll for Michaelmas, 2 Edward IV, about 3,650 out of 4,000 are such entries; in Michaelmas, 22 Edward IV, the number is about 5,100 out of 6,000. It does not necessarily follow from these figures that plaintiffs were generally unsuccessful in getting satisfaction. In private papers, such as the *Paston Letters*, there are frequent references to settlements out of court. Often, especially where the ultimate outcome was more or less certain as in debt on a written obligation, the defendant may have given the plaintiff satisfaction in order to avoid further vexation. There is no way of telling from the plea roll how many cases were so settled.

[59] *C. P. Att.* (1648), pp. 16, 19; *Compleat Att.* (1652), pp. 7–8, 10.
[60] This is Blackstone's explanation of why the original writ came to be omitted (*Commentaries,* bk. III, p. 282). It seems a good one.

CHAPTER XIII

Pleading

THE PERSISTENT PLAINTIFF who had succeeded in getting the defendant into court must next enter his declaration, and the defendant must answer it within a limited time set by the court.[1] This was the beginning of the pleadings. Depending on the circumstances the defendant had three main choices of answer. He could admit the cause of action; he could ask leave to imparl or talk the matter over until a later day; or he could enter a plea. If he chose the first course, he had not only to satisfy the plaintiff but also to pay a fine to the king for not appearing in response to the original writ. If he chose the second course, he was usually given a day in the following term. If he chose the third, he had three further decisions to make: he could plead in abatement of the writ; he could admit the facts and deny that they gave the plaintiff legal cause for action; or he could deny some or all of the facts alleged and so proceed to an issue of fact. Issues of law were uncommon in the fifteenth century. More often than not, the defendant or his attorney was not ready with his plea and had to ask leave to imparl.[2]

Probably many imparlances are accounted for by the difficulties of communication in mediaeval times. It took time for the de-

---

[1] Powell (*Academy*, p. 100) says that the plaintiff must declare within four days after reversal of outlawry and the defendant must answer within nine. I do not know what the fifteenth century rule was.

[2] In the roll for Mich., 2 Ed. IV, one defendant admitted the cause of action, two demurred in law, forty-nine pleaded to issue, and ninety-six asked for leave to imparl. In Mich., 22 Ed. IV, seventeen defendants admitted the plaintiff's cause of action, either on the day in court or later at the assizes. Attorneys were required to enter their warrants of attorneyship in the term of plea or imparlance or earlier (App. I [d]). The rolls show that the ordinance was normally observed.

fendant's attorney to consult with his master concerning his plea and to engage counsel and consult with them, referring their opinions back to his master. The Paston and Plumpton correspondence is full of such long-distance consultation. Entries of *non sum informatus* by attorneys after license to imparl had been granted in an earlier term suggest the same sort of difficulties.[3] Another possibility is that imparlances sometimes led to settlements out of court. John Paston on one occasion wrote concerning an adversary to Sir John in London: "I pray you let Whetley or somebody speak with him, and let him know that if he sues me softly this term, that he shall be payed or the next term be at an end." [4] Blackstone says, perhaps with his tongue in his cheek, that the practice of granting imparlances is supposed to have been adopted originally in accordance with the precept of the gospel "Agree with thine adversary quickly, whilst thou art in the way with him." [5] Since the plea roll does not record settlements out of court, there is no means of knowing how many cases were disposed of in this fashion. Some imparlances may have been vexatious, that is, merely to cause delay. In the majority of cases, however, imparlance was only for a term or two, and there is no justification for assuming without further proof that there was any abuse involved.

Ultimately the defendant must either plead or settle out of court. Pleading had been an elaborate ritual in the earlier middle ages. The most esoteric mysteries of it were understood only by experienced sergeants and justices. Whereas a party might conceivably prosecute his own case rather than employ an attorney to get for him his writs of process, for pleading he must employ a professional lawyer. Already in the fifteenth century, sergeants and justices seem to have begun to lose some of their interest in the ritual. By Edward IV's time pleading was often by exchange of papers between the parties, and the prothonotaries appear to have begun to supersede the ser-

---

[3] For examples, see C. P. 40/843, mm. 114, 130, 424. Five of the ninety-six entries of imparlances in Mich., 2 Ed. IV have a *postea* recording the later default of the defendant and a judgment for the plaintiff. In most cases there is no continuation and presumably a new entry was made when the defendant pleaded to issue or else the case was dropped. Cf. *Y. BB. Easter, 30 Hy. VI*, pl. 3, and *Mich., 32 Hy. VI*, pl. 1, where counsel imparls after pleading unacceptable pleas. Powell advises the attorney to enter an imparlance if he has no instructions (pp. 117–118).

[4] *Paston Letters*, No. 841.

[5] *Commentaries*, bk. III, p. 298.

geants as high priests of the mystery.[6] Sergeants were probably beginning to take their modern interest in trial, in the presentation of evidence to juries rather than in the formalities of pleading; but of this, no indication appears in the rolls of the court.

Chief Justice Hale referred to the period before 1500 as the "golden age of pleading," since, instead of being set down in paper books exchanged between the attorneys, pleadings were still settled by public battle in the court before the justices. He deplored the departed days of oral exchanges, which, he says, prevented the deceits, subtleties, and complexities which later became the rule. The degeneration, he says, began in the reign of Henry VI.[7] Just how fast and how far the degeneration progressed in the fifteenth century is hard to discover. The Year Books, which are case books of the science of pleading, last well into the sixteenth century. Professor Holdsworth found evidence in them of the introduction of paper pleadings at least as early as 38 Henry VI.[8] The combined evidence of Year Books, plea rolls, and the Exchequer list of fees, without much doubt a fifteenth century document,[9] is that by the reign of Edward IV exchange of paper books was rapidly becoming the customary method of pleading.

Professor Holdsworth discussed very fully the case in the Year Book of Easter, 38 Henry VI [10] in which the tenant in a writ of formedon asked his counsel to plead matter which they considered so suspect that they refused to put it forward on his behalf. The tenant then went to Cumberford, prothonotary, and asked him to make a paper of the matter, which he did. With the paper the tenant went to Choke, one of the sergeants, and asked him to put it before the court. Choke did so but refused to look at it or to take any responsibility for it. The paper was put in the hands of Copley, prothonotary, the clerk who had entered the declaration and earlier pleading. Reference to the plea roll shows that Copley entered the

---

[6] Several instances of consultation of the prothonotaries concerning the form of pleadings are cited in Ch. VIII above.

[7] Hale, *H. E. L.*, pp. 174–177; cf. *Co. Litt.*, 304b. For evidence that pleadings were sometimes put into writing even as early as the end of the thirteenth century, see Sayles, *Select Cases in K. B.*, vol. II, pp. ci–cii.

[8] *H. E. L.*, vol. III, pp. 642 ff.

[9] See App. I for discussion of probable date.

[10] *Y. B. Easter, 38 Hy. VI,* pl. 13.

suspicious matter like any other plea with no indication that the sergeants had refused to take notice of it.[11]

There are other references to "papers" in the Year Books, three of which may be quoted here. One is a report of a case of trespass in Easter, 2 Edward IV,[12] in which Littleton for the plaintiff, in reply to a plea in abatement on the ground that the place where the trespass was supposed to have been committed was not accurately named, said "le paper est Brampton en le Mersh." Billing for the defendant denied this and warned the court to take care that Littleton did not touch anything before the justices examined the plea. In another case from Michaelmas of the same year,[13] Littleton said "All this conveyance ought not to be entered *in the book;* for this is empty matter, because it suffices to maintain your plea in bar, as above, that at the time etc. it was your soil and free tenement *sans ceo q'* the defendant disseised the plaintiff." Billing for the defendant on advice of Danby, Justice, asked Littleton to agree to allow him to change the plea in the book. Littleton refused, and Billing was forced to "pray that all be entered in the book." In a third instance, a brief note in the Year Book of Easter, 21 Edward IV, in a case of debt, Copley, clerk, said: "Your paper is false because the plaintiff shows only one day of payment." [14]

Seventeenth century practice books refer to the pleadings either as "paper books" or "papers." At that time, apparently, the attorneys themselves drew up the paper pleadings when they were in the common form. Special pleas, however, must be "pleaded under the hand of one of the sergeants at law," that is, they must be signed by a sergeant. Furthermore, the plaintiff's attorney is warned to have the prothonotary of the office examine the "issue drawne into a Paper before he carries it to his sergeant" in order that the prothonotary may see whether it is well pleaded.[15]

The distinction between pleas in the common form and special pleas for which a sergeant must be responsible is also made in the Exchequer list of fees. The implication of this document is, how-

[11] *C. P.* 40/797, m. 273, Copley.

[12] *Y. B. Easter, 2 Ed. IV*, pl. 23, fol. 10.

[13] *Y. B. Mich., 2 Ed. IV*, pl. 3, fol. 14.

[14] *Y. B. Easter, 21 Ed. IV*, pl. 18, fol. 6.

[15] Powell, *Academy,* pp. 114–117; *C. P. Att.* (1648), pp. 50 ff.

ever, that at this earlier date filacers and prothonotaries, rather than attorneys, drew up both the pleas in the common form and the special pleas, and that their clerks made the paper copies of the pleadings which were exchanged between the parties. It lists the following fees of the prothonotaries for entries of pleas and judgments: "Inprimis for euerye comyn declaracion, comen' plea in barr; comen' replicacion and comen' reioynder in pleas personall, whether the Defend' appeare in proper person' or by Attorney, xijd. . . . And in euerye plea personall pleded by a Seriaunt ijs."

In the list of fees of "Clerkes of Prothonotaries & Philizers" is the following: "Item 5, for drawinge & makinge euerye paper leafe vppon' pleadings to be taken' of the playntiffe & the defendaunte of euerye of them after the rate of his owne pleadinge viijd." [16]

The introduction of paper pleadings did not mean that the prothonotary no longer made memoranda in court during the discussion at the bar. In the *Long Quinto* we find Littleton directly addressing Cumberford, one of the prothonotaries, and instructing him concerning the "titeling" or abstract of his plea.[17]

This fifteenth century evidence, meager and scattered though it is, makes possible a tentative description of the two methods of pleading in use at that time. Where the pleadings were in the common form, and where, therefore, no discussion at the bar was necessary, the plaintiff or his attorney went to the office of the prothonotary and entered his declaration. The defendant or his attorney within a certain time fixed by rule of the court also went to the office of the prothonotary, got a paper copy of the declaration, paid the usual fee for it, and put in his reply. Where the pleading was special, on the other hand, and must be presented before the justices at Westminster, papers were, at least sometimes, also exchanged, but merely for the convenience of the sergeants. Nothing was entered on the plea roll until after the matter had been argued

[16] Table of Fees, Appendix I (e). Holdsworth in *H.E.L.*, vol. III, p. 646, misquoted a seventeenth century printed version of this document (*Praxis Utriusque Banci* [London, 1674], p. 28) which unfortunately already contains an error, that is, xiis., iid., for the first item in the fees of prothonotaries. The Exchequer version is without doubt the correct one because charges seem for the most part to have been quantitative. A plea pleaded by a sergeant, being a special plea, would as a rule be longer, and might have to be amended in court. Pleas in the common form could be entered from a memorandum left by the parties with the help of a precedent book.

[17] *Long Quinto*, fol. 35.

in court. Afterwards the prothonotary made the entry, using as materials for it the abstract he had jotted down in court and the paper book turned over to him by counsel at the conclusion of the pleadings.[18]

This is substantially the picture of methods of pleading which can be reconstructed from the docket, remembrance, and plea rolls of the sixteenth century. For example, in the remembrance roll for Easter, 15–16 Henry VIII,[19] of John Jenour, prothonotary, on the second membrane of "Bills of pleas," there are entries as follows:

Wigorn'	ff	nisi def' inferat papirum aduersus Rice versus Agborough mercurij post leuacione Curie fiat breue de dampno
Suff'	ff	nisi def. inferat papirum ad' Reppes versus Bowes et al' ad mercurij post leuacione Curie fiat breue
Devon'	ff	nisi def. inferant papirum aduersus Comitisse Deuon' in curij [*sic*] post leuacione Curie fiat breue vjs. Epi' x s.
Norff'	ff	nisi Cosyn' inferat papirum aduersus Bokkyng et al' in curij post leuacione Curie fiat breue de dampnis

The corresponding entries on the docket roll giving the references to the plea roll are as follows:

Caldwell pro Ryce; Cokesey pro Agborough; reiondr' in trans' j ro' 533
Knyghtley pro Reppes; Sherman pro Bowes et al; plm' iij ro' et di' 439
Bonysaunt pro Comitissa Devon'; Ford pro Epo' Winton'; plm' in quare impedit 1 ro' 431
Knyghtley pro Bokkyng, Grote pro Cosyn; plm' ij ro' et pl 435 [20]

It seems from the docket and plea rolls that in each one of these cases the defendant brought in his paper, and the entry was subsequently made on the plea roll. The entries on the plea roll appear on the membranes as indicated in the docket roll,[21] and the pleas are as reported in abbreviated form in the docket (in the first case, an entry of trespass with the defendant's plea and rejoinder).

[18] Cf. *H. E. L.*, vol. III, pp. 643–646, and Reeves, *H. E. L.*, vol. II, pp. 621–622.
[19] C. P. 45/1, Easter, 15–16 Hy. VIII to Hil., 16 Hy. VIII, Bill of pleas, m. B.
[20] C. P. 40, Index 4, Docket rolls of J. Jenour, Easter, 12–13 Hy. VIII—Hil., 16 Hy. VIII.
[21] C. P. 40/1043, Easter, 15–16 Hy. VIII.

Other entries in the "Bills of pleas" in the prothonotary's remembrance are obviously memoranda from which pleas would later be entered on the roll. Similar memoranda are jotted down at the tops of Wydeslade's membranes of the Hilary, 1 Edward IV plea roll.[22] The late Isobel Thornley found evidence that the customary method of making memoranda of pleadings in court in Richard II's reign was to jot them down at the heads of the membranes, which were later pared off when the roll was bound up.[23] Probably the later fifteenth century practice was a transitional stage between this method and the sixteenth century procedure of drawing up special remembrance rolls. Wydeslade followed the practice described by Thornley, at least in the Hilary, 1 Edward IV roll, but other clerks, and even Wydeslade at other times, may have used special remembrance rolls which have not survived because it did not occur to anyone until the reign of Henry VIII that they should be preserved as records of the court. The series even after 15–16 Henry VIII is very irregular, and only the rolls of the second prothonotary, the appointee of the Custos Brevium, have survived with any completeness. Parchment was scarce and expensive. It is possible that earlier remembrance rolls were erased and used over again.

If a great deal of the pleading was already done by exchange of papers, it is easier to understand how so much business could have been got through in one term. In Michaelmas, 22 Edward IV nearly 700 cases were either pleaded to issue or were imparled after declaration. It seems unlikely that the justices could have heard the pleadings in all these cases in the seven weeks of Michaelmas term in addition to all the other business they had to deal with. Perhaps for the very reason that the court was so overloaded with business throughout the fourteenth and fifteenth centuries, the practice arose of pleading in writing where no particular point of difficulty needed the justices' consideration.

The prothonotaries were expected to enter the pleadings during the term or within a few days of its conclusion. An ordinance of 23 Henry VII [24] requiring that the membranes of the roll be in the

---

22 C. P. 40/803, Hil., 1 Ed. IV. See, for instance, mm. 108, 109, 113, 308, 313. Wydeslade was at this time first prothonotary.

23 *Y. B. 11 Ric. II* (Ames Foundation, Year Books Series, vol. V), pp. xxxiii–xxxviii.

24 App. II (d).

hands of the Clerk of the Estreats within seven or eight days of the last day of term suggests that there was some carelessness on the part of the clerks in making up their membranes of the roll. There is no question, however, that the entries were from term to term in the fifteenth century. Powell says that this was still true in his time of the Court of Common Pleas, although the King's Bench practice was otherwise.[25] The prothonotaries themselves testified in court in 5 Edward IV that the "entry is after the declaration."[26] A report from the Year Book of 4 Edward IV is incomprehensible unless the entry of pleading was from term to term. The case is one of debt in which the defendant had license to imparl to Easter. On the day in Easter term Littleton for the defendant demanded judgment of the count, "because in the roll of the court, no place is shown where the deed was made, etc." The justices consulted the Hilary roll and found a "windowe" where the name of the place should have been. Yonge for the plaintiff said that this must have been a mistake of the clerk, because he gave the name to the prothonotary when he delivered the obligation to him with the "box" (fee). He asked that the mistake be amended. Littleton protested against amendment on the ground that the declaration was of the previous term, and that the amendment should have been made then.[27] There seems little point to this argument or to the whole series of statutes of *jeofails,* which allowed parties to amend their pleas as soon as mistakes were discovered,[28] if the formal entry on the plea roll was not made in the term in which the case was pleaded.

Study of the rolls in connection with such writs as are available, therefore, fails to support Hubert Hall's hypothesis that the entry of pleadings was made after verdict and judgment, from memoranda on the dorse of the writ, sometimes after the passage of many years.[29] Most of the writs in the files are writs of process to get the defendant into court. These bear on the dorse only the returns of the sheriff and an occasional note of something procedural.

[25] Powell, *Academy,* pp. 103–104.

[26] *Long Quinto,* fol. 23.

[27] *Y. B. Easter, 4 Ed. IV,* pl. 23, fol. 14.

[28] 14 Ed. III, stat. 1, c. 6; 9 Hy. V, stat. 1, c. 4; 4 Hy. VI, c. 3; 8 Hy. VI, c. 12. The last three of these statutes allow amendment after judgment.

[29] *Studies in English Official Historical Documents* (Cambridge, 1908), pp. 325–326; cf. *H. E. L.,* vol. III, pp. 644 ff., and Thornley, *Y. B. 11 Ric. II* (Ames Foundation, Y. B. Series, vol. V), pp. xxxii ff.

The writs of *habeas corpora juratorum* and *distringas juratores,* however, have *schedulae* attached to them consisting of panels of jurors and sometimes also transcripts of records of the pleadings. On these are endorsed the record of trial at the assizes. A reference to the plea roll appears on the face of these transcripts, and a comparison of plea roll and transcript makes clear that the latter was made in the Common Pleas Treasury [30] and sent down to the Clerk of the Assizes. At the trial this clerk entered on the dorse the record of the proceedings there and returned it into the Bench where the endorsed matter was added on the plea roll as a *postea* to the original entry, which would often have been made a year or more earlier.[31]

Sometimes, to be sure, instead of continuing the first entry by adding the *postea,* the clerks made an entirely new entry of the case in another term. In the Year Book of Michaelmas, 39 Henry VI (pl. 43), Choke is quoted as saying:

Sir, there are two rolls: one roll in which the count and the plea and certain continuance was made and the roll which he has brought forward, which was made when the verdict was passed, in which the whole matter was entered anew in another term. And in the first roll the entry is 'qui heir il est' and, since the clerk has omitted this in the new roll, an amendment should be made because this is nothing but misprision of the clerk.

The first roll was viewed and was as Choke said. Therefore the roll was amended by advice of all the court. There are many examples of this practice of entering the whole matter in a new term in the plea rolls themselves. Sometimes the second entry is introduced "Alias prout patet" with a reference to the previous entry; probably more often, there is no mention of the previous entry.

The case of *Rither v. Sayer* illustrates admirably the way in which continuations of a case through several years might be entered in the

---

30 App. I (g).

31 For example, in a case of reversal of outlawry in process on a writ of debt (the procedure with respect to sending the record into the county for trial would be the same as in any other case), the entry of the challenge to the outlawry is in C. P. 40/805, m. 53, Mich., 1 Ed. IV. The writ of *habeas corpora juratorum* is enrolled *de recordo* (see above, Ch. X) on C. P. 40/805, m. 20, the roll for Trin., 2 Ed. IV. The returned writ and transcript are found in the bundle for the quindene of Mich., 2 Ed. IV marked *Oxon.*

plea rolls. It is a case of *formedon in the descender* in which the demandant's count was originally entered in the plea roll of Michaelmas, 27 Henry VI.[32] The tenant made no answer but asked leave to imparl to Hilary and again to Easter. The main part of the first entry stops with the note of the first request for leave to imparl, the second request being recorded in a *postea*. In Easter term the tenant answered the count, and both count and plea were entered in the Easter roll, no reference to any earlier entry in the case being noted.[33] The main part of the Easter entry ends with the sending out of the writ of *venire facias*, a long *postea* covering half the face of the membrane. The dorse records the continuations to Michaelmas, 38 Henry VI, more than ten years later. This part of the record consists mainly of notes that the jury was in respite because none of the jurors came but also relates that the tenant put in two successive royal protections. It concludes with the record of the defendant's default at the York assizes in August, 37 Henry VI, the issue in Michaelmas term of a *cape in manum domini Regis,* and a summons to the tenant to appear to hear the judgment against him.

Meanwhile, between Easter, 27 and Michaelmas, 38 Henry VI, continuations of the case had been entered from term to term by brief notes that the jury was in respite because none of the jurors came.[34] There is also the record of a subsidiary case of deceit in which the demandant accused the tenant of bringing in a fraudulent royal protection.[35]

The whole of the long *postea* to the entry in the Easter, 27 Henry VI plea roll, including the notes that the jury was in respite, was probably made when the demandant came into court in Michaelmas term, 37 Henry VI, asked the prothonotary or his clerk to search in the office of the Custos Brevium for the returned writ of *habeas corpora juratorum* and the transcript of the record with the endorsement telling of the tenant's default at the York assizes, paid the required fee for the search in the Treasury to find the earlier

[32] C. P. 40/751, m. 501.
[33] C. P. 40/753, m. 335.
[34] C. P. 40/756, m. 34; 757, m. 34; 764, m. 207; 766, m. 151d.; 769, m. 440d.; 771, m. 182d.; 772, m. 324; 774, m. 389d.; 777, m. 460d.; 779, mm. 149, 341; 780, m. 29; 782, m. 208; 787, m. 22; 793, m. 469d.
[35] C. P. 40/789, m. 460; 791, 78d.; 794, mm. 148, 210, Easter, 36 through Trin., 37 Hy. VI.

entries in the case and for the entry of the *postea*, and asked for a writ of *cape in manum domini Regis*.

In Easter, 38 Henry VI the demandant appeared to hear his judgment. The tenant, who also appeared, had entered in writing an excuse for his default so suspect that his counsel would not plead it for him.[36] This matter was apparently too long and complex to be entered as a continuation to the earlier entry of Easter, 27 Henry VI, and was therefore set down in roll of Easter, 38,[37] no reference being made to the earlier entry except the one implied in the introductory sentence which is as follows: "William Rither knight, *alias* in the King's court here sought against John Sayer. . . ." It continues with the record that the parties pleaded to issue, and that process was continued by juries in respite to Michaelmas quindene, 38 Henry VI, but that the tenant defaulted at the York assizes, that the writ of *cape in manum* was issued, and that the plaintiff came to hear his judgment. Then follows the tenant's suspicious plea and the demandant's demurrer to it. A *postea* records continuations for several terms because the justices "wish to advise," and for several years by a writ of resummons necessary because of the overthrow of Henry VI. The conclusion of the case is a marginal to the *postea* which records that it was not continued beyond the octaves of Michaelmas, 7 Edward IV. The defendant's persistence in wickedness seems to have been rewarded. For twenty years he had hedged and stalled to prevent the demandant from getting possession of the land. The record does not tell us the final outcome. It may be that by 7 Edward IV either one or both of the parties had died.

This case illustrates very well the methods of the clerks in entering pleadings and continuations of a case over a long period of years and shows conclusively that entries were made from term to term rather than after the conclusion of the case. It also does much to

---

[36] *Y. B. Easter, 38 Hy., VI*, pl. 13. The tenant pleaded that four days before the assize day, his attorney, Christopher Horbury, had come to him at Hertilpole and given him notice of the assizes to be held the following Monday at York. He and Horbury immediately set out to go to York, which, he says, was sixty leagues distant. On Friday they came to the river Tees, forty leagues from York, and found it in flood so that they were unable to get across until six o'clock Sunday evening. They then crossed in a boat and made their way to York, only to find that between nine and ten on Monday morning a default had been entered against them.

[37] C. P. 40/797, Easter, 38 Hy. VI, m. 273.

clarify the discussion of the Earl of Wiltshire's case, one which has caused much confusion about the time and method of making enrollments.

The facts in this case are as follows: [38] the Earl of Wiltshire brought an assize of novel disseisin against another. On the day before the justices of assize in the county the parties came, two of the jurors were sworn, and the rest failed to come. The matter was adjourned to the next assizes. On the later day both parties and all the jurors came, and the latter gave a verdict for the demandant. The tenant brought error on the ground that the record did not mention what had happened on the first day when the two jurors were sworn. A long discussion of the method of entering records followed. Finally Prysot, Chief Justice of the Common Pleas, called before him in the Exchequer Chamber the three prothonotaries of his court to give their opinion in the matter. Wydeslade, Cumberford, and Copley gave opinions.

Thornley's is the only earlier discussion of this case which takes notice of Sergeant Choke's remark that this is an assize which is different from an ordinary action in that both the parties and the jury appeared on the first day.[39] In an assize there was no pleading to issue and therefore no transcript of the record to be sent into the county to be endorsed with an account of the proceedings there. There was only the writ summoning the assize. The question under discussion in the Exchequer Chamber, therefore, was not whether pleadings should have been entered in the record before the assize, but whether afterwards, when the assize could not be held because the jurors (or assizors) defaulted, it was necessary for the Clerk of the Assizes to send a record of this into the central court.

Wydeslade, dean of the three prothonotaries, said that it was necessary only to make a note of the default on the dorse of the writ of summons. When the assize had actually been held, he would then make a record of it to send into the central court with the writ.[40]

---

[38] Y. B. Mich., 39 Hy. VI, pl. 22.

[39] Thornley, Y. B. 11 Ric. II, pp. xxxii ff. Cf. Hall, Studies, pp. 325–326, and H. E. L., vol. III, p. 645.

[40] This record would probably be attached to the writ as a schedula and sent with it to the central court. The formal entry in the plea roll would be a copy of this, beginning "Assisa venit recognoscere. . . ."

Cumberford's reply is interesting because he compared this case to one begun by pleadings in the Common Pleas and advocated the method of entering respites of the jury which was actually followed in the case of *Rither v. Sayer,* quoted above. He said that it was good practice to enter a brief record that the jury was in respite each time that the jurors defaulted and to make a note on the dorse of the writ. This is exactly what was done in the case of *Rither v. Sayer,* so far as one can tell from the rolls. The particular writs in this case could not be made available to the writer at the Record Office, but the writs of *habeas corpora juratorum* in the bundles examined are endorsed with such notes. Cumberford said that some of the records of assize which he had seen were like the one at hand, others were not. His opinion, although he had not been a Clerk of the Assizes, was that the correct method was to enter the record from day to day.

Copley, called on last, probably because he was the most recently appointed of the prothonotaries, said that his habit was to enter the record from day to day. The justices commended him, and after further discussion it was agreed that error should be allowed. Whether Wydeslade reformed his methods it is impossible to tell from the rolls. Copley, however, succeeded Wydeslade as first prothonotary about ten years later. This case may have been the first in which he made his mark in the eyes of the justices.

The technicalities of the mediaeval science of pleading are beyond the powers of a layman to discuss. And they are not essential to a study of the workings of the court. The elaborate ritual of plea, replication, rejoinder, and so forth, is so archaic as to hold little interest to a generation accustomed to the freer exchanges of a modern trial. It is to be remembered, however, that in the fifteenth century pleading still engaged the talents of the most highly trained men in the legal profession, and that, in the seventeenth century, so distinguished a lawyer as Sir Matthew Hale believed that the English common law had suffered a setback when oral pleadings were given up.

CHAPTER XIV

Trial, Judgment,
and Final Process

AFTER PLEADING came trial. Blackstone lists seven methods, as
follows: trial by record, by inspection or examination, by
certificate, by witnesses, by battle, by compurgators, and by jury.[1]
Although all these methods were in use in the fifteenth century,
jury trial was usual in actions in the Court of Common Pleas. Compurgation was narrowly restricted to actions in which the plaintiff
had nothing to support his action but his own word, and therefore
was not of much general use.[2]

The first step in compurgation was wager of law. The defendant
defended "the force and tort" [3] and then made a general denial.
After this, in the words of the record, he offered to prove his denial
in any way in which the court should decide. He then produced
pledges for his law, that is, "vadium" or wager that he would come
with his compurgators on the day set by the court.[4] This was the
"wager of law." On the day set, he must either appear in person or
essoin himself. If he had made his first appearance by attorney, the
latter was instructed to warn his master to come himself on the
day of the trial. It is perhaps this requirement which explains why
there are so few cases of trial by compurgation even where it was al-

[1] *Commentaries,* bk. III, p. 330.
[2] *H. E. L.,* vol. I, pp. 307–308.
[3] *Defendit vim et iniuriam.*
[4] From the few names available I could not tell whether these pledges were real
or not.

197

lowed.[5] Travel was difficult and expensive in the fifteenth century. Journeys to London from the more distant counties would not be undertaken lightly in order to avoid payment of a small debt. It may also explain a case in the Michaelmas, 22 Edward IV roll and another in Easter, 12 Edward IV, where the defendant did not appear with his compurgators on the day given, and the plaintiff recovered by default.[6] The normal outcome of this sort of trial was acquittal. Of course it is possible that in these two cases the plaintiff persuaded the defendant to settle out of court. If the defendant was on hand, there was no need to postpone the trial to the next term. He could be assigned a day to appear "to accomplish his law twelvehanded" in the same term.[7] In some ten of the twenty-eight cases from Michaelmas, 22 Edward IV, this seems to have been done.

From the plaintiff's point of view there was every disadvantage in trial by compurgation. Laicon, in a discussion held in Michaelmas term, 2 Edward IV, brought out some of these disadvantages.[8] In an action for detinue of chattels, Littleton for the defendant "rehearsed all the matter pleaded the first day and said that he wished to repudiate it all and make his law." Laicon protested that it was too late to do so since the defendant had already pleaded in bar. Danby, Chief Justice, said that he could relinquish his bar and traverse when he wished. To this Laicon agreed that he might relinquish his plea in bar of the action and plead to issue, but he would not agree to go to trial by compurgation, because, as he said, such trial would neither give the plaintiff a fair answer to his complaint, nor yet an opportunity of being nonsuited so that he might bring another action later.[9]

---

[5] Only six in Mich., 2 Ed. IV and twenty-eight in Mich., 22 Ed. IV, for example.

[6] C. P. 40/882, m. 121, *Edward v. Wynchecombe;* C. P. 40/842, m. 199d., *Hill v. Gawge* in debt on sale. In the former case, the plaintiff brought his action for arrears on account against Wynchecombe and his wife, Elizabeth, as executors of J. Smallewod. He counted that she was found to be in arrears when she was single. Husband and wife jointly waged their law and then defaulted. In the latter case the defendant, a chapman of Bury St. Edmunds, defaulted after waging his law in London.

[7] The Latin wording is "idem Iohannes perfecit inde legem suam duodecimo manus," etc.

[8] *Y. B. Mich., 2 Ed. IV,* pl. 1, fol. 14.

[9] Powell (*Academy,* p. 133) says: "But if the Plaintiffe will not abide his Oath, intending to charge him otherwise afterwards, the Plaintiffe may bee *Non suit,* pay the Defendant his Costs, and bee at libertie to begin anew againe at another time, and to

Although Laicon finally yielded and allowed the defendant to "have his law" in this particular case, the objection which he made to trial by compurgation was from a modern point of view a sound one. This form of trial was as final as trial by jury, and the plaintiff was, after judgment, precluded from bringing another suit based on the same cause of action, even although he had never received more than a general denial of his complaint, and although the only matter which was settled by this method of trial was that the compurgators believed the defendant to be a man of good faith. The possibilities of abuse of this method of trial are self-evident. It is no surprise to find that in the early seventeenth century, Powell advised attorneys that there was "an Officer here for the case of the subject, who will furnish the Defendant in this case of Wager of Law, with twelve such Compurgators as occasion shall require." [10] One of the reasons for the growth in popularity of *indebitatus assumpsit* at the expense of the older action of debt is that compurgation was not allowed in the former action, a derivative of trespass. Plaintiffs who wanted an answer to their complaints would try to avoid a method of trial which allowed the defendant merely to offer a general denial with no further explanation and no chance for discussion before the jury.

On the other hand, defendants had every reason to want to preserve compurgation as a method of trial. The preamble to a statute of 5 Henry IV [11] embodies a complaint that plaintiffs sometimes attempted to avoid trial by compurgation by falsely bringing debt on account, a form of the action in which compurgation was not allowed. An accounting by auditors was fictitiously supposed, apprentices or servants of the plaintiff acting as the alleged auditors. This, the statute says, worked an injustice on defendants who were thus deprived of their right to wage their law. The mention of the use of apprentices as fictitious auditors suggests that the fiction may have been an attempt by tradesmen to improve upon the legal

---

lay his action so (in some cases) that no Wager of Law shall lye therein." Blackstone (*Commentaries*, bk. III, p. 347), says: "Therefore one shall hardly hear at present of an action of debt brought upon a simple contract," the custom being to use trespass on the case where it was possible and a bill in equity elsewhere. There was no alternative action available in the fifteenth century.

[10] Powell, *Academy*, pp. 132–133.

[11] 5 Hy. IV, c. 8.

means available to them for recovering debts from gentlemen debtors who could all too easily escape their obligations by having their retainers act as their compurgators and swear their debts away. If the fiction really cloaked a "racket," as the tone of the preamble to the statute implies, the remedy enacted is exceedingly mild. The justices are to examine attorneys and then at their discretion to allow defendants either to wage their law or to order trial by jury.

There are several cases in the Michaelmas, 22 Edward IV plea roll of wager of law in debt on account, even where the accounting had been before auditors. In one, the defendant expressly pleads the statute, invoking its provision that the justices examine the attorneys or any others as they please in order to have the plaintiff examined on his count.[12]

The usual method of trial in the fifteenth century was by jury. The defendant, in the words of the record, "placed himself on the country," or asked that the question at issue "be inquired into by the country," and the plaintiff did likewise. The prothonotaries or their subordinates were directed to make out a writ of *venire facias* to the sheriff to impanel the jurors.

Jury trial in the fifteenth century was apparently nearly always at *nisi prius,* although the parties presumably still had the option allowed them in the statute of Westminster II except in causes "wherein small examination is required." [13] At any rate I have come upon no cases in the rolls which were tried at Westminster.[14] Trial at the assizes must have been generally more convenient. The writ of *venire facias* did not, however, summon the jurors to come to the assizes. It had been found that if this was done, the parties had no chance to see the names of the jurors and prepare their challenges.[15] The custom was, therefore, to summon the jury to appear at the next return day in the Bench. On that day the writ was returned into the Bench with the names of the men summoned for

---

12 C. P. 40/882, Mich., 22 Ed. IV, m. 409, *Eloure v. Underwode.*
13 13 Ed. I (Westm. II), c. 30.
14 Maitland and Turner, *Y. BB. 3 and 4 Ed. II* (S. S. vol. XXII), pp. xxiv–xxix; Turner, *Y. BB. 4 Ed. II* (S. S. vol. XLII), pp. lvi–lxviii. In Edward II's time, trial at Westminster was usual; after 14 Edward III, trial was always at *nisi prius* except in Middlesex cases or those of exceptional importance.
15 42 Ed. III, c. 11; *Y. B. Trin., 27 Hy. VI,* pl. 4.

the jury. An entry was made in the plea roll that the jury was in respite because none of the jurors came, and a writ of *habeas corpora juratorum* was issued. This second writ sometimes included the formula for the summons of the jurors to the assizes, i.e., that the sheriff was to have them before the justices at Westminster "or before our Justices assigned to hold the assizes at X according to the form of our statute thereto provided if they come on [date] [16] before" the return of the writ. Sometimes, depending, it is to be supposed, on the date of the assizes and the convenience of the court, the sheriff was not directed to have the jurors at the assizes until a further writ either of *habeas corpora* or of *distringas juratores* was sent out.

Gilbert, writing in the later eighteenth century, says that the "old practice" before his time was to continue the case with a *vicecomes non misit breue* until the time of trial at the assizes.[17] This kind of continuation is sometimes found in the fifteenth century plea rolls. The more common continuation, however, seems to be that the jury is in respite because none of the jurors came. Gilbert's "old practice" was perhaps adopted in response to complaints of jurors similar to those referred to in the statutes of 7 Richard II [18] and 8 Edward IV.[19] The first of these is a complaint that, because parties have juries empaneled and then do not pursue their cases but allow them to drag on from year to year, many persons so empaneled by repeated writs of *distringas juratores* lose the issues of their lands beyond what they can afford. The remedy enacted is that, after a writ of distraint has issued against them three times, they shall be able to sue out a writ of *nisi prius* themselves, thus forcing the parties to go to trial. This was cold comfort indeed. It is not surprising therefore, that complaints continued. The people of Middlesex complained again of the same evil, and in 8 Edward IV a new statute was enacted. The remedy this time was that the jurors were to be demanded on the fourth day whether the parties appeared or not, and their presence was to be recorded. More satisfactory than this from the jurors' point of view, for it would have

---

[16] The dates mentioned in the plea rolls fall into two groups, between Hilary and Easter terms and between Trinity and Michaelmas.

[17] Gilbert, *History and Practice of C. P.*, pp. 79 ff.

[18] 7 Ric. II, c. 7.

[19] 8 Ed. IV, c. 3.

relieved them of all responsibility, would have been Gilbert's remedy of an entry that the sheriff did not send the writ, and this is why it came to be the preferred practice as time went on.

In the term before the trial at the assizes the plaintiff must get his record from the Clerk of the Treasury. Probably he also asked at this time to have the *postea* summarizing the continuations by *jurata in respectum* entered on the original roll.[20] The next step was to deliver the transcript of the record to the Clerk of the Assizes. To this clerk also were delivered any documents in evidence, such as a *scriptum obligatorium*, which were in the keeping of the Custos Brevium.[21]

At the assizes both parties had to be present either in person or by an attorney. If the defendant failed to appear, judgment went by default for the plaintiff, and the jury assessed the damages and costs.[22] If the plaintiff failed to appear, the defendant was acquitted, the plaintiff was nonsuited and was in mercy for a false claim. When, as was more usual, both parties came, the first transaction was the swearing in of the jury. The principal qualification for jury service in the fifteenth century seems to have been freehold tenure in the shire where the cause of action arose. In actions in which the amount in debt, damages, or land rents was above 40 marks, they had to be 40s. freeholders. In actions where lesser amounts were at stake, they might have less freehold at the discretion of the justices. These requirements, which were in part intended as an insurance against bribery and in part as a means of making possible the use of the writ of distraint to make them appear, were certainly not always effective. Four must be of the hundred in which the cause of action arose. This was still the principle, although laxity seems to have been creeping into its enforcement (perhaps because of the difficulty of finding jurors who could not be challenged). It is implied in the terms used in fifteenth century statutes relating to the qualifications of jurors, that, except for the four from the hundred, they

[20] See above, Ch. XIII.

[21] See C. P. 40/842, Easter, 12 Ed. IV, mm. 276d and 193d, and many other cases where one of the parties delivered a *scriptum* to the Custos Brevium and that officer later delivered it to the Clerk of the Assizes.

[22] Chancery Miscellanea, C 47/68/19/624. If the defendant had defaulted on a second day at Westminster, it was necessary for the prothonotary to send a special writ to the sheriff to summon a jury to assess the damages. Cf. C. P. 40/806, m. 303. This was probably also the procedure on demurrer (Powell, *Academy*, p. 112).

were probably "common jurors," that is, that the same ones sat on several cases.[23] Many challenges to the jury were allowed. Either of the parties might challenge the array as showing partiality on the part of the sheriff. In this case, a writ was sent to the coroners, or if they, likewise, were suspected of partiality, to two clerks of the court or of the county who, upon oath, drew up an unchallengeable panel. Individual jurors might also be challenged for so many different reasons that time and space do not permit their discussion here.[24] The names of the jurors who appeared on the first day of the assizes were "pricked" or "pointed" in the panel.[25] If too few of the jurors appeared or too many were rejected on challenge, the case was postponed to the next assizes, and a writ of *decem tales* was sent to the sheriff to empanel more jurors.[26] If this failed, an *octo tales* would issue, and so on, until the required twelve jurors were sworn. When there was such difficulty in filling up the jury, the Clerk of the Assizes made a note on the dorse of the writ calling the jury. This writ with the panel and transcript was sent back to Westminster on the return day in the Bench, and an entry of *ponitur Jurata in respectum* entered on the plea roll. At least, this is the procedure which Cumberford and Copley, the prothonotaries, described as the correct one.[27] Writ, panel, and transcript were sent down again when the case came up at the next assizes, and the whole matter of

[23] The qualifications of fifteenth century jurors are described in Fortescue, *De Laudibus*, cap. 25; and in statutes 2 Hy. V, c. 3; 8 Hy. VI, c. 29, with which should be compared the earlier statutes: 13 Ed. I (Westm. II), c. 38, and 21 Ed. I. For four hundreders, see also *Y. B. Mich.*, 2 *Hy. IV*, pl. 22; *Mich., 4 Hy. IV*, pl. 2. In *Forthay v. Catesby* (C 47/59/6/242) trespass, 4–5 Ed. IV, in which the plaintiff claims £40 damages, there are five esquires and one knight in the panel of twenty-three names. In *Clerk v. Kerdeston*, C 47/70/2/59, false imprisonment, where the plaintiff claims 100 marks damages, no special note of the status of the jurors is made but the issues taken in distraint are 2s. each. In *Shepherd v. Power* (file of writs marked Oxon for Mich., 2 Ed. IV), a case of trespass, in which the plaintiff claimed only 20 marks damages, the issues to be levied from the jurors vary from 8d. to 12d. See Stow, *Survey*, Vol. I, p. 191.

[24] Fortescue, *De Laudibus*, cap. 25. Many Year Book reports relate discussion of challenges. For instance, see *Y. B. Easter, 4 Ed. IV*, pl. 17, fol. 11, and pl. 31, fol. 17; *Mich.*, 2 *Hy. IV*, pl. 53, fol. 13; *Mich., 3 Ed. IV*, pl. 4, fol. 12.

[25] *Y. B. Mich., 4 Ed. IV*, pl. 19, describes this practice, and the writs themselves show such "pricks" or "points" under the first letter of the names of jurors.

[26] A statute of 35 Hy. VIII, c. 6, authorized a writ of *tales de circumstantibus* of persons present in the court, but Powell says this was not allowed in the Common Pleas (*Academy*, p. 103).

[27] *Y. B. Mich., 39 Hy. VI*, pl. 22; cf. p. 196 above.

the difficulty about the jurors at the first assizes and the ultimate trial and verdict was entered on the dorse of the transcript and sent again to Westminster, there to be transcribed into the roll as a *postea* to the entry of the pleadings. Challenges to those who did appear were thus common causes of delay in fifteenth century actions.[28]

The most interesting stage in proceedings in a twentieth century court is undoubtedly the presentation of the evidence to the jurors. Modern lawyers' reputations are made or broken in this process of putting a case to the jury and striking the proper balance between the sound legal reasoning necessary to remain in the good graces of the justice on the bench, and the knowledge of human nature necessary to convince the twelve men (and, more recently, women) in the box. Fifteenth century records tell us almost nothing of trial. All we get from them is a brief note that the parties appeared, and the jurors gave the verdict, which is recorded, and assessed the damages, which are noted in the record. In fact, so far as the records go, we might be back in the time when the jurors gave their verdict entirely or almost entirely on their own knowledge of the facts, as neighbors.[29]

Fortescue's account of trial is disappointingly meager.[30] First, he says, the record is read to the jury in English "with a plain declaration of the issue of the plea, touching the truth whereof those sworne men shall certifie the Court." [31] Then either counsel or the parties themselves present the evidence. "And then may either party bring before the same Justices and sworn men, all and singular witnesses on his behalf, as he will produce, who by the Justices being charged upon the Holy Gospel of God, shall testifie all things proving the truth of the fact, whereupon the parties contend." If need be, the witnesses may be kept apart so that they may not influence one another.

---

[28] Among 120 entries of *jurata in respectum* in the plea roll of Mich., 2 Ed. IV, twenty-three note that a writ of *decem tales* was sent to the sheriff because the jury had not been filled.

[29] The early history of jury trial, its nature in the fifteenth century, and the rules relating to evidence are subjects best not discussed by a layman. The reader is referred to Thayer's famous *Preliminary Treatise on Evidence at the Common Law*.

[30] *De Laudibus*, cap. 26.

[31] The prothonotary or, at *nisi prius*, the Clerk of the Assizes read the record (*Y. B. Mich., 2 Ed. IV*, pl. 18).

After the presentation of the evidence and probably also some sort of instruction from the court,[32] the jurors retired to a suitable place "in keeping of the Ministers of the Court," who appear to have been the criers.[33] There they deliberated and, when they had come to a decision, they returned into the court in the presence of the justices and the parties and delivered their verdict. They also assessed the damages and costs. It is not clear where they got the necessary data for the assessment of costs. Later, in Powell's time, the plaintiff drew up a bill of costs and presented it to the prothonotary who examined it and made the assessment.[34] By the nineteenth century reviewing bills of costs was the most laborious duty remaining to the prothonotary.[35] The later method seems more calculated to insure fair assessment.

The happenings at the assizes were duly entered by the Clerk of the Assizes on the dorse of the transcript of the record and returned into the Bench with the panel of jurors and the writ of *habeas corpora juratorum* or of *distringas juratores*.

On the day of judgment the justices reviewed the record of the verdict and gave their decision. Often this involved a revision of the damages and costs. Ordinarily the justices added only an increment to the costs.[36] Sometimes, however, they increased or decreased the damages.[37] Sometimes, also, the justices were not ready to give a decision, and the note in the record is that "the justices wished to advise," and that a day was given later in the same term or in the following term. On occasion this postponement of the judgment seems to have been used as a means of forcing revision of a grossly unfair verdict. For example, in a case reported in the Year Book for Michaelmas term, 19 Henry VI, the court held up judgment until the plaintiff yielded a portion of the outrageous damages awarded by the jury.[38]

---

[32] *Y. B. Mich.*, *2 Ed. IV*, pl. 4.

[33] Table of Fees, App. I (l). See also E 101/518/4, Law Expenses of Thomas Roche and others against Wm. Fawke and others, 9 Hy. VIII, 2s. paid to the crier of the court for custody of the jury.

[34] *Academy*, p. 121. E 101/518/4 and E 101/514/17 in Exchequer Miscellanea are bills of costs from the fifteenth and early sixteenth centuries.

[35] *Parlt. Papers* (1819), Report on Fees in the Court of Common Pleas, p. 27.

[36] For examples, see C. P. 40/882, mm. 123, 250, 320.

[37] For example, see C 47/68/19/624 in Chancery Miscellanea; *Y. BB. Mich.*, *2 Hy. IV*, pl. 23; *Mich.*, *3 Hy. IV*, pl. 16; *Easter*, *2 Hy. VI*, pl. 1; *Mich.*, *10 Hy. VI*, pl. 84.

[38] *Y. B. Mich.*, *19 Hy. VI*, pl. 28.

If verdict and judgment were for the defendant, he went quit and the plaintiff was in mercy for a false claim, that is, he had to pay a fine to the king. But if, as was more often the case, verdict and judgment were for the plaintiff, he paid for the entry in the prothonotary's office and got his writ of execution. It was possible for the plaintiff to receive a verdict and judgment for part of his plea and to be in mercy for the rest.[39]

At any time between the defendant's first appearance and the recording of judgment, the plaintiff might be nonsuited. If he defaulted, the defendant asked to have him nonsuited.[40] He might also choose, himself, to suffer amercement rather than to prosecute the case further. A settlement out of court or the possibility of getting a more favorable verdict and judgment by bringing a new action later would usually be the factors in his decision.

The plaintiff had three main choices of procedure in execution of judgment. He might get a writ of *capias ad satisfaciendum* to have the defendant arrested and might even have him imprisoned or outlawed on such a writ.[41] It was possible, also, for him to proceed by a writ of *fieri facias*, which ordered the sheriff to levy from the land and goods of the defendant the amount awarded in damages and costs.[42] Finally, he might have a writ of *elegit*, which entitled him to all the goods except "oxen and beasts of his Plough" and one-half the lands of the defendant, as tenant by *elegit* until he should have received full satisfaction.[43] The plaintiff probably chose his method according to the defendant's assets. If the latter were a freeholder, either the *fieri facias* or the *elegit* were possible methods. *Capias ad satisfaciendum*, however, was the commonest method in the fifteenth century.[44] Those who failed to get their judgments

---

[39] For example, C. P. 40/806, m. 176d., and C 47/68/19/624 in Chancery Miscellanea.

[40] *Y. BB., Mich.*, 2 *Hy. IV*, pl. 13; *Mich.*, *33 Hy. VI*, pl. 1; *Mich.*, *3 Ed. IV*, pl. 2; *Easter*, 22 *Ed. IV*, pl. 2.

[41] C. P. 40/843, Trin., 12 Ed. IV, m. 360d., *Godard v. Castill; ibid.*, 119d. *Aleyn v. Browning;* C. P. 40/882, Mich. 22 Ed. IV, 321d., *Caudon v. Dobbys.* See also C 47/59/6/236; C 47/67/11/476; C 47/68/21/668; and C 47/68/18/598 in Chancery "County Placita." For discussion of process, see *Y. B. Mich., 4 Ed. IV*, p. 22.

[42] C. P. 40/843, Trin., 12 Ed. IV, m. 127d.

[43] Stat. 13 Ed. I (Westm. II), c. 18. No instances of execution by *elegit* were found in the fifteenth century records.

[44] In fifteen entries of final process in the plea roll of Mich., 2 Ed. IV, nine are of *capias ad satisfaciendum*, two are of *fieri facias*, and four are of *scire facias* on judgments delivered in the later years of Henry VI.

executed within a year must, before proceeding to execution, procure a writ of *scire facias* to warn the defendant to come and show reason why the judgment should not be executed.[45]

Capias ad satisfaciendum was a much more severe process than *capias* in mesne process. If the plaintiff was forced to have the defendant outlawed in order to get satisfaction, the defendant was not allowed bail but was imprisoned in the Fleet.[46] Even where he gave the plaintiff full satisfaction, he must surrender himself to the Warden of the Fleet and enter bail for his payment of a fine to the king.[47]

There were two means by which the losing party might reverse the judgement against him. He might attempt an attaint of the jury, a very serious and solemn process according to Fortescue, but one difficult to prosecute because of the problem of getting thirteen defendants into court at one and the same time.[48] I have found copies of the records of two unsuccessful attempts among the Chancery Miscellanea called "County Placita." [49] Both happen to be cases where, in the original suit, there was a plea in abatement on the ground that the plaintiffs were villeins. The verdict of the original jury was that they were not villeins; the verdict of the jury of twenty-four was that "the twelve jurors of the first inquest made a good and legal oath," and that the plaintiffs were free men. One of these attempts at attainder of the jury was by Joan, Countess of Kent.

The other method of reversal was by error into the King's Bench. An interesting case of this occurs on the roll of Easter, 12 Edward IV [50] in an assize of novel disseisin. Brayne, the prothonotary who had entered the case, when directed by the justices to stop execution, reported that he had already sent out several writs. William Wylkys *ex parte* the plaintiff in error asked for a writ of *supersedeas*

---

[45] C. P. 40/882, 22 Ed. IV, m. 406d., bears a memorandum of a writ of *scire facias* in execution of a judgment of Hil., 9 Hy. IV, in debt on an annual rent. In a case of which a part of the record appears on m. 316d. of C. P. 40/842, Easter, 12 Ed. IV, the plaintiff was stopped from her execution by the defendants' plea that one of the executors against whom she had recovered a debt had died since judgment. She was forced to get a new writ.

[46] 23 Hy. VI, c. 9.

[47] C. P. 40/880, m. 312; and "County Placita" referred to in n. 41 above.

[48] Stat. 11 Hy. VI, c. 4; 15 Hy. VI, c. 5.

[49] C 47/62/1/30; C 47/67/5/172.

[50] C. P. 40/842, m. 304.

on the ground that these writs had been sent out without the order of the court and without the justices' having seen the record of the assize. And although the justices admitted this to be true, they "wished to advise" until the octaves of Trinity before granting the *supersedeas*.

Many questions concerning the steps in bringing an action in the Court of Common Pleas in the later fifteenth century have necessarily been left unanswered or have been only tentatively answered. For instance, we should like to know more about the cost of bringing an action in a fifteenth century law court, more about how process was executed in the county, more of the relations between the courts and the sheriff's office and between the Court of Common Pleas and the local courts, and more of the court's relation to the other central courts and other administrative departments. Finally, we should like to know more of what people living in the fifteenth century thought about judicial administration in their time, something to bring into relation with each other the contradictory impressions created by the expressions of fear and distrust of lawyers in the proclamations of Jack Cade and his followers, on the one hand, and the respect and admiration for the English law and lawyers expressed by Fortescue in the *De Laudibus Legum Anglie* on the other.

PART IV

Handicaps and Weaknesses

CHAPTER XV

Delays and Hindrances to Justice

THE FUNDAMENTAL FACT about a fifteenth century action at law was that it was a contest in which each party was ready to use whatever means lay at hand to outwit the other. Devices for delaying, hindering, and obstructing altogether the work of the fifteenth century Court of Common Pleas were many. The account given in the foregoing chapters of the method of bringing a personal action in the court has for the most part ignored these hindrances. Parties, clerks, attorneys, sergeants at law, justices, and sheriffs and their bailiffs have been treated as abstractions rather than as human beings bound to be moved by desire for gain, the instinct of self-preservation (either in body or in honor), vengeance, friendship, lordship, or any of the other motivating forces in fifteenth century society. Consequently, the account above of the steps in an action at law bears somewhat the relation to the actualities of the contest that a treatise on the principles of baseball or cricket bears to the game played on the field.

The records do not reveal much concerning the people who made them. Rarely do they relax their stereotyped pattern sufficiently to allow human beings to emerge from the Latin verbiage. The clerk was drilled in the use of time-honored formulas which were like pigeonholes into which he thrust the information given him. His training was good insurance against carelessness in setting down essential information, but it made for sterility of human detail in the plea rolls.

Although the records tell little, the Year Books, statutes and petitions in Parliament, petitions in Chancery and council in cases where the common law courts had failed, and especially the family letters and papers do enable us to discover more about how the law was used and abused by litigants in their endeavors to secure or to evade justice.

There were many ways by which the defendant could impede the ponderous machinery for bringing him into court, inducing him to answer, and forcing him to give satisfaction to a victorious plaintiff. He could, for example, when warned of process for his arrest, disappear from his usual haunts in the county to which the writ was addressed, or he might escape altogether into another county.[1] Process by distraint he might avoid by putting all his movable goods into the safe-keeping of someone else so that the sheriff's bailiff would find nothing by which to distrain him, and the sheriff would be forced to return a *nihil habet*.[2] Meanwhile he would enjoy several months of grace while the plaintiff sued out a writ of *capias* returnable in the next term.

Such methods of evasion were easier for the man of little wealth and not much business than for the wealthy man of position. Sir John Paston, for example, who had lands and goods in Norfolk and business to attend to in London would not get beyond the reach of the law so readily as a lesser man would. His younger brother, John, in charge of his affairs in Norfolk, wrote to him in May, 1472 to complain that he could get no money from his tenants to pay "for green wax"[3] in one suit and for damages in another. He closed his letter with the warning: "Remember what pain it is to a man to lose liberty. The Fleet is a fair prison, but you had small liberty therein for you must needs appear when you were called."[4]

A more aggressive tactic than escape into another county was to bring a countersuit against the plaintiff in order to have him outlawed or imprisoned and thus disabled from further prosecution

[1] *Paston Letters,* Nos. 485, 497; *Stonor Letters and Papers,* 1290–1483, (ed. Kingsford; London, 1919), Nos. 118, 304.

[2] For an example, see *Paston Letters,* No. 434, Sir Robert Williamson to Agnes Paston, 1460–1464. He intends, he says, to evade arrest in an action of rescue falsely brought against him by enemies by going "as far as my feet may bear me" after he has put his movable chattels in "sure hands" for "truly I will not abide the jeopardy of the suit." In quotations from the *Paston Letters* and *Plumpton Correspondence,* modern spelling and punctuation are used.

[3] Used here to mean money owed to the sheriff on a writ of distraint.

[4] *Paston Letters,* No. 693, May 14, 1472.

of his suit. Sir Robert Wyngfield in 1440 carried through a particularly successful offensive of this kind against John Lyston, to whom he owed 700 marks in damages which the latter had recovered against him in an assize of novel disseisin. After Sir Robert had "subtly" succeeded in having Lyston outlawed, the Treasurer, certified of the outlawry, granted the claim for 700 marks, along with the rest of the outlawed man's goods, to the Duke of Norfolk for arrearages of pay. The duke released the damages to Sir Robert and then, says John Paston's correspondent, there "was great heaving and shoving by my lord of Suffolk and his counsel for to espy how this matter came about." [5] William Jenney, sergeant at law, onetime friend of Sir John Paston and later enemy, was particularly expert at such tactics. The younger John, Sir John's brother, wrote to his mother just after Edward's restoration in 1471 that Jenney was troubling Sir John's servants "with old actions and all such things as he can renew" in order to avoid payments due on sealed obligations.[6]

Even land assizes were not so solemn and final in their effect as the formal discussions of them would suggest. For example, Hugh Unton wrote to Sir William Stonor to warn him that, although his enemy, Thomas Worthe, had a writ to give him seisin of Woollston manor in execution of a judgment of the court of Common Pleas against him, he need not accept defeat. His counsel said that if Worthe entered the land "by his own authority," Sir William could put him out and take the profits of the land, "and if he enters by authority of the sheriff . . . you must suffer the sheriff's officers to enter by virtue of the writ of warrant, and, as soon as they be gone, enter ye again and take the profits." [7] Worthe's claim to the manor was flimsily founded according to the Stonor correspondents, and the suit was a vexatious one, a sufficient justification by the standards of the times for taking the law into private hands.

Both legal and extralegal means were at hand to delay the prosecution of both honest and dishonest suits. Entering the king's service was a popular device for fending off arrest. Sir Robert

5 *Ibid.*, No. 27, Nov., 1440. For other examples, see *ibid.*, Nos. 28, 117, 503, and *Plumpton Corr.*, Ser. II, No. XXVII.

6 *Paston Letters*, No. 678, Oct. 28, 1471. Cf. *Y. B. Easter, 4 Ed. IV*, pl. 27.

7 *Stonor Letters*, No. 313. For the whole story of the Worthe case, see vol. I, p. xxxii; vol. II, pp. 104–105, 109, 145–146.

Plumpton, for example, petitioned for an appointment as Knight of the Body in order to protect himself against arrest in one of his several suits at law.[8] Despite statutes providing safeguards against abuse of letters of protection [9] for service to the king or one of his officers, they could be easily procured and fraudulently used for delay. The plaintiff could sue a repeal, but that cost time and money.[10] He could also bring an action for deceit,[11] but that meant an even greater expenditure of time, patience, and money.

Essoins were another device which, although originally legitimate, had come to be used abusively. In the fifteenth century, however, they were not nearly so frequent as in the fourteenth.[12] For example, in the roll of Michaelmas, 2 Edward IV, there were but ten essoins entered at any stage of process in personal actions: two in debt, four in trespass, two in waste, one in breach of the statute of entries, and one in replevin. In other rolls examined, they appear to be equally infrequent.

The probable reason for the apparent obsolescence of essoins is that other methods were more widely effective. Essoins were not available in answer to judicial writs.[13] Presumably, also, since the writ which followed a person's failure to appear after he had once essoined himself was one of *distringas*, an essoin could be entered only where that process was allowed. Evidence has been given above to show that process by distraint was much less common than process by arrest and outlawry.[14] Thus, essoins were limited by the rules of procedure. They had also been hedged about by statutory limi-

---

[8] *Plumpton Corr.*, Ser. II, p. 165, n. a.

[9] 25 Ed. III, stat. 5, c. 19; 1 Ric. II, c. 8; 13 Ric. II, c. 16.

[10] The protection offered by the tenant in *Rither v. Sayer* (cf. above, Ch. XIII) was evidently fraudulent. In a case recorded in Easter term, 22 Edward IV (C. P. 40/880, m. 406) the defendant offered two successive protections, one claiming service to the victualer of Calais, the other to the Earl of Northumberland. The plaintiff got letters repealing the first. Trial was held in spite of the second and the plaintiff recovered £5 damages and £15 in losses and costs. In *Long Quinto*, fols. 1–5, the reporter has collected together a number of discussions of protections from earlier years of the century. One difficult problem raised by protections was whether to continue process against the jury after a protection had been brought in or to call a new jury later. The first alternative was vexatious to the jurors, the second, to the plaintiff.

[11] C. P. 40/791, m. 38d., and C. P. 40/794, mm. 148, 210.

[12] See *H. E. L.*, vol. III, p. 624, for the frequency of essoins in the fourteenth century.

[13] *Y. B. Hil., 33 Hy. VI*, pl. 17. All the justices agreed in quashing an essoin on a *venire facias* on the ground that it was a judicial writ on which an essoin did not lie.

[14] Ch. XII.

tations adopted in the late thirteenth and early fourteenth centuries. By the statute of Marlborough only one essoin was allowed after joinder of issue.[15] Fourching, or alternating in essoins by coparceners, was forbidden.[16] Essoins *de malo lectu* and for service to the king abroad were strictly regulated.[17] Executors were forbidden to essoin themselves.[18] The most important limitation of essoins, however, was that they might not be put in by attorneys. Appearance either of the party or of his attorney was ground for quashing an essoin.[19] In an age when most legal business was carried on through attorneys, this rule alone made the essoin relatively useless as a means of delay.

License to imparl, normally a legitimate concession to the defendant's need to prepare his case, also afforded opportunities for abuse which were no doubt increased by the fullness of the court's docket. One attorney, under prosecution by bill in the Court of Common Pleas, had license to imparl through thirty-four successive terms.[20] One suspects that he was exploiting his special knowledge of the court's machinery. On the other hand, another defendant with no apparent claim to special favor or knowledge had license to imparl through twenty-six terms. In the majority of the cases of imparlance recorded on the plea roll, however, the defendant answered, or the case was dropped within the next few terms.[21] Without more positive evidence it is impossible to say that imparlance was frequently used abusively.

Day-to-day continuances within the term, although not so expensive in time and money, could be irritating to the plaintiff. What person with experience of the law will not feel sympathy with Thomas Playter's complaint: ". . . and always days given them by

15 52 Hy. III, c. 13. Cf. 3 Ed. I, c. 42; 13 Ed. I, c. 28.
16 3 Ed. I, c. 43. "Coparceners" were persons to whom an estate of inheritance descended jointly.
17 3 Ed. I, c. 44; 13 Ed. I, c. 17; 5 Ed. III, c. 6.
18 9 Ed. III, c. 3.
19 See Year Books of Edward II and Edward III, Selden Society and Rolls Series, *passim*, especially 15 Ed. III (R. S.), p. 96 and 16 Ed. III (R. S.), pt. II, p. 86.
20 C. P. 40/842, Trin., 12 Ed. IV, m. 145.
21 In Mich., 2 Ed. IV (C. P. 40/806) there were ninety-six imparlances. In ten cases *posteas* record continuations through seven or more subsequent terms. Five records show that the plaintiff won his case on the later day. Nine more entries introduced with the note that the defendant is in mercy for earlier defaults suggest abusive use for delay.

the court to answer and then they took small exceptions, and trifled with the court, and always excused them because the bill is long and his counsel had no leisure to see it." [22]

The writ of *supersedeas* directing the sheriff to discontinue process against a defendant, although originally devised to save harmless of outlawry one who had given evidence of his intention to appear, was another instrument of justice often perverted. Such a writ could be issued by the Chancery, by the king under privy seal, by the justices of the peace in the county, or by any of the king's justices. The chief abuses seem to have been in connection with such writs from the Chancery and under privy seal. In Easter, 7 Edward IV, a frustrated plaintiff, who had sued out process of outlawry against the defendant three times only to be blocked by a writ of *supersedeas* from the Chancery, asked in understandable impatience for a special writ of *exigi facias* with a clause forbidding the sheriff to receive such a writ. The justices of the Common Pleas were very willing to grant the special writ, but whether the sheriff obeyed it we are not told.[23] The Chancery's authority to grant a *supersedeas* on process in the Court of Common Pleas had been a point in controversy much earlier in the century, for in Michaelmas, 7 Henry IV, Rickhill persuaded the court that a Chancery *supersedeas* was invalid because that office had no knowledge of the record.[24] The Chancery seems to have got around this objection by sending for the records by a writ of *certiorari*.[25] Unwillingness on the part of the court to recognize a *supersedeas* from the Chancery is certainly justifiable in view of the conditions described by Godfrey Grene in writing to Sir William Plumpton in 1475.[26] He advised Sir William to get a *supersedeas* from the justices of the peace in the county because of a new ruling that henceforth writs from the Chancery would be granted only on "sufficient surety," "and twenty of the old common sureties discharged." He complained in disgust that he had been swindled by "one which hath been of old a super-

---

[22] *Paston Letters*, No. 387, Thomas Playter to John Paston, May, 1461.
[23] *Y. B. Easter, 7 Ed. IV*, pl. 19.
[24] *Y. B. Mich., 7 Hy. IV*, pl. 32.
[25] See the many such records among Chancery Miscellanea.
[26] *Plumpton Corr.*, Ser. I, No. XXIV, July 10, c. 1475. Cf. *Stonor Letters*, No. 304, request of a servant of the Stonors that a writ of *supersedeas* be got from the Chancery to protect him from arrest for service done to Edmund Ramsey on Sir William Stonor's behalf.

sedeas monger" to whom he had agreed to pay 5s. for his services before he discovered the new ruling. "And I may not arrest him," he wrote to Sir William, "nor strive with him for money nor for the deceit because the matter is not worshipful. . . ." The "new ruling" of the Chancery seems to have been a needed remedy.

Writs of *supersedeas* under privy seal were luxuries for the rich and well connected since they must be secured through the favor of the king himself or someone of his council. By such a writ Lord Moleyns successfully obstructed John Paston's efforts to have his men indicted and punished for an outrageous attack on Paston's wife and servants at Gresham.[27] On the other hand, John Paston himself failed to avoid outlawry and imprisonment by such a writ of privy seal when William Jenney, sergeant at law, got a judgment against him in 1465. Jenney persuaded the sheriff to ignore the *supersedeas* and continue the process of outlawry. Paston eventually got his release from jail by bringing a writ of error into the King's Bench. Meanwhile he had avoided some of the worst consequences of outlawry by giving into the keeping of the prior of Norwich seven or eight thousand marks.[28]

Protections, essoins, imparlances, and writs of *supersedeas* had all originally been devised as legitimate protections to defendants. Very likely their potentialities for abuse were not foreseen. One of the heaviest burdens of government is to provide remedies for legitimate grievances with sufficient care also to prevent abuses. Fortescue was unduly boastful when he informed his young pupil that "the laws of England do not permit frivolous and unfruitful delays." And he was, perhaps, himself aware of this for he went on to say "that if less proper delays in pleas have occurred in this realm, they can be cut down in every parliament." [29] The most notable statute dealing with delays was that of 14 Edward III which had provided for the appointment of a special commission to deal with petitions of those who felt themselves aggrieved.[30]

More serious than attempts to evade or delay the law in its course were such attempts to pervert or corrupt it as bribery of officials, embracery of juries, and maintenance of suits. Bribery need not

27 *Paston Letters*, No. 164.
28 *Ibid.*, Nos. 491, 494, 495; *Y. BB. Mich.*, 4 Ed. IV, pl. 14; *Hil.*, 4 Ed. IV, pls. 3, 4.
29 *De Laudibus*, cap. 53.
30 14 Ed. III, stat. 1, c. 5.

be defined here. Maintenance and embracery were closely related offenses. The first, in nontechnical terms, was an unlawful upholding of another's suit by spoken word, writing, encouragement, or other act.[31] Embracery was any attempt to influence a jury to favor one side or the other by money, promises, threats, or persuasion.[32]

These evils were not new in the fifteenth century. The statutes against them go back to the reign of Edward I.[33] Even then, perversion of justice by these methods was clearly not a new phenomenon.[34] On the other hand, royal justice administered by the courts of common law was relatively new and was rapidly expanding at the expense of other jurisdictions, to the king's increasing profit and power. Regulation of public morals in relation to the administration of royal justice was essential to the preservation of its competitive force. The most important and comprehensive statutes dealing with maintenance and embracery were adopted in the reign of Edward III.[35] By the accession of Richard II both civil and criminal remedies were available for prosecution of embraceors, maintainors, and those guilty of champerty (a specialized kind of maintenance consisting in maintaining a suit in consideration of receiving a part of the land, damages, or things recovered). These evils continued to require regulation in succeeding reigns, however. The giving of liveries by great men was recognized as a closely associated evil a century after the first statutes dealing with maintenance, champerty, and embracery were adopted, and the statutory attempts to regulate this related abuse begin in Richard II's time and extend throughout the fifteenth century.[36]

Embracery is much more readily defined, recognized, and punished today than it was in the fifteenth century because the nature

---

[31] Winfield, *Conspiracy*, p. 136.

[32] *Ibid.*, p. 161.

[33] 3 Ed. I, c. 28, and 13 Ed. I, cc. 36, 49: maintenance and champerty; *S. R.*, vol. I, p. 216, *Statutum de Conspiratoribus:* maintenance; p. 145, 33 Ed. I, *Ordinacio de Conspiratoribus:* champerty.

[34] *H. E. L.*, vol. III, pp. 395–396.

[35] 1 Ed. III, stat. 2, c. 14; 4 Ed. III, c. 11; 20 Ed. III, cc. 4, 5, 6: maintenance. 20 Ed. III, c. 6; 34 Ed. III, c. 8; 38 Ed. III, stat. 1, c. 12: embracery. 20 Ed. III, cc. 1, 6: bribery.

[36] 1 Ric. II, c. 7; 13 Ric. II, stat. 3; 16 Ric. II, c. 4; 20 Ric. II, c. 2; 1 Hy. IV, c. 7; 2 Hy. IV, c. 21: 7 Hy. IV, c. 14; 13 Hy. IV, c. 3; 8 Hy. VI, c. 4; 8 Ed. IV, c. 2; 12 Ed. IV, c. 4.

and the functions of the jury are more clear and definite. Then, the jury was only in the process of evolution from its original character as a body of witnesses of facts already known to themselves to its modern character of a group of judges of facts presented in evidence at the trial. Obviously it is easier to decide what kinds of attempts to influence jurors are illegal now, when they are expected to make their decisions from the facts presented to them during the trial, than in the fifteenth century when, although the law still officially presumed that they knew the facts before the trial, actually they often knew little or nothing. The official records ignored the presentation of evidence and recorded only the verdict or speaking of the truth by the jurors; if they gave a wrong verdict, they were still in the fifteenth century as in the thirteenth, considered to have perjured themselves by saying what they knew to be untrue. The injured party could have against them an action of attaint. Is it reasonable under these circumstances to expect that parties would refrain from "laboring" juries to insure their knowing the facts favorable to themselves, especially where they suspected that their opponents had dictated the selection of the panel? [37]

Some of the pleadings reported in the Year Books in case of embracery and maintenance illustrate the ambiguity in the concept of the jury in the fifteenth century. For example, Brian, sergeant at law, pleading on a writ of *decies tantum* in Michaelmas, 6 Edward IV, said that the defendant was a man of law and that he took 6*s.* 8*d.* of the alleged sum of £20 "by force of which he swore the evidences of his client before the jury and asked them if they found in their consciences that what he said was true, they would find for his client." This, he said was the alleged "inducing and embracery," and he took nothing more.[38] A *dictum* of the judges of the King's Bench later in the reign is of like interest in illustrating the difference between present-day and fifteenth century concepts of the jury: "It was held by all the court that a juror may exhort his companions to pass with the plaintiff or the defendant according to where he thinks right is and this shall not be called maintenance. But if he gives money, either his own or that of

[37] For examples, see *Paston Letters*, Nos. 53, 133, 147, 151, 373; *Plumpton Corr.* Nos. C, CI, CIII, CX, CXVIII, CXXVII, letters dated from Jan. 28, 1498, to June 1501. Cf. Pickthorn, *Tudor Government: Henry VII*, p. 80.
[38] *Y. B. Mich., 6 Ed. IV*, pl. 14.

another, that shall be called maintenance whether it be for the best cause in the world." [39] This *dictum* is an unlikely product of a modern court, since it would neither occur to anyone to question that a juror might endeavor to persuade his co-jurors to agree with him, nor to doubt that the use of money to do so would be culpable.[40]

The civil remedy provided by the first statute of 38 Edward III [41] against the crudest form of embracery, that is, the giving or taking of money for a verdict, was the writ of *decies tantum*. The provision of a specific remedy for this particular kind of embracery, a very present evil at the time when the statute was adopted, seems to have had the effect of narrowing the scope of the general concept represented by the term embracery. Embracery remained the term to describe the giving or taking of money for a verdict, that is, the offense for which the writ *decies tantum* would lie. All other forms of embracery tended, in spite of the efforts of Hankford and Martyn, justices of the Common Pleas, to differentiate them, to be considered maintenance.[42] This is perhaps why there is no mention of embracery in the indices to the printed editions of the fifteenth century Year Books. Cases involving embracery are grouped either under the heading *decies tantum* or under maintenance.[43] *Decies tantum* was the usual action against jurors, and maintenance the usual one against those who tried to influence jurors.[44]

[39] *Y. B. Mich., 17 Ed. IV*, pl. 2. Cf. *Y. B. Easter, 18 Ed. IV*, pl. 23, where the justices reiterated the statement that giving money to persuade his companions by a juror is maintenance.

[40] For other interesting cases of maintenance in which the pleas are archaic, see *Y. BB. Easter, 18 Ed. IV*, pls. 6, 8. In the later case the defense is that the defendant was one of the jurors in the original action.

[41] C. 12.

[42] Hankford said in Hil., 13 Hy. IV (*Y. B.*, pl. 12) that an embraceor is properly one who takes upon himself to make the jurors appear, a person called in English "a leader of inquests." This *dictum* does not seem to have been supported by later decisions. Martyn in Mich., 11 Hy. VI (*Y. B.*, pl. 24), said that where an attorney gave 10s. of his own money to the jurors, that would be maintenance; where he gave his master's money, that would be embracery. Chief Justice Babington, and Justice Paston, thought that even where he gave his master's goods or money, it would be a case of special maintenance rather than embracery. See Winfield, *Conspiracy*, p. 168, and *H. E. L.*, vol. III, p. 399, for discussion of the distinction between maintenance and embracery.

[43] See, for example, Wight editions, 1601 and 1605, respectively, of later years of Henry VI and of Henry IV and V, and 1609 edition of first part of Henry VI (Stationers', London).

[44] Winfield, *Conspiracy*, pp. 168 ff.

There are very few cases of *decies tantum* in the fifteenth century reports.[45] Furthermore, I have found little evidence of payments to corrupt jurors in the correspondence of the period.[46] The Pastons, who were certainly not reticent about their misdemeanors speak of "laboring" jurors rather than of bribing them. "Laboring" may, of course, be a euphemism for bribery. More probably it is what it seems to be, that is, the use of argument and influence to persuade jurors to give a favorable verdict. It is the sort of action intended by the Earl of Oxford, who wrote to John Paston asking him to call before him the jury empaneled between a tenant of his and a butcher of Norwich and to "open the matter at large at my instance and desire them to do as conscience will and to eschew perjury." [47] Now, this is a clear case of embracery under the more general definition of that offense, and it is also clearly maintenance, but it is not embracery of the limited kind for which one could have as a remedy the writ *decies tantum*.

Indeed, why should parties have paid money and risked liability under *decies tantum* when they could accomplish the same results by less expensive means? Practically speaking, the most effective way to influence a jury in the fifteenth century was to get the protection of some great lord whose disfavor twelve men, however good and true, would hesitate to incur. A conversation of Edmund Paston with "Steward, the Chief Constable," reported by him to his brother John, makes this point very clear. Steward, having been empaneled on an assize between John Paston and another, consulted Edmund to ask what he should do because, as he said, the suit was maintained by Sir Thomas Tuddenham, a powerful man in the county. "I counselled him," reported Edmund, "to swear the truth of the issue that he shall be swore to, and then he needed

---

45 Only twelve altogether for Henry IV, Henry V, Henry VI, and Edward IV.

46 In a letter of Sir Richard Plumpton to Sir Robert in 1501 (*Plumpton Corr.,* Ser. II, No. CXXVI) discussing litigation against Empson, Sir Richard sadly predicted that the suit was likely to go against Sir Robert "except the great mercy of God, and great labour and cost." Frequently mentioned in the *Plumpton Correspondence* especially are attempts to win friends in the county by spending money there, the sort of thing which is described in Clement Tailour's case (*Y. B., Mich., 31 Hy. VI,* pl. 1) where J. delivered to Thomas Tuddenham and another 100s. to be distributed among the people of the county. These appear to be attempts to build up a friendly atmosphere rather than payments for particular verdicts.

47 *Paston Letters,* No. 373. The references to "labouring" juries in the correspondence of the period are many (see *Plumpton Corr.,* Ser. II, Nos. CIII, CXXVII).

never to dread him of no attaint." Steward then inquired of "the rule of my master Daniell and my lord of Suffolk [Daniell was a friend of Tuddenham's] and asked which I thought should rule in this shire: and I said both, as I thought, and he that surviveth to hold by the virtue of the survivor, and he to thank his friends and to acquit his enemies." [48] James Gloys, Paston family chaplain, reporting to John Paston on his "laboring" of a jury between Agnes Paston and another, said: "There be many of them will do their part, and there be some that will not pass thereupon for they are afraid the world should turn!" [49] The man empaneled on a fifteenth century jury had more to worry him than loss of time from business or the truth of the case before him. His security and the peaceable enjoyment of his possessions might depend on his giving the "right" verdict, that is the verdict favorable to the mightiest man.

It is not fair, however, to assume without studying the legal records more fully that acts of retributive violence, such as that described in a fourteenth century presentment before justices of the peace telling how Hugh Pipard attacked John atte Denne on the highway for giving a verdict against him in an assize of mort d'ancestor,[50] were widespread and frequent in the following century. On the other hand, that jurors sometimes had occasion to fear physical violence from such "gangsters" as Sir Thomas Tuddenham is evident from the petition of the Town of Swaffham in 1451 asking mercy for twenty-four men who, having been empaneled on an assize between Sir Thomas and John Aleyn, "for dread of the horrible menaces" [51] of the former, gave a false verdict. In a case in trespass between the Duke of Exeter and Lord Cromwell, Billing, for the latter, unsuccessfully attempted to persuade the justices that the trial should be held at Westminster rather than in the county before the justices of assize. "You know well that here in the Hall when the writ was returned, there was a great rout," he argued, and he feared that even greater mischief was likely to occur in the county "because my lord of Exeter is a great and prepotent prince in that county." Prisot, however, held that it was more im-

[48] *Paston Letters*, No. 53, Edmund to John Paston, June, 1447.
[49] *Ibid.*, No. 147, March 2, 1451.
[50] Putnam, *Proceedings*, p. 220.
[51] *Paston Letters*, No. 151. They also asked that the verdict of the assize be reversed without attaint of the twenty-four men who had given the false verdict.

portant to maintain the party's privilege of choosing trial at *nisi prius* than to see that the jury was protected from improper influence in this particular case.[52]

The juror was caught between the upper and nether millstones. If he gave a true verdict against a powerful man, he risked his displeasure, violent or not. If, on the other hand, he gave a false verdict, the wronged party could prosecute him for perjury by a writ of attaint, which entailed ferocious penalties. If the grand jury of twenty-four substantial men of the county [53] gave a verdict against the petty jurors for making "a false oath," the penalties were that they should be committed to prison, their goods should be seized, their houses and buildings torn down, their woods felled, and their meadows plowed up. Moreover, they themselves were to be forever after accounted infamous and barred from further jury service. Their verdict was, of course, reversed. "Who then," says Fortescue, "though he regard not his soul's health, yet for fear of so great punishment and for shame of so great infamy would not upon his oath declare the truth?" [54]

Who, indeed? And yet Steward, the constable, and the jurors in Agnes Paston's case hesitated, weighing the hazards of an unpopular verdict against those of an untrue one.[55] The fact was that an attaint against a jury was difficult to prosecute. Hard as it was to get two or three defendants into court in an ordinary suit, it must have been considerably harder to prosecute the thirteen who must appear together on a writ of attaint. Furthermore, once in court, the petty jurors could in turn plead "false and faint" pleas, all of which must be tried, some in foreign counties. The statutes of Henry VI attempted to remedy some of these defects of attaint by providing that the plaintiff could recover damages and costs against petty jurors for false pleas, that the distraints against the petty jurors should be heavy (i.e., 40s. on the first writ; 100s. on the second), and that the grand jury should be composed of substantial men unlikely "to be drawn or moved to perjury by brocage, power, or

---

[52] *Y. B. Mich., 32 Hy. VI,* pl. 14, "Prisot dit que ceo ne fuit pas pur que ilz fuer ouste de Nisi prius."

[53] £20 freeholders in cases where land of yearly rent value of 40s. or damages of £40 were involved (15 Hy. VI, c. 5).

[54] Fortescue, *De Laudibus,* cap. 26.

[55] *Paston Letters,* Nos. 53 and 149.

corruption." [56] Yet the difficulties of prosecuting an attaint continued, and the abuses of the process, also, as the more drastic legislation necessary in Henry VII's reign shows.[57] Sir John Fastolf not only rewarded the sheriff for a favorable grand jury panel, but also planned to get the two defendants, against whom the verdict had gone in the original action, into the household of the Duke of Norfolk, the better to influence the jury of attaint.[58] In another case, however, he lost 100 marks "by a suit of Margaret Brygg upon a defense of attaint because a quest passed against her of xij pennyworth land by year." [59]

The misdeeds so far discussed have been those of parties and jurors. The weakness of the jury as an instrument of justice in the fifteenth century was in part due to its dependence on the integrity of sheriffs. The sheriff's office was a focal point for corrupt intent to interfere with the workings of mediaeval justice. A full list of the sheriff's misdemeanors in relation to the courts is best found in the provisions of the comprehensive statute of 23 Henry VI.[60] Sheriffs were not to return their own servants on panels. They were not to take anything for omitting an arrest or attachment, or for letting a defendant out on bail, or for showing any special favor to persons arrested or to be arrested, except the customary 20d. for making an arrest, with 4d. to the bailiff for his task, and 4d. to the jailer if the prisoner was committed. They were to let out on bail all persons in their custody by force of writ, bill, or warrant "in any action personal or by cause of indictment of trespass upon reasonable sureties of sufficient persons having sufficient within the counties where such persons be let to bail or mainprise" with certain exceptions. They were not to take more than 4d. for the return of panels and for the copy of the panel. They were not to make or accept any "obligations" (i.e., agreements under seal) except in their own names and upon condition "that the said prisoner shall appear at the day contained in the said writ, bill, or warrant," and they were not to take for such obligations more than 4d. They were to ap-

[56] 11 Hy. VI, c. 4; 15 Hy. VI, c. 5.
[57] 11 Hy. VII, c. 24.
[58] *Paston Letters*, No. 224, Sir Thomas Howes to John Paston, Nov., 1454.
[59] *Ibid.*, No. 296, William Botoner to John Paston, Oct. 12, 1456.
[60] 23 Hy. VI, c. 9.

point deputies in the Chancery, King's Bench, Common Pleas, and Exchequer of Record to receive their writs for them, and if they made a return of *cepi corpus* or *reddidit se,* they were to have the prisoner in court on the return day not waiting for a writ of *habeas corpus.* The penalty for all save the last provision of the statute was treble damages to the injured party and £40 fine, of which the king would have half and the party the other half. Justices of both benches, justices of assize, and justices of the peace were empowered to inquire into, hear, and determine their offenses without special commission to do so. An earlier statute [61] had included embezzlement of writs in the list of misdemeanors and the empaneling of juries without sending warning to the jurors "to their great loss and damage" and had provided the remedy of double damages to the party injured. Justices of the peace had been given power to inquire into such misdemeanors but not to hear and determine. They were to certify such offenses before the "Justices of Deliverance," and offenders were to make fine and ransom to the king.

Earlier attempts to prevent bribery and excessive personal influence of important men of the county had taken the form of limitation of the term of office of sheriffs and their bailiffs to one year at a time,[62] provisions against reappointment within three years, and the requirement that sheriffs be substantial men resident in the county,[63] and therefore, presumably, less subject to the temptations of the money bag. The evils described in the statutes of Henry VI were evidently nothing new.

The problem was to find effective means of holding sheriffs responsible. This was a vain search. First justices of assize,[64] then justices of the peace,[65] were given power to inquire into their misdemeanors, but the evils continued. Eventually for most administrative purposes the justices of the peace superseded the sheriffs.[66] The latter continued, however, to be the agencies upon which the

[61] 4 Hy. VI, c. 1.
[62] 14 Ed. III, stat. 1, c. 7; 28 Ed. III, c. 7; 42 Ed. III, c. 9; 1 Ric. II, c. 11; 1 Hy. V, c. 4; 23 Hy. VI, c. 7.
[63] 4 Ed. III, c. 9; 5 Ed. III, c. 4; 14 Ed. III, stat. 1, c. 7. Cf. also 12 Ed. II, c. 5, and 9 Henry V, stat. 1, c. 5.
[64] 20 Ed. III, c. 6.
[65] Putnam, *Proceedings,* pp. xxxvi–xxxvii.
[66] Pickthorn, *Early Tudor Government: Henry VII,* pp. 59–66.

central court depended for the execution of writs of process, and this was probably the most critical weakness in the administration of justice in the fifteenth century.

The influences which worked for the sheriff's corruption were active before his selection. Justice Yelverton's voice was a cry in the wilderness of disorder in Norfolk in 1450, when he wrote to John Bocking to move Sir John Fastolf "that we may have a good sheriff and a good under-sheriff that neither for good favour nor fear will return for the king, nor betwixt party and party, none other men but such as are good and true and in no wise will be forsworn; for the people here is loath to complain until they have tidings of a good sheriff." [67] The election of a sheriff was already overdue when Yelverton wrote in November, and the sort of influence which made him fear the outcome is illustrated in the report James Gresham sent to John Paston that John Heydon, recorder of Norwich and notorious extortioner, had threatened to spend £1000 "rather than he should fail of a sheriff this year coming for his intent." [68]

According to the mediaeval principle that the richest man was the one least likely to yield to the temptations of bribery, the selection of sheriffs should have been above the corrupting influence of money. They were chosen by the king from three men nominated by the council.[69] In this method of selection the influence of great lords with interests in the county inevitably weighed heavily.[70]

Before undertaking his duties, the sheriff took an oath to exercise his office "well and faithfully and impartially" and to "take nothing of any other man than the king by colour or reason of his office." [71] How difficult it was for him to live up to this oath and to Justice Yelverton's requirement that he show no favor in empaneling juries is well illustrated in the case of John Jermyn, chosen sheriff of Norfolk in 1450.

All hopes for quieting the county centered on Jermyn, and William Jenney believed that he would be "ruled well enough." He did

[67] *Paston Letters*, No. 125.
[68] *Ibid.*, No. 117.
[69] Fortescue, *De Laudibus*, cap. 24.
[70] *Paston Letters*, Nos. 132, 591.
[71] Fortescue, *De Laudibus*, cap. 24. Cf. *S. R.*, vol. I, p. 247.

not prove a willing tool in the hands of the Pastons, however, and he could not prevent the King from acting on Lord Moleyns' behalf. The King wrote directly to John Paston [72] asking him to delay bringing charges against Moleyns for the riotous attack made by his servants on Paston's manor of Gresham, the destruction of the manor house, the carrying off of valuable goods, and the mistreatment of Margaret Paston, who had tried to hold the place. When proceedings finally began in the following year, the sheriff reported that he had a writing from the King "that he shall make such a panel to acquit the lord Moleyns." [73] (According to John Paston, writings of this sort could be had for a noble.) Jermyn was no Sir Francis Bacon, however. He did not take money for favors unperformed. John Osbern, who asked him on Paston's behalf to take a reward for past and future services in the matter of Moleyns, reported: "He thanked you and said his under-sheriff was at London, and himself had none deserved, and if he had he would have taken it." When reminded that John Paston had promised to "attempt to rear actions that should be to the avail of him and his office" and also "to save him harmless" of any possible consequences to the amount of £100, he said that Lord Moleyns was a great lord who had the King's favor and could soon and easily damage him to the amount of more than £100. An appeal to his sense of public duty also failed to move Jermyn. In reply to the reminder that in default of a sheriff, every man was in danger of his livelihood, he merely said that he "trusted to God to impanel such men as should to his knowledge be indifferent." [74]

Although the Pastons were sincerely anxious to rid the county of the extortions and maintenances of Heydon and Tuddenham and the riotous depredations of Charles Nowell and his gang, they were not above reproach themselves. Apparently they believed that the enforcement of the statutes against corruption of sheriffs was the responsibility of the itinerant justices and the justices of the peace. At any rate, they did not leave the sheriff's favor to chance. Influence, friendship, and money they used liberally to insure sup-

[72] *Paston Letters*, No. 111, Henry VI to John Paston, Sept. 18, 1450.
[73] *Ibid.*, No. 155, Debenham, Tymperley, and White to John Paston, May 2, 1451.
[74] *Ibid.*, No. 159, J. Osbern to J. Paston, May 27, 1451. Cf. No. 510, a similar refusal of a bribe.

port of their interests.[75] No doubt they argued, with some reason, that it was a question of survival. Where the King himself intervened to protect from punishment a lawbreaker such as Lord Moleyns, a sensible man looked to his fences even though he had to build them with silver for the sheriff. Hopes of reform at the top and center were repeatedly dashed.

The sheriff's favor was useful in many ways. He could, and would for a consideration, empanel jurors to suit the party.[76] He could, would, and did make false returns to writs [77] or no returns at all. Thomas Denys wrote in March, 1454, to John Paston to send to the sheriff on behalf of a kinsman of his arrested on a writ of process in debt for £100 "that my said kinsman may be eased and no return made against him but that he may answer the next term by attorney." [78] The slang expression for thus failing to return the writ seems to have been *per album breue*,[79] I suppose because the writ remained unendorsed. The frequent note in plea roll records of process (for example, in about one out of every five among 500 sample entries selected at random from the roll of Michaelmas, 2 Edward IV) that the sheriff did not send the writ may in some instances represent such entreaties to the sheriff.

Although the penalties for embezzlement were high and the

---

[75] *Ibid.*, No. 993, James Gresham to John Paston, 1449: "You had better come hither as soon as possible and get the favour of the sheriff that shall be next year." *Ibid.*, No. 144, memorandum of John Paston that it is useless to labour for indictments "but if ye be right secure of the sheriff's office." *Ibid.*, No. 281, J. Bockyng to John Paston, May 8, 1456: "Ye must surely entreat the sheriff, for we have much to do with him." *Ibid.*, No. 183, Agnes Paston to John Paston, Nov. 16, 1452: "Margaret Talfas . . . asked my counsel whether she might give the sheriff silver or not and I told her that if she did, I supposed she should find him the more friendly." *Ibid.*, No. 223, Sir Th. Howes to J. Paston, Nov. 13, 1454: "And sir, as ye think with advice of my Master Yelverton, Jenney, and others, my master's counsel therein, that the sheriff may be rewarded."

[76] *Ibid.*, No. 224, Same to same: "And also my master is agreed what reward you gave the sheriff and holdeth him content, wherefore that your reward may be the larger, so he will thereupon return the panel for the said attaint," *ibid.*, No. 222; No. 420, Richard Calle to John Paston, June, Oct., 1461. He wrote to young John that if Jenney had not prevented the holding of the gaol (jail) delivery, he would have been acquitted because of the favor of the sheriff "and a panel made after my advice."

[77] Case of *Jenney v. Paston* discussed above; C. P. 40/804, Easter, 2 Ed. IV.

[78] *Paston Letters*, No. 199.

[79] *Plumpton Corr.*, Ser. I, No. VII, Godfrey Grene to Sir Wm.: "also the writs were out, but I caused Horbury [attorney of the Common Pleas] *per album breue* so the sheriff shall have none paid for the writs by advice of Mr. Rocliff." The reference is to Bryan Rocliff, Sir William's legal adviser.

practice of delivering writs *de recordo* to deputies of the sheriff in the Bench provided a means of checking upon the sheriff, the evil seems to have continued and may explain other entries noting that the sheriff did not send the writ. In the case quoted above of John Paston against William Jenney, the sheriff embezzled the original copy of a writ of exigent.[80] Another sheriff is reported in the Year Book for Trinity, 5 Edward IV to have been amerced £20 for embezzlement and £10 each for the return of two unsealed copies of a writ.[81] Rewards to the sheriff would have to be substantial to cover his risk of penalties such as these.

The sheriff's derelictions of duty in failing to send prisoners to Westminster have been given some attention in an earlier chapter.[82] The most spectacular example which has come to my attention is the contumacy of Sir Robert Wingfield, sheriff of Norfolk in 1454 and again in 1471, and of his wife Margaret. Between them, despite repeated distraints, they neglected for thirty-three years in the case of one prisoner, and for nineteen in the case of another, to send them into the King's Bench.[83] In Alice of Salisbury's case (cited above in Chapter XII), the sheriff's return to the peremptory writ of *habeas corpus* was that his predecessor, not he, was responsible for the frivolous return of *languidus est*. These two cases illustrate a fundamental deficiency of the sheriff as an officer for the enforcement of process in suits at law. A sheriff held office for only one year at a time and was not responsible for the acts of his predecessor nor to his successor for turning over prisoners.[84] Wingfield's prisoners eventually escaped sometime in the reign of Richard III. The original reasons for their arrest, in one case a fine owed the king in trespass, in the other, an order to appear in the King's Bench to give security of the peace, seem scarcely to warrant such long-continued confinement. In Alice of Salisbury's case the sheriff could not produce the prisoner because he had let him escape, a more ordinary delinquency, and one which helps to lessen our con-

---

[80] For discussion of statutes and devices to insure safe delivery and return of writs, see above, Ch. XI.
[81] *Y. B. Trin.,* 5 Ed. IV, pl. 13.
[82] Ch. XII.
[83] Blatcher, *Bull. of the Inst. of Hist. Research,* vol. XIII (1935–1936), pp. 146–150.
[84] Normally commissions of gaol (jail) delivery must have provided some safeguard against abuses like the Wingfields' behavior.

cern over the inhumanities of mediaeval procedure. On the other hand, it cannot but increase our feeling that the sheriff was not a very reliable arm of the central courts of common law.

The sheriff was not primarily an officer of the law. His chief responsibility was the collection of the money for which he accounted to the Exchequer. It was the misfortune of the law courts that they were forced to depend for execution of writs of process on an officer who was not a trained servant of the government and, at best, had no special feeling of responsibility for the effectiveness of legal procedure. The clerks, attorneys, sergeants at law, justices, and other officers of the court, however, were members of a professional group which was building up standards of its own, and this hierarchy headed by the justices had as its chief function the administration of justice to the English people. What then can be said of the standards of responsibility of this group? What complaints were made against them, and how seriously are they to be taken?

The complaints concerning attorneys seem to have sprung from the conviction expressed in a Commons petition in Parliament that the "diverse errors, deceits, injuries" occurring daily in the courts and "extortions, expenses, and large losses" inflicted on the king's subjects were due to the large numbers of "unlearned" attorneys hunting for business and willing to stir up vexatious lawsuits if necessary to get it.[85] The shyster lawyer had apparently already made his appearance thus early in the history of the profession. He was probably an excellent tool in the hands of maintainers of suits like Heydon and Tuddenham. The remedy provided was that the justices should examine and swear in a certain number of attorneys to take care of the business of each county. The reply did not grant the request that the number of attorneys for each county be limited to an arbitrary number.[86] Such restriction was applied only to Norfolk, Suffolk, and Norwich, and in answer to a later petition.[87] This was perhaps because the answer was drawn up with the advice and consent of the justices. A request that the clerks who made enrollments should not be allowed to practice as at-

[85] *R. P.*, vol. III, 666a, 13 Hy. IV, and preamble to statute of 33 Hy. VI, c. 7.
[86] 4 Hy. IV, c. 18.
[87] *R. P.*, vol. III, pp. 642–643, 11 Hy. IV, and *R. P.*, vol. III, 666a, 13 Hy. IV.

torneys was similarly shelved by referring it to the justices.[88] An earlier complaint that the clerks who had the keeping of the rolls of the benches were charging fees for bringing the rolls into the court was met with the answer: "Let him who feels himself aggrieved complain to the Chancellor who will do for him right and reason." [89] The function of the justices as advisers to the king on the drawing up of legislation seems to have given them an opportunity to prevent too serious meddling with the internal affairs of the courts.

There are few complaints of extortion by court officers in the fifteenth century. The only one publicly complained of was the Chirographer.[90] His difficulties and the reasons for his misbehavior have been considered in an earlier chapter.[91] There were complaints also of embezzlement of documents in his care.[92] The two sins perhaps go together. Because of the difficulties which he and his clerks had in getting an adequate income, they may have been more susceptible to offers of money for destroying or stealing writs.

Although no general complaints have been found of such extortions on the part of other officers of the court, the list of fees which has come down to us in seventeenth century copies from the Black Book [93] was probably an answer to demands for certainty concerning the rewards to which officers were entitled. The danger that tips given for special favor might come to be expected as a matter of right must have been an ever-present one.

The statutes enacting measures intended to remove the justices from corrupt influences are mainly fourteenth century ones and they were fairly inclusive. The oath provided by the ordinance of 20 Edward I forbade their giving judgments through fear of favor and prohibited their taking gifts except "meat and drink of small value." [94] The injunctions against submitting to fear of favor were not so well obeyed that there was no repetition of complaints.[95] Statutes of Richard II's reign attempted to diminish the influence

88 *Ibid.*
89 R. P., vol. III, p. 202, 8 Ric. II.
90 R. P., vol. II, pp. 312–313, 46 Ed. III; vol. III, p. 471, 2 Hy. IV; stat. 5 Hy. IV, c. 14.
91 Ch. IX.
92 R. P., vol. III, pp. 495–496, 4 Hy. IV; p. 543, 5 Hy. IV.
93 App. I.
94 20 Ed. III. Cf. 5 Ed. II, c. 39, and 14 Ed. III, stat. 1, c. 5.
95 R. P., vol. III, p. 158, 7 Ric. II; p. 623, 11 Hy. IV.

at the assizes of powerful men of the county,[96] and to prevent sale of offices.[97] If these statutes were effectively enforced, they should have kept the judicial office reasonably free from partiality and corruption.

Attempts to influence the decisions of justices and accusations of partiality may be found in the *Paston Letters*. The Pastons and their friends left nothing to chance where the outcome of lawsuits was at stake. Sir John Fastolf wrote to Justice Yelverton in 1457 asking his favor on behalf of his chaplain Thomas Howes in a suit against Andrews.[98] He also wrote to Sir Richard Bingham's son-in-law to ask him to speak to the judge, his father-in-law, about the same matter.[99] Margaret Paston was a great believer in personal influence. She wrote often to her husband to urge him to solicit the favor of judges. In 1465 she enjoined him to see the justices of assize for Norfolk before they came into the county, in order to protect his servants Daubeney, Wykys, and Calle against charges made by enemies.[100] We are not told anywhere whether these importunings achieved the desired results. John Pullan, legal adviser to Sir Robert Plumpton in his controversy with Empson, urged him to labor the sheriffs and all his friends in the counties where his lands lay but beyond that to trust to God's steersmanship "in every righteous cause." [101]

William Paston, judge of the Common Pleas, was accused of taking various rewards and fees from persons and corporations within the counties of Norfolk: 1s. from the town of Yarmouth, 26s. 8d. from Saint Bennett's, 20s. from the Prior of Saint Fennes, 10s. from the prior of Norwich, 20s. from the Prior of Penteney, 40s. from the town of Lynn, 20s. from the Prior of Walsingham, and 10 marks from Katherine Shelton "to destroy the right of the king and his ward, that is for to say, Ralph, son and heir of John Shelton." [102] The charge was not proved against William Paston, but it is not altogether improbable that justices sometimes took special rewards

---

96 8 Ric. II, c. 2; 20 Ric. II, c. 3.
97 12 Ric. II, c. 2.
98 *Paston Letters*, No. 308, Oct. 29, 1457.
99 *Ibid.*, No. 309, Sir John Fastolf to Stephen Scrope.
100 *Ibid.*, No. 513, July 12, 1465.
101 *Plumpton Corr.*, Ser. II, Nos. CXIX and CXX, May 1501.
102 *Paston Letters*, No. 19, William Dalling's petition, 1434(?).

of this sort. A century earlier there is conclusive evidence of their receiving such rewards.[103]

The notorious instance of partiality described in the *Paston Letters* is Prisot's behavior on a commission of oyer and terminer in Norfolk in 1451. Prisot was Chief Justice of the Common Pleas at the time. He and his fellows, according to Thomas Howes's account, would not give so "much as a beck nor a twinkling of their eye" towards the "lawful exceptions" put in and declared by the city of Norwich, the town of Swaffham, Sir John Fastolf, the Pastons, and others but "took it to derision." They removed the sessions from Norwich to Walsingham, where Heydon and Tuddenham's influence was stronger. Heydon and Tuddenham came with four hundred mounted retainers, and their friends appeared in great numbers. Only John Paston among the plaintiffs dared to present himself. Furthermore, Prisot "would suffer no man that was learned to speak for the plaintiffs, but took it as a venom, and took them by the nose at every third word which might well be known for open partiality." [104] Counsel for the complainants in this case were neither the first nor the last ever to be taken by the nose at every third word by a judge. Furthermore, Prisot's position was difficult. If Walsingham was more open to the influence of Heydon and Tuddenham, Norwich was overwhelmingly for the complainants. It must have been difficult indeed for a judge to maintain any sort of impartiality in the midst of the factional strife of the time, where powerful interests were involved.

At any rate, the Paston correspondents seem to have had in varying degrees the conviction expressed by Sir John Fastolf to John Paston in May, 1455: "It would be a great rebuke if the matter of the ward went against us for nowadays ye know well that law goeth as it is favoured, and after that the attorneys be wise and discreet." [105] Certainly no sensible man depended only on law to protect his interests. He followed the advice of an anonymous correspondent to John Paston: "Make you so strong in lordship and in the law that ye reck not much whether he be good or bad." [106]

---

103 *The Knights Hospitallers in England*, p. 203.
104 *Paston Letters*, No. 158, May 9, 1451.
105 *Ibid.*, No. 235, Sir John Fastolf to John Paston, May 3, 1455.
106 *Ibid.*, No. 428, anon to John Paston, Dec. 1461(?).

The *Letters* are full of references to requests for the favor of the great.[107] Many expectations were formed of the Duke of York's "good lordship" when he returned from Ireland in 1450.[108] Margaret Paston, discouraged over the progress of the struggle for Drayton and Hellesden against the Duke of Suffolk, wrote to her husband: "Sundry folks have said to me that they think verily but if you have my lord of Suffolk's good lordship, while the world is as it is, you can never live in peace. . . ."[109] Two years later, the Duke's men were still in possession at Drayton and Hellesden, and it was rumored that he and Justice Yelverton, former ally of the Pastons but by this time "a good threadbare friend"[110] to them, were to come down to the county on a commission of oyer and terminer to indict and hang as many of the Duke's enemies as possible. Like many rumors, this proved to be an exaggeration. Richard Calle, who reported it, suggested that John Paston secure the good lordship of the Duke of Norfolk to counter the attack from Suffolk and Yelverton, even if he had to give him the profits of Drayton and Hellesden "for the keeping and some money beside."[111]

The influence of great men was forceful in persuading sheriffs, intimidating juries and witnesses, and overawing opponents. Lesser people did not lightly either commence or continue lawsuits in which a great lord might interfere on the other side. For example, Sir John Fastolf directed Sir Thomas Howes to discuss the matter with the Duchess of Norfolk before taking action against one Brome for taking and withholding Fastolf's sheep, the Duchess having written to him eight years before "desiring that the process I was purposed take against him should be respited and all that reason would he should obey."[112] There are a number of examples

---

[107] *Ibid.*, No. 233, Sir John Fastolf to the Duke of Norfolk to ask his favor in the matter of the wardship referred to in No. 235. *Ibid.*, No. 234, plea by the same to the Duke of Norfolk to get his favor for Sir Thomas Howes and John Porter, whose indictment for trespass Sir John was trying to have reversed by writ of attaint. In an earlier letter (No. 224), Howes had urged John Paston to get Jenney to move the Duke of Norfolk to take Howes and Porter into his household in order to speed the attaint "as well with the sheriff as with the great jury." *Plumpton Corr.*, Ser. I, No. XVI, Sept. 14, 146–(?), John Felton and John Ward to Sir William Plumpton, keeper of the castle of Knaresborough to ask protection for Thomas of the Logge.
[108] *Paston Letters*, Nos. 113 ff., especially No. 116.
[109] *Ibid.*, No. 472, May 6, 1463.
[110] *Ibid.*, No. 435, Margaret Paston to John Paston, Jan. 7, 1462.
[111] *Ibid.*, No. 512, Richard Calle to John Paston, July 10, 1465.
[112] *Ibid.*, No. 132, Dec. 20, 1450.

among the *Paston Letters* of this sort of letter in which a great personage asks a lesser one to discontinue process against some defendant in a lawsuit in return for a promise of good lordship in other matters.[113] The helplessness of the lesser people is testified by Justice Paston. A plaintiff in debt for arrears of rent, who had been attacked in two counter-suits and arrested, asked his advice. He urged the man to abandon his own suit and seek no remedy. "For if you do," he said, "thee shall have the worse, be the case never so true, for he is feed with my Lord of Norfolk and much is he of his counsel and also, thee canst no man of law in Norfolk nor in Suffolk to be against him and for sooth no more might I when I had a plea against him." [114]

Sometimes the support of lords extended to maintenance, that is the taking over of the responsibility for the suit by the maintainer. For example, Sir John Fastolf, in his suit against the Prior of Hikeling, only hoped that the sheriff would do his duty because the brothers had handed over all their evidences to Lord Scales and arranged for him to come and live in the manor in question.[115] William Wayte reported to John Paston in 1451 that Lord Scales was the maintainer of the notorious Sir Thomas Tuddenham.[116] Although cases of maintenance are infrequent in the rolls of the Court of Common Pleas,[117] there is frequent mention of it in the letters, and there are probably many examples in the records of the King's Bench and of the sessions.[118]

Illustrations of the use of physical force to establish or maintain a right are so numerous, especially in the correspondence, as to be impossible to present here. The need to show that one had held the last manor court, or that one had collected the rents continuously over a considerable number of years in a manor which was being fought over in the royal courts, led to violent forays by the one side

[113] *Ibid.*, No. 967, Lord Scales to Sir John Fastolf on behalf of his servant Dowbegyng in outlawry in debt; *ibid.*, No. 294, Archbishop Bourchier to John Paston, Sept. 7, 1456, on behalf of Robert Ufford appealed of the death of a clerk; *Plumpton Corr.*, Ser. I, No. XXI, Earl of Northumberland to Sir William Plumpton, June 6, 1471–1479, asking Sir William to stop process against his servant, Robert Birnand.

[114] *Paston Letters*, No. 28.

[115] *Ibid.*, No. 291, Sir John Fastolf to John Paston, July 31, 1456.

[116] *Ibid.*, No. 994, Jan. 3, 1451.

[117] The only one I have found is C. P. 40/801, Trin., 1 Ed. IV, *Copley* (prothonotary of the Bench) *v. Kyrton.*

[118] Putnam, *Proceedings*, p. 362, No. 392, and p. 408, No. 30.

and the other. Tenants of the Pastons must have been in a constant state of destitution and feaf, between the distraints and counterdistraints of the Pastons and their enemies and the brawls which occurred when the one side or the other attempted to hold a manor court. John Paston, the younger, got his apprenticeship as a landowner of the county in such struggles for the interests of his older brother and seems to have developed a considerable shrewdness in overcoming the superior physical force of his opponents.

Sufficient illustration has perhaps been given of the abuses possible in fifteenth century litigation. The elaborate procedure of the courts, the patience with defendants, and the technicality offered many opportunities to him who was shrewd enough to seize them. Officers of the courts, sheriffs, and justices were subject to the overwhelming influence of great lords. Jurors took bribes or were terrified by threats of force into giving verdicts contrary to their knowledge or their conviction of the truth. Influence of great lords, money, and physical force weighed too often against justice. These are heavy charges. On the other hand, these same accusations in general terms may be made against administration of justice in any time and place. The important and unanswered question is how prevalent they were in the fifteenth century. The Pastons wrote chiefly of Norfolk, and that shire had its gangsters in their time as Chicago has today. But the depredations of criminals in Chicago do not mean that life in the United States or even in Chicago is generally insecure because of lawlessness. The Pastons are famous for having left behind a set of letters which is unique for its time. It is possible that the conditions they describe are less typical than has sometimes been assumed. The legal records hold the answers to our questions, but the work of digging out their secrets will be a laborious and time-consuming task.

CHAPTER XVI

Evaluation

THE COURT OF COMMON PLEAS in the fifteenth century was not a fountain from which pure and absolute justice flowed over the land. It must often have failed to satisfy the demands of those who felt themselves aggrieved. Yet is this not true of any court in any time and place? Justice is, in most circumstances, a relative rather than an absolute quantity, and the rain falls on the more just and the less just. In the fifteenth century absolute justice must often have been particularly difficult to find. Then, a land-hungry gentry was engaged in transforming feudal landholdings into estates which could be more freely transferred and inherited. Moreover, families like the Pastons, the Littletons, and the Plumptons, were not content to keep what they had. They aimed to add to and consolidate their wealth and power. What they wanted of the law courts was not abstract justice but assistance in furthering their objectives. At the same time, a prosperous mercantile class was carrying on commercial enterprises which had escaped somewhat from the restraining interdicts of the mediaeval church against profit. And what the Celys and the Thomas Betsons, as well as the more humble people like fishmongers and bakers, wanted of the courts was also gain of some sort.

The Court of Common Pleas was largely occupied with the interests of all these people. Most of the actions carried on there were of debt. And many of the trespass cases were indirectly concerned with interest in land. Actions of trespass *quare clausum fregit* often clearly sprang from such altercations as were carried on by the Pastons over disputed titles to real property. A person who considered

237

that he had a claim in land which was in the possession of another asserted his claim by entering and acting as if he were the owner. The disseised person then had the choice of bringing action for title or one for damages. The records suggest that he often chose an action of trespass *quare clausum fregit.*

The rules of the common law which had to be applied to the needs and interests of these people were complex and difficult to understand, as anyone may discover by reading the mediaeval Year Books and plea rolls. The fifteenth century machinery for enforcing the rules was inherited from earlier centuries and had the defects which result from piece-by-piece construction over a long period of time. There are two main questions to answer in judging the health of the fifteenth century Court of Common Pleas as an institution for the administration of justice. On the one hand, what inherent weaknesses were there in the rules and the means available to enforce them? On the other, how well were they enforced by the judges and other officers who peopled the court in the fifteenth century?

It is not yet time to give more than a tentative answer to the second question. Holdsworth and others have been harsh in their judgments. According to this view, it was "no exaggeration to say that by the middle of the fifteenth century, the rules of the common law were either perverted in their application or so neglected that they ceased to protect adequately life and property." [1] Nonetheless, Holdsworth was puzzled by "the curious combination of legal development with political retrogression" which he found characterized both fourteenth and fifteenth centuries.

The merely exploratory study of the Common Pleas records which I have made does not justify a demand for a reversal of this severe judgment. It does, I think, justify a plea that the case be remanded for retrial on the ground that there is a wealth of further evidence which should be investigated and compared with similar evidence from other centuries. The Common Pleas records themselves will probably help little to further this inquiry. The ponderous regularity with which they record the proceedings in the court make it easier to agree with Denton's judgment than with Holdsworth's. To the former, few things seemed "more striking than to

[1] *H. E. L.,* vol. II, p. 408.

follow the calm dignity of the law and its official administration as judges passed from county to county, and to note the observance of most of the legal forms of courts of justice, even in the midst of the strife and noise of angry partisans." The records which should be most useful and pertinent to the inquiry are those of the King's Bench, the assizes, gaol delivery, oyer and terminer, and particularly the sessions of the justices of the peace. Miss Putnam's *Proceedings Before the Justices of the Peace in the Fourteenth and Fifteenth Centuries* shows what valuable materials there are to be discovered and studied.

I do not expect that the results of such investigation will be to confirm the laudatory view expressed by Chief Justice Fortescue in the volume which he dedicated to the proposition that the English law was the best in the world. On the other hand, they may show that the rise of a legal profession with standards established in an arduous course of training and the efforts which had been made in the fourteenth century to remedy by statute some of the more serious defects in the legal system had resulted in improvement rather than deterioration.

But there is no escaping the fact that the top layer of fifteenth century society was in a state of confusion and disorder, and that reforms were necessary when Henry Tudor seized the throne. Yet the enactments of Henry VII's reign were, for the most part, not new in principle. The philosophy on which they were based is best expressed in the words of the Chief Justice of the King's Bench before an assembly of the justices at Blackfriars, met to discuss how the law might be amended. He said: "The law will never be well-executed until all the lords spiritual and temporal are of one accord, for the love and dread that they have for God or for the king, or both, to execute them effectually, and when the king on his part and the lords on their part both want to do this—and do it." [2] Otherwise, he said, all would take them lightly, and, if they were chastised or punished, others would be ready to stand surety for them. As king's attorney in Edward IV's time he had seen the lords swear to keep the laws as compiled and an hour later in Star Chamber break their oaths by other oaths completely contrary to the first.

[2] *Y. B. Mich., 1 Hy. VII*, pl. 3.

The measures adopted by Henry VII's vigorous government were mainly new enactments of old remedies. The significant innovation was the steadfastness of purpose to enforce them in the upper levels of government. Moreover, neither the drastic legislation nor the new spirit at the heart of the administration accomplished spectacularly immediate results. Evidences of bribery and other forms of official corruption are just as strong in the *Plumpton Correspondence* as in the *Paston Letters*. Many of the evils complained of in the fifteenth century became worse in later times, and some are still with us. Some will always be with us until we are governed by the philosopher kings of Plato.

A judgment concerning the inherent defects in the rules and machinery for administration of justice in the fifteenth century is more nearly germane to the substance of this present study than any attempt to judge how well they worked. In describing the workings of the court many manifest weaknesses have been exposed.

In the first place, the cumbersome process described in Part III, above, allowed many opportunities for escape from justice. It was ponderously slow and not inevitably effective if prosecuted to a conclusion. Distress infinite might continue until the goods and patience of the plaintiff were as much exhausted as the defendant's. Process by *capias* and exigent inevitably made of the defendant an outlaw if he did not appear before proclamation, but it did not bring him into court to answer the plaintiff unless he found himself seriously inconvenienced by his outlawry. Both processes might take years. The rules concerning procedure were complex, so complex that justices and lawyers spent a good deal of time discussing them, as is clear from the Year Books of the period. There were signs of change, to be sure, not open and direct change as the result of conscious thought by forward-looking lawyers, but indirect and, in a sense, dishonest change through the substitution of fictions for steps which had become obsolete. This development, encouraged by competition for business among the central courts went so far by the eighteenth century that only in cases where arrest was forbidden was there any pretense of going through the elaborate sequence of process which had been required in mediaeval times. The signs that the development was already under way in the fifteenth century are the use of fictitious names of pledges and mainpernors in

240

sheriffs returns to writs and the probable omission of summons in process by *capias*, the writ being returned by the deputy sheriff and not sent into the county at all. Some foresight of the consequences of this substitution of fictions for the reality might have saved more laborious reform later on. It is asking a lot of fifteenth century men of law, however, to expect them to foresee in small beginnings such heavy consequences, and to remedy conditions of which they must scarcely have been aware, especially in a tradition-bound age when even statute law was thought of rather as definition of existing law than creation of new law.[3]

A second weakness of fifteenth century administration, which continued for a long time with increasing evil consequences, was the payment of officers by fee rather than by salary. Justices and other patent officers received salaries, to be sure, but the bulk of their income came from fees. This, with the frequent deputing of offices to subordinates and the multiplication through splitting off of functions, helped to make the cost of lawsuits increasingly prohibitive, even where there was no extortion, and where no bribes were necessary. In this respect, however, offices of the Court of Common Pleas did not differ from other administrative offices.

A third handicap to fifteenth century justice was the ambiguous nature of the jury, looked upon both as a body of witnesses and a group of judges of evidence. Officially, in the legislation concerning embracery and especially attaint, the jury was a body of witnesses responsible for knowing the facts. Practically, the courts recognized the inadequacy of this principle by allowing the presentation of evidence at trial. Until the jury became, as it did later, clearly a group of judges of evidence, the laws concerning embracery inevitably remained primitive.

Another consequence of the contemporary concept of the jury was that provisions for cases where justice went astray were inadequate. Judgment could be reversed in the common law courts only by two methods: first by attaint, because the jurors were supposed to have perjured themselves; second by writ of error because some mistake had been made in the procedure. The failure to make provision for the case where new evidence might be found or to allow for misunderstanding as well as dishonesty on the part of jurors was a

[3] Chrimes, *Const. Ideas*, pp. 192–199.

serious handicap to justice in the courts of common law. Appeal could be had to the council or to Parliament to be sure, but some of the difficulties of such appeal have been suggested above.

A more serious handicap to administration of justice in fifteenth century courts of common law than any of the foregoing was the dependence of the courts on the sheriff for execution of process. His office predates the organization of the central courts and was not especially well adapted to their use. For one thing, he was appointed annually in the middle of Michaelmas term. In the early fifteenth century, before 12 Edward IV, this meant that if the new sheriff did not take up his duties immediately, there was a period in which no one was responsible for the return of writs.[4] In a statute of 12 Edward IV, later confirmed, it was provided that writs should be returned in the name of the old sheriff until the new one should appear. Annual appointments of sheriffs and bailiffs with provision against immediate reappointment may perhaps have had its advantages in keeping the sheriff free from influences of local landowners, although it does not seem to have been notably successful in that purpose. On the other hand, it was inefficient from the point of view of getting done the local business of the courts. A professionally trained man with knowledge of the law would have been better from their point of view. Increasing supervision of the sheriff by the justices of the peace accomplished some reform of the office.[5] How much it helped to remedy the weaknesses which hampered the central courts is a question to be answered only from later records.

Several other questions concerning the sheriff make clear the need for continuation of the history of the office begun by Morris. For example, the curious case discussed above of Robert[6] and Margaret Wingfield, who refused for a period of many years to produce two prisoners at Westminster in spite of repeated distraints, suggests serious inefficiency in the arrangements for surrender of prisoners by a sheriff to his successor. There are many evidences in the plea rolls of the difficulties of holding an ex-sheriff responsible for omissions, errors, or deliberate wrongdoing. Miss Blatcher has

[4] 12 Ed. IV, c. 1; 17 Ed. IV, c. 7.
[5] 23 Hy. VI, c. 9, and 11 Hy. VII, cc. 15, 24, are the pertinent statutes dealing with the sheriff's functions in relation to the central courts.
[6] Ch. XV, p. 229.

described the difficulties caused by the practice of postponing the collection of distraints until the writs of green wax issued from the Exchequer.[7] Lord Fitzwalter's letter to Sir John Paston the younger, urging him to collect "such money as was coming toward you of right for the time that you were sheriff" elsewhere than by distresses within the Duchy of Lancaster,[8] rouses curiosity concerning the whole question of financial responsibility of the sheriff.

The statutes of Henry VII did not reform any of these defects of fifteenth century administration. They did nothing to shorten or clarify procedure, nothing to remedy the situation about fees, nothing to change the ideas about responsibility of jurors, nothing about the sheriff's office except to increase the supervision of the justices of the peace. They were not based on any new conception of the responsibility of the courts of common law. As the Chief Justice said, there were enough laws already. What was needed was better enforcement and a changed spirit among the lords spiritual and temporal. How Henry achieved these results through Star Chamber prosecutions, through execution of troublemakers, and through taxation, is a well-known story which needs no telling here.

The basic weaknesses in Common Pleas procedure and in the system of office-holding in this court and throughout the administration was left for later centuries to reform. The attorneys who were the authors of the *Proposals* of 1650 saw some of the problems and suggested helpful although not thoroughgoing remedies. Their proposals seem, however, to have been lost sight of in the more exciting interests of a period of revolution. Sir Matthew Hale, a little later, saw more of the problems and analyzed them more thoughtfully.[9] His proposals likewise came to nothing. Hence the two evils of obsolete procedure and privilege in office-holding settled down the more heavily upon the Court of Common Pleas until the reorganization of the early nineteenth century.

There are perhaps two reasons more fundamental than others for the persistence of the evils in spite of attacks upon them. One is that a law of precedent is inevitably backward-looking. The

[7] *Bull. of the Inst. of Hist. Research,* vol. XIII (1935–1936), pp. 146–150.
[8] *Paston Letters,* No. 902.
[9] M. Hale, "Considerations Touching the Amendment or Alteration of Laws," in Hargrave, *Tracts,* vol. I, pp. 249 ff.

reverence for the past in a law which requires each new decision to be made in the light of earlier decisions in similar cases makes for stability of principles. It also makes for stability in the ways of doing things, even when such ways are not very efficient. The other cause of persistence of weaknesses in the English court system was the human tendency to blame individuals for what went wrong. Parties complained of heavy fees and blamed the officers of the court or the sheriff. The officers took their stand on ancient custom and privilege and said they took only what was their due. Sheriffs retired from office and evaded responsibility.

No reform could have been accomplished without realization that it was often not bad men who were responsible but lack of imagination and effort directed towards improvement of the legal system. Jack Cade blamed the lawyers. The lawyers were at fault, not so much for what they did as for what they did not do. They saw the way to get around the crotchets of the law in the interests of their clients, but they did not see that it would have been better to get rid of more of the crotchets. Inevitably more of them were interested in fees than in reform and in safeguarding the mysteries of the profession than in simplifying them for the sake of justice.

Appendices

List of Fees of the

Officers of the Court

from the Black Book of the Common Pleas

Transcribed in the Early Seventeenth Century

The document below is the second of three copies of the list of fees which is among the records produced by the commission of fees appointed under James I to investigate the offices of the various courts of record (E 215 under arrangement).* The second copy was chosen for transcription because it appears to be the most complete and accurate. It is supplemented and corrected from the other two. The first copy begins with section (e), omitting the first seven paragraphs. In the left-hand margin beside the heading is the following: "An° 35° Hen: 6. Theis ordinances are inrolled in the Roll mencioned in the Blacke booke in the Treasurie of the Court of Common Pleas./ Upon search of the number Roll it appeareth that none of theis Fees." This first copy ends with the word "Courtesie" corresponding to "Curtesye" under the heading "The Cryors" in the copy here transcribed. Otherwise, variations are slight. The third copy is almost identical with the second. It is subscribed "examinatur cum Record'/Edv/Ayscoghe/Moyle" and endorsed as follows: "A Copy taken out of the black book" and "Orders and fees taken out of the blacke Booke in the Treasury is/" This final mark "is" seems to be the successor to the Latin "est" found so frequently in earlier documents. The same mark in the same handwriting appears beside Item 4 under "Clerks of the Prothonotaries and Philizers." The writing seems to be that of J. Moyle.

No other mention has been found of the Black Book of the Court of

* This list of fees came to my attention through the kindness of Professor Jean S. Wilson of Smith College.

Common Pleas. Richardson (*Attorney's Practice* [London, 1758], vol. I, p. 5), says of the prothonotary: "He draws up the general rules of the court made for regulating and settling the practice in the proceedings therein, and causes the same to be ingrossed and hung up in the treasury chamber at Westminster, gives copies thereof to the judges and to the other prothonotaries and officers of the court, if required without any fee." The preamble to the ordinance of 23 Henry VII (App. II [d]) suggests that this duty may have been entrusted to the prothonotary at that time, and that the engrossment of the rules in a book may also have begun at that time. The prothonotary was required by the ordinance to read the earlier ordinance of 35 Henry VI and the one of 23 Henry VII once in each term. The earlier ordinance had been enrolled on the plea roll (C. P. 40/786, m. 494). It would have been extremely difficult for the prothonotary to find the required plea rolls and have them carried into court in order that he might read the rules each term. It is altogether probable that the Black Book was begun as a result of this ordinance of 23 Henry VII.

There is still a problem as to when the lists of fees were drawn up. Seventeenth century books (*Praxis Utriusque Banci*, 1674; *Rules, Orders, and Notices of the Court* [3d ed., 1724], pp. 1 ff.) ascribe them to Trinity, 35 Henry VI, but the versions given are incorrect and incomplete. They conclude with the second item under "Filacers for Common Process" and continue with an ordinance of Michaelmas, 6–7 Elizabeth. This establishes a probability that they were drawn up before 6–7 Elizabeth.

Internal evidence does not help to narrow down the span of years between Trinity, 35 Henry VI and Michaelmas, 6–7 Elizabeth. The spelling is probably at least partly early seventeenth century spelling because the three Exchequer copies available differ in this particular. A hypothesis that the list of filacers' fees must have been drawn up after 19 Henry VII, because of the mention of the fee for writs of exigent in actions on the case and statutory trespass (supposed not to have been allowed until a statute of that year authorized them) falls to the ground when search in the rolls reveals that, statute or no statute, process by outlawry was employed in these forms of trespass throughout the reign of Edward IV.

Thomas Jakes's memoranda (App. II) include a list of fees of the Clerk of the Warrants and Estreats which does not appear in any of the other lists and, in addition to the ordinance of Trinity, 35 Henry VI, an ordinance of 23 Henry VII, which likewise does not appear anywhere else, probably because it became obsolete as a result of the issue of a later ordinance altering its provisions in 15 Elizabeth (*Rules, Orders, and Notices,* 15 Eliz.).

A reason for believing, in spite of our lack of certainty, that the lists of fees were drawn up in the fifteenth century is to be found in parallel developments in other administrative departments. Jack Cade and his followers complained not only of corruption of the justices but also of extortionate fees taken by administrative officers of the Exchequer and of the courts (*Three Fifteenth Century Chronicles,* pp. 94–99), and in 34 Henry VI the Commons asked to have the fees of the officers of the Exchequer defined to prevent extortion (*R. P.,* vol. V, p. 323, 34 Hy. VI, 1455). Reforms of the Household were also being mooted at this time (Nichols, *A Collection of Ordinances and Regulations for the Government of the Royal Household Made in Divers Reigns from King Edward III to King William and Queen Mary* [London, 1780], p. 15).

It is almost certain that the lists were drawn up between 35 Henry VI and 6–7 Elizabeth, and it is probable, because Moyle, the prothonotary in 1625 who had access to the Black Book, accepted them as of 35 Henry VI, and because of a similar defining of the fees of Exchequer officers in 34 Henry VI, that the fees as well as the order concerning officers of the court are of that year.

(a) A true Copye of ordinances and Rules written' in a booke called the blacke booke remayninge in the treasurye of the Courte of Comon' pleas as followeth

(b) Hereafter doe insue the good ordinances and Rules made as well by the kinges Justices of the sayd [1] courte of the comen' place in tyme past as by the sayd Justices nowe being for the good rule and order of the same Courte which same nowe Justices doe Chardge and commaunde euerye of the sayde officers and attorneys surelye well and truelye to obserue and keepe vpon' the paynes lymyted in the foresayd Ordinances
Ordinaciones sequentes irrot[u]lantur Termino sancte Trinitatis Anno Regni Regis Henrici sexti post conquestum xxxv^to Rotulo cccclxxxxiiij° vt patet ibidem Iohanne Prisott tunc capitali Iusticiario de communi Banco et Nicholao Ayston P[etro] [1] Arden' Roberto Danvers Roberto Danby Waltero Moyle et Iohanne Nedham Iusticiariis de eodem Banco

(c) Memorandum that forasmuche as greate troubles subtletyes falsehoodes and deceites haue bin' caused and doone before this tyme

---

[1] Document torn. [Footnote numbers are repeated here to avoid repetition of footnotes.]

in the kinges courte of the comen' pleas as well for lacke of attendance of the Officers of the same place as by Comers and sitters
within the same that be not sworne [ne] [2] have not to doe within
There ben' certeyn' ordinaunces made at this vtas of saynt John'
the bap[tist] [1] the yeare of the raigne of kinge Henry the sixte
after the conquest the xxxv[th] by John' Prysett Cheife Justice òf
the sayd place by the advyse of all the Judges of the same in forme
followinge/
First that euerye prenotarie Philizer Exigenter kinges Clarke and
euerye other officer of the same pl[ace] [1] such as they and theire
predecessors have vsed to occupie theire offices in theire proper
person' and they [or] [1] theire deput[ies] [1] sworne that have vsed to
occupye theire offices by theire deputyes from hensforth attend
vpon' there sayd offices in theire places accustomed for the same
and occupye them in ther[e] [1] proper person' vpon payne of for-
feature and lesinge of theire sayd offices always forseene that if
any of the sayd officers (or deputies) [3] for sicknes or other causes
resonable be licenced or had excused by the Cheife Justice of the
same place for the tyme being that he bee not preiudised by this
ordinaunce
Item that none of the sayd officers or deputyes take vpon' them
to licence or doe sett any clarke or oth[er] [1] in any of there places
or by them to occupye in there sayd offices or for any other cause
without licence of the Cheife Justice for the tyme being savinge
such as (haue) [3] beene accustomed to have there Clarkes sitti[ng] [1]
by them that is to witt eueryche of the ij prenotaries ij Clarkes
the Clarke of Streates ij Clarkes the keeper of the writtes or his
deputie one Clerke vpon' payne of ymprisonment and makinge
fyne to the kinge therefore Nether that noe man' take vppon' him
to sitt within the sayd Comon' place that i[s] noe officer ne hath
no place within without leave of the sayd Cheife Justice or
Justices vpon' the same payne.
Item that none Attorney ne none other make any manner writt
or proces in any officers name of the same place savinge only
euerye officer in his owne name ne intromitte in any other manns
office ne of any thinge that perteyneth thereto without leve
of the Cheife Justice of the same place for the tyme being or the
same Officer in whose name he writeth and (that) [3] the sayd Of-

[2] Document torn; "ne" in the third copy.
[3] Interlineated in the second and third copies.

ficer wille allowe [4] and affirme the same vpon' payne of Imprisonment and makinge fyne to the kinge as is aforesayd

(d) Memorandum For As much as many greate Inconvenyences and
Errors daylye bee founde as well in the kinges benche as in the
Comen' place for not puttynge in of Warrentes of Attorney It is
ordeyned and agreed by the assent of all the Justices of both the
sayd places that in euerye plea or ymparlance entred by any person' as attorney in any of the sayd Courtes that he [*sic*] soe named
attorney putt in his warrant the same terme of plea or imparlance
vnder payne of forgoinge the office of Attorneyshipp' of that place
and to bee Comytted to prison and to make fyne after discrecion
of the Judges where any suche default shall happen' to fall.
Theise ordinaunces are inrolled in the rolle mencioned in the
booke

(e) Prothonot̄aries for Entries of pleas and iudgmentes

1. Inprimis for euerye comyn' declaracion
   comen' plea in barre comen' replicacion
   and comen' reioynder in pleas personall
   whether the Defend' appeare in proper
   person' or by Attorney   xij*d.*
2. And for euerye plea reall   ij*s.*
3. And in euerye plea personall pleded by
   a Seriaunt   ij*s.*
4. And if it bee matter conteyninge a whole
   rolle or more both partyes to pay for a
   rolle after the rate of euerye rolle   vj*s.* viij*d.*
5. And for euerye Judgement or satis-
   faccion in accions personall   ij*s.*
6. And for euerye Judgement or satis-
   faccion in accions reall   iiij*s.*
7. And for euerye exemplificacion in
   writtes of Entre vpon' vouchers or
   confession'   ij*s.*
8. And to the writer of the same
   exemplificacion   viii*d.*
9. And for euerye other exemplificacion
   vpon' a double vo[ucher] [1]   [iiijs.]
10. And to the writer of the same exempli-
    ficacion   xij*d.*

[4] Altered in the second copy to "avowe" but not in the third.

11. And for euerye other exemplificacion of
greate lengthe to take for the same after
the rate of the lengthe thereof
(f) Custos breuium
Inprimis yt is considered that by reason' of writtes put in after the
day many men be arrested to the greate rebuke of attorneyes and
slander of the Courte wherefore there is sett a direccion by the
Courte that none originall writt nor plur' Capias be put in after
the last day of the terme
Item the sayd Officer Oweth dayly to bringe to the Courte the
bundell of writtes of the terme present to bee seene and occupyed
by suche as have auctority soe to doe without payeing any thinge
therefore
Item for seeing of a bundell of the last
terme he Oweth to haue but   j*d.*
Item for seeinge of a bundell of euerye other
olde terme he oweth to have but   v*d.*
Item he oweth to haue nothinge for any
exigend' though yt cometh in retorned
after the day because yt is for the kinges
advantage
Item he Oweth to give attendance in his Owne
person' or by his sufficient deputy att all
convenyent tymes that Officers may take out
writtes for proces and other necessary
causes without any mony payeinge therefore
Item he Oweth to take for the receite of a
hole retorne of one Sheire comynge in after
the daye   viij*d.*
Item he Oweth to take for the retorn' of an
exigend' retorned Owtlawed in an ould terme   xx*d.*
(g) The Clerke of the Tresourhouse and his Clerkes
Inprimis for exemplificacions and writinges
of the same to take therefore as afore yt is
lymyted to the prenotaries and nothinge to
be payde for the searche if the partye
bringe the nomber rolle with him
Item for euerye record of Nisi prius   ij*s.* j*d.*
Item to the secondary for writinge and
examininge the same   iiij*d.*
Item for a scire facias vpon' a Charter

of pardon'	vj*d.*
Item for a supersedeas vppon' Mayneprise	
which should not be taken excepte the	
Defendant be in proper person'	ij*s.*
Item for a bill of bayle therevpon'	iiij*d.*
Item for writinge examynynge and certe-	
fyeinge of euery writt of Error	xij*s.* j*d.*
Item for Fees of a charter of pardon'	vj*s.* xj*d.*
that is to saye for the certyfycate of	
the record ij*s.* j*d.* and to the Warden'	
of the Fleete ij*s.* iiij*d.* and for his	
favour xx*d.* and for the scire facias vj*d.*	
and for the bill of bayle iiij*d.*	
Item Officers and Attorneys owe to see	
the Essoyne rolles and other rolles of olde	
termes for the assurances of theire matters	
and processes without any thinge payinge therefore	

(h) Comen' process'

Inprimis for euery capias pone and distresse	
in Accions of debte detinewe accounte and	
trespasse of comen process'	iij*d.*
Item for a capias and a pone or a capias and	
a distresse in one writt in euerye of the	
sayd Accions	vj*d.*
Item for euerye capias pone and distresse in	
writtes of covenaunt annuity detinewe of	
charters [accions vpon the case accions in	
qu][1]are impedit replegiare graund cape petit	
cape venire fac' vppon' an yssue joyned writtes	
of rauishment of warde writtes in all reall	
accions or mixte with realtie capias ad satis-	
faciend[um] fieri facias habere facias seisinam	
habere facias visum summoneas ad Warrantum Sum-	
moneas ad sequendum simul habeas corpus vpon' the	
retorn of a Cepi corpus or a languet Ducens tecum	
vpon' the same habeas Corpora Iuratorum Dis-	
tringas ad deliberandum Distringas balliuum vel	
vicecomitem ad habendum corpus a pone or distresse	
after Essoyne an' exigend' an' allocat' venire	
facias Clericum' and euerye other process' vpon'	
the same	vj*d.*[1]

Item for euerye wrytt of Supersedeas quia
impervide or [5] erronice Scire facias vpon
execucions Elegit withernam' writt of privi-
ledge cerciorare extendum facias Summoneas ad
auxiliandum wryttes of Bastardy into the
chauncery and to the bushoppe (a writt to the
bushopp) [6] in a quare impedit a writt de retorn'
habend' a wrytt of second delyuerance with the
entryes of the same writtes de retorn' habend'
and of second delyuerance   ijs.
Item vpon' euery exigend' vpon' Statutes and
vpon' the case   xijd.
(i) The Clerke of the Owtlawryes
Inprimis for euerye capias vtlagat' he Oweth
to haue   vjd.
and nothinge to be paide for the seale thereof
because yt is for the kinge
Item for markinge of a Trauerse Error or pardon'
in his remembrance   iiijd.
Item for a Cerciorare vpon' an Owtlawrye   vjd.
Item for a capias pro fine vpon' a writt of
Rescous to bee retorned by the sheriffe   vjd.
(j) Clerkes of the Prothonotaries and Philizers
  1. Inprimis for Copies of titelinges of one plea
     yf ytt bee not aboue one laefe [sic] of
     paper   iiijd.
  2. Item for a Copy of an ymparlance of the
     comen' rate   iiijd.
  3. And if yt bee aboue the comen' rate to
     paye after the rate of the length thereof
  4. Item for a Copy of euerye other matter of
     the comen' rate wherein is a replicacion
     vjd. and wherein is a reioynder viijd.
     and if yt be aboue the comen' rate then
     to take after the rate of the length
     thereof
  5. Item for drawinge and makinge euerye paper
     leafe uppon' pleadinges to be taken' of the
     playntiffe and the defendaunte of euery of
     them after the rate of his owne pleadinge   viijd.

[5] "Erronire" struck through.
[6] Interlineated in the second copy.

6. Item for the Copy of a plea of the lengthe
of a rolle of the nomber till yt cometh to
the nomber of CCCC   xx*d.*

7. Item for the copye of euerye rolle of the
nomber of CCCC and aboue   ij*s.*

(k) The Clerke of the Essoynes
Inprimis for the entry of euerye Essoyne   iiij*d.*
and for the adiornament of the same   ij*d.*
Item for euerye of the Idem dies   ij*d.*
Item for euery bill of Excepcion   vj*d.*
Item for euery supersedeas as the Clarke
of the Treasourhouse doth receive   ij*s.* iiij*d.*
Item for euery terme of the Cheife
Justice for markinge and ingrossinge of
the same term for his [attendance] [1]   xiij [*s* iiij*d.*] [1]
Item for euery nonsuite   ij*s.* iiij*d.*[7]

(l) The Cryors
Inprimis for euery Judgment and euery
Nonsuite they ought to have   iiij*d.*
Item for euerye fyne   viij*d.*
Item for euery fynall' iudgment   xij*d.*
Item for callinge and swearinge of a Jury
they owe to haue nothinge and for keepinge
of the Jurors after (that) [8] they (be) [9] full
sworne and chardged they can nothinge aske
of dutye but of Curtesye at the pleasure of
the partye.

(m) examinatur (by Mr. Askewe and) [10] cum Record'
                  Edw. Ayscoghe [11]
                      Moyle
            this name Moyle
          vnder the name of Ed' Ascoughe is my hand writing
          and the particulers mencioned in this paper weare
xiij^to Aprilis examyned by Mr. Askough and myselfe by the blacke
1630 [12]   booke by direccion and in the presence of my lord
          Hobarte about fyve yeares sithens   J. Moyle

---

[7] Although this item appears to have been inserted later in copy 2, it appears in the
third copy in normal form.

[8] Interlineated.

[9] Interlineated above "are," which is struck through.

[10] Struck through.

[11] In a different hand.

[12] In the margin of the document in this position.

Thomas Jakes's Memoranda

These memoranda were found in the Public Record Office, in the first pages of the paper book entitled "Recoveries 7 Henry VIII—22 Henry VIII." [1] The name of Thomas Jakes, Clerk of the Warrants and Estreats and Keeper of the Common Pleas Treasury during the Chief Justiceship of Frowyk, later married to Frowyk's widow,[2] is written, apparently in his own hand, on several of the pages.[3]

(a) Nomina officiariorum et Quot Rotulos quilibet officiarius occupat Et valor' eorundem [4]

Willelmus Mordaunt . . . . . . Ro j° Cj vsque Cxx		xxli
Iohn [5] Muscove . . . . Ro ij Cxxj vsque Clx		xxli
Simon' Fitz . . . . Ro iij Clxj vsque Clxvi	x marc'	
( ) [6] Underhull . . . . . . Ro iiij^to CCj vsque CCviij	v li'	
Willelmus [5] Tassell . . . . . Ro v° xxiij vsque xxxv	—— [7]	
( ) [6] Partriche . . . . Ro vj° (vsque) [8] lxxvj vsque lxxxvij	iiij li'	
Willelmus Clerkson' . . . . Ro vij° Clxxxiij vsque Clxxxxij	v li	
Henricus Smyth . . . . Ro viij° Clxxxxix vsque CC	v li	
Thomas Glantham . . . . . Ro ix° CCxxj vsque CCxxxij	x marc'	

[1] P. R. O. Index 17180.

[2] D. N. B.

[3] The hand is the same as that found in several books, now in the British Museum, which at one time belonged to Thomas Jakes.

[4] The first twenty-one surnames and the name Ric' Elryngton are in a precise, formal hand. The heading, Christian names, roll numbers, and values were added later in an informal hand or hands.

[5] Christian name added later in darker ink and perhaps a different hand.

[6] Blank space left for Christian name.

[7] No sum listed.

[8] Crossed out.

Thomas [5] Jubbes (numbers of mm. not listed)   x li

Willelmus Temple ...... Ro xi° lxxxviij° vsque

    lxxxx Cxxxiij   v li

Iohn Caryll .... Ro xij° Cxlj vsque Clx   xx li'

Iohn Acton' .... Ro xiij° xxxvj vsque li   x li

Iohn Agmondesham ..... Ro xiiij° lxxxxvj vsque C   xx li

Iohn Ienour .... Ro xv Clxxxxiij vsque

    Clxxxxviij   x li'

Robt' Elryngton' .... Ro xvj° lij° vsque lxxv   xx marc'

Fraunces [5] Moundesford .. Ro xvij Clxxxij° et CCix

    vsque CCxx   xx marc'

Thomas Boynham .... Ro xviij° Clxxv vsque Clxxx   v li

Thomas [5] Sprotte ....   iiij li

Thomas Soper .... Ro xx CCxxxiiij° vsque

    CCxxxv   v li

Iohn Hall .... Ro xxj Clxvij vsque

    Clxxiiij   v li

    Ric' Elryngton[9]   x marc'

    Thomas Iakes [10] clericus warr'   xx li

    Iohn' Gardyner cirograffar'   xx li

Edwardus [5] Gelgelt .... Ro v^{to} xxiij vsque xxxv   ——— [7]

( ) [6] Byllysby capitalis clamator   xx li

Ricardus Dicons Custos breu'   xx li

Oliuer [5] Woode Gardian' de Flete   xx li

Philippus [5] Coorff v li

    Thomas Iakes clericus inferni   xx li

(b) Anno xxj h vij^{mi}

    Feoda pertinenta Officio Clerici Warrantorum et Extractorum
de Communi Banco

    In primis pro Irrotulacione Carte feoffament' non in-
dentat' et sine littera attornati in eadem Carta .... ii *s.*

Item pro Irrotulacione carte indentate .... iiij *s.*

Item pro Irrotulacione Carte cum littera attornati in
eadem contenta .... iiij *s.*

Item pro Irrotulacione indenture .... iiij *s.*

Item pro Irrotulacione scripti obligatorii simplicis .... ij *s.*

Item pro Irrotulacione scripti obligatorii cum condicione . iiij *s.*

---

[9] The names of Richard Elryngton, Thomas Jakes, and John Gardyner are set in as shown; the original margin of the list seems to have been the beginnings of these names.

[10] Elaborate flourish after the name.

Item pro Irrotulacione Scripti relaxacionis .... ij *s.*
Item pro Irrotulacione Scripti acquietancie .... ij *s.*
Item pro quolibet Warranto in placito debiti et alio
warranto .... iiij *d.*
Item pro Warranto ad cognoscendum se fore satisfactum .. viij *d.*
Item pro Warranto gardiani qui sequitur pro infante
infraetat' .... viij *d.*
Item pro warranto voc' ad Warr' .... viij *d.*
Item pro warranto de attinct' .... viij *d.*
Item pro Warr' super Casum .... viij *d.*
Item pro Warr' vic' pro quolibet Com' .... iiij *d.*
Item pro exemplificacione cuiuslibet Carte Irrotulac'
in eodem termino .... ij *s.*
Item pro exemplificacione cuiuslibet Warr' eodem
termino .... ij *s.*
Item de Maior' London' pro intraccione Warr' eiusdem .. xx *d.*
maioris vna toga ex secta generos' et clerico eiusdem
clerici (xx*d.*) [11] ....
Item de Maior et Civitate London' singulis annis
solut' per le Secundari le Counte in termino
Trinitatis [12] .... xiij *s.* iiij *d.*
Item pro regardo pro script' extract' etc. per patenc'
domini Regis prout per litteras patentes domini Regis
Henrici vj xxxvj^to Skypwhitth quondam clericus Warr'
fact' patet. Et alloc' super Compotum' vic' Norwic'
prout patet eodem anno

> Per Purse quondam Clericus
> Iohannis Foster clerici eorundem'
> Et per Smetheley nunc Cleric'
> subtus   Thomas Woodmance

(c) Certein' ordinances made in the tyme of Sir Iohn' Prisott Chef
Justice of the Common Place touchyng the officers there [13]
Memorandum that for as muche as greate troublez soteltez. . . .[14]
. . . fyn to the kyng as is be for' seid.
Ordinaciones predicte irrotulantur Termino Trinitatis anno
regni regis Henrici Sexti post conquestu xxxv^to Rotulo
cccclxxxxiiij ut patet ibidem.

---

[11] Crossed out.
[12] Ink a different color.
[13] This is written in a careless hand, possibly that of Thomas Jakes.
[14] What follows is identical with App. I (c) except for spelling.

Johannes Prysott Nicholaus Asshton' Petrus Ardern' Robertus
Danvers Robertus Danby Walterus Moyle and Iohannes Nedham' tunc Iusticiarii de eodem Banco existentes

(d) Here after foloyth certen' Ordinances mad this present terme of
Seynt Mychell the Archaungele the xxiij yer' of the Reign' of
Kyng Henry the vij^th by Sir Robert Rede knyght' then' beyng
Cheiff' Justic' of the Commen' place by the aduyse and assent of
all the Juges of the same place from this day forward to be put in
execution

Fyrst that the seid ordenaunces mad' in the vtas of Seynt John'
Baptist the xxxv^th yere of the Reign of kyng Henry the sexte be
trewly obserued and kepte and to thentent that thei may be better
obserued we will that the Cheiff prenotary of the same place
euery terme from hens forward ones in the terme In the presence
of all the Justices of the same place rede or cause to be redd openly
the seid ordinaunces and also thes ordinaunces nowe made. Also
wheras it expressed in the seid ordenaunces made in the seid xxxv
yere of kyng Henry the sexte howe many clerkes euery of the
prenotaries the Clerk of the Stretys and the keper of the Writtes
shalbe syttyng w^tyn the seid Commen place we wyll that the same
Clerkes fyrst at ther' admittans be sworn' as all other officers of
the same place beyn' and that from hensforth the same clerk' that
shalbe so sworn' or assigned to sytt dayly in the seid place w^th
ther' masters and non other shalle haue ther recourse into hell'
at ther pleasures syttyng the court to entre ther Iugementes and to
geve over ther days and that non' other person' ne person excepte
he be an' officer' of the seid place (ente) [15] entermytte or medill'
w^t any of the recordes of the same place nother w^thin the place
nother in hell w^tout licence of the Justices of the same place or of
the clerk of hell upon' payn of enprisonment and to abyd suche
ferther direccion' as the Cheiff Justice of the same place shall
assign' conuenient for theym'

Item (that) [16] wher' as of old tyme it (hah) [15] hath ben' used and
accustomed that euery officer of the Commen place as prenotarys
and philosours for the tym' beyng shuld delyuer all ther Rolles
to the Clerk' of the Strettes then beyng w^thin vij or viij days Im-
mediatly after the ende of euery terme and the seid Clerke of
the Strettes then' hauyng the same Rolles shuld kepe them with'
hym' ij dayes them to Estrete and furthermore then' the seid

[15] False start.
[16] Crossed out.

Clerk shuld delyuer the same Rolles to the Clerk of the Essonez
to Bynd and so he to haue them by the space of other ij days and
then he to deliuer the holle recorde to the Clerk of hell' it is nowe
agreyd assented and inacted by the seid Iustices that the seid use
custome and Ordinance from hensforth be accordyngly in euery
(poynt) [17] obserued and kepte upon' the payn' herafter foloy-
ing' [18]

[17] Inserted above the line.

[18] The remaining memoranda of Thomas Jakes in the first fifteen folios of this
paper book relate to the clerk of Hell and the delivery of records to the Chief Justice
by the executors of his predecessor. They are in a very careless hand, almost completely
illegible at times, possibly that of Thomas Jakes himself.

Clerks of the Court

during the Reigns of Edward IV, Edward V, and Richard III

C. P. 40/799 Mich., 39 Henry VI	C. P. 40/800 Hil., 39 Henry VI	C. P. 40/801 [1] Trin., 1 Edward IV
m. 1 Wydeslade [2] Cumberford	Wydeslade	....
m. 2 Wydeslade [2] Cumberford	Cumberford	....
m. 3 ( ) [2]	Hethe	....
m. 4 Brown	....[3]	Aleyn
m. 5 Aleyn	Cheke	Forster
m. 6 Praers	( ) [4]	Gegge
m. 7 Forster	....	Fililode
m. 8 Hervy	....	Praers
m. 9 Ferrers	....	....
m. 10 Forster [5]	( ) [4]	Burton
m. 11 Gegge	....	Burton-Pittes
m. 12 Copley	....	....
m. 13 Fililode	....	Pulter
m. 14 Pulter	....	Vaus
m. 15 Glyn	....	....
m. 16 Vaus	....	Elryngton

[1] The roll of Easter, 1 Ed. IV is missing.
[2] Document torn.
[3] Italics or dotted lines indicate that the clerk is the same as in the preceding term.
[4] No "signature."
[5] Writs of *exigi facias* are enrolled on this membrane.

C. P. 40/799	C. P. 40/800	C. P. 40/801 [1]
Mich., 39 Henry VI	Hil., 39 Henry VI	Trin., 1 Edward IV
m. 17 Elryngton	Elryngton, J. [6]	Elryngton, J.
m. 18 Elryngton	. . . .	Elryngton
m. 19 B [2]——	Burton	( ) [4]
m. 20 Audeley	( ) [4]	. . . .
m. 21 Waldyene	( ) [4]	( ) [4]
m. 22 Cumberford [8]	. . . . [7]	( ) [4]
Roll of warrants		
Skypwyth	. . . .	. . . .

C. P. 40/802	C. P. 40/803	C. P. 40/817 [9]
Mich., 1 Edward IV	Hil., 1 Edward IV	Mich., 5 Edward IV
m. 1 *Wydeslade*	. . . .	. . . .
m. 2 *Cumberford*	. . . .	. . . .
m. 3 *Hethe*	. . . .	Chambre
m. 4 Brown	. . . .	. . . .
m. 5 Aleyn	. . . .	. . . .
m. 6 Praers	. . . .	. . . .
m. 7 Forster	. . . .	. . . .
m. 8 Hervy	. . . .	. . . .
m. 9 *Ferrers*	. . . .	. . . .
m. 10 Forster	. . . . [10]	. . . .
m. 11 Gegge	. . . .	Saynton
m. 12 *Copley*	. . . .	. . . .
m. 13 Fililode	. . . .	. . . .
m. 14 Pulter	. . . .	. . . .
m. 15 *Glyn*	. . . .	. . . .
m. 16 Vaus	. . . .	. . . .
m. 17 Elryngton, J.	Elryngton	. . . .
m. 18 Elryngton	Elryngton, J.	. . . .
m. 19 Burton	. . . .	. . . .
m. 20 *Audeley*	. . . .	. . . .
m. 21 Waldyene	. . . .	. . . .
m. 22 ( ) [4]	Cumberford	. . . .
Roll of warrants		
Skypwyth	. . . .	. . . .

6 It is not clear whether there were two Elryngtons, or only one who sometimes added a "J" to his name.

7 Notes of licenses to levy fines from all counties are enrolled on this membrane.

8 Respites of juries from all counties are enrolled on this membrane.

9 So many intervening terms omitted because no changes took place.

10 All the entries on this membrane are writs addressed to the sheriff of Middlesex.

C. P. 40/821 Mich., 6 Edward IV	C. P. 40/825 Mich., 7 Edward IV	C. P. 40/829 Mich., 8 Edward IV
m. 1 *Wydeslade*	....	Copley [11]
m. 2 *Cumberford*	....	....
m. 3 Chambre	....	....
m. 4 Broun	Danby	....
m. 5 Aleyn	....	....
m. 6 Praers	....	....
m. 7 *Forster*	....	....
m. 8 *Hervy*	....	....
m. 9 *Ferrers*	....	....
m. 10 *Forster*	....	....
m. 11 *Saynton*	....	Thornburgh
m. 12 *Copley*	....	Brayne
m. 13 Conyers	....	....
m. 14 *Pulter*	....	....
m. 15 *Glyn*	....	....
m. 16 *Vaus*	....	....
m. 17 *Elryngton*	....	....
m. 18 *Elryngton, J.*	....	....
m. 19 *Burton*	....	( ) [2]
m. 20 *Audeley*	....	Acton
m. 21 *Waldyene*	....	....
m. 22 *Cumberford*	....	....
Roll of warrants		
Skypwith	....	....

C. P. 40/833 Mich., 9 Edward IV	C. P. 40/837 Mich., 49 Henry VI	C. P. 40/842 [9] Easter, 12 Edward IV
m. 1 *Copley*	....	....
m. 2 *Cumberford*	....	....
m. 3 *Chambre*	....	....
m. 4 *Danby*	Conyers	Danby
m. 5 Cheke	....	....
m. 6 *Praers*	....	....
m. 7 *Forster*	....	....
m. 8 *Hervy*	....	....
m. 9 *Ferrers*	....	....
m. 10 *Forster*	....	Beell

[11] Copley replaced Wydeslade as first prothonotary between Trinity and Michaelmas terms, 8 Edward IV. Brayne succeeded Copley as third prothonotary.

C. P. 40/833	C. P. 40/837	C. P. 40/842 [9]
Mich., 9 Edward IV	Mich., 49 Henry VI	Easter, 12 Edward IV
m. 11 Thornburgh	....	Orston
m. 12 *Brayne*	....	....
m. 13 *Conyers*	....	....
m. 14 *Pulter*	....	....
m. 15 *Glyn*	....	....
m. 16 *Vaus*	....	....
m. 17 *Elryngton*	Elryngton, J.	....
m. 18 *Elryngton*	....	....
m. 19 *Burton*	....	....
m. 20 *Acton*	....	....
m. 21 *Waldyene*	....	....
m. 22 Snaythe	....	....
Roll of warrants		
Skypwyth	....	....

C. P. 40/844	C. P. 40/848	C. P. 40/852
Mich., 12 Edward IV	Mich., 13 Edward IV	Mich., 14 Edward IV
m. 1 ( )[2]	....	....
m. 2 Brent [12]	....	....
m. 3 *Chambre*	....	Gurney
m. 4 Monmouth [13]	....	....
m. 5 *Cheke*	....	....
m. 6 *Praers*	....	....
m. 7 *Forster*	Staynford	....
m. 8 *Hervy*	....	....
m. 9 *Ferrers*	....	....
m. 10 *Beell*	....	....
m. 11 *Orston*	....	....
m. 12 *Brayne*	....	....
m. 13 *Conyers*	....	Acton
m. 14 *Pulter*	....	....
m. 15 Wydeslade	....	....
m. 16 *Vaus*	....	....
m. 17 *Elryngton, J.*	....	....
m. 18 *Elryngton*	....	....

[12] Brent replaced Cumberford in Trinity term on m. 137 of the roll.
[13] Monmouth replaced Danby between Trinity and Michaelmas terms.

C. P. 40/844	C. P. 40/848	C. P. 40/852
Mich., 12 Edward IV	Mich., 13 Edward IV	Mich., 14 Edward IV
m. 19 *Burton*	....	....
m. 20 *Acton*	....	Danby
m. 21 *Waldyene*	....	Aleyn
m. 22 *Snayth*	....	Underhill
		m. 23 Torold [14]
Roll of warrants		
Skypwyth	Forster	....

C. P. 40/860	C. P. 40/864	C. P. 40/868
Mich., 16 Edward IV	Mich., 17 Edward IV	Mich., 18 Edward IV
m. 1 *Copley*	....	....
m. 2 *Brent*	....	....
m. 3 *Gurney*	....	....
m. 4 *Monmouth*	....	....
m. 5 *Cheke*	....	....
m. 6 *Praers*	....	....
m. 7 *Staynford*	....	....
m. 8 *Hervy*	....	....
m. 9 *Ferrers*	....	....
m. 10 *Beell*	....	....
m. 11 *Orston*	....	....
m. 12 *Brayne*	....	Broun
m. 13 *Acton*	....	....
m. 14 *Pulter*	....	....
m. 15 *Wydeslade*	....	....
m. 16 *Elryngton*	....	*Elryngton, J.*
m. 17 Vaus	....	Vaus
m. 18 Vaus	....	Adam
m. 19 *Burton*	....	....
m. 20 *Danby*	....	....
m. 21 *Aleyn*	Bedford	....
m. 22 *Underhill*	....	....
m. 23 *Torold*	....	....
Roll of warrants		
Forster	....	....

[14] Entries on this membrane are of pleas of debt in which Thomas Torold appears as attorney.

265

C. P. 40/874	C. P. 40/878	C. P. 40/884
Mich., 20 Edward IV	Mich., 21 Edward IV	Easter, 1 Edward V
m. 1 *Copley*	....	....[15]
m. 2 *Brent*	....	....
m. 3 Lister	....	Copley
m. 4 Knyght	....	Cheke
m. 5 *Cheke*	....	Pulter
m. 6 *Praers*	....	Staynford
m. 7 *Staynford*	....	Orston
m. 8 *Hervy*	....	Acton
m. 9 *Ferrers*	....	Praers
m. 10 *Beell*	....	Conyngesby
m. 11 *Orston*	....	Conyngesby
m. 12 Brown	Conyngesby	Burton
Conyngesby		
m. 13 *Acton*	....	Vaus
m. 14 *Pulter*	....	Elryngton, J.
m. 15 *Wydeslade*	....	Ferrers
m. 16 *Elryngton*	Elryngton, J.	Cheke
m. 17 *Vaus*	....	Bedford
m. 18 *Adam*	....	Elryngton, J.
m. 19 *Burton*	....	[No more membranes]
m. 20 *Danby*	....	
m. 21 *Bedford*	....	
m. 22 *Underhull*	....	
Roll of warrants		
Forster	....	

C. P. 40/885A	C. P. 40/885B	C. P. 40/887
Trin., 1 Edward V	Trin., 1 Richard III	Hil., 1 Richard III
m. 1 *Copley* [16]	....	....
m. 2 *Brent*	Copley	Brent
m. 3 *Lyster*	Conyngesby	Lister
m. 4 ....[17]	[No more membranes]	Knyght
m. 5 *Cheke*	Roll of warrants	Cheke
m. 6 *Praers*	*Forster*	Praers
m. 7 *Staynford*		Staynford

[15] "Thynk and thank God" is written at the foot of this membrane.
[16] "Thynk and thank God" is written inside the C of Copley.
[17] The membrane is blank but is numbered "iiij."

C.P. 40/885A	C. P. 40/885B	C. P. 40/887
Trin., 1 Edward V	Trin., 1 Richard III	Hil., 1 Richard III
m. 8 ....[18]		Hervy
m. 9 *Ferrers*		Ferrers
m. 10 ....[19]		( )[20]
m. 11 *Orston*		Orston
m. 12 *Conyngesby*		Conyngesby
m. 13 *Acton*		Acton
m. 14 *Pulter*		Pulter
m. 15 ( )[4]		Wydeslade
m. 16 *Elryngton, J.*		Elryngton, J.
m. 17 ....[2]		Vaus
m. 18 ....[2]		Adam
m. 19 *Burton*		Burton
m. 20 ....[19]		Danby
m. 21 *Bedford*		Bedford
m. 22 ....[19]		Woodmance
Roll of warrants		Roll of warrants
Forster		*Forster*

C. P. 40/890	C. P. 40/894	C. P. 40/895
Mich., 2 Richard III	Mich., 3 Richard III	Hil., 1 Henry VII
m. 1 *Copley*	( )[2]	Copley
m. 2 *Brent*	....	Brent
m. 3 *Lister*	....	....
m. 4 *Knyght*	....	....
m. 5 *Cheke*	....	....
m. 6 *Praers*	....	Praers
m. 7 *Staynford*	....	....
m. 8 Wyghtman [21]	Elryngton	Wyghtman
m. 9 *Ferrers*	....	....
m. 10 Beell	Elryngton	Beell
m. 11 *Orston*	....	....
m. 12 *Conyngesby*	....	....
m. 13 *Acton*	....	....
m. 14 *Pulter*	( )[4]	....

[18] The membrane is blank but is numbered "viij."
[19] Membrane is missing.
[20] The membrane is blank but numbered "x."
[21] Succeeded Hervy between Hilary and Easter, 1 Richard III.

C. P. 40/890	C. P. 40/894	C. P. 40/895
Mich., 2 Richard III	Mich., 3 Richard III	Hil., 1 Henry VII
m. 15 *Wydeslade*	Blount [22]	....
m. 16 *Elryngton, J.*	Elryngton	Elryngton, J.
m. 17 *Vaus*	....	....
m. 18 *Adam*	....	....
m. 19 *Burton*	....	....
m. 20 *Danby*	( )⁴	....
m. 21 *Bedford*	( )⁴	....
m. 22 ( )²	Burton	....
Roll of warrants		
Forster	Belyngton	....

[22] Succeeded Wydeslade between Michaelmas and Hilary, 2 Richard III.

268

Return Days in the Bench

An official list of common return days is printed in *Statutes of the Realm* among statutes of uncertain date.[1] This list, which in mediaeval editions of the statutes was thought to date from 51 Henry III, seems to have been looked upon as still valid in the fifteenth century.[2] Moreover, it corresponds precisely with a list of return days drawn up from the continuations of cases in the plea rolls. According to both there were eight return days in Michaelmas term and fewer in the other terms, the sequence being as follows:

Michaelmas: October 6 to November 28 [3]

1. In Octabis Sancti Michelis .... Oct. 6–12
2. A die Sancti Michelis in xv dies *or*
   in quindena Sancti Michelis [4] .... Oct. 13–19
3. A die Sancti Michelis in tres septimanas .... Oct. 20–26
4. A die Sancti Michelis in unum mensem *or*
   in mense Sancti Michelis [4] .... Oct. 27–Nov. 2
5. In crastino Animarum .... Nov. 3–11
6. In crastino Sancti Martini .... Nov. 12–17
7. In octabis Sancti Martini .... Nov. 18–24
8. A die Sancti Martini in xv dies *or*
   in quindena Sancti Martini [4] .... Nov. 25–28

[1] *S. R.*, vol. I, p. 208. Cf. *H. E. L.*, vol. III, App. VII.
[2] *Y. B. Easter, 8 Ed. IV*, pl. 9, fol. 4.
[3] The dates of opening given in Frye's *Almanack* are three days later because, although the official day of opening was as above, the justices did not sit until the fourth day. If the first day fell on a Sunday, the term opened on the Monday following.
[4] The first form given is from the fifteenth century plea rolls; the alternative is the form found in the statute *De dies* and frequently also in the Year Books.

Hilary: January 20 to February 12

1. In octabis Sancti Hillarii . . . . Jan. 20–26
2. A die Sancti Hillarii in xv dies *or*
   in quindena Sancti Hillarii [4] . . . . Jan. 27–Feb. 2
3. In crastino Purificacionis beate Marie . . . . Feb. 3–9
4. In octabis Purificacione beate Marie . . . . Feb. 10–12

Easter: Variable according to the date of Easter, beginning on any day from April 5 to May 9, ending on any day from May 4 to June 7

1. A die Pasche in xv dies *or* in quindena Pasche [4]
2. A die Pasche in tres septimanas *or* in tres septimanas Pasche
3. A die Pasche in unum mensem *or* in mense Pasche [4]
4. In crastino Ascensionis domini *or* in quinque septimanas Pasche [4]

Trinity: Variable according to the date of Easter, beginning on any day from May 24 to June 27 and ending on any day from June 17 to July 21

1. In octabis Sancte Trinitatis
2. A die Sancte Trinitatis in xv dies *or* in quindena Sancte Trinitatis
3. In crastino Sancti Iohannis Baptiste . . . . June 25–30
4. In octabis Sancti Iohannis Baptiste . . . . July 1–8
5. A die Sancti Iohannis Baptiste in xv dies . . . . July 9–14 [5]

[5] Whether or not there was a morrow, octave, and quindene of St. John the Baptist depended on the date of Trinity Sunday. If Trinity were early, there might be in the term only an octave, quindene, and third week of Trinity. If Trinity were late, on the other hand, there might be no octave, quindene, etc., of Trinity, but only a morrow, octave, and quindene of St. John the Baptist.

Keepers of the Writs
and Chirographers

*of the Court of Common Pleas from the Reign of Henry III
through the Reign of Henry VII*[1]

A. Keepers of the Writs

DATES OF TENURE	NAMES	ORIGINAL GRANT, CONDITIONS OF TENURE, ETC.	REFERENCES
1246–1253 or 1258?	Roger de Whitcestre.	May 23, 1246. £10 a year at the Exchequer so long as he keeps the rolls and writs.	*C. P. R., 1232–1247,* p. 480.
		Jan. 8, 1251. Robes to be delivered to him.	*C. C. R., 1247–1251,* p. 395.
		June 21, 1253. To deliver to Justice Thurkelby the first roll, to keep the second roll and the king's writs.	*C. C. R., 1251–1255,* p. 374.
			Other references:[2] *C. C. R., 1242–1247,* p. 247.
1258–1260 or 1266?	John Blundel.[3]	Payments of fees for period from Mich., 1258; to Mich., 1260.	Liberate Rolls: No. 35, mm. 8, 4, 2; No. 36, mm. 6, 2.
		Oct. 17, 1259; Dec. 6, 1260. Livery of gowns to him.	Close Rolls: No. 74, m. 2; No. 77, m. 22.
			Other references: *C. C. R., 1256–1259,* p. 17.

[1] Lists for the reigns of Edward I and Edward II may be found in Sayles, *Select Cases in K. B.,* vol. I, pp. cxlviii–cxlxix, and in Tout, *Place of Edward II,* p. 330. The material used here for these reigns is in part drawn from these earlier lists.

[2] Items for which the reference is given under this heading do not relate to the office in the Court of Common Pleas but may be useful in further research. I have not attempted to make them complete but have included only those references casually found in compiling this list.

[3] Sayles, *Select Cases in K. B.,* vol. I, pp. lxxxiii, cxlviii.

DATES OF TENURE	NAMES	ORIGINAL GRANT, CONDITIONS OF TENURE, ETC.	REFERENCES
1266–1276	Roger de Leicester.[4]	Payments of fees, maintenance, and expenses for period from Mich., 1266, to Mich., 1275.	Liberate Rolls: No. 43, mm. 8, 2; No. 48, m. 7; No. 52, mm. 5, 11.
1276–1278	William de Middelton, king's clerk.	June 6, 1276. During pleasure. Leicester to deliver writs, rolls, etc., to him.	C. P. R., 1272–1281, p. 146.
		July 23, 1276. Discharged of levy of tallage of Jews because of his office in the Bench.	Ibid., p. 163.
		Jan. 18, 1278. Acquitted of 5 marks for carriage of writs and rolls from London to Shrewsbury and of other monies given him for expenses.	C. C. R., 1272–1279, p. 438.
1278–1285	Elias de Bekingham,[5] king's clerk.	Aug. 10, 1278. During pleasure. Middelton to deliver to him rolls, writs, etc., of the Bench.	C. P. R., 1272–1281, p. 276.
		Nov. 16, 1278. Orlandinus de Podio et al., merchants of Lucca, to pay 10 marks of his fee.	Ibid., p. 283.
		Payments of fees for period from Mich., 1279, to Mich., 1284.	Liberate Rolls: No. 55, m. 2; No. 56, m. 5; No. 57, m. 8; No. 60, m. 4; No. 61, m. 8.
		Oct. 14, 1285. Appointed a justice of the Bench.	C. P. R., 1281–1292, p. 196.
1285–1290	Robert de Littelbury.[6]	Oct. 14, 1285. Appointed during pleasure.	Ibid., p. 196.
		Payments of fees for Mich., 1286, and Easter, 1287.	Liberate Roll: No. 63, m. 2.
		Nov. 29, 1289. Delivery of records into Treasury.	L. T. R. Mem. Rolls: No. 61, m. 4d.
1290–1292	John Luvel,[7] king's clerk.	Jan. 20, 1290. Received records from Littelbury.	Ibid., m. 5d.
		Payments of fees for Easter and Mich., 1290.	Liberate Rolls: No. 66. m. 1.
		Feb. 12, 1290. Order to Treasurer and Chamberlains to deliver to Bekingham and Luvel "or to him who supplies his place in the Bench" the rolls of Thomas Weyland's time.	C. C. R., 1288–1296, p. 69. Other references: C. P. R., 1281–1292, pp. 323, 327, 339, 419, 485.
1292–1313	John Bacon,[8] king's clerk.	April 17, 1292. During pleasure. Mandate to Luvel to de-	Ibid., p. 485.

[4] Ibid., p. cxlviii.
[5] Ibid., p. cxlviii.
[6] Ibid., pp. cxlviii, cxlii.
[7] Ibid., pp. xlvi, lix, cxxii, cxxxii, cxlix, clxii, clxix.
[8] Ibid., pp. cxl, cxlix, lx.

DATES OF TENURE	NAMES	ORIGINAL GRANT, CONDITIONS OF TENURE, ETC.	REFERENCES
		liver rolls to him by chirograph.	
		Payment of fees for period from Mich., 1292, to Mich., 1306.	Liberate Rolls: No. 69, mm. 2, 3; No. 70, m. 2; No. 75, m. 2; No. 83, m. 2.
		June 6, 1306. To appoint a deputy while expediting personal business in Rome.	*C. C. R., 1302–1307,* p. 391.
		Sept. 6, 1307. Order to continue in office and to take the oath on Wednesday after Michaelmas.	*C. C. R., 1307–1313,* p. 41.
		Sept. 6, 1307. Reappointed by Edward II during pleasure.	*C. P. R., 1307–1313,* p. 2.
		Sept. 18, 1309. Charged to keep a counterroll of pleas and essoins in the Bench.	*C. C. R., 1307–1313,* p. 231.
		Feb. 19, 1313. Appointed a justice of the Bench.	*C. P. R., 1307–1313,* p. 552. Other references: E 403/152; *Mem. de Parl.,*[9] pp. 166–167.
1313–1314	William de Rasen, king's clerk.	Feb. 19, 1313. During pleasure.	*C. P. R., 1307–1313,* p. 552.
1314	Robert de Hauville, king's clerk.	Mar. 21, 1314. During pleasure.	*C. P. R., 1313–1317,* p. 94.
1314–1322	Adam de Herwynton, king's clerk.	Oct. 3, 1314. During pleasure. Hauville to deliver writs and rolls to him.	*Ibid.,* p. 185. Other references: Tout, *Place of Edward II,* p. 331.
1322–1323	Robert Ayleston, king's clerk.	June 11, 1322. During pleasure. Herwynton to deliver writs and rolls to him.	*C. P. R., 1317–1321,* p. 133.
1323–1327	John de Shordich, king's clerk, advocate of the Court of Arches, professor of both laws.	Sept. 11, 1323. During pleasure.	*C. P. R., 1321–1324,* p. 340.
		1330. Petition for restoration of office.	*R. P.,* vol. II, p. 41.
		Hil., 5 Ed. III. Revocation of grant to Richard de Haukeslowe (*q.v.* in list of chirographers) in favor of Shordich.[10]	C. P. 40/284, m. 1. Other references: *C. P. R., 1327–1330,* pp. 440, 446, 491. *C. C. R., 1327–1330,* pp. 500, 510, 586. Tout, *Place of Edward II,* p. 331.

[9] *Records of the Parliament (Memoranda de Parliamento) holden at Westminster on the 28th Day of February in the 33d Year of the Reign of Edward I* (ed. Maitland; London, 1893).

[10] Shordich's petition was favorably answered (*R. P.,* vol. II, p. 41), and the grant to Haukeslowe was disallowed, but Peter de Lodyngton's grant was not referred to in these proceedings, and he apparently continued to exercise the office until 1334.

DATES OF TENURE	NAMES	ORIGINAL GRANT, CONDITIONS OF TENURE, ETC.	REFERENCES
1327–1334	Peter de Lodyngton, king's clerk.	Feb. 4, 1327. During pleasure.	*C. P. R., 1327–1330,* p. 17; C. P. 23/1 (Hil., 1 Ed. III), m. 1.
		Aug. 18, 1327. To array writs and rolls to go to York.	*C. C. R., 1327–1330,* p. 161.
		Oct. 20, 1328. To array writs and rolls to return to Westminster.	*Ibid.,* p. 325.
		Sept. 3, 1329. Order to deliver writs of eyre of Northants to Steyngrave (*q.v.* below) and those of Notts to William de Scothowe.	*Ibid.,* p. 493.
		May 7, 1330. Similar orders re eyres of Beds and Derby.	*C. C. R., 1330–1333,* p. 31.
		June 9, 1330. Order to Steyngrave to return writs of eyre to Lodyngton.	*Ibid.,* p. 158.
		Mich., 7 Ed. III. Lodyngton's name appears on Rex rolls as keeper of the writs and rolls.	C. P. 23/11.
1334–1341	Adam de Steyngrave, king's clerk.	July 14, 1334. During pleasure. Mandate to William de Burgh and William de Poynton [11] to deliver to him writs and rolls.	*C. P. R., 1330–1334,* p. 562.
		Oct. 1, 1338. Order to transfer writs and rolls to Westminster while king is beyond seas.	*C. C. R., 1337–1339,* pp. 501–502.
		Feb. 16, 1339. Order to deliver writs and rolls to the Treasurer and Chamberlains, by indenture.	*C. C. R., 1339–1341,* p. 13.
		Jan. 26, 1341. To be admitted as clerk of eyre of London.[12]	*Ibid.,* p. 606.
1341–1354	William de Herlaston.	Jan. 26, 1341. To deliver to Steyngrave all writs touching citizens of London.	*C. C. R., 1341–1343,* p. 103.
		Oct. 11, 1348. To deliver to Chief Justice Stonor all writs touching men of Kent.	*C. C. R., 1346–1349,* p. 559.
		Dec. 1, 1348. Return of above writs to Herlaston.	*Ibid.,* p. 597.

11 Executors of Peter de Lodyngton?

12 On the same date Nicholas de Greseleye was ordered to deliver all the rolls, writs, and memoranda of the Common Bench which were in his custody under the seals of Robert de Sadington, Chief Baron of the Exchequer; William Basset, one of the justices of the Bench; and William de Poynton, one of the clerks of the Bench, to Roger Hillary, the new Chief Justice (*C. C. R., 1339–1341,* p. 604). This order must relate to the writs, rolls, and memoranda which were commonly in the Chief Justice's keeping. (See above, Ch. IX.) Nicholas de Greseleye may have been the Chief Justice's clerk or a prototype of the later keeper of the Common Pleas Treasury.

DATES OF TENURE	NAMES	ORIGINAL GRANT, CONDITIONS OF TENURE, ETC.	REFERENCES
		April 6, 1354. Commission to William de Sandeford (*q.v.* below) to survey writs, rolls, etc., relating to Herlaston's office, as the king is informed that the latter is dead.	*C. P. R., 1354–1358*, p. 27.
1354–1375	William de Sandeford, king's clerk.	April 9, 1354. During pleasure.	*Ibid.*, p. 29.
		June 14, 1362. Sent note of a fine to the Chancery.	*C. P. R., 1361–1364*, p. 355.
		Trin., 37 Ed. III (1363), name appears on Rex rolls. Easter, 49 Ed. III (1375).	C. P. 23/10; C. P. 23/82.
1375–1387	Richard de Treton, king's clerk.	July 27, 1375. During pleasure.	*C. P. R., 1374–1377*, p. 132; C. P. 40/467 (Trin., 1 Ric. II).
		June 26, 1377. Reappointed by Richard II during pleasure.	*C. P. R., 1377–1381*, p. 1.
		Jan. 30, 1381. Grant during good behavior.	*Ibid.*, p. 590.
1386	William de Culham.	Sept. 15, 1386. For life.	*C. P. R., 1385–1389*, p. 211.
		Sept. 24, 1386. Revocation because of earlier grant to Treton.	*Ibid.*, p. 226.[13]
1387–1397	Thomas Haxey, knight.	June 18, 1387. For life with assent of Treton; later vacated and canceled with assent of Thomas because he obtained no benefit of the grant.	*Ibid.*, p. 314.
		Jan. 25, 1392. Witness of release of personal actions, referred to as Sir Thomas Haxey, Chief Clerk of the Common Bench.	*C. C. R., 1389–1392*, p. 551.
		June 7, 1392. Writ of aid re removal of writs and rolls to York.	*C. P. R., 1391–1396*, p. 63.
		Oct. 25, 1392. Order to return to Westminster with writs, rolls, etc.	*C. C. R., 1392–1396*, p. 76.
		Other evidences of his incumbency.	C. P. 40/507 (Mich., 11 Ric. II) m. 364; C. P. 40/535 (Mich., 18 Ric. II) m. 95; C. P. 23/38. Other references: Haxey's case in Parliament, *R. P.*, vol. III, pp. 339, 341, 407, 430, 434; Tout, *Chapters*, vol. IV, p.

---

13 Both the grant and the revocation were by signet letter.

DATES OF TENURE	NAMES	ORIGINAL GRANT, CONDITIONS OF TENURE, ETC.	REFERENCES
			18, n. 2; Neale, *Free Speech*,[14] p. 259.
1397–1399	Robert Manfield, king's clerk.	Feb. 8, 1397. For life. Vacated by surrender and canceled because, with his assent, Henry IV granted the office to Robert Darcy (*q.v.* below).	*C. P. R., 1396–1399*, p. 81; C. P. 23/135; C. P. 23/136.
1399–1409	William Pountfrett,[15] king's clerk.	Oct. 4, 1399. For life.	*C. P. R., 1399–1401*, p. 7.
		Nov. 21, 1401. Payment of fees.	Issue Rolls:[16] No. 571, R. 9.
		July 1, 1406. Pountfrett made return to Chancery as Custos Brevium.	Chancery Miscellanea, C 60/4/103.
1409–1410	Robert Manfield.	April 26, 1409. Revocation of grant at suit of Manfield.	*C. P. R., 1408–1413*, p. 69.
1410–1413	Robert Darcy.	April 24, 1410. For life on surrender of Manfield's patent.	*Ibid.*, p. 219.
		June 15, 1414. Grant of annuity to Darcy in lieu of office, which had been granted to Hotoft (*q.v.* below).	*C. P. R., 1413–1416*, p. 333.
1413–1422	John Hotoft, king's esquire.	Mar. 23. 1413. During pleasure.	*Ibid.*, p. 1.
		Nov. 1, 1430. Grant of annuity of 100 marks in compensation for loss of office recovered by Darcy at death of Henry V. This grant vacated Feb. 1, 1431, by grant of office of Chamberlain of the Receipt of the Exchequer.	*C. P. R., 1429–1436*, p. 101. *Ibid.*, p. 102. Other references: Wedgewood and Holt, *Biographies*.
1422–1440	Robert Darcy.	Nov. 1, 1430. Original grant reasserted at death of Henry V.	*C. P. R., 1429–1436*, p. 101.
		Nov. 27, 1436. Payment of fees in arrears for thirteen years.	Issue Rolls: No. 725, R. 7.
		May 26, 1447. Payment of arrears of fees.	Issue Rolls: No. 757, R. 4. Other references: *Y. B. Easter, 19 Hy. VI*, pl. 16; Nicolas, *Privy Council*, vol. II, p. 169; Wedgewood and Holt, *Biographies*.

14 J. E. Neale, "The Commons Privilege of Free Speech in Parliament," *Tudor Studies* (ed. Seton-Watson; New York, 1924).

15 William Pountfrett evidently exercised the office from Oct. 4, 1399, to April 26, 1409, when Manfield's patent was reasserted.

16 I owe this reference and the others below from Chancery Miscellanea and from Issue Rolls to the members of Professor Williams' seminar in English legal history at the Institute of Historical Research (London). They have collected a file of miscellaneous material concerning the clerks of the courts.

DATES OF TENURE	NAMES	ORIGINAL GRANT, CONDITIONS OF TENURE, ETC.	REFERENCES
1440–1461	Robert Darcy and Henry Fylongley.	Oct. 16, 1440. In survivorship, in lieu of earlier grant to Darcy alone.	*C. P. R., 1436–1441,* p. 471.
		Trin. and Mich., 24 Hy. VI (1446). Action against Thomas del Rowe (*q.v.* below) for recovery of office.	C. P. 40/738, m. 528d.; C. P. 40/739, mm. 337–339d.
		Mich., 36 Hy. VI (1457). Evidence that Fylongley was still Custos Brevium.	C. P. 40/787, m. 371. Other references: *Paston Letters,* No. 324. Sir J. Fastolf refers to Fylongley as his nephew.
1444	John Ulveston and Thomas del Rowe, king's servants. Former called receiver of Eton College, latter one of the clerks of the Common Pleas.	Oct. 17, 1444. Grant in survivorship.	*C. P. R., 1441–1446,* p. 316.
1461–1472	John Fogge, esquire, king's servant.	April 14, 1461. For life.	*C. P. R., 1461–1467,* p. 11.
		Mar. 26, 1465. Indenture re delivery of fines into the Treasury.	E 101/336/12; Palgrave, *Kalendars,* vol. III, p. 388.
		July 1, 1472. Exemplification of the above grant because he had accidentally lost his letters patent.	*C. P. R., 1467–1477,* p. 339; cf. Canceled Letters Patent, C 202, H 63/35.
1472–1483	John Fogge, knight, and John Fogge, esquire, his son.	July 11, 1472. For term of both their lives. Vacated by surrender and canceled, Mar. 12, 1485 (2 Ric. II).	*C. P. R., 1467–1477,* p. 339; C 66/529, m. 10.
1483–1485	John Kendale, esquire, king's servant.	July 5, 1483. For life.	*C. P. R., 1476–1485,* p. 463. Cf. *Grants of Edward V,* p. xxix.[17]
1486–1501	John Heyron and John Fogge, esquire.	Oct. 1, 1486. In survivorship. Sept. 22, 1501. Mandate to Keeper of the Great Seal and Keeper of the Rolls of Chancery not to allow Fogge to exercise the office now at the death of Heyron since his name was fraudulently inserted in the patent without the king's knowledge, and the office has now been granted to Decons (*q.v.* below).	*C. P. R., 1485–1494,* p. 123.
		1495–1504 Attainder and restoration of Heyron.	Stat. 11 Hy. VII, c. 64; 19 Hy. VII, c. 37.
1501–1509	Richard Decons, esquire, king's servant.	Sept. 23, 1501. For life, for services to king and queen.	*C. P. R., 1494–1509,* p. 265.

[17] *Grants, etc., from the Crown during the Reign of Edward the Fifth* (ed. Nichols; Camden Society; London, 1854).

B. Chirographers

DATES OF TENURE	NAMES	ORIGINAL GRANT, CONDITIONS OF TENURE, ETC.	REFERENCES
1307	John de Bradford, clerk.	Oct. 6, 1307. During pleasure.	*C. P. R., 1307–1313,* pp. 7, 36.
1307–1312	Robert de Hauville, king's clerk.	Nov. 21, 1307. During pleasure.	*Ibid.,* p. 22.
1312–1328 ?	Robert de Foxton, king's clerk.	March 24, 1312. During pleasure.	*Ibid.,* p. 448.
		Oct. 28, 1313. For life during good behavior.	*C. P. R., 1313–1317,* p. 31.
		April 22, 1327. Confirmation of grant of late king.	*C. P. R., 1327–1330,* p. 94.
		April 15, 1332. Grant of £50 annuity until he recovers the office of chirographer granted without his consent to Haukeslowe (*q.v.* below).	*C. P. R., 1330–1334,* p. 281.
		Sept. 30, 1334. Annuity to be paid from farm of Northampton.	*C. P. R., 1334–1338,* p. 30.
1328–1330	Richard de Haukeslowe.[1]	Jan. 30, 1327. During pleasure.	*C. P. R., 1327–1330,* p. 2.
		Feb. 6, 1328. Grant at the request of Roger de Mortuo Mari in succession to Foxton, who has surrendered it.	*Ibid.,* p. 229.
1330–1345	John de Shordich, king's clerk. (See above, Keepers of the Writs.)	Dec. 20, 1330. Grant in recompense of £50 annuity lately granted him for service to the king, after revocation in Parliament of Haukeslowe's grant.	*C. P. R., 1330–1334,* p. 36.
		June 11, 1332. Grant for life. Not to be disturbed by Foxton, who has surrendered his patent, or by Haukeslowe, whose grant was revoked by Parliament.	*Ibid.,* p. 308.
		Feb. 3, 1333. To keep office although he has by king's command taken the order of knighthood.	*Ibid.,* p. 398.
		Oct. 1, 1341. Revocation of grant because he has been satisfied of part of yearly sum due him from another source and "he has borne himself ill by adhering to rebels against the King."	*C. P. R., 1340–1343,* p. 292.

[1] As in the case of the Keepers of the Writs, new grants of the office were sometimes made without regard to the claims of earlier incumbents. This led to some confusion about the tenure of the office in the early years of Edward III. Only by searching the Exchequer records for notes of payments of fees to the clerks could one ascertain which of the three claimants exercised the office in this confused period.

DATES OF TENURE	NAMES	ORIGINAL GRANT, CONDITIONS OF TENURE, ETC.	REFERENCES
		April 23, 1345. Restoration on death of Brok (*q.v.* below). License to discharge office by attorney in his absence.	*C. P. R., 1343–1345,* p. 458. *Ibid.,* p. 480.
1341–1345	Ralph de Brok, king's clerk.	Oct. 4, 1341. For life.	*C. P. R., 1340–1343,* p. 292.
		Nov. 6, 1342. Grant of power to discharge office by substitute during pleasure because he wants to continue his studies at university.	*Ibid.,* p. 563.
1345–1361	Thomas de Brembre, king's clerk.	July 27, 1345. During pleasure (on decease of Shordich) with proviso that if he stays continually in the king's service, he may perform the office by deputy.	*C. P. R., 1343–1345,* p. 534.
		Jan. 28, 1350. Grant for life.	*C. P. R., 1348–1350,* p. 467.
1361–1372	William de Wykeham, king's clerk.	Oct. 24, 1361. For life to hold in same manner as Brembre, deceased.	*C. P. R., 1361–1364,* p. 99.
1372–1376	John Woderove, the king's confessor.	Aug. 26, 1372. For life in lieu of an annuity which he has surrendered.	*C. P. R., 1371–1374,* p. 199; *C. P. R., 1358–1361,* p. 40.
1376–1383	William Strete, king's sergeant and controller.	Nov. 10, 1376. For life.	*C. P. R., 1374–1377,* p. 372.
		Dec. 20, 1380. Grant to Strete that he shall still hold office granted him by late king, to which Richard II has appointed Russhok (*q.v.* below) in belief that Strete was dead.	*C. P. R., 1377–1381,* p. 583.
1380	Thomas Russhok, the King's confessor.	Oct. 6, 1380. For life.	*Ibid.,* p. 559.
1383–1384	Richard Medford, "one of the clerks of the king's chapel."	Sept. 18, 1383. For life. Vacated by surrender because at Medford's request, the office was granted to Beauchamp (*q.v.* below).	*C. P. R., 1381–1385,* p. 307.
1384–1388	John Beauchamp, knight.	Jan. 5, 1384. For life.	*Ibid.,* p. 367.
1388–1391	John de Wendelyngburgh, the elder, king's clerk.	May 12, 1388. During pleasure for good service to the late king and at the request of several prelates and magnates of the realm.	*C. P. R., 1385–1389,* p. 446.
		June 5, 1388. For life at the special request of several prelates, etc., as above.	*Ibid.,* p. 421.
		Feb. 6, 1392. Vacated by surrender and canceled in favor of an annuity of 40 marks un-	*C. P. R., 1391–1396,* p. 36. Other references:

DATES OF TENURE	NAMES	ORIGINAL GRANT, CONDITIONS OF TENURE, ETC.	REFERENCES
		til he is restored to the office.	*ibid.,* pp. 116, 118, 299.
1391–1399	Henry Godard, esquire.	July 4, 1391. For life with power to execute by deputy, the king having been informed that Wendelburgh so exercised it and that it was not void since Beauchamp (*q.v.* above) was still living.	*C. P. R., 1388–1392,* p. 471.
1399–1413	Peter de Bukton, king's knight.	Oct. 15, 1399. For life.	*C. P. R., 1399–1401,* p. 16.
		Parliament of 1400–1401. To occupy by deputy "sufficient and knowing." After his death, office to be occupied in person.	*R. P.,* vol. III, pp. 495–496.
1413–1419	John Rodenhale, king's knight.	April 12, 1413. During pleasure.	*C. P. R., 1413–1416,* p. 14.
		April 17, 1415. Petition to king to grant him lordship of old Shoreham. He already has the office of chirographer of the Bench, water bailiff of Wyngate, and "Gaugeour de Lyne," the custody of the castle of Launceston in Cornwall, and the alien priory of Hayling in Southants, for which he paid annually to the king and his father 100 marks. Granted.	Council and Privy Seal Documents, File 31, 3 Hy. VI.[2]
1419–1420	Nicholas Merbury, esquire.	Nov. 7, 1419. *Vice* Rodenhale, deceased.	*Deputy Keeper's Reports,* vol. XLII, app. II, p. 381.[3] (Grant not found in *C. P. R.*)
1420–1421	Robert Kirkeham.	Oct. 16, 1420. During pleasure.	*C. P. R., 1416–1422,* p. 299.
1421–1436	William Pope, king's esquire and servant.	Dec. 16, 1421. For life as Merbury had it in lieu of annuities granted to him of £10 at Exchequer of Chester and 20 marks from issues of Duchy of Lancaster, surrendered. Vacated by surrender and canceled because of grant (*q.v.* below) by Henry VI.	*Ibid.,* p. 409.
		Feb. 21, 1423. For life as granted by Henry V. He has been unable for various reasons (*q.v.* below) to exercise earlier grant.	Nicolas, *Privy Council,* vol. III, p. 41.

2 Professor Williams' seminar.
3 From the same source.

DATES OF TENURE	NAMES	ORIGINAL GRANT, CONDITIONS OF TENURE, ETC.	REFERENCES
		Feb. 24, 1424. For life, to be exercised in person or by deputy. Earlier grant invalid because "mention was not made in it of any statute or ordinance to the contrary notwithstanding," or of the yearly value of the office.	*C. P. R., 1422–1429,* p. 194.
		Oct. 1, 1444. Pope to receive £10 annually from subsidy and ulnage of cloth in London as compensation for £10 annuity at hands of Chamberlain of Chester and 20 marks from issues of Duchy of Lancaster, surrendered in order that he might take office of chirographer and other offices, the profits whereof are so uncertain that they cannot be valued, "so that he lost more than £10 a year." The king "considering the premises and his great age and his service to the Crown for fifty years" has granted to him compensation.	*C. P. R., 1441–1446,* pp. 297, 350.
		May 10, 1445. Complaint of Sir John Fortescue that Pope and his servant, John Gervys, charged the extortionate sum of 8s. in a fine levied between Fortescue and Nicholas Ayston, Justice of the Common Pleas and others.	C. P. 40/737 (Easter, 23 Hy. VI), m. 438.
1436–1455	William Pope and Ralph Legh.	May 14, 1438. In survivorship. In lieu of a grant to Pope alone, surrendered.	*C. P. R., 1436–1441,* p. 170.
1455–1461	Henry Unton.	May 24, 1455. For life in lieu of a grant to Pope and Legh now surrendered.	*C. P. R., 1452–1461,* p. 242; C. P. 40/778, m. 115. Other references: Macklin, *Brasses,*[4] Sculthorpe, Norfolk, 1470.
1461–1472	Henry Unton, John Scotte, knight and William Beaufitz.	Dec. 1, 1461. For life.	*C. P. R., 1461–1467,* p. 79.
1472–1483	John Scotte, knight, Vincent Fynch, and Robert Worthington.	Dec. 1, 1472. For life, in lieu of a grant to John Scotte and William Beaufitz, and Henry Unton, now deceased.	*C. P. R., 1467–1477,* p. 376.

[4] W. H. Macklin, *The Brasses of England.*

DATES OF TENURE	NAMES	ORIGINAL GRANT, CONDITIONS OF TENURE, ETC.	REFERENCES
1483–1485	Robert Worthington.	July 2, 1483. During pleasure.	*C. P. R.*, *1476–1485*, p. 463.
		Mar. 30, 1484. For life.	*Ibid.*, p. 390.
1485–1493	John Payn, king's servant.	Nov. 5, 1485. For life.	*C. P. R.*, *1485–1494*, p. 41.
1493	William Vampage.	Jan. 28, 1493. For life.	Chancery Warrants: [5] C 82/102 (Jan. 18, 1493); *C. P. R.*, *1485–1494*, p. 408.
1493–1497	William Vampage and Robert Bygge.	June 24, 1493. For term of both their lives. June 21, 1494. Quit claim by Vampage to Bygge.	Chancery Warrants: C 82/107 (June 24, 1493); Close Rolls: C 54/354, m. 16d.
1497–1501	William Vampage and Thomas Wodyngton.	Nov. 28, 1497. Joint grant for term of their two lives because Bygge has died and Vampage as Knight of the Body has to wait on the king.	Chancery Warrants: C 82/170 (13 Henry VII).
1501–1508	John Gardyner.	Sept. 5, 1501. For life on surrender of Vampage's and Wodyngton's patent.	*C. P. R.*, *1494–1509*, p. 213.
1508 *et seq.*	John Pakyngton.	Sept. 26, 1508. For life.	*C. P. R.*, *1494–1509*, p. 607.

[5] This reference and the others below from Chancery Warrants and Close Rolls were given to me by Miss M. Blatcher.

Sources for the Study
of the Court of Common Pleas
in the Fifteenth Century

The list given below is only a partial one of the records, manuscripts, and published works consulted in the preparation of this study, but it gives the main titles which have provided material of value. The record sources have been fully described and discussed in Chapter IV of the text. For comment on the legal treatises, etc., the reader is referred to Winfield, *Chief Sources of English Legal History*.

A. Documents preserved in the Public Record Office:

Chancery Miscellanea, Brevia Regia et Recorda or County Placita, Edward I to Elizabeth (C 47/47–88).[1]

Curia Regis Rolls, 5 Richard I to 56 Henry III (K. B. 26/1–223).

De Banco Rolls, 1 Edward I to 38 Victoria (C. P. 40/1 *et seq.*).

Docket Rolls of the Court of Common Pleas, Easter 12–13 Henry VIII to Hilary, 16 Henry VIII (C. P. 40/Index 4, No. 1) MS: Index to docket rolls, prepared by the Record Commission, 1800 (Index, 6649).

Essoin Rolls of the Court of Common Pleas, 11 Henry III to 38 George III (C. P. 21/1 *et seq.*). Marked unfit for production. Only C. P. 21/11 was examined carefully.

Exchequer Miscellanea:

E 101/508/1   Sums paid to John de Stonard, justice of the Common Pleas and assize for fees, 20 Edward III to 36 Edward III.

E 101/513/22   1–7 Henry V, accounts of payments to John Cokayn, justice of the Common Pleas and of assize.

E 101/514/17   4–7 Henry VI, account of the expenses of Hugh Dalby, attorney of John, Duke of Norfolk, in a suit

---

[1] Record Office classification.

against John Botiller of Coventry, a tenant of the manor of Calondon.

E 101/518/4   Law expenses of Thomas Roche and others against William Fawke and others, 9 Henry VIII.

E 101/216/15 Accounts of the Clerk of the Hanaper, 12 Edward IV.

E 101/332–336 Treasury of the Exchequer, Contents and Administration of, Henry III to George III.

E 101/110–112 Fines and Amercements of the Court of Common Pleas, Henry III to Anne.

E 215 (under arrangement). Documents relating to the commission of fees appointed temp. James I.

Issue Rolls of the Exchequer, Henry III to 1797 (E 403).

Recoveries 7 Henry VIII—22 Henry VIII, Index 17180.

Remembrance Rolls of the Court of Common Pleas, 1524–1871 (C. P. 45/1 *et seq.*).

Returna Brevium, Exchequer Miscellanea, T. R. 8 Augmentation Office, vol. CLXVIII (E 315/169, fol. 13 ff.).

Rex Rolls of the Court of Common Pleas

    1. 51 Henry III—20 Edward II among Curia Regis Rolls and de Banco Rolls, marked "Rex" (K. B. 26/1–223; C. P. 40/1 *et seq.*).

    2. 1 Edward III—10 Henry IV, "Extract Rolls" (C. P. 23/1 *et seq.*).

Tellers Rolls, 20 and 22 Edward IV (E 405/69 and 71).

Writs of the Court of Common Pleas

Under process of sorting and classification.

B. Early lawbooks (manuals, treatises, Year Books, etc.)

Ashe, Thomas, Promptuarie, or Repertory Generall de les Annales, et Plusors Auters Livres del Common Ley Dengleterre. London, 1614.

The Attourney of the Court of Common Pleas or, Directions and Instructions concerning his Practice therein. By G. T. of Staple Inne and T. P. of Barnard's Inne. London, 1648.

Bacon, Nicholas, Cary, Robert, and Denton, Thomas, Report on the Inns of Court Presented to Henry VIII, c. 1540. *In* Fortescutus Illustratus, by Edw. Waterhouse. London, 1663, pp. 543 ff.

Blackstone, William, Commentaries on the Laws of England. 4 vols. London, 1765–1769.

The Book of Oaths and the Several Forms thereof, both Antient and Modern, faithfully Collected out of sundry Authentike Books and

Records, not heretofore extant, compiled in one Volume. London, 1649.

Boote, R., Historical Treatise of an Action or Suit of Law and of the Proceedings used in the King's Bench and Common Pleas, 6th ed. London, 1823.

Bracton, Henricus de, De Legibus et Consuetudinibus Anglie. Edited by G. E. Woodbine. 4 vols. New Haven, 1928–1942.

——, Bracton's Notebook. Edited by F. W. Maitland. 3 vols. London, 1887.

A Calendar of the Inner Temple Records. Edited by F. A. Inderwick. London, 1896.

A Calendar of the Middle Temple Records. Edited by C. H. Hopwood. London, 1903.

Certaine Proposals of Divers Attorneys of the Court of Common Pleas, for the Regulating the Proceedings at Law and Remedying some Inconveniences Whereby the Clyent Will Be Much Secured. . . . Presented to the Honourable Committee for the regulating proceedings in Law, Dec. 5, 1650. London, 1650.

Coke, Edward, Institutes of the Laws of England. 4 parts. London, 1628–1644. 19th ed.; 2 vols. London, 1832.

Cooke, Sir G., Rules, Orders, and Notices in the Court of Common Pleas at Westminster from the Thirty-fifth of King Henry VI to Trinity Term, the Twenty-first of King George II, 1747 inclusive. 2d ed. London, no date.

Cowell, John, The Interpreter, or Booke Containing the Signification of Words. Cambridge, 1607.

——, A Law Dictionary. London, 1708.

Crompton, R., L'Authoritie et Iurisdiction des Courts de la Maiestie De La Roygne: Nouelment collect & compose per R. Crompton del milieu Temple, Esquire, Apprentice del Ley. London, 1594.

Dugdale, William, Origines Juridiciales, or Historical Memorials of English law, Courts of Justice Forms of Trial, Inns of Court, etc. London, 1666. 3d ed.; London, 1680.

Fitzherbert, Sir Anthony (?), Diversité de Courtz et Lour Jurisdictions et Alia Necessaria et Utilia. London, 1523.

——, La Novelle Natura Brevium. London, 1534.

Fortescue, Sir John, De Laudibus Legum Anglie. Edited and translated with introduction and notes by S. B. Chrimes. Cambridge, 1942.

——, The Governance of England, Otherwise called the Difference between an Absolute and a Limited Monarchy. Edited by Charles Plummer. Oxford, 1885.

Gilbert, Sir G., History and Practice of the Court of Common Pleas. London, 1737. 2d ed., 1761.

Hale, Sir Matthew, "Considerations touching the Amendment or Alteration of Lawes," Hargrave Law Tracts, vol. I, pp. 249 ff. Dublin, 1787.

——, "Discourse concerning the Courts of King's Bench and Common Pleas," Hargrave Law Tracts, vol. I, pp. 357–376. Dublin, 1787.

——, The History of the Common Law of Engand. London, 1713.

Herbert, W., Antiquities of the Inns of Court and Chancery. London, 1804.

Ingpen, A. R., Master Worsley's Book on the History and Constitution of the Honorable Society of the Middle Temple. London, 1910.

Jacob, Giles, The Compleat Attorney's Practice in English in the Courts of King's Bench and Common Pleas at Westminster. 2d ed.; 2 vols. London, 1674.

——, A New Law Dictionary. 9th ed. London, 1772.

Lincoln's Inn, Black Books, 1422–1845. 4 vols. London, 1897–1902.

——, Records of the Honorable Society. Admissions, 1420–1893, and Chapel Registers. 2 vols. London, 1896.

Officina Brevium. London, 1679.

Powell, Thomas, Attourney's Academy, or Manner and Forme of Proceeding Practically, upon any Suite, Plaint, or Action, in any Court of Record, especially in the Great Courts at Westminster, with Fees. London, 1623.

The Practick Part of the Law shewing the Office of a Compleat Attorney . . . most part of which was composed and collected by G. T. of Staples Inne, and T. P. of Barnards Inne, with some new additions to the same. London, 1652.

Praxis Utriusque Banci. The Ancient and Modern Practice of the two Superior Courts at Westminster viz. the King's Bench and Common Pleas. . . . 2d ed. London, 1674.

Reeves, John, A History of English Law. 2 vols. London, 1783–1784.

Registrum Omnium Brevium tam Originalium quam Judicialium. 2 parts. London, 1531. 4th ed., 4 parts, 1687.

Returna Brevium. Redman edition, London, 1538.

Robinson, Henry, Certain Considerations in Order to a More

Speedy, Cheap, and Equal Distribution of Justice Throughout the Nation, most Humbly Presented to the High Court of Parliament of the Most Hopeful Commonwealth of England, by Henry Robinson. London, 1651.

Rules and Orders for the Court of Common Pleas at Westminster Made and Published by the Judges of the Said Court in the Term of St. Michael in the Year One Thousand Six Hundred and Fifty Foure. London, 1654.

Rules, Orders, and Notices of the Several Courts of King's Bench, Common Pleas, Chancery, and Exchequer. 3d ed. London, 1724.

Waterhouse, Edward, Fortescutus Illustratus or a Commentary on that Nervous Treatise, De Laudibus Legum Angliae, Written by Sir John Fortescue, Knight, First Lord C. J., after Lord Chancellour to Hy. the Sixth. London, 1663.

Year Books:

1. Black-letter edition

Le Premier Part de les Reports del Cases en Ley que Furent Argues en le Temps de le Tres Haut et Puissant Prince Roye Edward le Tierce. London, 1679.

Le Second Part de les Cases, *etc.*

Les Reports del Cases en Ley que Furent Argues en le Temps de Tres Haut et Puissant Princes Les Roys Henry le IV et Henry le V. London, 1679.

La Premiere Part des Ans du Roy Henry le VI. London, 1679.

Les Reports des Cases Contenus en les Ans Vingt Premier, et Apres en Temps du Roy Henry le VI. Communement appelles: The Second Part of Henry the Sixth. London, 1679.

Les Reports des Cases en Ley que Furent Argues en Temps du Roy Edward le Quart. London, 1679.

Les Reports des Cases en les Ans des Roys Edward V, Richard iij, Henrie vij, et Henrie viij. London, 1679.

2. Modern Editions:

Bolland, W. C., Year Books of Edward II. 5–8 Edward II. Selden Society, vols. XXXI, XXXIII, XXXVI, XXXVII, XLI, XLIII. London, 1915–1927.

Deiser, G. F., Year Books of Richard II. 12 Richard II, 1388–1389. Edited for the Ames Foundation. Cambridge, 1914.

Horwood, A. J., and Pike, L. O., Year Books of the Reign of King Edward the Third. Years 11 and 12. Rolls Series. London, 1883.

Maitland, F. W., Year Books of Edward II. 2–3 Edward II. Selden Society, vols. XIX and XX. London, 1904–1905.
Maitland, F. W., and Turner, G. J., Year Books of Edward II. 3–4 Edward II. Selden Society, vol. XXII. London, 1907.
Neilson, N., Year Books of Edward IV. 10 Edward IV and 49 Henry VI. Selden Society, vol. XLVII. London, 1931.
Pike, L. O., Year Books of the Reign of King Edward the Third. Years 12–18. Rolls Series. London, 1885–1904.
Plucknett, T. F. T., Year Books of Richard II. 13 Richard II. Ames Foundation. London, 1929.
Thornley, I. D., Year Books of Richard II. 11 Richard II. With a commentary upon the cases by T. F. T. Plucknett. Ames Foundation. London, 1937.
Turner, G. J., Year Books of Edward II. 4 Edward II. Selden Society, vols. XXVI and XLII. London, 1911 and 1926.
Williams, C. H., Year Books of Henry VI. 1 Henry VI. Selden Society, vol. L. London, 1933.

C. General

Agard, Arthur, Repertorie of Records Remaining in the 4 Treasuries on the Receipt Side at Westminster, the two Remembrancers of the Exchequer. Edited by Thomas Powell. London, 1631.
Beale, J. W., A Bibliography of Early English Law Books. Compiled for the Ames Foundation. Cambridge, Mass., 1926.
Bennett, H. S., The Pastons and Their England. Cambridge, 1922.
Bolland, W. C., "The Training of a Mediaeval Justice," Cambridge Legal Essays. Cambridge, Mass., 1926.
Calendars of Close Rolls preserved in the Public Record Office, prepared under the superintendence of the Deputy Keeper of the Records. London, H. M. Stationery Office, 1892 et seq.
Calendar of Patent Rolls preserved in the Public Record Office, prepared under the superintendence of the Deputy Keeper of the Records. London, H. M. Stationery Office, 1891 et seq.
Chrimes, S. B., English Constitutional Ideas in the Fifteenth Century. Cambridge, 1936.
Cohen, Herman, The History of the English Bar and Attornatus to 1450. London, 1929.
Denton, William, England in the Fifteenth Century. London, 1888.
Douthwaite, W. R., Gray's Inn: Its History and Associations. London, 1866.

Fletcher, R. G., Pension Book of Gray's Inn: Records of the Society, 1569–1810. 2 vols. London, 1901–1910.

Foss, Edward, The Judges of England. 9 vols. London, 1848–1864.

Fowler, G. H., "Rolls from the Office of the Sheriff of Beds and Bucks, 1332–1334," Quarto Memoirs of the Bedfordshire Historical Record Society, vol. III. Old House in Aspley Guise, 1929.

Gairdner, James, editor. The Paston Letters: 1422–1509 A.D. 3 vols. London, 1872–1875.

Galbraith, V. H., "The Tower as an Exchequer Record Office in the Reign of Edward II," Essays in Mediaeval History Presented to Thomas Frederick Tout. Edited by A. G. Little and F. M. Powicke. Manchester, 1925.

Giuseppi, M. S., Guide to the Manuscripts Preserved in the Public Record Office. 2 vols. London, 1923–1924.

Hall, Hubert, Studies in English Official Historical Documents. Cambridge, 1908.

Holdsworth, W. S., "The Development of Written and Oral Pleading," Select Essays in Anglo-American Legal History. Boston, 1918.

——, A History of English Law. 3d ed., rewritten in 9 vols. London, 1922 et seq.

Kingsford, C. L., Prejudice and Promise in Fifteenth Century England. Oxford, 1925.

Maitland, F. W., Collected Papers. 3 vols. Cambridge, 1911 et seq.

——, English Law and the Renaissance. Cambridge, 1901.

——, Equity, Also the Forms of Action at Common Law. Edited by A. H. Chaytor and W. J. Whitaker. Cambridge, 1909.

——, "Materials for the History of English Law," Select Essays in Anglo-American Legal History, vol. II.

Manning, James, Serviens ad legem. London, 1840.

Maxwell-Lyte, H. C., Historical Notes on the Use of the Great Seal of England. London, 1926.

Nicolas, Sir N. H., Proceedings and Ordinances of the Privy Council of England. London, 1834–1837.

North, Roger, The Lives of the Right Hon. Francis North, Baron Guilford, the Hon. Sir Dudley North, and the Hon. and Rev. Dr. John North. Edited by Augustus Jessop. 3 vols. London, 1890.

Palgrave, Sir Francis, The Antient Kalendars and Inventories of the Treasury of His Majesty's Exchequer. . . . London, 1836.

Parliamentary Papers, 1810 (Misc.). Report from the Commissioners on the Saleable Offices in the Courts of Law, 15 June 1810. Parliamentary Papers, 1819–1820, vol. II. Report of the Commissioners for Examining into the Duties, Salaries, and Emoluments, of the Officers, Clerks, and Ministers of the Several Courts of Justice in England, Wales, and Berwick-upon-Tweed; as to the Court of Common Pleas, 3 July 1819.

Parliamentary Papers, 1860, vol. XXXI. Minutes of Evidence taken before Commissioners Appointed to Inquire into the Expediency of Bringing Together in one Place or Neighborhood all the Superior Courts of Law and Equity, etc.

Pickthorn, Kenneth, Early Tudor Government: Henry VII. Cambridge, 1934.

——, Some Historical Principles of the English Constitution. London, 1925.

Plucknett, T. F. T., A Concise History of the Common Law. Rochester, N.Y., 1929.

——, "The Lancastrian Constitution," Tudor Studies. Edited by R. W. Seton-Watson. London, 1924.

——, "New Light on the Old County Court," Harvard Law Review, vol. XLII, 1928–1929, pp. 639 ff.

——, "A Note on the County Court Rolls." Harvard Law Review, vol. XLIII, 1929–1930, pp. 1111 ff.

Pollock, Sir Frederick, and Maitland, F. W., The History of English Law before the Time of Edward I. 2 vols. Cambridge, 1895.

Pulling, Alexander, Order of the Coif. London, 1897.

Putnam, B. H., "Early Treatises on the Practice of the Justices of the Peace in the Fifteenth and Sixteenth Centuries," Oxford Studies in Social and Legal History, vol. VII. Oxford, 1924.

——, Proceedings before the Justices of the Peace in the Fourteenth and Fifteenth Centuries, Edward III to Richard III. London, 1938.

Record Commission Papers relative to the Project of Building a General Record Office. London, 1835.

Richardson, H. G., "An Oxford Teacher of the Fifteenth Century," Bulletin of the John Rylands Library, vol. XXIII, No. 2, October. 1939, pp. 436 ff.

——, "Year Books and Plea Rolls as Sources of Historical Information," Royal Historical Society Transactions, Fourth Series, vol. V. London, 1922.

Rotuli Parliamentorum ut et Petitiones et Placita in Parliamento. Record Commission ed. London, 1767–1777.

Sayles, G. O., editor, Select Cases in the Court of King's Bench under

Edward I. 3 vols. Selden Society, vols. LV, LVII, and LVIII. London, 1936–1939.

Smith, Sir Thomas, De Republica Anglorum: A Discourse on the Commonwealth of England. Edited by L. Alston. Preface by F. W. Maitland. Cambridge, 1906.

Stapleton, Thomas, editor, Plumpton Correspondence: A Series of Letters Chiefly Domestick, Written in the Reigns of Edward IV, Richard III, Henry VII, and Henry VIII. Camden Society. London, 1839.

Statutes of the Realm. Record Commission edition, 1810 et seq.

Stubbs, William, The Constitutional History of England. 5th ed. Oxford, 1896.

Thayer, J. B., A Preliminary Treatise on Evidence at the Common Law. Boston, 1896.

Thorne, S. E., "Courts of Record and Sir Edward Coke," Toronto Law Journal, vol. II, No. 1, 1937, pp. 24 ff.

Tout, T. F., "Beginnings of a Modern Capital." The Raleigh Lecture, 1923. Proceedings of the British Academy, vol. X. Also in Collected Papers, vol. III.

——, Chapters in the Administrative History of England. 6 vols. Manchester, 1920–1933.

——, Collected Papers. 3 vols. Manchester Historical Series. Manchester, 1932–1934.

——, The Place of Edward II in English History. 2d ed., revised throughout by Hilda Johnstone. Manchester, 1936.

Wedgewood, Josiah, in collaboration with Holt, Anne D., "Biographies of Members of the House of Commons, 1439–1509," History of Parliament. London, 1936.

Wilkinson, B., The Chancery under Edward III. Manchester, 1929.

——, "The Seals of the Two Benches under Edward III," English Historical Review, vol. XLII, 1927, pp. 397 ff.

Winfield, P. H., The Chief Sources of English Legal History. Cambridge, Mass., 1925.

——, The History of Conspiracy and Abuse of Legal Procedure. Cambridge, Mass., 1921.

Woodbine, G. E., "County Court Rolls and County Court Records," Harvard Law Review, vol. XLIII, 1929–1930, pp. 1083 ff.

——, "The Origin of Trespass," Yale Law Journal, vol. XXXIII, 1930, pp. 799 ff.; vol. XXXIV, 1931, pp. 343 ff.

——, Review of G. O. Sayles, Select Cases in the Court of King's Bench under Edward I (vol. I), Yale Law Journal, vol. XLVI, 1937, pp. 1264 ff.

Index

SUBJECTS